The **Rough Guide** to

Rome

written and researched by

Martin Dunford

ROUGH
GUIDES

NEW YORK · LONDON · DELHI

www.roughguides.com

Contents

Colour maps following p.352

Baroque Rome colour section following p.64

Food and drink colour section following p.160

◄◄ Scooting through the city ◄ Fontana del Nettuno, Piazza Navona

Introduction to

Rome

Rome is the most fascinating city in Italy, which arguably makes it the most fascinating city in the world. An ancient place, packed with the relics of well over two thousand years of inhabitation, you could spend a month here and still only scratch the surface. Yet it is so much more than an open-air museum: its culture, its food and its people make up a modern, vibrant city that would be worthy of a visit irrespective of its history. As a historic place, it is special enough, but as a contemporary European capital, it is utterly unique.

Evenly placed between Italy's North and South, Rome is perhaps the ideal capital for a country only fully united in 1870 and possessing no shortage of rival cities. Once the seat of the most powerful empire in history, and still the home of the papacy within the Vatican city state, Rome is seen as a place somewhat apart from the rest of the country, spending money made elsewhere on the bloated government machine. Romans, the thinking seems to go, are a lazy lot, not to be trusted and living very nicely off the fat of the rest of the land.

For the traveller, all of this is much less evident than the sheer weight of history that the city supports. Beginning with the city's celebrated classical features, most visibly the Colosseum, and the Forum and Palatine Hill, Rome boasts an almost uninterrupted sequence of spectacular monuments – from early Christian basilicas, Romanesque churches, Renaissance palaces, right up to the fountains and churches of the Baroque period, which perhaps more than any other era has determined the look of the city today. There is the modern epoch too, with the ponderous Neoclassical architecture of the post-Unification period and the self-aggrandizing edifices of the Mussolini years. All these various eras crowd in on one another to an almost overwhelming degree: there are medieval churches atop ancient basilicas above Roman palaces; houses and apartment blocks incorporate fragments of eroded Roman columns, carvings and inscriptions; roads and piazzas follow the lines of ancient amphitheatres and stadiums.

All of which means the capital is not an easy place to absorb on one visit, and you need to take things slowly, even if you have only a few days here. Most of the sights can be approached from a variety of directions, and part of the city's allure is stumbling across things by accident, gradually piecing together the whole, rather than marching around to a timetable on a pre-determined route. In any case, it's hard to get anywhere very fast. Despite regular pledges to ban motor vehicles from the city centre, the congestion can be awful. On foot, it's easy to lose a sense of direction winding about in the twisting old streets, but you're so likely to come upon something interesting it hardly makes any difference.

Rome doesn't have the nightlife of, say, Paris or London, or even of its Italian counterparts to the north – culturally it's relatively provincial – and its food, while delicious, is earthy rather than refined. But its atmosphere is like no other city – a monumental, busy capital and yet an appealingly relaxed place, with a centre that has yet to be taken over by chain stores and big multinational hotels. Indeed, there has perhaps never been a better time to visit the city, whose once notorious infrastructure is looking and functioning better than it has done for some time. This process began with the feverish activity that took place in the last months of the twentieth century to have the city centre looking its best for the Church's millen-nium jubilee – a lot of it the work of the-then mayor, Francesco Rutelli. This work was continued by Rome's current mayoral incumbent, Walter Veltroni, who has done his best to haul Rome into the twenty-first cen-tury. Museums, churches and other buildings that had been "in restoration" as long as anyone can remember have reopened, and some of the city's historic collections have been re-housed. Plus, the city's cultural life has been enhanced, with frequent open-air concerts, a new film festival, and initiatives like September's "Notte Bianca" helping to restore Rome's pride. Transport, too, is being tackled, with the construction of a third metro line and various other initiatives – although it will be some time before these reach fruition.

Whether all this will alter the character of the city remains to be seen – the enhanced crowds of visitors, spurred on by the growth of cheap flights in recent years, are certainly having a go. But for now at least there's definitely no place like Rome.

Ancient Rome

Everyone who visits Rome wants to see the sites of the ancient city, and these are easy enough to find – they literally litter the city centre. There is, however, one concentrated sector that could keep you busy for a couple of days on its own: the Forum (pictured), the heart of the city during the Republic, and the adjacent Palatine Hill, where the ultra-rich lived – and where the city was founded, as legend has it, by Romulus and Remus. These two areas are surrounded by the columns and plinths of other fora built during Imperial times that are under continuous excavation, as well as the iconic bulk of the Colosseum, and some recently opened Roman houses up on the Celian Hill. Just beyond, the Baths of Caracalla and Domus Aurea both give a perfect impression of the gargantuan building tendencies of the late Empire and its despots (though the Domus Aurea is unfortunately closed at the moment), while back in the city centre the giant dome of the Pantheon demonstrates the ingenuity of its architects. A short trip outside the city, the ruins of Ostia, Rome's former port, are also strikingly well preserved, indeed one of the best examples of an ancient Roman city that you'll find. And the Via Appia Antica, to the south, is littered with ancient Roman sights. Once you have seen what's left of the monuments and buildings of the Romans, take some time to visit the city's amazing classical museums – the two main branches of the Museo Nazionale Romano, the Palazzo Altemps and Palazzo Massimo, plus the Capitoline Museums and their branch at Centrale Montemartini. Together they house the most awesomely complete collection of Roman sculpture, frescoes and other relics that you'll find anywhere – all unmissable.

Orientation

Rome's city centre is divided neatly into distinct blocks. The warren of streets that makes up the **centro storico** occupies the hook of land on the left bank of the River Tiber, bordered to the east by Via del Corso and to the north and south by water. From here Rome's central core spreads east: across Via del Corso to the major shopping streets and alleys around the Spanish Steps – the **Tridente** – down to the main artery of Via Nazionale; to the major sites of the ancient city to the south; and to the huge expanse of the Villa Borghese park to the north. The left bank of the river is distanced from the main hum of this part of the city, home to the **Vatican** and Saint Peter's, and, to the south of these, **Trastevere** – even in ancient times a distinct entity from the city proper and the focus of a good part of the city centre's nightlife.

▼ Fontana di Trevi.

To see most of this, you'd be mad to risk your blood pressure in any kind of vehicle, and really the best way to get around the city centre is to walk. The same goes for the ancient sites,

7
■

and probably the Vatican and Trastevere, too – although for these last two you might want to jump on a bus going across the river. Keep **public transport** for the longer hops, down to Testaccio, EUR or the catacombs and, of course, for trips out of the city – to the excavations at Ostia and Tivoli, or one of the nearby beaches.

Modern Rome

Strolling in central Rome you could be forgiven for thinking that nothing new had been built for at least a century. But there are modern aspects of the city that are well worth searching out. Probably the most spectacular is the Mussolini-era EUR quarter on the southern edge of the city, where broad boulevards cut a rectangular grid between hulking white marble buildings designed to glorify – and to some extent mimic – the Roman legacy while at the same time looking to the future in an uncompromisingly modern way. It's a great example of the period, and has aged relatively well, and it is also home to the Zaha Hadid-designed MAXXI, or Museum of Twenty-First Century Art, due to open soon after myriad delays. This is just one of a number of prestige projects by big-name architects that the city has seen over recent years. The best-known and perhaps most controversial is Richard Meier's structure to house the Ara Pacis Augustae, which opened in 2005 and provides a suitably airy backdrop for the Augustan-period altar, as well as adding a welcome dose of modernism to the ancient centre. The Auditorium (pictured) was opened to much fanfare in 2006 – the work of the internationally acclaimed Italian architect Renzo Piano, it is designed to enhance Rome's cultural clout around the world, giving it the large-scale concert halls it so desperately needed. The Auditorium – and its so-called Parco della Musica – also provides a focus for the northern edge of the city centre, in much the same way as the forthcoming redevelopment of the central markets in Ostiense will in the south. This huge project, to turn the vast site of the city's former wholesale food markets into a retail and cultural park, is already underway. In true Roman style, no one quite knows when it will be finished, but when it is it will surely help to propel the city further into the modern era.

So much to see, so little time

As you'll see from our "22 things not to miss" (p.11), you can't see everything on a first visit to Rome. The best thing is to enjoy the city: take in the attractions that interest you most at an easy pace, and look forward to the next time you're here when you can see what you missed.

The following suggested itineraries give you an idea of what's possible in a day. They're mainly designed around the key sights and include suggestions for where and when to have lunch. But don't be afraid to skip the galleries and monuments and just wander!

Three days
• Galleria Doria Pamphilj; Pantheon; centro storico (lunch); Piazza Navona; Palazzo Altemps.
• Forum; Palatine (picnic lunch); Capitoline Museums; Jewish Ghetto; Campo de' Fiori.
• St Peter's; Borgo/Prati (lunch); Vatican Museums.

Six days
As above plus...
• Galleria Barberini; Fontana di Trevi; Piazza di Spagna (lunch); Piazza del Popolo; Castel Sant'Angelo.
• Via del Corso; Via Veneto; Pincio Gardens; Galleria Borghese; Villa Borghese (picnic lunch); Villa Giulia.
• Colosseum; Monti (lunch); Santa Maria Maggiore; Palazzo Massimo.

Nine days
As above plus...
• Villa Farnesina; Galleria Corsini; Trastevere (lunch); Janiculum Hill.
• Aventine Hill; Baths of Caracalla; Testaccio (lunch); Ostia Antica.
• San Clemente; San Giovanni in Laterano (lunch); Aurelian Wall; Via Appia Antica.

When to go

R ome is a year-round city, and you can really visit at any **time of year**. Some months, however, are better than others. If you can, you should avoid visiting Rome in July and August, when the weather is hot and sticky, and those Romans who don't make their living exclusively from the tourist industry have left town; many businesses are closed, and in those places that are open most of the patrons will be fellow tourists. The weather is more comfortable in May, June and September,

▲ Piazza del Popolo

when most days will be warm but not unbearably so, and less humid, though you'll still find the city busy during these times; April, outside Easter, and October, are quieter and the weather can still be clement – making this in many ways the ideal time to come. The winter months can be nice, with many of the city's more popular sights relatively uncrowded: you may have some rain but the temperatures are usually mild. Whenever you visit, you'd be well advised to book your accommodation in advance.

What to wear is almost as important as when to come. Sturdy, comfortable shoes are essential – you're going to be doing a lot of walking – and, if you're here during the summer, you should wear loose, cool clothes, and a sunhat. Bear in mind that some sights – the catacombs, even some churches – can be unlit and cold, even when it's warm outside, so dress in layers; and bear in mind also that even on the hottest days you are required to cover up to enter many churches. Be frugal with your possessions when sightseeing, and only take out as much money, or jewellery, as you can bear to lose; pickpockets can be rife during the high season.

Average monthly temperatures and rainfall

	Jan	Feb	Mar	Apr	May	Jun	Jul	Aug	Sept	Oct	Nov	Dec
Average daily temperature												
max (°C)	12	13	15	18	23	23	30	30	27	22	16	13
min (°C)	3	4	5	8	11	15	17	18	15	11	7	4
max (°F)	53	55	59	65	73	81	87	87	80	71	61	55
min (°F)	37	38	41	46	52	58	63	64	59	51	44	39
Average rainfall												
inches	4	4	3	3	2	1	1	1	3	4	5	4
mm	103	98	68	65	48	34	23	33	68	94	130	111

22

things not to miss

It's not possible to see everything that Rome has to offer in one trip – and we don't suggest you try. What follows, in no particular order, is a selective taste of the city's highlights, from outstanding museums and ancient sites to Roman food and shopping. They're arranged in five colour-coded categories to help you find the very best things to see, do, eat and experience. All highlights have a page reference to take you straight into the guide, where you can find out more.

01 Ara Pacis Augustae Page **85** • Open again in a smart new purpose-built structure, this ancient hunk of stone from the Augustan era gives us perhaps the greatest glimpse of the Roman Imperial family.

02 Galleria Borghese Page **155** • A fantastic collection of Bernini sculptures together with a fine collection of Renaissance paintings, in a beautifully restored seventeenth-century villa.

03 St Peter's Page **182** • It's not the most beautiful church you'll ever visit, but it overwhelms with its grandeur and significance.

05 Fontana di Trevi Page **86** • Squeezed into the narrow streets of the city centre, this is Rome's flashiest and largest fountain – especially impressive if you stumble upon it by accident.

04 Ice cream Page **237** • The best way to finish off an evening out in Rome.

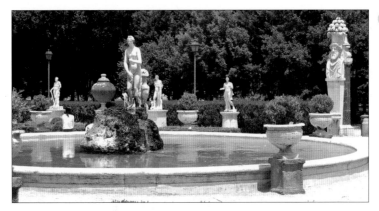

06 Villa Borghese Page **153** • The city centre's largest open space has plenty to do – a couple of superb galleries, a zoo, balloon rides – but also lots of quiet spaces to snooze if you just need to chill out.

07 Football Page **279** • Roma-Lazio derbies at the Stadio Olimpico are extreme, passionate affairs: not to be missed if you're lucky enough to be here at the right time, and can get hold of a ticket.

08 Coffee Page **233** • Even if you don't normally drink coffee you should do so in Rome – it's a way of life, and tastes better, too!

10 Keats-Shelley House Page **80** • An artist's garret that was occupied by Keats when he died, and which has been lovingly preserved as a shrine to the poet and his Romantic chums.

09 Pasta See *Eating and drinking* **colour section** • The basis of the Roman diet, and of some typical Roman dishes such as *Cacio e Pepe* and *Amatriciana*.

13

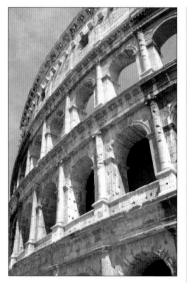

11 **Colosseum** Page **102** • The most photographed of Rome's monuments, but deservedly so. The completeness and ingenuity of this forerunner of all arenas mean it doesn't disappoint.

12 **Vatican Museums** Page **187** • Highlights of this giant complex include the stunning Raphael Stanze and Michelangelo's famous Sistine Chapel.

13 **The Forum** Page **92** • The heart of the ancient world is almost unrecognizable now, but is no less evocative for that.

14 Pizza See *Eating and drinking* **colour section** • There's nothing quite like Roman pizza – thin, crispy, and utterly delicious.

15 The Pantheon Page **55** • By far the most intact of Rome's – perhaps the world's – ancient Roman monuments.

16 Campo de' Fiori Page **71** • Held each morning, the market here is one of Rome's oldest, while in the evening the square's bars and restaurants form one of the city centre's main nightlife hubs.

17 Trastevere Page **167** • Wandering through the streets and tiny piazzas of Trastevere is what a visit to Rome is all about.

18 Museo Nazionale Romano

Page **65** & **133** • Palazzo Altemps and Palazzo Massimo, the two main sites of the Museo Nazionale Romano, hold some of the city's finest ancient finds.

20 Santa Maria Maggiore

Page **143** • One of the most important and impressive of Rome's patriarchal basilicas.

21 Piazza Navona Page **59** • If

Rome has a centre, this is probably it. Drinking a coffee here and watching the world go by is the quintessential Roman experience.

19 San Clemente Page **150** •

The epitome of Rome – an ancient temple under an ancient basilica topped by an ancient church.

22 Capitoline museums

Page **48** • Two amazing museums in one, situated at the heart of the ancient Roman Republic – one displaying Roman sculpture, the other Roman sculpture and Italian paintings.

Basics

Basics

Getting there

BASICS | Getting there

The easiest way to get to Rome **from the UK and Ireland** is to fly: and the lowest-priced air tickets are generally cheaper than those for the long train or bus journey. **From the US and Canada** there are direct flights to Rome, although you could consider flying via London or another European gateway and picking up a cheap onward flight from there. There are no direct flights to Italy **from Australia or New Zealand**, but plenty of airlines fly to Rome via Asian or European cities.

Flights from the UK and Ireland

There are plenty of **flights** from the **UK** and **Ireland** to Rome. Of the scheduled airlines, British Airways (BA) and Alitalia between them fly several times a day from London. Of the low-cost carriers, easyJet fly from London, Bristol, East Midlands and Newcastle; Ryanair fly from London, Dublin, East Midlands and Glasgow; bmibaby fly from Birmingham; Aer Lingus has daily direct flights from Dublin to Rome; while Alitalia covers the same route three to five times a week depending on the season. It is possible to find deals from Ireland if you book early, but prices are usually significantly higher and unless you're in a hurry it can sometimes make more sense to pick up an inexpensive flight to London or Birmingham and get a connecting flight from there. Alternatively, you could fly direct from Ireland to Brussels with Ryanair, who operate a cheap service from Brussels to Rome.

Prices depend more than ever on how far in advance you book and the time of year: a ticket to anywhere between June and August, when the weather is best, will cost more than in the depths of winter (excluding Christmas and New Year). Note also that it is generally more expensive to fly at weekends. As always the cheapest tickets come with restrictions: any changes incur additional fees, and tickets are rarely valid for longer than a month. Book far enough in advance with one of the low-cost airlines and you can pick up a ticket for under £100 return plus taxes, even in summer; book anything less than three weeks in advance and this could triple. Scheduled airline fares, booked within

a month of travel, will cost £120–160 out of season and £250–300 in summer.

Flights from the US and Canada

Alitalia fly the widest choice of direct routes between the **USA** and Rome, with daily flights from New York, Miami, Chicago, Boston and Miami; Delta fly from New York direct, and from Chicago and LA with stopovers in New York. In addition, many European carriers fly to Italy (via their capitals) from all major US and Canadian cities – for example British Airways (via London), Lufthansa (via Frankfurt), KLM (via Amsterdam), and so on.

The **direct scheduled fares** charged by each airline don't vary as much as you might think, and you'll often be basing your choice around flight timings, routes and gateway cities, ticket restrictions, and even the airline's reputation for comfort and service. It's a long flight, around nine hours from New York, Boston and the eastern Canadian cities, twelve hours from Chicago, and fifteen hours from Los Angeles, so it's as well to be fairly comfortable and arrive at a reasonably sociable hour. The cheapest **round-trip fares** to Rome, travelling midweek in low season, start at around $550 from New York or Boston, rising to about $750 in spring and fall and over $1000 during the summer. Add another $100–200 for flights from LA, Miami and Chicago. Note that these prices do not include taxes.

Air Canada and Alitalia have **direct** flights from **Toronto** to Rome for a low-season fare of Can$650 midweek, increasing to around Can$1000 in high season without taxes.

Flights from Australia, New Zealand and South Africa

Round-trip fares to Rome from the main cities in **Australia** go for Aus$1500–1850 in low season, and around Aus$2000 in high season. You are likely to get most flexibility by travelling with Alitalia, Malaysian, Thai, British Airways or Qantas, which offer a range of discounted Italian tour packages and air passes, although you can sometimes find cheaper offers with Garuda and Sri Lanka Airlines. There are no direct flights to Italy from Australia. **Round-trip fares** to Rome from **New Zealand** cost from around NZ$2000 during low season to around NZ$3000 in high season. Of the national carriers, Air New Zealand flies in conjunction with KLM and Alitalia, with stops in Japan and Amsterdam; Alitalia with other carriers from Auckland via Sydney and Bangkok/Singapore; British Airways from Auckland via Singapore/Bangkok or LA; Qantas from Auckland, Christchurch or Wellington via Sydney or Melbourne; JAL from Auckland (with an inclusive overnight stop in Tokyo/Osaka); Malaysia and Thai from Auckland via Kuala Lumpur and Bangkok respectively. Finally there are no direct flights from **South Africa** to Rome, and most flights make one European stop using one of the big carriers – Lufthansa, KLM, Olympic and South African Airways all offer decent deals. Reckon on paying around R7000 return from Johannesburg, around R8000 from Cape Town.

Trains

Travelling **by train** to Rome won't save much money, but it can be an enjoyable and leisurely (as well as environmentally friendly) way of getting there, and you can stop off in other parts of Europe on the way. As you'd expect, the choice of routes and fares is complex, but most trains from the UK pass through Paris and head down through France to northern Italy and then on to Rome. Advance booking is essential (and can often save you quite a lot of money; there are also discounts (for under-26s) and special offers are common. Using slower trains won't cut the cost very significantly and neither will the cross-Channel ferry route, which is now barely used and accordingly badly timetabled. If you travel via Paris on Eurostar you will have to change stations, which means lugging your bags on the metro from the Gare du Nord to the Gare de Lyon.

The journey takes around 21 hours and the best way to do it is to leave London on the lunchtime Eurostar train, which arrives in Paris later that afternoon, and then leave Paris on the early evening train, travelling overnight to Rome. A return ticket from London to Rome can be had for a total of £120–180 for the two legs (London–Paris from £60 return, Paris–Rome for £60–120 return). If you want to travel in style, take the Palatino sleeper from Paris to Rome, which costs £120 to £230 return depending on whether you travel in a six-berth couchette or a two-berth sleeper. The train has a decently priced restaurant car and is a wonderfully comfortable way to travel to Rome.

Details on all international rail tickets and passes are best obtained by calling personally at major train stations or by contacting the agents listed below. Don't expect much help from travel agents on planning routes, however, or the Italian State Railways office to answer the phone. A good place to start looking, if you fancy the idea of getting to Paris in time for dinner before taking the evening sleeper to Rome, is the excellent European rail website, Ⓦ www.seat61.com.

Buses

It's difficult to see why anyone would want to travel to Rome by **bus** from the UK, unless they had a phobia of flying – and of trains. National Express Eurolines do, however, have occasional bargain offers, and regular tickets are in any case cheap – £69 to Rome if booked a week in advance, £98 for a fully refundable and flexible ticket. The service departs four times a week and takes around 30 hours.

Packages and organized tours

There's no great need to take a package to Rome these days; it's easy to find flights online, and most websites offering cheap flights give plenty of hotel and other options too. Nonetheless, a plethora of operators sell short-break deals to Rome, including specialists offering small-group tours focusing on art, gastronomy or archeological

Fly less – stay longer! Travel and climate change

Climate change is the single biggest issue facing our planet. It is caused by a build-up in the atmosphere of carbon dioxide and other greenhouse gases, which are emitted by many sources – including planes. Already, flights account for around 3–4% of human-induced global warming: that figure may sound small, but it is rising year on year and threatens to counteract the progress made by reducing greenhouse emissions in other areas.

Rough Guides regard travel, overall, as a global benefit, and feel strongly that the advantages to developing economies are important, as are the opportunities for greater contact and awareness among peoples. But we all have a responsibility to limit our personal "carbon footprint". That means giving thought to how often we fly and what we can do to redress the harm that our trips create.

Flying and climate change

Pretty much every form of motorized travel generates CO_2, but planes are particularly bad offenders, releasing large volumes of greenhouse gases at altitudes where their impact is far more harmful. Flying also allows us to travel much further than we would contemplate doing by road or rail, so the emissions attributable to each passenger are greater. For example, one person taking a return flight between Europe and California produces the equivalent impact of 2.5 tonnes of CO_2 – similar to the yearly output of the average UK car.

Less harmful planes may evolve but it will be decades before they replace the current fleet – which could be too late for avoiding climate chaos. In the meantime, there are limited options for concerned travellers: to reduce the amount we travel by air (take fewer trips, stay longer!), to avoid night flights (when plane contrails trap heat from Earth but can't reflect sunlight back to space), and to make the trips we do take "climate neutral" via a carbon offset scheme.

Carbon offset schemes

Offset schemes run by **climatecare.org**, **carbonneutral.com** and others allow you to "neutralize" the greenhouse gases that you are responsible for releasing. Their websites have simple calculators that let you work out the impact of any flight. Once that's done, you can pay to fund projects that will reduce future carbon emissions by an equivalent amount (such the distribution of low-energy lightbulbs and cooking stoves in developing countries). Please take the time to visit our website and make your trip climate neutral.

www.roughguides.com/climatechange

sights. These are well worth considering, especially as they often give access to places that aren't otherwise open. For an ordinary city break, you can reckon on spending £600–800 for two staying for three nights in a 3–4-star hotel between April and October, including flights, though special offers can sometimes cut prices drastically, especially for late bookings. Specialist tours with guest lecturers tend to cost around £1500 for a week. Travelling from the US, you can expect to pay from around $1500 for a week in a three-star hotel in Rome, which may not include air fares, although tours limited to Rome can be hard to find – most take in Tuscany and other Italian highlights, or focus on the three cities of Rome, Florence and Venice.

UK

ACE Study Tours ☎ 01223/835 055, ⓦ www.study-tours.org.
Citalia ☎ 0870/909 7555, ⓦ www.citalia.co.uk.
Eurobreak ☎ 020/8780 7700, ⓦ www.eurobreak.com.
Martin Randall Travel ☎ 020/8742 3355, ⓦ www.martinrandall.com.

North America

Abercrombie & Kent ☎ 1-800/323-7308 or 630/954-2944, ⓦ www.abercrombiekent.com.

Central Holidays ☎1-800/935-5000, ⓦwww.centralholidays.com.
Cross Culture ☎1-800/491-1148 or 413/256-6303, ⓦwww.crosscultureinc.com.
Europe Through the Back Door ☎425/771-8303, ⓦwww.ricksteves.com.

Australia and New Zealand

Abercrombie and Kent Australia ☎03/9536 1800 or 1300/851 800, New Zealand ☎0800/441 638, ⓦwww.abercrombiekent.com.au.
CIT Australia ☎02/9267 1255, ⓦwww.cittravel.com.au.
Explore Holidays Australia ☎02/9857 6200 or 1300/731 000, ⓦwww.exploreholidays.com.au.

Airlines, agents and operators

Online booking

ⓦwww.expedia.co.uk (in UK),
ⓦwww.expedia.com (in US),
ⓦwww.expedia.ca (in Canada)
ⓦwww.lastminute.com (in UK)
ⓦwww.opodo.co.uk (in UK)
ⓦwww.orbitz.com (in US)
ⓦwww.travelocity.co.uk (in UK),
ⓦwww.travelocity.com (in US),
ⓦwww.travelocity.ca (in Canada)
ⓦwww.zuji.com.au (in Australia),
ⓦwww.zuji.co.nz (in New Zealand).

Agents and operators

ebookers UK ☎0800/082 3000, Republic of Ireland ☎01/488 3507, ⓦwww.ebookers.com, ⓦwww.ebookers.ie. Low fares on an extensive selection of scheduled flights and package deals.
North South Travel UK ☎01245/608 291, ⓦwww.northsouthtravel.co.uk. Friendly, competitive travel agency, offering discounted fares worldwide. Profits are used to support projects in the developing world, especially the promotion of sustainable tourism.

STA Travel US ☎1-800/781-4040, UK ☎0871/2300 040, Australia ☎134 STA, New Zealand ☎0800/474 400, SA ☎0861/781 781. Worldwide specialists in independent travel; also student IDs, travel insurance, car rental, rail passes, and more. Good discounts for students and under-26s. ⓦwww.statravel.com.
Trailfinders UK ☎0845/058 5858, Republic of Ireland ☎01/677 7888, Australia ☎1300/780 212, ⓦwww.trailfinders.com. One of the best-informed and most efficient agents for independent travellers.

Airlines

Aer Lingus Republic of Ireland ☎0818/365 000, ⓦwww.aerlingus.ie.
Air Canada ☎1-888-247-2262, UK ☎0871/220 1111, Republic of Ireland ☎01/679 3958, Australia ☎1300/655 767, New Zealand ☎0508/747 767, ⓦwww.aircanada.com.
Air New Zealand Australia ☎13 24 76, New Zealand ☎0800/737 000, ⓦwww.airnz.co.nz.
Alitalia US ☎1-800-223-5730, Canada ☎1-800-361-8336, UK ☎0870/544 8259, Republic of Ireland ☎01/677 5171, New Zealand ☎09/308 3357, South Africa ☎11/721 4500, ⓦwww.alitalia.com.
British Airways UK ☎0870/850 9850, Republic of Ireland ☎1890/626 747, US & Canada ☎1-800/AIRWAYS, Australia ☎1300/767 177, New Zealand ☎09/966 9777, ⓦwww.ba.com.
bmibaby UK ☎0871/224 0224, Republic of Ireland ☎1890/340 122, ⓦwww.bmibaby.com.
Delta US and Canada ☎1-800-221-1212, UK ☎0845/600 0950, Republic of Ireland ☎1850/882 031 or 01/407 3165, Australia ☎1300/302 849, New Zealand ☎09/379 3370, ⓦwww.delta.com.
easyJet UK ☎0905/821 0905, Republic of Ireland ☎0870/600 0000, ⓦwww.easyjet.com.
Malaysia Airlines US ☎1-800/5529-264, UK ☎0870/607 9090, Republic of Ireland ☎01/6761 561, Australia ☎13 26 27, New Zealand ☎0800/777 747, South Africa ☎11-8809 614, ⓦwww.malaysia-airlines.com.
Qantas Airways US and Canada ☎1-800-227-4500, UK ☎0845/774 7767, Republic of Ireland

Airline offices in Rome

Many of the big airline offices are located on and around Via Bissolati/Piazza Barberini.

Air Canada ☎06.6501.0991
Alitalia domestic ☎06.2222
American ☎06.6605.3169
British Airways ☎199.712.266

Delta ☎800.477.999
EasyJet ☎848.887.766
Ryanair ☎899.88.99.73

☏ 01/407 3278, Australia ☏ 13 13 13, New Zealand ☏ 0800/808 767 or 09/357 8900, South Africa ☏ 11/441 8550, ⓦ www.qantas.com.
Ryanair UK ☏ 0871/246 0000, Republic of Ireland ☏ 0818/303 030, ⓦ www.ryanair.com.
South African Airways US and Canada ☏ 1-800-722-9675, UK ☏ 0870/747 1111, Australia ☏ 1800/221 699, New Zealand ☏ 09/977 2237, SA ☏ 11/978 1111, ⓦ www.flysaa.com.

Rail contacts

Eurostar UK ☏ 0870/518 6186, ⓦ www.eurostar.com.

European Rail UK ☏ 020/7387 0444, ⓦ www.europeanrail.com.
International Rail UK ☏ 0870/084 1414, ⓦ www.international-rail.com.
Rail Europe UK ☏ 0870/837 1371, ⓦ www.raileurope.co.uk.
Trainseurope UK ☏ 0900/195 0101, ⓦ www.trainseurope.co.uk.

Bus contacts

Eurolines UK ☏ 0870/580 8080, ⓦ www.nationalexpress.com/eurolines.

Arrival

Reaching the centre of Rome is pretty straightforward for air and rail travellers. You'll most likely end up at **Termini** station – very close to the top attractions and the bulk of accommodation. If arriving by **taxi** or **bus**, remember Rome's notorious traffic can add significantly to your journey time.

By air

Rome has two **airports**: Leonardo da Vinci, better known as Fiumicino, which handles the majority of scheduled flights, and Ciampino, where you'll arrive if you're travelling with one of the low-cost airlines or on a charter flight.

Fiumicino Airport

Fiumicino, or FCO (enquiries ☏ 06.6595.3640) is Rome's largest airport and is about 30km southwest of the city centre, close by the coast. There are three terminals: A serves domestic flights, B international flights within the EU and C all other international flights. The airport is connected to the centre of Rome by direct trains, which take thirty minutes to get to Termini and cost €11; services begin at 6.35am and then leave half-hourly until 11.35pm. Alternatively, there are more frequent but slower trains to Ostiense and

Tiburtina stations, each on the edge of the city centre; tickets cost €5. Both stations are stops on Rome's metro (€1, see p.25), or you can catch city bus #175 from Ostiense, or city bus #492 or #649 from Tiburtina, to the centre of town (again €1). These cheaper alternatives do inevitably involve a certain amount more bag-hauling. **Taxis** from Fiumicino to the city centre cost a flat €40 and the journey time to the city centre is about 30 minutes.

Ciampino Airport

The city's second airport, **Ciampino**, or CIA (enquiries ☏ 06.794.941) has three terminals: Departures, Arrivals and General Aviation, and is only 15km southeast of Rome. However, there are no direct connections between the airport and city centre, and if you're travelling with one of the low-cost airlines the best thing you can do is take the Terravision **shuttle bus**, timed to coincide with arrivals and departures to Termini (€8

★★★

Hotel delle Muse

*located in a very quiet, green residential area –
57 rooms with w.c. and shower, telephone, sat TV,
hairdryer, air conditioning/heating, Internet access,
elevator, safe, bar, restaurant, garden, garage,
internet point.*

Contact details:
Hotel delle Muse
Via Tommaso Salvini 18
00197 Roma
Telephone: +(39) 06 80 88 333
Fax: +(39) 06 808 57 49
Skype: hotel-delle-muse
(from 09.00 until 15.00 – Italy local time)
info@hoteldellemuse.com
www.hoteldellemuse.com

single, €14 return). Otherwise ATRAL buses run from the airport to the Anagnina metro station, at the end of line A, every forty minutes (€1), from where it's a twenty-minute ride into the centre (a further €1). **Taxis** cost a flat €30 and the journey time to the city center is 30–40 minutes. However, beware that many drivers don't like taking people into the city centre from Ciampino, especially for this fixed rate, and it can sometimes be hard to persuade someone to take you; stand your ground if no one seems to want to put their hand up; and don't pay more than €30 plus tip; once cajoled, some drivers may be tempted to inflate the fare.

By train

Travelling by **train** from most places in Italy, or indeed Europe, you arrive at the central **Stazione Termini**, meeting-point of the two metro lines and many city-bus routes. There are **left-luggage** facilities here, by platform 1 and platform 24 (both open daily 7am–midnight; €2.50–3 per piece). Among **other train stations** in Rome, Tiburtina is a stop for some north–south intercity trains; selected routes around Lazio are handled by the Regionali platforms of Stazione Termini (a further five-minute walk beyond the end of the regular platforms); and the Roma-Nord line station on Piazzale Flaminio runs to Viterbo.

By bus

Arriving by **bus** can leave you in any one of a number of places around the city. The main station for trains from outside the Rome region is Tiburtina, also the city's second railway station. Others include Ponte Mammolo (trains from Tivoli and Subiaco); Lepanto (Cerveteri, Civitavecchia, Bracciano area); EUR Fermi (Nettuno, Anzio, southern Lazio coast); Anagnina (Castelli Romani); Saxa Rubra (Viterbo and around). All of these stations are on a metro line, except Saxa Rubra, which is on the Roma-Nord line and connected by trains every fifteen minutes with the station at Piazzale Flaminio, on metro line A.

By road

Coming into the city by road can be quite confusing and isn't really advisable unless you're used to driving in Italy and know where you are going to park (see p.28). If you are on the A1 highway coming from the north take the exit "Roma Nord"; from the south, follow exit "Roma Est". Both lead you to the Grande Raccordo Anulare (GRA), which circles the city and is connected with all of the major arteries into the city centre – the Via Cassia from the north, Via Salaria from the northeast, Via Tiburtina or Via Nomentana from the east, Via Appia Nuova and the Pontina from the south, Via Prenestina and Via Casilina or Via Cristoforo Colombo from the southeast, and Via Aurelia from the northwest. From **Ciampino**, either follow Via Appia Nuova into the centre or join the GRA at junction 23 and follow the signs to the centre. From **Fiumicino**, just follow the A12 motorway into the city centre; it crosses the river just north of EUR, from where it's a short drive north up Via Cristoforo Colombo to the city walls and, beyond to the Baths of Caracalla.

Getting around

As in most Italian cities, the best way to get around Rome is to **walk** – you'll see more and will better appreciate the city. Rome wasn't built for motor traffic, and it shows in the congestion, the pollution, and the bad tempers of its drivers. However, it has good public transport on the whole – a largely efficient blend of buses, a few trams and a small two-line metro.

ATAC: buses, trams and metro

ATAC (*Agenzia dei Transporti Autoferrotranviari del Commune di Roma*) runs the city's bus, tram and metro service. There is a toll-free enquiries line (Mon–Sat 8am–8pm; ☏800.431.784 – as with most Italian numbers, you may struggle to find an English-speaking operator), and ⓦwww.atac.roma.it has tourist information in English, route maps, an excellent route planner and links to the individual trambus and metro sites (see below), and an information booth in front of Termini on Piazza dei Cinquecento (daily 9am–8pm; ☏06.4695.2252), as well as basic transport information displayed outside.

Buses and trams

The bus and tram service, **"trambus"** (ⓦwww.trambus.com), is on the whole pretty good – cheap, reliable and as quick as the clogged streets allow. Remember to board through the rear doors and punch your ticket as you enter. There is also a small network of electric minibuses that negotiate the narrow backstreets of the old centre. Around midnight, a network of nightbuses clicks into service, accessing most parts of the city up to about 5am. They normally have conductors so you can buy a ticket on board, although it's worth keeping spare tickets handy just in case; they are easily identified by the owl symbol above the "bus notturno" schedule. For useful bus and tram routes, see p.26–27.

Metro

Rome's **metro** or "Met.Ro" as it calls itself (ⓦwww.metroroma.it), runs from 5.30am to 11.30pm daily, except on Saturdays, when it closes down at 12.30am. The metro currently consists of two lines – A (orange) and B (blue) – and they're working on line C, which should be finished by 2012. Due to engineering works, buses replace trains on Line A after 9pm until around January 2008. The system also incorporates the major **overground trains** that head out to the suburbs – the

Tickets and passes

Flat-fare **tickets** cost €1 each and are good for any number of bus or tram rides and one metro ride within 75 minutes of validating them. You need to punch your ticket before you ride on the metro and as you get on a bus or tram; otherwise you can be fined. Tickets are available from tobacconists, newsstands and ticket machines located in all metro stations, at major bus stops and on most buses. You can also get a day pass (BIG), valid on all city transport until midnight of the day purchased, for €4, a three-day pass (BTI) for €11, or a seven-day pass (CIS) for €16. Monthly passes cost €30, while monthly passes that can be used by anyone cost €46. Finally, it's worth knowing that there are hefty spot fines of up to €100 for **fare-dodging**, and pleading a foreigner's ignorance will get you nowhere. BIRG tickets (regional transport passes) for COTRAL and ATAC services are well worth buying if you are going out of Rome for the day; see box, p.28.

Useful transport routes

Buses

#23 Piazza Clodio–Piazza Risorgimento–Ponte Vittorio Emanuele II–Ponte Garibaldi–Via Marmorata–Piazzale Ostiense–Centrale Montemartini–Basilica di S. Paolo.

#30 Express Piazza Clodio–Piazza Mazzini–Piazza Cavour–Corso Rinascimento–Largo Argentina–Piazza Venezia–Luntotevere Aventino–Via Marmorata–Piramide–Via C.Colombo–EUR.

#40 (Express) Termini–Via Nazionale–Piazza Venezia–Largo Argentina–Piazza Pia.

#62 Piazza Bologna–Via Nomentana–Porta Pia–Piazza Barberini–Piazza San Silvestro–Via del Corso–Piazza Venezia–Corso V. Emanuele II–Borgo Angelico–Piazza Pio.

#64 Termini–Piazza della Repubblica–Via Nazionale–Piazza Venezia–Largo Argentina–Corso Vittorio Emanuele II–Stazione S. Pietro.

#75 Via Poerio (Monteverde)–Via Induno–Porta Portese–Testaccio–Piramide–Circo Massimo–Colosseo–Via Cavour–Termini–Piazza Indipendienza.

#175 Termini–Piazza Barberini–Via del Corso–Piazza Venezia–Colosseo–Circo Massimo–Aventine–Stazione Ostiense.

#271 S. Paolo–Via Ostiense–Piramide–Viale Aventino–Circo Massimo–Colosseo–Piazza Venezia–Ponte Sisto–Castel Sant'Angelo–Via Vitilleschi–Piazza Risorgimento–Ottaviano–Foro Italico.

#492 Stazione Tiburtina–Piazzale Verano–Termini–Piazza Barberini–Via del Corso–Piazza Venezia–Largo Argentina–Corso del Rinascimento–Piazza Cavour–Piazza Risorgimento–Cipro.

#660 Largo Colli Albani–Appia Nuova–Via Appia Pignatelli–Via Appia Antica.

#590 Same route as metro line A but with access for disabled; runs every 90 minutes.

#660 Largo Colli Albani–Appia Nuova–Via Appia Antica.

#714 Termini–Santa Maria Maggiore–Via Merulana–San Giovanni in Laterano–Viale Terme di Caracalla–EUR.

#910 Termini–Piazza della Repubblica–Via Piemonte–Via Pinciana (Villa Borghese)–Piazza Euclide–Palazzetto dello Sport–Piazza Mancini.

Minibuses

These **small buses** negotiate ciricular routes through the narrow streets of Rome's centre.

#116 Porta Pinciana–Via Veneto–Via del Tritone–Piazza di Spagna–Piazza San Silvestro–Corso Rinascimento–Campo de'Fiori–Piazza Farnese–Lungotevere Sangallo–Terminal Gianicolo.

#117 San Giovanni in Laterano–Piazza Celimontana–Via Due Macelli–Via del Babuino–Piazza del Popolo–Via del Corso–Piazza Venezia–Via Nazionale–Via dei Serpenti–Colosseo–Via Labicana.

#119 Piazza del Popolo–Via del Corso–Piazza Venezia–Largo Argentina–Via del Tritone–Piazza Barberini–Via Veneto–Porta Pinciana–Piazza Barberini–Piazza di Spagna–Via del Babuino–Piazza del Popolo.

Trams

#3 Stazione Trastevere–Via Marmorata-Piramide–Circo Massimo-Colosseum–San Giovanni–San Lorenzo–Via Nomentana–Parioli–Viale Belle Arti.

Roma-Lido line, which connects the city to Ostia, and the Roma-Laziale and Roma-Nord lines, which run respectively east and north of the city centre. The metro itself is focused on ferrying commuters out to the suburbs, not transporting tourists around the city

#8 Casaletto–Stazione Trastevere–Piazza Mastai–Viale Trastevere–Largo Argentina.

#19 Porto Maggiore–Piazzale Verano–Viale Regina Margherita–Viale Belle Arti–Via Flaminia–Ottaviano–Piazza Risorgimento.

Tourist buses

Three main **tourists buses** circle Rome and its major sights. They're in competition with each other, but you can get combined tickets for two of them and you can get information on each at ⓦwww.trambusopen.com or from ☏800.281.281. See p.32 for more information on tours.

Bus #110 Good for general orientation and a quick glance at the sights, this ATAC-run open-top bus has a guided commentary. It leaves from Piazza dei Cinquecento outside Stazione Termini and stops at all the major sights, including Piazza di Spagna, Castel Sant'Angelo, the Vatican and Appia Antica. The whole round trip takes two hours, and in summer departures are every twenty minutes from 8.40am until 8.20pm daily, including holidays and Sundays. Tickets cost €13 and allow you to get on wherever you like and hop on and off throughout the day. Combined #110 and Archeobus tickets cost €20. Tickets can be bought on board, or before you get on at Piazza dei Cinquecento.

Archeobus The Archeobus is another hop-on-hop-off service that links some of the most compelling Roman sights, and is much the best way of seeing some of the monuments on and around the Via Appia Antica. Like the other tourist lines, it starts at Piazza dei Cinquecento, bang in front of Termini, and heads down to the southern edge of the city via Piazza Venezia, Piazza Bocca della Verità, Circo Massimo–Terme di Caracalla and the Porta San Sebastiano. On Via Appia, there are stops at Domine Quo Vadis–Catacombe di S. Callisto, Catacombe di S. Sebastiano, Circo di Massenzio, Casal Rotundo–Aquedotti Romani and the Villa dei Quintili. Buses run daily every hour between 9am and 4pm. Tickets cost €8, and integrated tickets are available, including the #110 bus and various museums and so on, with different lengths of validity. They can be bought on board, or at Piazza dei Cinquecento.

Christian Rome The Vatican's tourist bus service links Rome's major basilicas and other Christian sights, starting, like the others, in front of Termini on Piazza dei Cinquecento. Services run daily every thirty minutes between 8.30am and 7.30pm, and tickets cost €13 for the day (€20 for two days €28 for three); they can be bought on board, at Piazza dei Cinquecento or at the Info Points on Piazza Pio XII, next to St Peter's Square, and San Giovanni in Laterano. More information at ⓦwww.orpnet.org.

Night buses

#29N Piazzale Ostiense–Lungotevere Aventino–Lungotevere De'Cenci–Via Crescenzio–Via Barletta–Piazza Marina–Via Belle Arte–Viale Liegi–Viale Regina Margherita–Via dei Marruccini–Via Labicana–Viale Aventino–Piazzale Ostiense.

#40N Same route as metro line B.

#55N Same route as metro line A.

#78N Piazza Clodio–Piazzale Flaminio–Piazza Cavour–Largo di Torre Argentina–Piazza Venezia–Via Nazionale–Termini.

centre, and is therefore not as useful as you might think. Nonetheless, there are a few useful city-centre stations: Termini is the hub of both lines, and there are stations at the Colosseum, Piazza Barberini and Piazza di Spagna.

BIRG/CIRS tickets

If you're considering travelling outside Rome, the Lazio transport system is divided into six zones, which spread concentrically out from the city. It's possible to buy season tickets – either by the day or week – to travel within them. The **BIRG** (Biglietto Integrato Regionale Giornaliero) is valid all day for unlimited travel on the state railway, COTRAL buses and the Rome metro, and prices range from €2.50 to €10.50, depending on the zone. A €7 ticket, covering four zones, for example, ferries you between Rome and Viterbo. Weekly passes – the CIRS (Carta Integrata Regionale Settimanale) – cost from €9 to €41 depending on the zones you want to cover. Vendors – train and bus ticket offices, newspaper stands and tobacconists – can advise you on the required zone, as can the ATAC website ⓦ www.atac.roma.it.

Taxis

The easiest way to get a **taxi** is to find the nearest taxi stand (*fermata dei taxi*) – central ones are listed on below. Alternatively, you can call a taxi (☎06.3570, 06.4157, 06.6645, 06.8822 or 06.5551), but these usually cost more, as the meter starts ticking the moment the taxi is dispatched to collect you. Meters start at around €2.50 (more at night and on Sundays), plus a charge of about €1 per item of luggage; the meter clicks up at the rate of €1 or so every 140m. Most cabs are white, and a journey from one side of the city centre to the other should cost around €10, or around €15 on Sunday or at night. Note that all taxis carry a rate card in English giving the current tariff, and the extra charges for luggage, late-night, Sundays and holidays, and airport journeys.

By car, bicycle and scooter

Car rental

All the usual suspects have desks at Fiumicino, Ciampino, Termini and elsewhere in the city.

City centre taxi ranks

Piazza dei Cinquecento (Termini)
Piazza Venezia
Largo Argentina
Piazza del Popolo
Piazza di Spagna
Piazza San Silvestro
Piazza Barberini
Via Veneto (Porta Pinciana)
Piazza Belli (Trastevere)

Avis ☎199.100.133; Termini ☎06.481.4273; Ciampino ☎06.7934.0368; Fiumicino ☎06.6501.1531.
Europcar ☎800.014,410; Termini ☎06.488.2854; Ciampino ☎06.7934.0387; Fiumicino ☎06.6501.0879.
Hertz ☎199.112.211; Termini ☎06.474.0389; Ciampino ☎06.7934.0616; Fiumicino ☎06.6501.1553.
Maggiore ☎848.867.067; Termini ☎06.488.0049; Ciampino ☎067934.0368; Fiumicino ☎066501.0678.
Sixt ☎800.900.666; Termini ☎06.474.0014; Ciampino ☎06.7934.0838; Fiumicino ☎06.6595.3547.

Car repair

Call ☎116 for emergency breakdown service. Otherwise, consult the Yellow Pages (Pagine Gialle) under "Autoriparazioni" for specialized repair shops.

Parking

Only residents are allowed to **park** for free in central Rome so you will always need to pay. You can park on the street for around €1 an hour (8am–8pm), and there are plentiful pay-and-display parking meters. There are parking garages in the Villa Borghese (around €1 per hour) in front of Stazione Termini (€5 for 2 hours, then €1.50 per hour), and next to each of the terminal metro stations, from where it's easy to get into the city centre.

Bicycle and scooter rental

Renting a bike or moped/scooter can be a more efficient way of nipping around Rome's clogged streets, and there are plenty of places offering this facility, although you'll need to have a full driving licence. Rates are up to around €3–4 an hour/€10 a day for bikes, and about €30 a day for mopeds, €40–50 a day for scooters.

Barberini Villa della Purificazione 84 ⓣ06.488.5485 rents bicycles, mopeds and scooters. Bikes cost €10 per day, mopeds €30, scooters €50.

Bici e Baci Via di Viminale 5 ⓣ06.482.8443. Bicycles for €3–4 an hour, €9–11 a day; mopeds from €19 a day, scooters from €45. Daily 8am–7pm.

Collalti Via del Pellegrino 80a/82 ⓣ06.6880.1084. Bike rental and repairs by the hour or day. Closed lunchtimes and all day Mon.

Cyclo Via Cavour 80 ⓣ06.481.5669. Bikes from €12 a day, moped from €37, scooters from €47.

Treno e Scooter Rent Piazza dei Cinquecento, Stazione Termini ⓣ06.4890.5823. On the right as you come out of the station, this offers both scooter and bike rental – bikes for €5 an hour/€10 a day, mopeds/scooters for €8/13 an hour and €35/42 a day. Daily 7am–7pm.

Sights and museums

It's likely that you'll be spending a fair amount of your time in Rome visiting its dazzling array of **museums, galleries, churches** and **ancient sites**. They are not all that the city has to offer, but they are, inevitably, one of the main reasons people visit – and rightly so: nowhere in the world, perhaps, has such a collection of treasures from so many different eras.

Museums, galleries and ancient sites

Most **museums and galleries** are closed on Mondays. Opening hours for state-run museums are generally 9am–7pm, Tuesday to Saturday, and 9am–1pm on Sunday. Most other museums roughly follow this pattern, too, although they are more likely to close for a couple of hours in the afternoon, and have shorter opening hours in winter. Many large museums also run late-night openings in summer (till 10pm or later on Tues–Sat, or 8pm on Sun). The opening times of **ancient sites** are more flexible: most sites open every day, often including Sunday, from 9am until late

Chiuso per restauro

Although the situation is much better than it used to be in Rome, you may find buildings of all kinds **closed for restoration** (*chiuso per restauro*), and it's usually pretty uncertain when they might reopen. The most notable casualties at the time of writing were the Museo Barracco (though this should be open by the time of publication) and the Domus Aurea, but openings change all the time and by the time you read this these may well be open and others closed. If there's something you really want to see, and you don't know when you might be back in Rome, it might be worth trying to persuade a workman or priest/curator to show you around even if there's scaffolding everywhere.

evening – frequently specified as one hour before sunset, and thus changing according to the time of year.

Passes

There is no museum pass that will get you into all the main attractions in Rome. However, some sights are grouped together to make it easier and cheaper to visit them. For example, Rome's ancient sculpture and other artefacts have been gathered together in the **Museo Nazionale Romano**, which operates on three main sites: Palazzo Massimo, the Terme di Diocleziano, opposite Termini station and the Palazzo Altemps, in the centro storico. You can buy a ticket from

Look out for the **"Notte Bianca"**, when many sights – a lot of them rarely ever open to the public – open their doors all night over one weekend in September.

each location that permits entry to all the others for just €7 and is valid for three days.

Again, there's no city-wide pass to get you into all the main **ancient sites**, but the Colosseum and Palatine can be visited on a combined ticket, and you can buy an Archeological Card for €20 that gives entry to the Colosseum, Palatine Hill, Baths of Caracalla, Villa dei Quintili, Tomba Cecilia Metella, Palazzo Altemps, Palazzo Massimo, Crypta Balbi and Terme di Diocleziano – perhaps the city's best bargain.

Finally, the **Roma Pass**, available from major sights and tourist information kiosks (☎06.8205.9127; ⊛www.romapass.it), also costs €20 and is valid for three days. It entitles you to travel for free on buses, trams and the metro, gives free admission to two museums or sites of your choice (the vast majority of places participate) and reduced entry to others – and, perhaps most importantly, the opportunity not to queue at the first two sights you visit (quite a lifesaver at

Rome's special churches

In the course of visiting and reading about Rome you may come across the concept of the four **patriarchal basilicas** of Rome: St Peter's, San Giovanni in Laterano, San Paolo fuori le Mura and Santa Maria Maggiore. These are the four most important churches in Rome, and therefore of the Catholic church, and they symbolically represent the various parts of the world where the Catholic faith has reached. Apart from Santa Maria Maggiore, each one is technically part of the Vatican state (ie not Italian territory), and each has a Holy Door that is only opened – by the pope – every 25 years. San Giovanni in Laterano used to be the home of the pope and the Vatican, and is still technically the cathedral of Rome. Over the centuries pilgrims have always made a point of visiting these churches, plus the three other so-called "pilgrimage" churches - San Lorenzo fuori le Mura (occasionally included as a patriarchal basilica), Santa Croce in Gerusalemme and San Sebastiano fuori le Mura. It's a tradition that continues to this day, though Christian visitor numbers are these days swelled several-fold by tourists and other visitors.

the Colosseum). Some sites and museums also give discounts or even free admission to students and EU citizens under 18 or over 65 – but you need to make sure you have the relevant ID.

Churches

Rome is very used to tourists, but the rules for visiting **churches** are much as they are all over Italy. Dress modestly, which usually means no shorts (not even Bermuda-length ones) for men or women and covered shoulders for women, and try to avoid wandering around during a service. We've given opening hours throughout the guide, but most major Roman churches open in the early morning, at around 7 or 8am, and close around noon, opening up again at 4pm and closing at 6 or 7pm. Like ancient sites and some museums, hours may be shorter during the winter months. At any time of year some of the less-visited churches will open only for early morning and evening services, and some are closed at all times except Sundays and on religious holidays; if you're determined to take a look, you may have to ask around for the key, or make an appointment with the custodian.

Tourist information

There are tourist information **booths** at Fiumicino, at terminal B (daily 8.15am–7pm), and by platform 4 at Termini (daily 8am–9pm), although the long queues that often develop at both mean you're usually better off heading straight for the **main tourist office** at Via Parigi 5 (Mon–Sat 9am–7pm; ☎06.8205.9127, ⓦwww.romaturismo.it), five minutes' walk from Termini. They have free maps that – together with our own – should be ample for finding your way around, and lots of other printed information, and can help with accommodation if necessary. There are also **information kiosks** (daily 9am–6pm) in key locations around the city centre (see box, below) that are useful for free maps, directions (the staff usually speak English) and details about nearby sights – though they can be pretty clueless if you have anything other than an obvious need. Another good source of information is the privately run **Enjoy Rome**, Via Marghera 8a (Mon–Fri 8.30am–7pm, Sat 8.30am–2pm; ☎06.445.1843, ⓦwww.enjoyrome.com), whose friendly, English-speaking staff hand out lots of free information; they also operate a free room-finding service, organize tours, have a left-luggage service for customers and run a shuttle bus to Fiumicino.

Rome online

ⓦ**www.capitolium.org** The official website of the forums, with pictorial reconstructions of how the ruins would have looked in their day, material on life in ancient Rome, and even a live web view of the forum.

Information kiosks

Castel Sant'Angelo Piazza Pia ☎06.6880.9707.
Fontana di Trevi Via Minghetti ☎06.678.2988.
Fori Imperiali, Piazza del Tempio della Pace ☎06.6992.4307.
Piazza Navona Piazza delle Cinque Lune ☎06.6880.9240.
San Giovanni Piazza San Giovanni in Laterano ☎06.7720.3535.
Santa Maria Maggiore Via dell'Olmata ☎06.474.0955.
Trastevere Piazza Sonnino ☎06.5833.3457.
Via del Corso Largo Goldoni ☎06.6813.6061.
Via Nazionale Palazzo delle Esposizioni ☎06.4782.4525.

Ⓦ www.catacombe.roma.it Official site of Rome's Christian catacombs, with visuals, historical descriptions, and explanations of ancient symbols.

Ⓦ www.comune.roma.it Italian-language website of the Rome city authorities but with information in English, and particularly useful material if you're spending longer in the city.

Ⓦ www.enjoyrome.com Site of the helpful tourist organization, with information on accommodation and tours – and links to other popular Rome websites.

Ⓦ www.romaclick.com Decent Rome-specific accommodation booking engine.

Ⓦ www.romeguide.it Site of the "Il Sogno" cooperative, which aims to place young people in work in the tourist industry in Rome. A useful resource whether you're after a walking tour of the city centre, a guide to a particular monument or gallery or even the chance to go on a "ghost tour" of Rome. Good for up-to-date information on concerts and events too.

Ⓦ www.stpetersbasilica.org Site devoted to the wonders of St Peter's, with lots of photos and an interactive floorplan.

Ⓦ www.siamoroma.com General Rome site with lots of information for both English-speaking visitors and ex-pats.

Ⓦ www.vatican.va Slick, multilingual website of the Holy See, with material – some still under construction – on the Vatican Museums, the institutions of the city state and its online newspaper.

Ⓦ www.en.venere.com/hotels_rome/ Good general site for accessing Rome hotels online.

Tourist offices abroad

Australia Level 4, 46 Market St, Sydney, NSW 2000 ℡ 02/926-21666, Ⓔ italia@italiatourism.com.

Canada 175 Bloor St East, Suite 907, South Tower, Toronto, ON M4W 3R8 ℡ 416/925 4882, Ⓔ enitto@italiantourism.com, Ⓦ www.italiantourism.com.

UK 1 Princes St, London W1R 2AY ℡ 0207/408 1254 or 00800/00482542, Ⓔ italy@italiantouristboard.co.uk.

US 630 Fifth Avenue, Suite 1565, New York NY 10111 ℡ 212/245 4822, Ⓔ enitny@italiantourism.com; 12400 Wilshire Boulevard, Suite 550, Los Angeles, CA 90025 ℡ 310/820 1898, Ⓔ enitla@italiantourism.com, Ⓦ www.italiantourism.com; 500 North Michigan Ave, Suite 2240, Chicago IL 60611 ℡ 312/644-0996, Ⓔ enitch@ataliantourism.com, Ⓦ www.italiantourism.com.

Tours

A number of companies run organized trips around the city centre, though these are, for the most part, quite pricey and for general orientation and a glance at the main sights,

the ATAC-run #110 Open bus is much better value. See p.27 for more on this and other bus tours operated by ATAC.

Enjoy Rome Via Marghera 8a; Mon–Fri 8.30am–7pm, Sat 8.30am–2pm; ℡ 06.445.1843, Ⓕ 06.445.0734, Ⓦ www.enjoyrome.com. Enjoy Rome-run inexpensive walking tours of the city given by native English speakers in groups of no more than 25 people. Standard three-hour tours of places such as the Vatican, Ancient Rome, Trastevere or the old centre cost €18 per person; tours of the Via Appia, Gastronomic Rome, or special themes like Carvaggio's or Bernini's Rome cost a bit more and have to be booked further in advance. Enjoy Rome also act as an agent for Vastours bus tours (see below).

Institute of Design and Culture ℡ 940/202-4700, Ⓦ www.idcrome.org. US-based organization offering a great range of city courses with a cultural slant led by experts on Rome. They mostly last half a day and are not cheap, but you get what you pay for; choose from anything from the Baroque to Ancient Rome to *Tosca* – even offers cooking classes with visits to the city's markets.

Il Sogno Viale Regina Margherita 192 ℡ 06.8530.1758, Ⓦ www.romeguide.it. This long-established cooperative runs a range of tours of individual sights and is perhaps the best for a guided tour of a specific place.

Rome Revealed ℡ 06.324.741, Ⓦ www .romerevealed.com. Informative and entertaining walking tours run by native English speakers. Standard tours include the Vatican, the catacombs, the Fountains of Rome and several others, but you can also attend a thrice-weekly cookery workshop, or they can put together individual tours to your specifications. Prices for the standard tours go for €25–40 per person.

Through Eternity ℡ 06.700.9336. Ⓦ www .througheternity.com. Everything from straightforward visits to the Vatican and Capitoline Museums for €25–40 a head to themed tours like Rome at Twilight.

Vastours Via Piemonte 32 ℡ 06.481.4246, Ⓦ www .vastours.it. This nationwide tour company operates a wide range of themed city-centre excursions by coach with English-speaking guides, at a cost of €30–40 a head. They also do decent excursions to outlying sights like Ostia Antica and Tivoli for around €50 per person, as well as themed tours of the city that include papal audiences and Rome by Night. Or you could just opt for their Bus 'n' Boat open tour, where for a daily price of €13 you can hop on and off buses and boats that navigate six stops along the river and nine in the city centre every hour.

International Wine Academy Vicolo del Bottino 8 ℡ 06.699.0878. Wine courses, tours of Lazio vineyards, rooms (see p.225), and a bar and restaurant too – right in the heart of Rome just off Piazza di Spagna.

Travel essentials

Crime

Rome is a pretty safe city by any standards, but particularly when compared to its counterparts in the US and UK. The main thing is to make sure you're not too obvious a target for petty criminals by taking some common-sense **precautions**. Most of the crime you're likely to come across will be bag-snatching, where gangs of either street kids or *scippatori* or "snatchers" operate; *scippatori* work on foot or on scooters, disappearing before you've had time to react; the kids are more likely to crowd you in a group, trying to work their way into your bags or pockets while you're trying to shoo them away. As well as handbags, they whip wallets, tear off visible jewellery and, if they're really adroit, unstrap watches. You can minimize the risk of this happening by being discreet: don't flash anything of value, keep a firm hand on your camera, and carry shoulderbags, as Italian women do, slung across your body. It's also worth being vigilant when withdrawing money from ATMs. Be aware of anyone standing too close or trying to distract you during a withdrawal – they may be trying to read your PIN or clone your card using a "skimmer" machine. Contact your bank or credit card provider immediately if you suspect you're a victim of card fraud.

There are not really any parts of town you should avoid, and although some of the areas around **Termini** can be a bit rough, the neighbourhood is changing and in any case it's more uncomfortable than dangerous. Deserted stretches around **Ostiense** or **Testaccio** are probably worth avoiding at night, but again this is just to be on the safe side rather than because of any track record of violent crime in these areas.

If the worst happens, you may be forced to have some dealings with the **police**. In Italy this is principally divided between the Vigili Urbani, mainly concerned with directing traffic and issuing parking fines; the Polizia Statale, the main crime-fighting force; and

the Carabinieri, with their military-style uniforms and white shoulder belts, who also deal with general crime, public order and drug control. The Polizia enjoy a fierce rivalry with the Carabinieri and are the ones you'll perhaps have most chance of coming into contact with, since thefts should be reported to them. You'll find the address of the Questura or police station in the telephone directory.

Entry requirements

British, Irish and other EU citizens can enter Italy and stay as long as they like on production of a valid **passport**. Citizens of the United States, Canada, Australia and New Zealand need only a valid passport, too, but are limited to stays of three months. All other nationals should consult the relevant embassy about **visa requirements**. Legally, you're required to register with the police within three days of entering Italy, though if you're staying at a hotel this will be done for you.

Embassies

Australia Via Bosio 5 ☏ 06.852.721.
Britain Via XX Settembre 80a ☏ 06.4220.0001.
Canada Via G.B. de Rossi 30 ☏ 06.445.981.
Ireland Piazza Campitelli 3 ☏ 06.697.9121.
New Zealand Via Zara 28 ☏ 06.441.7171.
USA Via Veneto 119a ☏ 06.46.741.

Italian embassies and consulates abroad

Australia Embassy: 12 Grey St, Deakin, Canberra, ACT 2600 ☏ 02/6273 3333, ⊛ www.ambcanberra .esteri.it. Consulates in Melbourne ☏ 03/9867 5744; Sydney ☏ 02/9392 7900; Adelaide ☏ 08/8337 0777; Brisbane ☏ 07/3299 8944.
Canada Embassy: 275 Slater St, Ottawa, ON, K1P 5H9 ☏ 613/232-2401, ⊛ www.ambottawa .esteri.it. Consulates in Montreal ☏ 514/849-8351 and Toronto ☏ 416/977-1566.
Ireland Embassy: 63–65 Northumberland Rd, Dublin 4 ☏ 01/660 1744, ⊛ www.ambdublino.esteri.it.

New Zealand Embassy: 34–38 Grant Rd, PO Box 463, Thorndon, Wellington ☎04/473-5339, ⓦwww.ambwellington.esteri.it.
South Africa Embassy: 796 George Ave, 0083 Arcadia, Pretoria ☎012/423-0000, ⓦwww.ambpretoria.esteri.it.
UK Embassy: 14 Three King's Yard, London W1Y 2EH ☎020/7312 2200, ⓦwww.amblondra.esteri.it. Consulate in Manchester ☎0161/236 9024.
USA Embassy: 3000 Whitehaven St NW, Washington DC 20008 ☎202/612-4400, ⓦwww.ambwashingtondc.esteri.it/. Consulates in Boston ☎617/722-9201, Chicago ☎312/467-1550, New York ☎212/737-9100, San Francisco ☎415/931-4924 and other cities nationwide.

Health

As a member of the European Union, Italy has free reciprocal **health** agreements with other member states. EU citizens are entitled to free treatment within Italy's public health-care system on production of a European Health Insurance Card (EHIC), which you can obtain by picking up a form at the post office, calling ☎0845 606 2030, or applying online at ⓦwww.dh.gov.uk. Allow up to 21 days for delivery. The EHIC is free of charge and is valid for at least three years, and it basically entitles you to the same treatment as an insured person in Italy. The Australian Medicare system also has a reciprocal health-care arrangement with Italy. Vaccinations are not required, and Rome doesn't present any more health worries than anywhere else in Europe; the worst that's likely to happen to you is suffering from the extreme heat in summer or an upset stomach. The water that you'll see flowing from public fountains all over town is perfectly safe to drink, though look out for *acqua non potabile* signs, indicating that the water is unsafe to drink. It's worth taking insect repellent, too, as the countryside around

Rome is rather prone to mosquitoes. A **pharmacist** (*farmacia*) is well qualified to give you advice on minor ailments and to dispense prescriptions, and there are a number that are open outside normal hours (see below). If you need treatment, go to a **doctor** (*medico*); if you are seriously ill or involved in an accident, go straight to the **Pronto Soccorso** (casualty) of the nearest hospital, or phone ☎113 and ask for *ospedale* or *ambulanza*.

Dentist

Absolute Dentistry Dr Andrea Chiantini, Via G. Pisanelli 1/3, has a 24hr emergency service ☎06.3600.3837 or ☎339.250.7016.

Doctors

AlphaMed Via Zanardelli 36 ☎06.6830.9493. Ultra-central medical practice with English-speaking doctors. Mon–Fri 9am–8pm.
Tobias Wallbrecher Via Domenico Silveri 30 ☎06.638.0569. General English-speaking family doctor close to the Vatican. Mon–Fri 9am–1pm & 4–7pm.

Hospitals

The most central hospitals with emergency facilities are:
Fatebenefratelli Isola Tiberina (☎06.683.7299).
Rome American Hospital Via E. Longoni 81 (☎06.22.551). A private multi-speciality hospital with bilingual staff. Has a 24hr emergency line.
San Giovanni Via A. Aradam 8 ☎06.49.971.
Santo Spirito Lungotevere in Sassia 1 (☎06.68.351), near the Vatican.

Pharmacies

The following pharmacies are open 24hr, year-round:

Emergencies

For help in an emergency, call one of the following national telephone numbers:
Police or any emergency service, including ambulance (Soccorso Pubblico di Emergenza) ☎113.
Carabinieri ☎112.
Ambulance (Ambulanza) ☎118.
Fire (Vigili del Fuoco) ☎115.
Road assistance (Soccorso Stradale) ☎116.

Farmacia della Stazione Piazza dei Cinquecento 51 ☏06.488.0019.
Internazionale Piazza Barberini 49 ☏06.4825456.
Piram Via Nazionale 228 ☏06.488.0754.

Insurance

Even though EU health care privileges apply in Italy, you'd do well to take out an **insurance policy** before travelling to cover against theft, loss, illness or injury. A typical policy usually provides cover for the loss of baggage, tickets and – up to a certain limit – cash or cheques, as well as cancellation or curtailment of your journey. Most policies exclude so-called **dangerous sports** unless an extra premium is paid: in Italy this can mean scuba-diving, windsurfing and trekking. Many policies can be chopped and changed to exclude coverage you don't need – for example, sickness and accident benefits can often be excluded or included at will. If you do take medical coverage, ascertain whether benefits will be paid as treatment proceeds or only after your return home, and whether there is a 24-hour medical emergency number. When securing baggage cover, make sure that the per-article limit – typically under £500 – will cover your most valuable possession. If you need to make a claim, you should keep receipts for medicines and medical treatment, and in the event you have anything stolen, you must obtain an official statement from the police (*polizia* or *carabinieri*).

Rough Guides has teamed up with Columbus Direct to offer you **travel insurance** that can be tailored to suit your needs. Products include a low-cost **backpacker option** for long stays; a **short-break option** for city getaways; a typical **holiday-package option**; and others. There are also annual **multi-trip policies** for those who travel regularly. Different sports and activities (trekking, skiing, etc) can usually be covered if required. See our website (Ⓦwww.roughguidesinsurance.com) for eligibility and purchasing options. Alternatively, UK residents should call ☏0870/033 9988; Australians should call ☏1300/669 999 and New Zealanders should call ☏0800/55 9911. All other nationalities should call ☏+44 870/890 2843.

Internet

Internet cafés are as ubiquitous as in any European city so you should never be stuck for a place to get online. Reckon on paying around €2.50 an hour on average.
Bibli Via dei Fienaroli 28 (Mon 5.30pm–midnight, Tues–Sun 11am–midnight).
Easy Internet Café Via Barberini 2 (daily 7–1am).
Internet Train Piazza Sant'Andrea delle Valle 3 (Mon–Fri 10am–11pm, Sat 10am–8pm, Sun noon–8pm).
Internet Café Via Cavour 213 (daily 9–1am) ☏06.4782.3051.
Pole2Pole Via Santa Maria Maggiore 129 (daily 9am–11pm).

Laundries

You can usually get your laundry done in your hotel if you're staying at anywhere but the cheapest places but if you can't, try **Onda Blu**, Via Vespasiano 50, near the Vatican (daily 8am–10pm); or **Wash and Dry**, Via Della Pelliccia 35 & Via della Chiesa Nuova 15/16 (both daily 8am–10pm). All offer a wash including soap and tumble-drying for around €10 for a 6kg (15lb) load.

Libraries

The **British Council**, Via delle Quattro Fontane 20 (Mon–Tues & Thurs–Fri 10am–1pm, Wed 2–5pm; closed Aug & Christmas; ☏06.478.141), has a small video library. But the best library is the one at the American church of **Santa Susanna**, Via XX Settembre 14 (☏06.482.7510), which costs around €18 a year, and also has a good noticeboard for finding work, accommodation and so on (Tues 10am–1pm, Wed 3–6pm, Fri 1–4pm, Sat & Sun 10am–12.30pm). Reference libraries include those of the **American Studies Center**, Via M. Caetani 32 (☏06.6880.1613) and the **British School at Rome**, Via Gramsci 61 ☏06.326.4939 (Mon–Thurs 9am–1pm & 2–6.30pm, Fri 9am–1pm & 2–5pm), although it can be hard to get access unless you're a scholar.

Lost property

For property lost on a train call ☏06.4730.6682 (daily 7am–11pm); on a bus ☏06.581.6040 (Mon & Fri 8.30am–1pm, Tues–Thurs 2.30–6pm); on the metro ☏06.487.4309.

Mail

General information on Italian postal services is available on ☎803.160 or at ⊛www.poste .it. Rome's main post office on Piazza San Silvestro is open Monday to Saturday 8am to 7pm; other post office hours vary, but tend to be Monday to Friday 8.30am to 2pm, Saturday 8.30am to 1pm. Stamps (*francobolli*), are sold in *tabacchi* too, as well as in some gift shops; they will often also weigh your letter. The Italian postal system is one of the slowest in Europe, and if your letter is urgent make sure you send it "posta prioritaria", which has varying rates according to weight and destination. If you don't want to trust the Italian post at all, in Rome at least you have a choice: the Vatican postal system is quicker, loses less, and you get the benefit of an exotic postmark. However, not unreasonably, you have to use Vatican stamps and post your items from the Vatican itself. For this there are post offices and boxes in Piazza San Pietro and in the Vatican Museums.

Maps

For **walking around the city** you should find the maps in this book more than adequate for your needs. If you require something more detailed, then the best choice (though we would say this) is *Rome: The Rough Guide Map*, which is waterproof, rip-proof and includes the locations of most of the recommendations in this book keyed onto the map. Another option is the 1:12,500 *TCI* map (€7), which includes more coverage of the outskirts and suburban neighbourhoods. For **public transport**, metro maps are posted up in every station, and we've printed

one at the end of this book. If you're going to use the system a lot, especially the buses, it may be worth investing in the excellent and detailed *Lozzi* transport map (€6), available from most newsstands and bookshops.

Media

The city has three daily free (Italian language) **newspapers** – *City*, *Metro* and the newer and slightly more highbrow *EPolis* available in bars and cafés, and from street bins, all over town. All have weather reports, what's on info and useful phone numbers. If you want to get into things in a bit more depth, or to practice your Italian, you might want to dip into one of the Italian dailies – though be advised that however good your Italian is, most of the country's national newspapers offer a pretty turgid read. Of the big nationals, the posh paper is the right-of-centre *Corriere della Sera*, to which *La Repubblica* is the left-of-centre alternative – both have Rome news supplements daily. The Rome papers are the popular *Il Messagero*, the right-leaning *Il Tempo*, and the Vatican daily *L'Osservatore Romano*, which also prints an English edition once a week. You'll notice that the sports coverage in all these papers is relatively thin. If you want in-depth football reporting you need to try one of three national sports dailies – either the pink *Gazzetto dello Sport*, the Rome-based *Corriere dello Sport*, or *Tuttosport*.

If all you want is **what's on information**, the city's best source of listings is the weekly *Romac'è* (€1.20), which has a helpful section in English giving information on tours, clubs, restaurants, services and weekly events, and

---

Central post offices

Piazza San Silvestro 12 ☎06.6976.6320.
Corso Vittorio Emanuele II 330 ☎06.6840.2920.
Largo Brancaccio 82 (Via Marmorata) ☎06.4890.3635.
Via Arenula 4 ☎06.684.0501.
Via Cavour 277 ☎06.462.0741.
Via Giolitti 14 ☎06.488.8741.
Via del Quirinale 30 ☎06.474.0226.
Via Milano 18 (Via Nazionale) ☎06.474.5631
Via della Scrofa 61 ☎06.6840.9220.

a decent website – ⓦwww
.romace.it. The twice-monthly English ex-pat
magazine, Wanted in Rome (€0.75) –
ⓦwww.wantedinrome.com – is also a useful
source of information, especially if you're
looking for an apartment or work. Both are
available at most newsstands. For those with
a bit of Italian, the daily arts pages of *Il
Messaggero* list movies, plays and major
musical events, and *La Repubblica* includes
the "Trova Roma" supplement, another
handy guide to current offerings, in its
Thursday edition.

Finally, **English-language newspapers** are
available the same day of publication, usually
after lunch, at newsstands all over town. *The
International Herald Tribune*, available at most
newsstands, is printed in Italy and includes
an Italian news supplement.

Money

Italy's currency is the **euro** (€). The euro is
split into 100 cents. There are seven euro
notes – in denominations of 500, 200, 100,
50, 20, 10, and 5 euros, each a different
colour and size – and eight different **coin**
denominations, with 2 and 1 euros, then 50,
20, 10, 5, 2, and 1 cents. Euro coins feature
a common EU design on one face, but
different country-specific designs on the other
(including one for the Vatican). At the time of
writing the working rate of exchange is £1 =
€1.49; US$1 = €0.76; Aus$1 = €0.60; NZ$1
= €0.53. For the latest rates check: ⓦwww
.oanda.com or ⓦwww.xe.com.

If you're travelling from the UK it's a good
idea to have some euros on you when you
arrive; otherwise to get euros just use your
debit card in the local ATM machines
(*Bancomats*); there's usually a charge but
you won't spend more getting money this
way than any other. Travellers from
elsewhere, or on longer stays, may prefer to
use **traveller's cheques**. American Express
and the Thomas Cook and Visa alternatives
are widely accepted. Buying online in
advance usually works out cheapest. Make
sure you keep the purchase agreement and
a record of cheque serial numbers safe and
separate from the cheques themselves. In
the event that cheques are lost or stolen,
the issuing company will expect you to
report the loss immediately to their office in

Lost or stolen credit cards and traveller's cheques

Credit cards
American Express ☎800.914.912.
Mastercard ☎800.870.866.
Visa ☎800.819.014

Traveller's cheques
American Express ☎800.914.912.
Thomas Cook ☎800.872.050.
Visa ☎800.874.155.

Italy; most companies claim to replace lost
or stolen cheques within 24 hours. It's
advisable to buy euro traveller's cheques
rather than dollars or pounds sterling since
you won't have to pay commission when
you cash them. **Credit cards** are a very
handy backup source of funds, and can be
used either over the counter or in ATMs,
providing you have a PIN number that's
designed to work overseas. Remember that
all cash advances are treated as loans, with
interest accruing daily from the date of
withdrawal; there is often a transaction fee
on top of this.

Banking hours are normally Monday to
Friday mornings from 8.30am until 1.30pm,
and for an hour in the afternoon (usually
between 2.30pm and 4pm). Outside banking
hours, the larger hotels will change money or
traveller's cheques, or there are plenty of
exchange bureaux – normally open evenings
and weekends. Try American Express,
Piazza di Spagna 38 (Mon–Fri 9am–5.30pm,
Sat 9am–12.30pm); Thomas Cook, Piazza
Barberini 21a (Mon–Sat 9am–8pm, Sun
9.30am–5pm), and Via della Conciliazione
23 (Mon–Sat 8.30am–7.30pm, Sun 9.30am–
5pm). Post offices will exchange American
Express traveller's cheques and cash
commission-free. The last resort should be
any of the many *Ufficio Cambio* kiosks,
almost always offering the worst rates
(despite "no commission" signs).

Opening hours and public holidays

The city's **opening hours** are becoming
more flexible, but much of Rome still follows
a traditional Italian routine. Most shops and
businesses in Italy open Monday to Saturday

from around 8am until 1pm, and from about 4pm until 7 or 8pm, although many shops close on Saturday afternoons and Monday mornings; a few of the more international businesses follow a nine-to-five schedule. Traditionally, everything except bars and restaurants closes on Sunday, though there's usually a *pasticceria* (pastry shop) open in the mornings and in general Sunday opening is becoming more common. For the opening hours of churches and museums, see p.29. The other factors to be aware of are national holidays and the fact that in August, particularly during the weeks either side of *Ferragosto*, most of Rome flees to the coast, many shops, bars and restaurants close and the only people around are other tourists. On official national holidays everything closes down except bars and restaurants.

Phones

Public telephones, run by Telecom Italia, come in various forms in Rome, but they usually have clear instructions in English. Coin-operated machines are increasingly hard to find and you will probably have to buy a **telephone card** (*carta* or *scheda telefonica*), available from *tabacchi* and newsstands in denominations of €5 and €10. You always need to dail 06, the code for Rome, regardless of whether you are in the city. All **telephone numbers** listed in this guide include the Rome code. Numbers beginning ℡800 are free, ℡170 will get you through to an English-speaking operator, ℡176 to international directory enquiries. Italian **phone tariffs** are expensive, especially if you're calling long-distance or internationally, and even Rome residents use **phone calling cards** if they're calling long-distance. You can buy these easily from *tabacchi* for upwards of €5. Commons cards include the *Columbus* for calls to Western Europe and North America, the standard *Scheda Telefonica Internazionale* for the rest of the world, and the *Europa Card* for calls to Europe, US and Canada only. To use one of these cards, you dial a central number and then enter a pin code given on the reverse of the card, before dialling the number you want to reach. Finally, you can make international reversed charge or collect calls (*chiamata con addebito destinatario*) by dialling ℡170 and following the recorded instructions.

You can use your **mobile phone** – or *telefonino* – in Italy, and indeed you will hardly ever see an Italian without his or her mobile clasped to the ear. You are likely to be charged extra for incoming calls when abroad, as the people calling you will be paying the usual rate. If you want to retrieve messages while you're away, you might have to ask your provider for a new access code. For further information about using your phone abroad contact your network or check out Ⓦwww.telecomsadvice.org.uk. Locally, any numbers that start with three digits beginning with a 3 will most likely be a mobile and consequently a more expensive call.

National holidays

January 1 (New Year's Day)
January 6 (Epiphany)
Pasquetta (Easter Monday)
April 25 (Liberation Day)
May 1 (Labour Day)
June 2 (Republic Day)
August 15 (*Ferragosto*; Assumption of the Blessed Virgin Mary)
November 1 (*Ognissanti*; All Souls Day)
December 8 (*Immaccolata*; Immaculate Conception of the Blessed Virgin Mary)
December 25 (*Natale*; Christmas)
December 26 (*Santo Stefano*; St Stephen's Day)

International calls

Calling home from Italy
Australia + 61 + city code.
Ireland + 353 + city code.
New Zealand + 64 + city code.
UK and Northern Ireland + 44 + city code.
USA and Canada + 1 + area code.
South Africa + 27 + city code.

Calling Italy from abroad
To call Italy **from abroad**, dial the access code ☎00 from the UK, Ireland and New Zealand, ☎011 from the US and Canada, ☎0011 from Australia, followed by 39, then the area code **including the first zero** and finally the subscriber number.

Study

American Academy Via Angelo Masina 5, 00153 Rome ☎06.58.461 ⓦwww.aarome.org.
British School at Rome Via Gramsxi 61, 00197 Rome ☎06.326.4939 ⓦwww.bsr.ac.uk.

Time

Rome is one hour ahead of GMT, six hours ahead of Eastern Standard Time, and nine hours ahead of Pacific Standard Time.

Toilets

Caught short? There's a free public lavatory on Piazza Zanardelli, just north of Piazza Navona – something of a rarity in Rome. Apart from the facilities in McDonalds, which are always worth trying if you're desperate, the only other public loos in anything like a central location are those in Termini station.

Travel agents

For discount tickets, try the CTS offices at Via Genova 16 ☎06.462.0431 and Corso Vittorio Emanuele II 297 ☎06.687.2672, both open Saturday mornings, when other travel agents are closed. Other good places to try are Viaggiare, Via San Nicola da Tolentino 15 ☎06.421.171, who have some English-speaking staff, and Elsy Viaggi, Via di Torre Argentina 80 ☎06.689.6460.

Travellers with disabilities

Rome can be quite a challenge for those with disabilities: there are lots of steps, pavements are uneven, and Italy as a whole is just not as accessible as a lot of northern Europe and North America. The Consorzio Cooperative Integrate (COIN), Via degli Zingari 59 (☎06.712.9011, ⓦwww.coinsociale.it) makes things a bit easier, with a 24hr information line, a website and a disabled guide to the city, *Roma Accessible*, which contains information on accessibility to major sites, museums, hotels and restaurants.

Only two stops on metro line A are accessible for disabled persons (Cipro-Musei Vaticani and Valle Aurelia), but bus #591 does the same route and can accommodate those with disabilities. On line B, Circo Massimo, Colosseo and Cavour do not have accessibility, but bus #75 stops at those sights and has new buses that can accommodate those with disabilities (although you may have to wait for a few of the older buses to go by).

The City

The City

Piazza Venezia and the Capitoline Hill

For many people the modern centre of Rome is **Piazza Venezia**. It's not so much a square as a road junction, and a busy one at that, but it's a good place to start your wanderings, close to both the medieval and Renaissance centre of Rome and most of the city's ancient ruins. Flanked on all sides by imposing buildings, the piazza is a dignified focal point for the city in spite of the traffic, and a spot you'll find yourself returning to time and again – by some way the best landmarked open space in Rome, with the great white bulk of the Vittorio Emanuele Monument marking it out from almost anywhere in the city. The **Vittoriano**, as it's known, is now open to the public, and despite being a widely disliked building is one of the best sights in the city – both for its views and for the alternative route it gives to the Piazza del Campidoglio and the unmissable **Capitoline Museums** on the Capitoline Hill, the first-settled and most central of Rome's seven hills.

Piazza Venezia

There's not much need to linger on **Piazza Venezia** itself: it's more a place to catch a bus or pick up a taxi than soak up the atmosphere. A legacy of nineteenth-century Rome, it looked quite different a couple of hundred years ago, when it was the domain of the Venetian pope, Paul II, whose Palazzo Venezia dominated this part of the city, its gardens reaching around its south side, where the Vittoriano now stands. On the northern side, the canyon of Via del Corso, Rome's main street, begins its mile-and-a-half journey to the other side of the city centre at the Piazza del Popolo, its opening stretch flanked by the nineteenth-century **Palazzo Bonaparte** on the left, with its green shuttered balcony. It was from here that Napoleon's mother Letizia Bonaparte, who lived here after he was deposed until her death in 1836, used to keep an eye on the comings-and-goings outside, though nowadays it's privately owned and the shutters are usually closed.

Palazzo Venezia

Forming the western side of the piazza, **Palazzo Venezia**, Via del Plebiscito 118 (Tues–Sun 8.30am–7.30pm; €4), was the first large Renaissance palace in the city, built in the mid-fifteenth century and for several centuries the embassy of the Venetian Republic. Famously, Mussolini moved in here while in power, occupying the vast Sala del Mappamondo and making his declamatory speeches to the huge crowds below from the small balcony facing on to the piazza proper. In those days the palace lights would be left on to give the impression of constant activity in what was the centre of the Fascist government and war effort. Now it's a more peripheral building, a venue for good temporary exhibitions and home to a **museum of Renaissance arts and crafts** made up of the magpie-ish collection of Pope Paul II. The **paintings** include a lot of fifteenth-century devotional works from central and northern Italy. Among numerous *Crucifixions* and *Madonnas*, look out for an arresting double portrait of two young men by Giorgione in the first room; a late-sixteenth century *Deposition of Christ* by Borgianni in room 6, in which Christ is viewed from the feet up by way of clever use of perspective (a copy, basically, of Mantegna's painting of the same subject); and, in a small ante-room, Algardi's 1650 bust of a severe-looking Innocent X. There are also a number of polychromatic wooden statues, notably two figures from a Magi group from the Marche and a lovely Madonna and Child from Lazio, both thirteenth century. The ceiling paintings in room 7 are by Vasari, and depict Ceres, the Roman goddess of agriculture and the various months and seasons; they were in fact designed for another building and moved here in the late nineteenth century.

Beyond here, a corridor lined with ceramics skirts the courtyard to link with the palazzetto next door, where you can find a couple of rooms of beautifully displayed bronzes – a wide array of figures, animals and copies of ancient sculptures by Bernini and Giambologna among others. Around the corner are more sculptural pieces, including a tortured head of Seneca by Guido Reni and Algardi's representation of St Philip Neri with an angel, a study of St Theresa for Bernini's statue in the church of Santa Maria Vittoria and some designs for the Trevi Fountain by Pietro Bracci; and finally some rooms full of weapons and ceramic jars from an ancient monastic pharmacy. You can walk out to the palace's upper **loggia** for a view over the palm-filled courtyard – the loggia is crammed full of ancient sculptural fragments and the gardens are some of the prettiest in Rome.

San Marco

Adjacent to the palace on its southern side, the church of **San Marco** (daily 8am–noon & 4–7pm; closed Mon am & Wed pm), accessible from Piazza San Marco, is one of the oldest basilicas in Rome. This dark, cosy church was founded in 336 AD, on the spot where the apostle is supposed to have lived while in the city. It was rebuilt in 833 and added to by various Renaissance and eighteenth-century popes – Paul II restored it and added the graceful portico and gilded ceiling. The apse mosaic dates from the ninth century and shows Pope Gregory IV offering his church to Christ, above a gracious semicircle of sheep that bear more than a passing resemblance to llamas. Back outside, tucked away in the corner, the statue of the busty harridan is "**Madam Lucretia**", actually an ancient depiction of Isis. Like Pasquino a few hundred metres away, she is one of Rome's so-called talking statues (see box, below) commenting in a satirical fashion on the affairs of the day.

Vittorio Emanuele Monument

The rest of the buildings on Piazza Venezia pale into insignificance beside the marble monstrosity rearing up across the street from San Marco – the **Vittorio Emanuele Monument** or Vittoriano (daily 9.30am–6pm; free), erected at the turn of the nineteenth century as the "Altar of the Nation" to commemorate Italian Unification. It has been variously likened to a typewriter (because of its shape), and, by American GIs, to a wedding cake (the white marble used will never mellow with age). King Vittorio Emanuele II, by all accounts a modest man, probably wouldn't have thought much of it. Indeed, the only person who seems to have benefited from the building is the prime minister at the time, who was a deputy for Brescia, from where (perhaps not entirely coincidentally) the marble was supplied.

After years out of bounds to the public, the Vittoriano is now open, which is just as well as at least this gives it a (kind of) purpose. It's great to clamber up and down the sweeping terraces and flights of steps which before you could only gaze at from the street. There are things to see inside the monument (see below) but it's the outside of the structure that should command most of your

---

Rome's talking statues

As the home of the papacy, Rome has long been a political city, and its people have always enjoyed commenting on and arguing about the important issues of the day. In Renaissance times, the antics of the Church, in particular the pope and the powerful Roman families who vied to fill the post, were the subject of intense curiosity and scrutiny. A number of "**talking statues**" – usually ancient, unidentified pieces, among them Madam Lucretia outside the basilica of San Marco, Pasquino just off Piazza Navona, the "baboon" on Via del Babuino, and Marforio, now in the courtyard of the Palazzo Nuovo – were a focus for this, hung as they were with witty rhymes and notes commenting on the hubris and foolishness of the movers and shakers of the papal city: a kind of gossip column-cum-parliamentary sketch where people would gather to talk and laugh at their political masters.

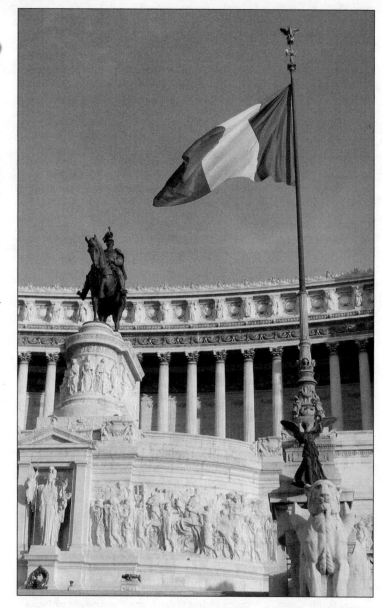

△ Vittorio Emanuele Monument

attention, full as it is of the weighty symbolism that was typical of the period. The figures either side of the entrance represent the two seas that surround Italy – the Tyrrhenian (on the right) and the Adriatic (on the left). At the top of the stairs is the Tomb of the Unknown Soldier, flanked by eternal flames and a permanent guard of honour. Up another flight of stairs sits the figure of Vittorio Emanuele II on horseback, at 10m x 12m one of the world's largest statues – his moustache alone is 3m long, and apparently twenty people once had lunch in the horse's belly – on a plinth friezed with figures representing the major cities of the Italian Republic. Above here, the huge, sweeping gallery stretches the width of the monument, with figures symbolizing the regions of Italy. The whole thing is undeniably impressive, if only for the sheer audaciousness of its conception, and there's a café around the back, from where you can now take a very useful shortcut through to Piazza del Campidoglio behind. Wherever you stand, though, the views of the city are the thing, perhaps because it's the one place in Rome from which you can't see the Vittoriano.

Inside the Vittoriano, the engaging **Museo di Risorgimento** follows the long corridor that runs around the back of the building, full of busts, weaponry and mementoes of the Unification struggle and beyond. Plus there are regular temporary art and other exhibitions held in the echoing chambers of the so-called **Complesso del Vittoriano**, which makes up the southeastern wing of the monument, accessible from the Via di San Pietro in Carcere.

The Capitoline Hill

The real pity about the Vittorio Emanuele Monument is that it obscures views of the **Capitoline Hill** behind – once, in the days of imperial Rome, the spiritual and political centre of the Roman Empire. The upside of this is that it gives a perfect route to the Capitoline, via the café right behind the Vittoriano and a passageway that delivers you right by the back entrance of Santa Maria in Aracoeli (see below), and just above the Piazza del Campidoglio.

The Capitoline's name derives from its position as the "caput mundi" or "head of the world", and its influence and importance resonate to this day, not least in language – "capitol" and "capital" originated here, as did "money", which comes from the temple to Juno Moneta that once stood on the hill and housed the Roman mint. The Capitoline also played a significant role in medieval and Renaissance times: the flamboyant fourteenth-century dictator, Cola di Rienzo, stood here in triumph in 1347, and was murdered here by an angry mob seven years later – a humble nineteenth-century statue marks the spot where he is said to have died. Michelangelo gave the hill's Piazza del Campidoglio its present form, redesigning it as a symbol of Rome's regeneration after the city was sacked by the troops of Holy Roman Emperor Charles V in 1527. These days the Capitoline forms a tight, self-contained group of essential attractions, with the focus on its pair of museums and the church of Santa Maria in Aracoeli.

Santa Maria in Aracoeli

The church of **Santa Maria in Aracoeli** (daily 9am–12.30pm & 3–6.30pm) crowns the highest point on the Capitoline Hill, and is built on the site of a temple to Jupiter where, according to legend, the Tiburtine Sibyl foretold the birth of Christ. It is reached by a flight of steps erected by Cola di Rienzo in 1348, the **Aracoeli Staircase**, although this is one of the city's steepest climbs and it's worth knowing that you can also access it from Piazza del Campidoglio, or direct from the Vittoriano. The church, one of Rome's most ancient basilicas, is worth it. Inside, in the first chapel on the right, there are some fine, humane frescoes by Pinturicchio recording the life of San Bernardino, with realistic tableaux of landscapes and bustling town scenes. The church is also known for its role as keeper of the so-called "Bambino", a small statue of the child Christ that was carved from the wood of a Gethsemane olive tree. Said to have healing powers, the statue was traditionally called out to the sickbeds of the ill and dying all over the city, its coach commanding instant right of way through the heavy Rome traffic. The Bambino was stolen in 1994, however, and a copy now stands in its place, in a small chapel to the left of the high altar.

Piazza del Campidoglio

Next door to the Aracoeli Staircase, the **Cordonata** is an elegant, smoothly rising ramp, and as such a much gentler climb. Topped with Roman statues of Castor and Pollux, it leads to **Piazza del Campidoglio**, one of Rome's most perfectly proportioned squares, designed by Michelangelo in the last years of his life for Pope Paul III, who was determined to hammer Rome back into shape for a visit by the Holy Roman Emperor, Charles V. In fact, Michelangelo died before his plan was completed (the square wasn't finished until the late seventeenth century), but his designs were faithfully executed, balancing the piazza, redesigning the facade of what is now Palazzo dei Conservatori and projecting an identical building across the way, known as Palazzo Nuovo. These buildings, which have been completely renovated in recent years, are home to the **Capitoline Museums** and feature some of the city's most important ancient sculpture. Both are angled slightly to focus on **Palazzo Senatorio**, Rome's town hall, with its double staircase and fountain, flanked by statues representing the Tiber and the Nile. In the centre of the square, Michelangelo placed an equestrian statue of Emperor Marcus Aurelius, which had previously stood unharmed for years outside San Giovanni in Laterano; early Christians had refrained from melting it down because they believed it to be of the Emperor Constantine (the first Roman ruler to acknowledge and follow Christianity). The original is now beautifully displayed in the new wing of the Palazzo dei Conservatori, and a copy has taken its place at the centre of the piazza.

The Capitoline Museums

If you see no other museums of ancient sculpture in Rome, at least try to see the **Capitoline Museums** (Tues–Sun 9am–8pm; €6.50, €8.50 for joint ticket with Centrale Montemartini – see p.115, valid for one visit to each museum over seven days; Ⓦwww.museicapitolini.org), perhaps the most venerable of all the city's collections. They're divided into two parts, one devoted only to sculpture, the other more extensive and wide-ranging with a gallery of paintings as well. You should if possible see both areas of the museum rather than choosing one, and tickets remain valid all day so you can easily take a break for a stroll around the Roman Forum in between.

Palazzo dei Conservatori

The **Palazzo dei Conservatori** on the right is perhaps the natural place to start, home as it is to the museums' ticket office and the larger, more varied collection, with ancient sculpture on the first floor and in the new wing at the back and paintings on the second floor. It has undergone quite a transformation in recent years with the incorporation of the Palazzo Clementio-Caffarelli into the museum, with its new wing housing some large ancient statuary and the newly discovered foundations of the Capitoline's original temple of Jupiter.

Ground and first floor

Some of the museum's ancient sculpture is littered around the ground floor courtyard by the entrance – most impressively the feet, hand and other fragments of a gigantic statue, believed to be of the Emperor Constantine, and one of the most popular images of Rome. Upstairs, the first room you enter is the massive *Hall of the Orazie e Curiaze*, where the curators of the collections used to meet, appropriately decorated with giant late-sixteenth-century frescoes showing legendary tales from the early days of the city – *The Discovery of the She-wolf*, at the western end, faces the *Rape of the Sabine Women* at the opposite end, while presiding over all are colossal statues of Pope Urban XIII and his successor Innocent X, by Bernini and Algardi respectively. Appropriately, it was the venue for the signing of the Treaty of Rome in 1957, and for the presentation of the EU's ill-fated draft constition nearly fifty years later.

The rooms that follow have more friezes and murals showing events from Roman history. Notably, the corner room contains the so-called *Spinario*, a Roman statue of a boy picking a thorn out of his foot, and a striking bronze head known as *Brutus* from the fourth century BC. The sacred symbol of Rome, the Etruscan bronze she-wolf nursing Romulus and Remus, the mythic founders of the city, gets a room to itself next door; the twins themselves are not Etruscan but were added by Pollaiuolo in the late fifteenth century, while on the walls the *Fasti* are an amazing record of magistrates and other political figures from the height of the Augustan age, rescued from the Forum. The next-door room is given over to two bronze Roman geese and a bust of Michelangelo, which Daniele da Volterra based on the artist's death mask, while further on there are more Roman bronzes – eagles this time – in a room with a Roman sculpture of the breast-laden Diana of Ephesus.

Retrace your steps slightly for the Hannibal Room, covered in wonderfully vivid fifteenth-century paintings recording Rome's wars with Carthage, and so named for a rendering of Hannibal seated impressively on an elephant, before moving on to the wonderfully airy new wing, where the original statue of Marcus Aurelius, formerly in the square outside, takes centre stage. Alongside it stand a giant bronze statue of Constantine – or at least its head, hand and orb – and a rippling bronze of Hercules, found near the Circus Maxentius. Behind are part of the foundations and a retaining wall from the Capitoline's original temple of Jupiter, discovered when the work for the new wing was undertaken.

There are some great exhibits around the main hall here: some remnants from the Iron Age on the Capitoline, statuary rescued from ancient gardens on the Esquiline Hill, including a statue of the emperor Commodus – the son of the decidedly more heroic Marcus Aurelius – as Hercules, the milk-white *Esquiline Venus*, and plenty more besides; and when museum fatigue sets in you can climb up to the second floor café, whose terrace commands one of the best views in Rome.

Second floor

The second-floor picture gallery or **pinacoteca** holds Renaissance painting from the fourteenth to the late seventeenth century – well-labelled, with descriptions of each work in Italian and English. The collection fills nine rooms, and highlights include a couple of portraits by Van Dyck and a penetrating *Portrait of a Crossbowman* by Lorenzo Lotto; a pair of paintings from 1590 by Tintoretto – a *Baptism of Christ*, and a *Flagellation*; some nice small-scale work by Annibale Carracci; and a very fine early work by Ludovico Carracci, *Head of a Boy*. There are also several sugary pieces by Guido Reni, done at the end of his life, including *St Sebastian*. In one of two large galleries, there's a vast picture by Guercino depicting the *Burial of Santa Petronilla* (an early Roman martyr who was the supposed daughter of St Peter), which used to hang in St Peter's and arrived here via the Quirinale palace and the Louvre. It is displayed alongside several other works by the same artist, notably a lovely, contemplative Persian Sibyl and a wonderful picture of Cleopatra cowed before a young and victorious Octavius (later Augustus). In the same room, there are also two paintings by Caravaggio, one a replica of the young *John the Baptist* which hangs in the Palazzo Doria Pamphilj, the other a famous canvas known as the *Fortune-Teller* – an early work that's an adept study in deception. The large room at the back holds paintings from the Sacchetti collection, which includes a number of works by Pietro da Cortona, among them portraits of Matteo Sacchetti and Pope Urban VIII and a *Triumph of Bacchus*.

Palazzo Nuovo

The same ticket gets you into the **Palazzo Nuovo** across the square – also accessible by way of an underground **walkway** that takes in yet more sculpture, the remains of a Roman temple, and a terrace which has probably the best, and certainly the most close-up, views of the Roman Forum just below. The Palazzo Nuovo is the more manageable of the two museums, its first floor concentrating some of the best of the city's Roman sculpture into half a dozen or so rooms and a long gallery crammed with elegant statuary. There's the remarkable, controlled statue of the *Dying Gaul*, a Roman copy of a Greek original; a naturalistic *Boy with Goose* – another copy; an original, grappling *Eros and Psyche*; a *Satyr Resting*, after a piece by Praxiteles, that was the inspiration for Hawthorne's book *The Marble Faun*; and the red marble *Laughing Silenus*, another Roman copy of a Hellenistic original. In the main *salone*, statues of an old and a young centaur face each other, and a naturalistic *Hunter* holds up a rabbit he has just killed. Walk through from here to the **Sala degli Imperatori**, with its busts of Roman emperors and other famous names, including a young Augustus, a cruel Caracalla, and, the centrepiece, a lifesize portrait of Helena, the mother of Constantine, reclining gracefully. Also, don't miss the *Capitoline Venus* – a coy, delicate piece, again based on a work by Praxiteles, housed in a room on its own. Finally, the **palace courtyard** is dominated by the large *Fountain of Marforio*, a bearded figure who was known as one of Rome's "talking statues" (see box, p.45), renowned in Renaissance times for speaking out in satirical verse against the authorities.

The Tarpeian Rock and San Pietro in Carcere

After seeing the museums, walk around behind the Palazzo Senatorio for another great view down over the Forum, with the Colosseum in the background. There's a copy of the statue of Romulus and Remus suckling the she-wolf here, while on the right, Via del Monte Tarpeio follows the brink of the old **Tarpeian Rock** – named after Tarpeia, who betrayed the city to the Sabines – from which traitors would be thrown in ancient times.

Steps lead down from here to the little church of **San Pietro in Carcere** (daily 10am–7pm; donation expected for the prison). The low-vaulted church itself doesn't attract much interest; it's the ancient Mamertine Prison beneath that people come to see. Here spies, vanquished soldiers and other enemies of the Roman state, including St Peter and St Paul, were incarcerated. More steps lead down into the murky depths of the jail, where you can see the bars to which St Peter was chained, along with the spring the saint is said to have created to baptize other prisoners; there's an altar which shows these baptisms, and a cross – upside-down, because this was how Peter was crucified. At the top of the staircase, hollowed out of the honeycomb of stone, is an imprint claimed to be of St Peter's head as he tumbled down the stairs (though when the prison was in use, the only access was through a hole in the ceiling). It's an unappealing place even now, and you won't be sorry to leave – through an exit cunningly placed to lead you through the gift shop.

Santi Luca e Martina

Opposite San Pietro, the church of **Santi Luca e Martina** is two churches in one, an elegant building that has been here since the eighth century, when it was dedicated to the little-known Christian martyr Martina, who preached on this site back in the third century AD. Later, it was given by Sixtus V to the artists' group, Accademia San Luca, who dedicated it to St Luke, the patron saint of painters, as well, and had it rebuilt in the mid-seventeenth century by Pietro da Cortona, who in turn is buried in the church in a tomb of his own design. These days the upper church is dedicated to Santa Martina, with a statue of the saint on the altar, and the lower to St Luke, with an altar by Pietro da Cortona and two works by Alessandro Algardi: a newly restored bas-relief of the *Deposition of Christ* and a terracotta *Pietà*.

The centro storico

he real heart of Rome is the **centro storico** or "historic centre", which makes up the greater part of the roughly triangular knob of land that bulges into a bend in the Tiber, above **Corso Vittorio Emanuele II** and to the west of **Via del Corso**, Rome's main street. In the days of ancient Rome, when it was known as the Campus Martius, this low-lying area lay outside the city centre and was mostly given over to barracks and sporting arenas, together with several temples – including the Pantheon. It became the heart of the Renaissance city, and today is the part of the town that is densest in interest, an unruly knot of narrow streets and alleys that holds some of the best of Rome's classical and Baroque heritage and its most vivacious **nightlife**.

It's here that most people find the Rome they have been looking for – the Rome of small crumbling piazzas, Renaissance churches and fountains, blind alleys and streets humming with scooters and foot-traffic. Whichever direction you wander in there's something to see; indeed it's part of the appeal of the centre of Rome that even the most aimless ambling leads you past some breath-lessly beautiful and historic spots.

From Via del Corso to the Pantheon

The eastern boundary of the historic centre, **Via del Corso** is Rome's main thoroughfare, linking Piazza Venezia at its southern end with the Piazza del Popolo to the north. You can follow it all the way up, dipping into the centro storico as and when you feel like it. The streets on this side of the centre focus on the ancient Roman dome of the **Pantheon**, and further north on the offices of the **Italian parliament** and prime minister.

Via del Corso

On its eastern side, **Via del Corso** gives onto the swish shopping thoroughfares that lead up to Piazza di Spagna; on its western side, a web of streets tangles its way down to the Tiber. Named after the races that used to take place along here during Renaissance times, the street has had its fair share of famous residents during the years: Goethe lived at no. 18 for two years, close to the Piazza del Popolo end (see p.84); the Shelleys – Percy and Mary – lived for several years in the Palazzo Vesporio, at Via del Corso 375 (now a bank), during which time they lost their son William to a fever (see p.114). Since the middle of the last

THE CENTRO STORICO

RESTAURANTS & CAFÉS

Da Alfredo e Ada	20
Armando al Pantheon	30
Il Bacaro	8
Da Baffetto	44
Bevitoria Navona	28
Boccondivino	9
Camilloni	39
La Campana	5
Capranica	16
Il Convivio da Troiani	6
Le Cornacchie	19
Davezzio	7
Delfino	47
Enoteca Corsi	45
Enoteca del Corso	35
La Focaccia	22
Da Francesco	31
Giolitti	12
Il Leoncino	1
Maccheroni	14
La Montecarlo	41
Myosotis	10
Obikà	4
Della Palma	17
Pascucci	46
Rosa Rosae	18
La Rosetta	15
Riccioli	40
Caffè Sant'Eustachio	43
Supperclub	26
Tapa Loca	23
La Tazza d'Oro	13
Da Tonino	36
El Toulà	2
Tre Scalini	27
Lo Zozzone	34

ACCOMMODATION

Abruzzi	G
Cesári	F
Due Torri	A
Genio	D
Mimosa	I
Navona	J
Nazionale	E
Pantheon	H
Portoghesi	B
Santa Chiara	K
Zanardelli	C

BARS

Anima	33
Bloom	38
Bar del Fico	29
Bar della Pace	25
Le Coppelle	42
Cul de Sac	11
Jazz Café	11
Jonathan's Angels	32
Miscellanea	21
La Trinchetta	24
Trinity College	37

century, it has become Rome's principal shopping street, home to a mixture of upmarket boutiques and chain stores that make it a busy stretch during the day, full of hurrying pedestrians and crammed buses, but a relatively dead one come the evening. The good news is that the top end, beyond Piazza Colonna, where the bulk of the shops are, is pedestrianized, making shopping and strolling much easier and more enjoyable.

The Palazzo and Galleria Doria Pamphilj

Walking north from Piazza Venezia, the first building on the left of Via del Corso, the **Palazzo Doria Pamphilj**, is among the city's finest Rococo palaces, with a facade added in 1734 to a building that was the product of years of construction and re-modelling dating back to Roman times, when a storehouse stood on this site. The Doria Pamphilj family were (and are) one of Rome's most illustrious, and still own the building and live in part of it. They were also prodigious collectors of art, and inside, through an entrance on Piazza di Collegio Romano, the **Galleria Doria Pamphilj**, Via del Collegio Romano 2, is one of Rome's best late-Renaissance art collections (Mon–Wed & Fri–Sun 10am–5pm; €8, including audio guide in English; private apartment tours every 30min 10.30am–12.30pm; €3.50; Ⓦwww.doriapamphilj.it).

The private apartments

The first part of the gallery is made up of a series of **private apartments**, furnished in the style of the original palace, through which you're guided by way of the gallery's free half-hourly audio tour, narrated by the urbane Jonathan Pamphilj. It takes in the large and elegant reception hall of the original palace, off which there is a room where the Pamphilj pope, Innocent X, used to receive guests, complete with a portrait of the great man. There are also a couple of side salons filled with busts and portraits of the rest of the family; a late – and probably by Rococo standards, rather poky – ballroom, complete with a corner terrace from which the band played; and a private chapel, which contains the apparently incorruptible body of St Theodora, swathed in robes, and the relics of St Justin under the altar.

The picture gallery

Beyond the apartments, the **picture gallery** extends around a lush courtyard, the paintings mounted in the style of the time, crammed in frame-to-frame, floor-to-ceiling. The labelling is better than it once was, with some paintings labelled, and others numbered and described on the audio tour, but it's still deliberately old-fashioned, and perhaps all the better for it. Just inside, at the corner of the courtyard, there's a badly cracked bust of Innocent X by **Bernini**, which the sculptor apparently replaced in a week with the more famous version down the hall, in a room off to the left, where he appears to have captured the pope about to erupt into laughter. In the same room, **Velázquez**'s famous painting of the same man is quite different, depicting a rather irritable character regarding the viewer with impatience.

The rest of the collection is just as rich in interest, and there are many works worth lingering over. These include perhaps Rome's best concentration of **Dutch** and **Flemish** paintings, among them a rare Italian work by Brueghel the Elder, showing a naval battle being fought outside Naples, complete with Vesuvius, Castel Nuovo and other familiar landmarks, along with a highly realistic portrait of two old men, by Quentin Metsys, and a Hans Memling

Deposition, in the furthest rooms, as well as a further Metsys painting – the fabulously ugly *Moneylenders and their Clients* – in the main gallery. You can also see a *St Jerome*, by the Spanish painter Giuseppe Ribera, one of 44 he is supposed to have painted of the saint; Carracci's bucolic *Rest during the Flight into Egypt*, painted shortly before the artist's death; *Repentant Magdalene* and *John the Baptist* by Caravaggio; and *Salome with the head of St John*, by Titian. Spare some time, too, for the marvellous classical statuary, busts, sarcophagi and figurines, displayed in the Aldobrandini room and on the Via del Corso side of the main gallery. All in all, it's a marvellous collection of work, displayed in a wonderfully appropriate setting.

Sant'Ignazio

Via del Caravita, the next left off Via del Corso after the palace, leads into **Piazza di Sant'Ignazio**, a lovely little square, laid out like a theatre set and dominated by the facade of the Jesuit church of **Sant'Ignazio** (daily 7.30am–12.30pm & 4–7.15pm). The saint isn't actually buried here; appropriately, for the founder of the Jesuit order, he's in the main Jesuit church, the Gesù, a little way south (see p.70). But it's a spacious structure, worth visiting for a marvellous Baroque ceiling, by Andrea del Pozzo, showing the entry of St Ignatius into paradise. This spectacular work employs sledgehammer trompe l'oeil effects, notably in the mock cupola painted into the dome of the crossing. Stand on the disc in the centre of the nave, the focal point for the ingenious rendering of perspective: figures in various states of action and repose, conversation and silence, fix you with stares from their classical pediment.

The Pantheon

On the other side of Piazza di Sant'Ignazio lies **Piazza di Pietra**, a pleasant triangular open space dominated by the giant Corinthian columns of an ancient Roman temple, still supporting their frilled peristyle and incorporated in true Roman style into the building behind, now Rome's stock exchange. The temple was built by Antoninus Pius in 145 AD in memory of his father, Hadrian.

From here it's a short walk west, down Via dei Pastini, to **Piazza della Rotonda**, one of the city's most picturesque squares, and perhaps suffering because of it, invariably thronged as it is with sight-weary tourists, hawkers and street musicians, besieging the café tables that fringe the edge. The waters of the fountains in the middle, an eighteenth-century construction topped by yet another obelisk, are a soothing influence, but the main focus of interest is the **Pantheon** (Mon–Sat 8.30am–7.30pm, Sun 9am–6pm; free), which forms the square's southern edge, easily the most complete ancient Roman structure in the city and, along with the Colosseum, visually the most impressive. Though originally a temple that formed part of Marcus Agrippa's redesign of the Campus Martius in around 27 BC – hence the inscription – it's since been proved that the building was entirely rebuilt by the emperor Hadrian and finished around 125 AD. It remains a formidable architectural achievement, although like the city's other Roman monuments, it would have been much more sumptuous in its day. It was consecrated as a Christian site in 609 AD and dedicated to Santa Maria ai Martiri in an allusion to the Christian bones that were found here; a thousand years later, the bronze roof was stripped from the ceiling of the portico by Pope Urban VIII, to be melted down for the baldachino in St Peter's and the cannons of the Castel Sant'Angelo. Interestingly, some of the "stolen" bronze later found its way back here when, after Unification, the cannons were in turn melted down to provide materials for the tombs of two Italian kings, which are housed in the right and left chapels.

Inside, you get the best impression of the engineering expertise of Hadrian: the diameter is precisely equal to its height (43m), the hole in the centre of the dome – from which shafts of sunlight descend to illuminate the musty interior – a full 9m across. Most impressively, there are no visible arches or vaults to hold the whole thing up; instead they're sunk into the concrete of the walls of the building. Again, it would have been richly decorated, the coffered ceiling heavily stuccoed and the niches filled with the statues of gods. Now, apart from the sheer size of the place, the main point of interest is the **tomb of Raphael**, between the second and third chapel on the left, with an inscription by the humanist bishop Pietro Bembo: "Living, great Nature feared he might outvie Her works, and dying, fears herself may die." The same kind of sentiments might well have been reserved for the Pantheon itself.

Santa Maria sopra Minerva

There's more artistic splendour on view behind the Pantheon. Bernini's diminutive **Elephant Statue** is the Baroque artist's most endearing piece of work, if not his most characteristic, showing a cheery elephant trumpeting under the weight of the obelisk he carries on his back – a reference to Pope Alexander VII's reign and supposed to illustrate the fact that strength should support wisdom.

Behind it is the far grander **Santa Maria sopra Minerva** (Mon–Sat 7am– 7pm, Sun 8am–7pm), modelled on the church of Santa Maria Novella in Florence. It is Rome's only Gothic church, and worth a look just for that, though its soaring lines have since been overburdened by marble and frescoes. Built in the late thirteenth century on the ruins of a temple to Minerva, it is also one of Rome's art-treasure churches, crammed with the tombs and self-indulgences of wealthy Roman families. Of these, the Carafa Chapel, in the south transept, is the best known, holding Filippino Lippi's late fifteenth century fresco of *The Assumption*, a bright, effervescent piece of work. Below, one painting shows a hopeful Carafa (the religious zealot who became Pope Paul IV) being presented to the Virgin Mary by Thomas Aquinas; another depicts Aquinas confounding a group of heretics in the sight of two beautiful young boys. The children, visible in the foreground on the right, are the future Medici popes Leo X and Clement VII – the equestrian statue of Marcus Aurelius, destined for the Capitoline Hill, is just visible in the background.

The lives of Leo and Clement come full circle in the church, where they are both buried, and remembered by two very grand tombs either side of the high altar – Leo on the left, Clement on the right, and both of them proof, if any were needed, that beautiful boys don't always grow up to be beautiful men. You should look, too, at the figure of *Christ Bearing the Cross*, on the left-hand side of the altar, a serene work that Michelangelo completed for the church in 1521, and the tomb of Catherine of Siena underneath, who died in a convent here in 1380. The room where she died is viewable through the sacristy, though you may need to ask someone to open it for you.

You can leave the church by the passage to the left of the altar, taking in the tomb of Fra Angelico, who also died here in 1455, just in front of a chapel that contains a very soothing *Madonna and Child* by Benozzo Gozzoli, from 1449. You emerge on Via Sant'Ignazio, just around the corner from the church of the same name (see above).

Clerical fashions

Opposite the church of Santa Maria sopra Minerva, Via dei Cestari and Via Santa Chiara host Rome's **clerical fashion district**, long-time home to a number of shops selling liturgical garments to priests, monks and nuns. Oddly enough anyone is welcome to browse and even buy: should you be interested, a full set of cardinal's outfits, including a change of cassocks, a skullcap and something for special occasions, will set you back about €1500. Perhaps the most famous store of all is *Gammarelli*, on Via Santa Chiara, in business since 1798 and apparently the personal favourite of John Paul II. Interestingly it's *Gammarelli* who are charged with delivering several sizes of white garments to the Vatican during papal elections to ensure that, whoever is elected, there will be something ready in the new pope's size.

Sant'Ivo alla Sapienza

A few steps west of the Pantheon, on Corso del Rinascimento, the rather blank facade of the **Palazzo della Sapienza** cradles the church of **Sant'Ivo** (Mon–Fri 8.30am–5pm, Sat & Sun 9am–noon) – from the outside at least, one of Rome's most impressive churches, with a playful facade designed by Borromini. Though originally built for the most famous Barberini pope, Urban VIII, the building actually spans the reign of three pontiffs. Each of the two small towers is topped with the weird, blancmange-like groupings that are the symbol of the Chigi family (representing the hills of Monti Paschi), and the central cupola spirals helter-skelter-fashion to its zenith, crowned with flames that are supposed to represent the sting of the Barberini bee, their family symbol. Inside, it's comparatively featureless but very cleverly designed – impressively light and spacious given the small space the church is squeezed into, rising to a tall parabolic cupola.

San Luigi dei Francesi

Just north of Sant'Ivo, there's a constant police presence around the seventeenth-century **Palazzo Madama**, which holds the offices and chamber of the Italian upper house or Senate. Cutting back towards the Pantheon, on to the bottom end of **Via della Scrofa**, the French national church of **San Luigi dei Francesi** (daily except Thurs afternoon 8.30am–12.30pm & 3.30–7pm) is worth a look, mainly for the works by Caravaggio that have hung here since they were painted in the last years of the sixteenth century. In the last chapel on the left are three paintings: the *Calling of St Matthew*, in which Christ points to Matthew, who is illuminated by a shaft of sunlight; Matthew visited by an angel as he writes the Gospel; and the saint's martyrdom. Caravaggio's first public commission, these paintings were rejected at first, partly on grounds of indecorum, and it took considerable reworking by the artist before they were finally accepted. These days they are considered to be among the artist's greatest ever works, especially *The Calling of St Matthew*, which manifests the simple, taut drama, as well as the low-life subject matter, that Caravaggio became so well-known for.

Sant'Agostino

Further north up Via della Scrofa, off to the left, the Renaissance facade of the church of **Sant'Agostino** (daily 7.45am–noon & 4–7.30pm) takes up one side of a drab piazza of the same name. It's not much to look at from the outside, but a handful of art treasures might draw you in: this was the church of Rome's creative community in the sixteenth century and as such drew wealthy patrons and well-connected artists. Just inside the door, the serene statue of the *Madonna del Parto*, by Sansovino, is traditionally invoked during pregnancy, and is accordingly surrounded by photos of newborn babes and their blissful parents. Further into the church, take a look at Raphael's vibrant fresco of *Isaiah*, on the third pillar on the left, beneath which is another work by Sansovino, a craggy *St Anne, Virgin and Child*. But the biggest crowds gather around the first chapel on the left, where the *Madonna di Loreto*, painted in 1605 by Caravaggio, is a characteristic work of what was at the time almost revolutionary realism, showing two peasants praying at the feet of a sensuous *Mary and Child*, their dirty feet and scruffy clothes contrasting with the pale, delicate feet and skin of Mary.

Torre della Scimmia

Just beyond Sant'Agostino on Via dei Portoghesi, take a look at the **Torre della Scimmia** – literally the "Tower of the Monkey" – which grows almost organically out of a fork in the road above an ivy-covered palazzo. The story goes that in the seventeenth century a pet monkey kidnapped a child and carried it to the top of the tower; the father of the child called upon the Virgin for help and the monkey promptly clambered down, delivering the child to safety. By way of thanks, the man erected a shrine to the Virgin, which you can still see at the top of the tower, accompanied by a glowing lamp that is to this day kept constantly burning.

Piazza di Montecitorio

A couple of minutes' walk east from the Torre della Scimmia, the obelisk in the centre of **Piazza di Montecitorio** was brought to Rome by Augustus to celebrate his victory over Cleopatra and set up in the Campus Martius, where it formed the hand of a giant sundial. The square takes its name from the bulky **Palazzo di Montecitorio** on its northern side, a Bernini creation from 1650 and home since 1871 to the lower house of the Italian parliament (open the first Sun of each month 10am–6pm; free). You have to take a 45-minute tour to visit the parliament and, given that it's in Italian, you might feel you'd be better off exploring the surrounding streets. But for those who know Rome well, and have even the slightest interest in Italy's notoriously shaky parliamentary system, a visit can be very worthwhile.

The building is in fact two knocked into one: the original, Bernini-designed structure, and another incorporating the main Hall of Deputies. The main building is full of grand reception rooms around a large courtyard, of which the *Sala della Lupa*, used for press conferences and presidential meetings with foreign dignitaries, is so called for its frescoes glorifying Rome as the country's capital, and the she-wolf that stands centre stage – a Mussolini addition. On the other side of the courtyard, the first-floor *Sala della Regina* is a massive room lined with tapestries that contains the entrance to the presidential part of the Hall of Deputies next door.

The Hall itself is an impressive nineteenth-century space with seats for 635 deputies arranged in a semi-circle under an art nouveau skylight; above the speaker's platform, a bronze representing the spirit of Italy, flanked by regal military groupings, does a great job of enhancing the solemnity the chamber tries hard to exude.

Piazza Colonna

Just east here, by Via del Corso, the **Piazza Colonna** is flanked on its north side by the late sixteenth-century **Palazzo Chigi**, the official residence of the prime minister and as such not open to the public. The **Column of Marcus Aurelius**, which gives the square its name, was erected between 180 and 190 AD to commemorate military victories in northern Europe, and, like the column of Trajan which inspired it, is decorated with reliefs depicting scenes from the campaigns. The statue of St Paul on top was added by Sixtus V, made from bronze from the ancient doors of the church of Sant'Agnese fuori le Mura (see p.138). The square used to be the site of the city's principal coffee-roasters' market, so was always a busy spot, and it still has an elegant backdrop in the **Palazzo Wedekind**, home to the offices of Rome's *Il Tempo* newspaper, whose dozen or so Ionic columns, originally Roman, support a gracious balustraded terrace.

San Lorenzo in Lucina

A little further up Via del Corso, on the left, the wedge-shaped **Piazza San Lorenzo** is a surprisingly spacious and relatively peaceful escape from the bustle of the Corso. On its left side, the church of **San Lorenzo in Lucina** (daily 8am–noon & 4–7.30pm), with its manifestly ancient campanile and columned portic, stands out among the largely undistinguished buildings around; it originally dates from the fifth century but was rebuilt in the twelfth century. Inside, like so many Roman churches, it doesn't look or feel nearly so old – indeed much of it dates from the seventeenth century – but there are several features of interest, not least a section of the griddle on which St Lawrence was roasted (see p.136), in the first chapel on the right – though this is almost impossible to see. A little further down on the same side, the tomb of the French painter Nicholas Poussin is a delicate nineteenth-century marble affair by his compatriot Chateaubriand; Poussin spent much of his life in Rome, and died here in 1665. Beyond, take a look also at Bernini's bust of the doctor of Innocent X, Fonseca, in the next chapel but one, and the *Crucifixion* by Guido Reni in the apse.

Piazza Navona and around

The western half of the centro storico focuses on and around **Piazza Navona**, Rome's most famous square – a pedestrianized oval that is as picturesque as any piazza in Italy, lined with cafés and restaurants and often thronged with tourists, street artists and pigeons. The best time to come is at night, when the inevitably tourist-geared flavour of the place is at its most vibrant, with crowds hanging out around the fountains or clocking the scene while nursing a pricey drink at a table outside one of the bars, or watching the buskers and street artists entertain the throng.

Piazza Navona

Piazza Navona takes its name from the Greek word for 'struggle', 'agone', due to the games that were traditionally held here, and its shape from the first-century AD Stadium of Domitian, the principal venue of the athletic events and later chariot races that took place in the Campus Martius (see p.52). Until the mid-fifteenth century the ruins of the arena were still here, overgrown and disused, but the square was given a facelift in the mid-seventeenth century by the Pamphilj Pope Innocent X, who built most of the grandiose palaces that surround it, including the largest, the **Palazzo Pamphilj**, which fills much of the southwestern side of the square. It's now home to the Brazilian embassy and is not open to the general public – which is a shame given the fact that one of its state rooms has a lavish frescoed ceiling by Pietro da Cortona, depicting the adventures of Aeneas, which you can glimpse at night if the lights are on in the embassy.

The Pamphilj pope also commissioned the church of **Sant'Agnese in Agone** next door to the palace (daily 9.30am–12.30pm & 4–7pm), initially from Carlo Rainaldi and later from Carlo Borromini, who took over after Rainaldi was sacked for being too slow. The story goes that the 13-year-old St Agnes was stripped naked before the crowds in the stadium as punishment for refusing to marry, whereupon she miraculously grew hair to cover herself. She was later martyred by a sword blow to her throat; nowadays she is the patron saint of young girls. This church, typically squeezed into the tightest of spaces by Borromini, is supposedly built on the spot where it all happened.

Opposite, the **Fontana dei Quattro Fiumi**, one of three that punctuate the square, is a masterpiece of 1651 by Bernini, Borromini's arch-rival. Each figure represents one of what were considered at the time to be the four great rivers of the world – the Nile, Danube, Ganges and Plate – though only the horse, symbolizing the Danube, was actually carved by Bernini himself. It's said that all the figures are shielding their eyes in horror from Borromini's church facade (Bernini was an arrogant man who never had time for the work of the less successful Borromini), but the fountain had actually been completed before the facade was begun. The grand complexity of rock is topped with an Egyptian obelisk, brought here by Pope Innocent X from the Circus of Maxentius.

Bernini also had a hand in the fountain at the southern end of the square, the so-called **Fontana del Moro**, designing the central figure of the Moor in what is another fantastically playful piece of work, surrounded by toothsome dolphins and other marine figures. The fountain at the opposite end of the square, the **Fontana del Nettuno**, is equally fanciful, depicting Neptune struggling with a sea monster, surrounded by briny creatures in a riot of fishing nets, nymphets, beards, breasts, scales and suckers.

Piazza Pasquino

Just south of Piazza Navona, immediately behind the Palazzo Braschi, it's easy to miss the battered torso of **Pasquino**, even in the small triangular space of **Piazza Pasquino**, in the corner of which it still stands. Pasquino is perhaps the best known of Rome's "talking statues" of the Middle Ages and Renaissance times, upon which anonymous comments on the affairs of the day would be attached – comments that had a serious as well as a humorous intent (see box, p.45). Pasquino gave us the word "pasquinade"; whether the graffitied comments and photocopied poems that grace the statue these days live up to it or not is debatable.

Museo di Roma

Backing on to Piazza Navona, the eighteenth-century Palazzo Braschi is the home of the **Museo di Roma**, Piazza San Pantaleo 10 (Tues–Sun 9am–7pm; €6.50; ⓦwww.museodiroma.comune.roma.it), which has a permanent collection relating to the history of the city from the Middle Ages to the present day.

To be honest, it's a large museum and is only sporadically interesting. Indeed the building – particularly the magnificent **Sala Nobile** where you go in, the main staircase, and one or two of the renovated rooms, not least the exotically painted *Sala Cinese* and *Sala Egiziana* – is probably the main event. But there's interest in some of the **paintings**, which show the city during different eras – St Peter's Square before Bernini's colonnade was built, jousting in Piazza Navona and the Cortile Belvedere in the Vatican, big gatherings and processions in the Campidoglio and Piazza del Popolo – and **frescoes** from demolished palaces provide decent enough highlights. There are also portraits and busts of the most eminent Roman families, most of whom made pope at one time or another – not only Braschi, but also the Corsini, Chigi and Odelaschi. These names resonate around historic parts of the city, and their faces gaze out of the rooms here with deadly and penetrating self-importance.

Sant'Andrea della Valle

Across the road towards Largo Argentina, the church of **Sant'Andrea della Valle** (Mon–Sat 7.30am–noon & 4.30–7.30pm, Sun 7.30am–12.45pm & 4.30–7.45pm) has the distinction of sporting the city's second-tallest dome (after St Peter's), built by Carlo Maderno, and of being the location for the first scene of the opera *Tosca* by Puccini. Inside, it's one of the most Baroque of Rome's churches, a high, barn-like building whose dome is decorated with paintings of the *Glory of Paradise* by Giovanni Lanfranco. The marvellous set of frescoes in the apse illustrating the life of St Andrew are by his contemporary, Domenichino, and centre on the monumental scene of the saint's crucifixion on the characteristic transverse cross. In a side chapel on the right, you may recognize some good-looking copies of not only Michelangelo's *Pietà* (the original is in St Peter's), but also of his figures of *Leah* and *Rachel* from the tomb of his patron, Julius II, in the church of San Pietro in Vincoli (see p.142).

Museo Barracco

Immediately across the road from the Palazzo Braschi, Piazza dei Baullari 1 is the so-called **Piccola Farnesina** palace, built by Antonio Sangallo the Younger. The palace itself actually never had anything to do with the Farnese family, and took the name "little Farnese" because of the lilies on the outside of the building, which were confused with the Farnese heraldic lilies. Recently thoroughly restored, it's home to the **Museo Barracco** (Tues–Sat 9am–7pm, Sun 9am–1pm; €10), a small but fine-quality collection of ancient sculpture that was donated to the city at the turn of the century by one Baron Barracco. There are ancient Egyptian and Greek pieces, including two sphinxes from the reigns of Hapsupset and Rameses II, an austere head of an Egyptian priest, a bust of a young Rameses II and statues and reliefs of the God Bes from various eras. Look out for ceramics and statuary from the Greek classical period – essentially the fourth and fifth centuries BC – which includes a lovely, almost complete figurine of Hercules, a larger figure of an athlete copied from an original by Policlitus, a highly realistic bitch washing herself from the fourth century BC and a complete and very beautiful votive relief dedicated to Apollo. A small room at the front of the building contains later Roman pieces, most notably a small figure of Neptune from the first century BC and an odd, almost Giacometti-like column-sculpture of a hermaphrodite. The charming busts of two young Roman boys opposite date from the first century AD.

△ Torre dell'Orologico

Palazzo della Cancelleria

Further west along Corso Vittorio Emanuele II is the grand **Palazzo della Cancelleria**, the seat of the papal government that once ran the city; Bramante is thought to have had a hand in its design, and this gorgeous edifice exudes a cool poise quite at odds with the rather grimy nature of its location. You can't get in to see the interior, but you can stroll into the marvellously proportioned, multi-tiered courtyard, which is a treat enough in itself, although the adjacent church of **San Lorenzo in Damaso** (daily 7.30am–12.30pm & 4.30–8pm) also forms part of the complex and is one of the oldest churches in Rome. It was rebuilt with the palace at the start of the sixteenth century and has since been greatly restored, the last time at the end of the nineteenth century, and has a painting by Federico Zuccaro over the altar, *The Coronation of the Virgin*, and a twelfth-century icon of the Virgin Mary in another chapel.

Via del Governo Vecchio and around

Back in the heart of the old city, **Via del Governo Vecchio** leads west from Piazza Pasquino through one of Rome's liveliest quarters. The street was named for the Palazzo Nardini at no. 39, which was once the seat of the governors of Rome. It's being restored at the moment but normally you can wander in to look at its elegant courtyard. However, this part of Rome is best-known for the **nightlife** that fills its narrow streets and vigorous restaurants and bars.

A little way down on the left, the delightful small square of **Piazza del Orologio** is so called because of the quaint clocktower that is its main feature. The clock is part of the **Oratorio dei Filippini**, designed by Carlo Borromini, which backs onto the Chiesa Nuova (see below) and is part of the same complex: the followers of Filippo Neri (founder of the Chiesa Nuova) attended musical gatherings here as part of their worship, hence the musical term "oratorio". Nowadays it's given over to a library of nineteenth-century literature and hosts temporary exhibitions – take the time to sneak in and rest for five minutes in its elegant orange-tree-shaded courtyard. Just off the square, there's a scatter of antique and bric-a-brac shops, which signal that you're just around the corner from Rome's antiques quarter, Via dei Coronari (see p.64).

Chiesa Nuova and around

The **Chiesa Nuova** (daily 8.30am–noon & 4.30–7pm) backs onto Via del Governo Vecchio and is another highly ornate Baroque church – which is strange, because its founder, **St Philip Neri**, didn't want it decorated at all. Neri was an ascetic man, who tended the poor and sick in the streets around here for most of his life and commissioned this place of worship on the site of an earlier structure, Santa Maria in Valicella, which had been donated to him and his followers by Pope Gregory XIII in 1577. Neri died in 1595, and this large church, as well as being his last resting-place (he lies in the chapel to the left of the apse), is his principal memorial. Inside, three paintings by Rubens hang at the high altar, centring on the *Virgin with Angels*. Pietro da Cortona's ceiling paintings, meanwhile, show the *Ascension of the Virgin* in the apse, and, above the nave, the construction of the church and Neri's famous "vision of fire" of 1544, when a globe of fire entered his mouth and dilated his heart – a physical event which apparently affected his health thereafter.

San Giovanni dei Fiorentini

The architect Borromini is buried 300m to the west, in the church of **San Giovanni dei Fiorentini**, set on its own small square, Piazza d'Oro, beyond which is the river. Its eighteenth-century facade is as monumental as any of Rome's churches, but inside it is a relatively plain affair, originally built by Sansovino on the orders of the Medici pope, Leo X, who wanted to see an expression of Florentine pride in what was then the heart of Rome. The church was finished in the early 1600s by Carlo Maderno, who added the dome (and is buried here), beneath which Raggi's flamboyant seventeenth-century altarpiece depicts *The Baptism of Christ*. In the nearby south transept, Salvatore Rosa's *Martyrdom of Saints Cosma and Damian* – the patrons of the Medici – has a fleeing male nude figure in the foreground that Rosa challenged Michelangelo to better: "Let Michelangelo come and see if he can paint a better nude than this!" The chapel to the right of the high altar has a faded fresco by Filippino Lippi that is said to have miraculous powers. Look out, too, for the naive statue of a young John the Baptist in the south aisle, above the sacristy door, next to which there's a bust of another Florentine pope, Clement XII, carved by Bernini. San Giovanni extends a special welcome to pets, and you'll often see churchgoers wandering in with cat baskets and the like.

Via dei Coronari

Carlo Maderno lived across the road at Via Banchi Nuovi 4, and there's a plaque marking the house. Turn left from here and head north, and you find yourself at the end of narrow **Via dei Coronari**, which leads back through the centro storico to the top end of Piazza Navona. This is the fulcrum of Rome's antiques trade, and, although the prices are as high as you might expect in such a location, there are a huge number of shops (Via dei Coronari consists of virtually nothing else), selling a tremendous variety of stuff, and a browse along here makes for one of the city's absorbing bits of sightseeing.

Santa Maria dell'Anima

A few steps right off Via dei Coronari is Via dell'Anima, where the church of **Santa Maria dell'Anima** (daily 9am–1pm & 3–7pm) takes its name from the statue of the Virgin on its facade, between two pleading souls in purgatory. It's another darkly cosy Roman church, wide and squat and crammed into an impossibly small space. Nowadays it's the German national church in Rome, and a richly decorated affair, almost square in shape, with a protruding main sanctuary flanked by Renaissance tombs. The one on the right, a beautiful, rather sad concoction, is that of the last non-Italian pope before John Paul II, the Dutchman Hadrian VI, who died in 1523, while at the far end, above the altar, you can just about make out a dark and glowing *Virgin with Saints* by Giulio Romano.

Santa Maria della Pace

Just off to the left of Via dei Coronari, the church of **Santa Maria della Pace** (Tues–Sat 8.30am–noon & 4–8pm) dates originally from the late fifteenth century but has a facade and portico that were added a couple of hundred years later by Pietro da Cortona. It's often closed when it shouldn't be, but if you're lucky enough to find it open, you can see Raphael's frescoes of various sibyls above the Chigi chapel (first on the right), executed in the early sixteenth century. But perhaps the most impressive part of the church is the attached **chiostro del Bramante**, finished in 1504, a beautifully proportioned, two-tiered cloister that is given over to fairly decent temporary art exhibitions and is at least the one part of the building you can be sure of seeing.

Baroque Rome

The Baroque was one of the great defining periods in Rome, an era of flamboyance and drama in art and architecture that grew out of the Catholic Church's need to re-establish itself during the Counter Reformation in the mid to late sixteenth century, when Protestantism was sweeping northern Europe. The Catholic Church defended itself by re-establishing obedience to its teachings through the Inquisition, and by making itself more approachable to ordinary people, attempting to welcome them into its fold rather than putting them off with a wagging finger. These sentiments informed the art of the day, which from the late sixteenth century onwards was more dramatic – and, above all, more immediately understandable to the common man.

Early flourishes

One of the first buildings of the Baroque era was the church of the Gesù, built in 1575, whose facade, designed by Giacomo della Porta, became a model for Roman churches for the next hundred or so years. Its interior decorative flourishes typified, on a vast scale, the Jesuit approach of celebrating the glory of God in a way that everyone could understand – the ceiling in particular is one of the city's most flamboyant. On a much smaller scale, the other great work of the early Baroque era is Bolognese artist **Annibale Carracci**'s fresco of the *Loves of the Gods* (1597–1603) in the Palazzo Farnese, whose fleshy theatricality helped kick-start the Baroque in the domestic arena.

The Baroque vision

The first pope of the seventeenth century, Camillo Borghese, took the title Paul V in 1605, and became the patron of a young man called **Gianlorenzo Bernini**, the son of a Neapolitan sculptor. Paul V had high hopes for Bernini, comparing him to Michelangelo, and his faith was not unfounded, for Bernini went on to become perhaps the most brilliant sculptor and architect of the seventeenth century. Paul V's name lives on most prominently on the facade of the new St Peter's, much of which he oversaw. Originally designed by the great late-Renaissance architect Carlo Maderno, it also features work by the young Bernini, whose playful and dramatic baldachino or canopy over St Peter's tomb is the epitome of the Baroque era. (Bernini is also known for trying to add towers to the building and cracking the facade – not his finest moment.) Paul V's nephew, Scipione Borghese, a cardinal and an avid collector of art, was another great supporter of Bernini, commissioning some of his finest secular sculptures and stashing them in his country villa (now the Villa Borghese), where they remain to this day.

"Bernini was made for Rome, and Rome for him". So said Maffeo Barberini, who ascended the papal throne as Pope Urban VIII in 1623, and who would prove to be Bernini's greatest patron. In fact, Bernini was more than just a favoured sculptor and architect for Urban VIII: the two were close friends, and would spend a great deal of time together discussing the pope's grand plans for the Counter Reformation city. Under Urban VIII, Bernini grew to be Rome's most sought-after artist, and almost the house sculptor of the Barberini family, leaving his mark on their palace as well as the neighbourhood around – with his sculpture of the Barberini bees at the bottom of Via Veneto, and the histrionic Triton sculpture on Piazza Barberini itself, both completed in the 1640s.

With the death of Urban VIII and the accession of the Pamphilj pope, Innocent X, to the throne, Bernini became a more peripheral figure. Innocent X at first deliberately preferred other sculptors and architects to Bernini, including Francesco Borromini. Innocent X commissioned Borromini to finish building a church next door to the Pamphilj family palace on Piazza Navona, Sant'Agnese in Agone. It is a typically small and ingenious building – Borromini became known for squeezing churches into the unlikeliest of places. He built the churches of San Carlo alle Quattro Fontane (1634) and Sant'Ivo (1650), both intricately fitted into small sites, and worked on

▲ Santa Maria della Vittoria

a famous trompe l'oeil perspective in the gardens of the Palazzo Spada, whereby a tunnel of columns looks four times its true length due to the architect's tricks of light and perspective. This sort of technical wizardry was typical of the Baroque period, and there are other examples in Rome, not least the church of Sant'Ignazio, where Andrew Pozzo's ingeniously painted ceiling does a good job of imitating a dome.

Piazza Navona was being developed at the time that Innocent X was renovating his family palace, and the story goes that a number of people made sure the pope got to see Bernini's designs for one of the fountains, the Fountain of the Four Rivers, which he loved – and immediately commissioned – thus restoring Bernini to a seat at Rome's top table. Bernini went on to produce a number of his most successful works during the reign of Innocent X (the church of Sant'Andre delle Valle and the statue of Saint Theresa in the church of Santa Maria della Vittoria being only the two best-known examples) but it was under the Chigi pope, Alexander VII, who ascended the throne in 1655, that he would construct perhaps his most lasting legacy – the colonnade of St Peter's, whose elliptical arms reach out from the mother church to symbolically embrace pilgrims to her breast. Undoubtedly the most theatrical open space in the city, the square was Bernini's last major accomplishment.

Bernini vs Borromini

The two great men of seventeenth-century Rome were **Gianlorenzo Bernini** and **Francesco Borromini**, both brilliant architects but otherwise unlike each other in just about every way. Where Bernini was a worldly man, perfectly at home in the company of his patrons, Borromini was by all accounts sullen, irritable and insecure, and he lost no opportunity to criticize his rivals. Bernini was always immaculately turned out and supremely confident, while Borromini was inarticulate and scruffy, and just couldn't hack life among Rome's aristocrats. As such, it was often Bernini who landed the plum jobs. Bernini and Borromini never worked together, but they came close in the **Palazzo Barberini**, in which each designed a staircase on either side of the building: Bernini's is a sweeping angular construct that still provides the main entry to the building, while Borromini's is a more retiring, circular affair that is ingenious but lacks the grandeur of his rival's effort.

Top ten Baroque splendours

Stadium of Domitian

At the far end of Via dei Coronari, just off the north side of Piazza Navona, there are some visible remains of the **Stadium of Domitian**, which used to occupy the whole of the piazza. You can visit these on occasional guided tours in English or Italian, and in doing so you can learn a little more about the stadium and its relationship with present-day Piazza Navona. But, to be honest, there's not a lot more to see than you can view from the street.

Palazzo Altemps

Just across the street from the north end of Piazza Navona, **Piazza Sant'Apollinare** is the home of the beautifully restored **Palazzo Altemps** (Tues–Sun 9am–7pm; €7, includes Palazzo Massimo, Terme Diocletian, Crypta Balbi, valid 3 days). Begun in 1477 and completed just under a hundred years later, it now houses a branch of the Museo Nazionale Romano, a relatively new addition to the sights around Piazza Navona. It houses the cream of Museo Nazionale's collections of Roman statuary, and is well worth a visit. Divided between two storeys of the palace, in rooms which open off an elegant courtyard, most of what is on display derives from the collection of the seventeenth-century Roman cardinal, Ludovico Ludovisi. It's a mix of pieces he purchased to adorn his villa on the Quirinal Hill and found in the grounds of the villa itself, which occupied the site of a former residence of Julius Caesar.

The ground floor

First up, at the far end of the courtyard's loggia, is a statue of the emperor Antoninus Pius, who ruled from 138 to 161 AD, and, around the corner, a couple of marvellous heads of Zeus and Pluto, a large bronze bust of Marcus Aurelius, a bust of Julia, the disgraced daughter of Emperor Augustus, and a grave-looking likeness of the philosopher Demosthenes, from the second century AD. Further rooms hold more riches: there are two almost identical statues of *Apollo the Lyrist*, a magnificent statue of Athena taming a serpent, pieced together from fragments found near the church of Santa Maria sopra Minerva, an *Aphrodite* from an original by Praxiteles, a frieze from a third-century sarcophagus showing the labours of Hercules, and, in the far corner of the courtyard, a shameless *Dionysus* with a satyr and panther, found on the Quirinal Hill.

The first floor

Upstairs, you get a slightly better sense of the original sumptuousness of the building – some of the frescoes remain, and the north loggia retains its original late-sixteenth-century decoration, simulating a vine-laden pergola, heavy with fruit, leaves and gambolling cherubs and now home to a series of busts of Roman emperors. The objects on display are if anything even finer than those on the downstairs. The **Painted Views room**, so called for the bucolic scenes on its walls, has a fine statue of Hermes, restored in the seventeenth century in an oratorical pose according to the fashion of the time. The **Cupboard Room**, next door, with its fresco of a display of wedding gifts against a floral background, has a wonderful statue of a warrior at rest called the *Ludovisi Ares*, which may represent Achilles and was restored by Bernini in 1622, and, most engagingly, a charmingly sensitive portrayal of *Orestes and Electra*, from the first century AD by a sculptor called Menelaus – his name is carved at the base of one of the figures.

Beyond are even more treasures, and it is hard to know where to look first. One room retains a frieze telling the story of **Moses** as a cartoon strip, with each scene displayed by nude figures as if on an unfurled tapestry. In the room itself is a colossal head of **Hera**, now thought to be a head of Antonia (Mark Anthony's daughter and mother of Caligula and Claudius), and – what some consider the highlight of the entire collection – the famous *Ludovisi throne*: an original fifth-century BC Greek work embellished with a delicate relief portraying the birth of **Aphrodite**. She is shown being hauled from the sea, where she was formed from Uranus's genitals, while on each side reliefs show a flute player and a woman sprinkling incense over a flame – rituals associated with the worship of Aphrodite.

Further on, there is a depiction of **Aphrodite** after a bath, a first-century AD boy strangling a goose, and a relief of **Dionysos** in the former cardinal's bedroom, a bold, almost modern profile of a face in red marble. Beyond the bedroom is the **Fireplace Salon**, whose huge fireplace is embellished with caryatids and ibex – the symbol of the Altemps family – and holds the *Suicide of Galatian*, apparently commissioned by Julius Caesar to adorn his Quirinale estate. At the other end of the room, an incredible sarcophagus depicts a battle between the Romans and barbarians in graphic, almost visceral sculptural detail, while in the small room next door there are some quieter, more erotic pieces – a lovely *Pan and Daphne*, a *Satyr and Nymph*, and the muses *Calliope* and *Urania*. Once you've made it to here, you'll be ready for a quick peek at the **Altemps chapel**, off the opposite end of the fireplace room, and a skim back through your favourite pieces, before leaving what is one of Rome's best collections of classical art.

Palazzo Primoli

Around the corner from Palazzo Altemps, at the end of Via Zanardelli, the sixteenth-century **Palazzo Primoli** was the home of a descendant of Napoleon, Joseph Primoli. Newly restored, it houses two minor museums that may command your attention on the way to the Vatican, just across the Tiber from here. The first, the **Museo Mario Praz**, on the top floor (Tues–Sun 9am–1pm & 2.30–7.30pm, Mon 2.30–7.30pm; obligatory tours every hour on the hour in the morning, on the half-hour in the afternoon; free), was the home of one Mario Praz, a teacher of English literature, art historian and writer who lived here for fifteen or so years until his death in 1982. It is kept pretty much as the elegant and cultured Praz left it, its nine or so rooms stacked to the gills with books, magazines, paintings and ornate furniture; Praz lived in a larger apartment in the Palazzo Ricci on Via Giulia before moving here and amassed heaps of stuff – a period described in his signature book, *La Casa della Vita*. Tours of the apartment take around thirty minutes and give you a glimpse of the vanished way of life of a connoisseur.

Next door, the ground floor **Museo Napoleonico** (Tues–Sat 9am–7pm; €3) is not that interesting unless you're an enthusiast for the great Frenchman and his dynasty. Rome was home for the Bonapartes in the 1820s, after Pauline married Camillo Borghese; Napoleon's mother, Letizia, also lived nearby (on Via del Corso) – and this is a rather weighty assortment of their personal effects. There's a letter from Napoleon himself from his exile in St Helena, a bad portrait of Pauline, a stirring depiction of Napoleon III, portraits of Count Primoli's mother, Carlotta Bonaparte, sketchbook in hand, hung amongst a number of her own quite adept drawings and even a Napoleonic bike. All things considered, though, it takes a pretty gritty determination, or a peculiar fascination with the family, to get through it all – though as the Swedish writer Bo Lundin has it: "Where else can you find a plaster cast of Pauline Borghese's left breast, done in situ by Canova?"

Campo de' Fiori, the Ghetto and around

This chapter is really Rome's old centre part two, covering the area which lies between the Corso Vittorio Emanuele II – the main thoroughfare which dissects the historic city core – and the Tiber. As in the centro storico, cramped streets, ripe for wandering, open out onto small squares flanked by churches, although it's more of a working quarter – less monumental, with more functional buildings and shops, as seen in its main square, **Campo de' Fiori**, whose fruit and veg stalls and rough-and-ready bars form a marked contrast to the pavement artists and sleek cafés of Piazza Navona. Across the river to the west lies the Vatican and to the south Trastevere, both covered in separate chapters. To the east it merges into the gloomy streets and scrabbly Roman ruins of the old **Jewish Ghetto**, a small but atmospheric neighbourhood that nuzzles close to the city's giant central synagogue, while just north of here lies the major traffic intersection and ancient Roman site of **Largo di Torre Argentina**.

Largo di Torre Argentina and around

Largo di Torre Argentina is a good-sized square, frantic with traffic that circles around the ruins of four (Republican-era) temples and the channel of an ancient public lavatory, now home to a thriving colony of cats. It's more a place to catch a bus or tram than to linger deliberately. You can visit the **cat sanctuary** (daily noon–6pm; Ⓦ www.romancats.com) down the steps on the southwestern corner, and if you wish donate money or buy a catty gift from their small shop, or even 'adopt' a cat for a monthly fee. Around 300 cats live in the excavations here, most of them domestic creatures dumped by their owners, and the people who look after them are all volunteers and receive no support from the city. In fact, the helpers here care for all of the city centre's 4000 or so cats, whose colonies spread from the Forum to the ruins at Piazza Vittorio Emanuele. As for the **temples**, you can take a guided tour in English (daily at 5pm, 1hr), although to be honest they don't add much to what you can see from the road.

On the far side of the square, the **Teatro Argentina** was the venue for the first performance of Rossini's *Barber of Seville*, in 1816. It was not a success: Rossini was apparently booed into taking refuge in a nearby pastry shop. Built in 1731, today

CAMPO DE' FIORI, THE GHETTO & AROUND

BARS

L'Angelo Divino	21
Le Bain	20
Bartaruga	25
Black & White	8
La Curia del Bacco	11
The Drunken Ship	14
Mad Jack's	28
Rock Castle Café	32
Taverna del Campo	17
Vineria	15

RESTAURANTS & CAFÉS

Acchiappafantasmi	2
Arnaldo ai Satiri	9
Bernasconi	23
Bruschetteria degli Angeli	27
La Carbonara	7
La Dolceroma	31
Il Drappo	1
Caffé Farnese	16
Dar Filletaro a Santa Barbara	19
Il Forno di Campo de' Fiori	6
Da Giggetto	33
Govinda	26
Grappolo d'Oro	5
L'Insalata Ricca	4
Osteria ar Galletto	13
Der Pallaro	12
Piperno	34
Al Pompiere	30
La Primavera	10
Roscioli	22
Sora Margherita	29
Da Sergio	18
Thien Kim	24
Sciam	3

ACCOMMODATION

Arenula	J
Campo de' Fiori	D
Casa di Santa Brigida	F
Della Lunetta	B
Residenza Farnese	I
In Parione	E
Pomezia	G
Smeraldo	H
Sole	C
Teatro di Pompeo	A

it is one of the city's most important theatres, and has a small museum that can be visited by appointment. It is also thought, incidentally, that it was built over the spot in Pompey's theatre (see p.71) where Julius Caesar was assassinated.

Via del Plebiscito and the Gesù

Via del Plebiscito, a dark, rather gloomy thoroughfare, links Largo Argentina with Piazza Venezia, 500m or so away. Halfway down on the left, flanking the north side of **Piazza del Gesù**, the grey decaying bulk of the **Palazzo Altieri** was a monster of a project in its time that − a contemporary pasquinade quipped − looked set to consume Rome by its very size. The Altieri pope, Clement X, had the palace built around the house of an old woman who refused to make way for it: the two spyhole windows that were left can still be seen above the ground-floor windows, three windows to the right of the main entrance. Unfortunately, you can't visit the palace, which is now used as offices.

Lording it over the piazza (said to be the windiest in Rome) is the church of the **Gesù** (daily 6am–12.30pm & 4–7.15pm), the first Jesuit church to be built in Rome, and an appropriately dramatic symbol of the Counter Reformation. High and wide, with a single-aisled nave and short transepts edging out under a huge dome, it was ideal for the large, fervent congregations the movement wanted to draw; indeed, it has since served as the model for Jesuit churches everywhere and is still well patronized. The facade is by Giacomo della Porta, the interior the work of Vignola, and the glitzy tomb of the order's founder, St Ignatius, in the north transept, is topped by a huge globe of lapis lazuli – the largest piece in existence. Opposite, the tomb of sixteenth-century Jesuit missionary St Francis Xavier, decorated with a painting by Carlo Maratta showing his death on a Chinese island, holds a reliquary containing the saint's severed arm; the rest of his (incorruptible) body remains a focus of pilgrimage in Goa, India. Otherwise, it's the staggering richness of the church's interior that you remember, especially the paintings by the Genoese painter Baciccia in the dome and the nave, *Triumph in the Name of Jesus*, an ingenious trompe l'oeil which oozes out of its frame in a tangle of writhing bodies, flowing drapery and stucco angels stuck like limpets.

The Rooms of St Ignatius

Next door to the Gesù church, the **Rooms of St Ignatius** (Mon–Sat 4–6pm, Sun 10am–noon; free) occupy part of the first floor of the **Jesuit headquarters**. St Ignatius lived here from 1544 until his death in 1556, and there are just three simple chambers, where the saint and founder of the Jesuit order studied, worshipped and received visitors. One was his **private chapel**, and the other two hold **artefacts** from his life – his shoes, vest and cloak, the robe he was buried in, his writing desks and original documents, and a bronze bust of the great man based on his death mask. But the true draw here is the **decorative corridor** just outside. Designed by Andrea Pozzo in 1680, it's a superb exercise in perspective, an illusion of a grand hall in what is a relatively small space. Stand on the rose in the centre and the room's architectural fancies, putti, garlands and scallop shells are precise and true; walk up and down and the ceiling beams bend, the figures stretch and the scrollwork buckles – giving the bizarre feeling of a room shifting before your eyes. It's a feast of technical trickery and grandiose brushwork – all in weird contrast to the basketball courts that occupy the quadrangle down below.

Crypta Balbi

Cutting back to Largo Argentina, following Via delle Botteghe Oscure, the **Crypta Balbi**, on the corner of Via Caetani (Tues–Sun 9am–7pm; €4), is the site of a Roman theatre, the remains of which later became incorporated in a number of medieval houses. There's a ground-floor exhibition which takes you through the evolution of the site in painstaking, sometimes excruciating, detail, with lots of English explanation, along with bits of pottery, capitals and marble plaques. You have to take one of the hourly tours down into the site proper, where excavations are ongoing, and you can try to glean what you can from the various arches, latrines, column bases and supporting walls that make up the cellar of the current building. The real interest is in the close dissection of one city block over two thousand years – an exercise that could presumably be equally well applied to almost any city corner in Rome.

Campo de' Fiori and around

From Largo Argentina you can either push on down Corso Vittorio Emanuele II or cut left along Via Arenula towards the Tiber and right at Piazza Cairoli into the network of streets that centres on **Piazza Campo de' Fiori** – in many ways Rome's most appealing square. Home to a lively fruit and vegetable **market** (Mon–Sat 8am–1pm), it's surrounded by restaurants and cafés, and is busy pretty much all day, although its function as heart of the area's nightlife, and the consequent glut of bars and outdoor drinkers has taken away much of its unique appeal, in the evenings at least.

No one really knows how the square came by its name, which means "field of flowers". One theory holds that it was derived from the Roman Campus Martius which used to cover most of this part of town. Another claims it is after Flora, the mistress of Pompey, whose theatre used to stand on what is now the northeast corner of the square – a huge complex by all accounts, which stretched right over to Largo Argentina, and where **Julius Caesar** was famously stabbed on the Ides of March, 44 BC. You can still see the foundations in the basement of the *Da Pancrazio* restaurant, on the tiny Piazza del Biscione, and the semicircular Via de' Grotta Pinta retains the rounded shape of the theatre. Later, Campo de' Fiori was an important point on papal processions between the Vatican and the major basilicas of Rome (notably San Giovanni in Laterano) and a site of public executions. The most notorious killing here is commemorated by the statue of **Giordano Bruno** in the middle of the square. Bruno was a late-sixteenth-century freethinker who followed the teachings of Copernicus and was denounced to the Inquisition; his trial lasted for years under a succession of different popes, and finally, when he refused to renounce his philosophical beliefs, he was burned at the stake.

Piazza Farnese

Just south of Campo de' Fiori, **Piazza Farnese** is a quite different square, with great fountains spurting out of carved lilies – the Farnese emblem – into marble tubs brought from the Baths of Caracalla, and the sober bulk of the **Palazzo Farnese** itself (Mon & Thurs visits in French or Italian at 3pm, 4pm, 5pm; free; book in advance at Via Giulia 250, on the river-side of the palace, via ⑦06.6880.9791 or at Ⓔvisitefarnese@france-italia.it). Commissioned in 1514 by Alessandro Farnese – later Paul III – from Antonio di Sangallo the Younger, the building was worked on after the architect's death by Michelangelo, who added the top tier of windows and cornice. It now houses the French Embassy, and access needs to be organized well in advance, but even from the outside it's a tremendously elegant and powerful building – indeed, of all the fabulous locations that Rome's embassies enjoy, this has to be the best.

If you're here for long enough, it is worth organizing a tour. The Farnese were great enthusiasts and collectors, and Classical statuary litters the hallways and salons of the palace: on the first floor or *piano nobile*, the *Salone del Ercole* has a copy of the so-called *Farnese Hercules* (the original of which used to stand here but is now in Naples), surrounded by busts of Roman emperors in a room decorated with the feats of Hercules by Federico Zuccari. Zuccari also had a hand in the room next door, the *Sala dei Fausti Farnesiani* or "room of the Farnese deeds", which is decorated with frescoes by Francesco Salinati illustrating the great acts of the family – though this is sadly not always open for tours because it's used for official functions. But the building's real treasure is at the back of the building – the Bolognese painter Annibale Carracci's *Loves of the Gods*, finished in 1603, and a work of such magnificent vitality, with complex and dramatically arranged figures, great swathes of naked flesh and vivid colours, that it is often seen as the **first great work of the Baroque era**. Commissioned by Odouardo Farnese, the main painting, centring on the *Marriage of Bacchus and Ariadne*, which is supposed to represent the binding of the Aldobrandini and Farnese families, leaps out of its frame in an erotic hotchpotch of cavorting, a fantastic, fleshy spectacle of virtuoso technique and perfect anatomy, surrounded by similarly fervent works illustrating various classical themes. Between and below them, nude figures peer out – amazing exercises in perspective that seem almost to be alongside you in the room. Carracci did the main plan and the central painting himself, but left the rest to his brother and cousin, Agostino and Lodovico, and assistants like Guido Reni and Guercino, who went on to become some of the most sought-after artists of the seventeenth century. It's a fantastic piece of work, perhaps only eclipsed in Rome by the Sistine Chapel itself, and it's sad to note that Carracci, disillusioned by the work, and bitter about the relative pittance that he was paid for it, didn't paint much afterwards, and died penniless a few years later.

Galleria Spada

If you can't get in to the Palazzo Farnese you'll have to make do with the **Palazzo Spada**, a couple of blocks east down Via Capo di Ferro. The **Galleria Spada** (Tues–Sun 8.30am–7.30pm; €5; ☎06.855.5952) is inside – walk right through the courtyard to the back of the building. Although its four rooms, decorated in the manner of a Roman noble family, aren't spectacularly interesting unless you're a connoisseur of seventeenth- and eighteenth-century Italian painting, it does have one or two items of interest. Highlights include two portraits of Cardinal Bernadino Spada by Reni and Guercino, alongside a *St Jerome*, also by Reni, works by Italian-influenced Dutch artists like Jan Van Scorel, and, among bits and pieces of Roman statuary, a seated philosopher. The building itself is great: its facade is frilled with stucco adornments, and, left off the small courtyard, there's a crafty **trompe l'oeil** by Borromini – a tunnel whose actual length is multiplied about four times through the architect's tricks with perspective, though to see this you have to wait for one of the guided tours (held every every 45min). The **state rooms** on the first floor are also open, by appointment, on the first Sunday of each month, and contain, among many other things, some ancient Hellenistic reliefs, a series of seventeenth-century frescoes and a large statue of Pompey, at the feet of which it was for a long time believed that Julius Caesar died.

Ponte Sisto

Immediately behind the Palazzo Spada lies the river, and a pedestrian bridge across to Trastevere, the **Ponte Sisto**. Built by Pope Sixtus IV in 1479 on the site of a ruined structure, it was the first bridge to be built across the Tiber since Roman times. A relatively narrow structure, the inscriptions on each side of the entrance recall Sixtus IV's achievements, although they do not record the fact that the money to build it came from cardinal Juan de Torquemada – uncle of the notoriously grisly tyrant of the Inquisition. One thing you can't see from the bridge itself is a large round hole in the middle – placed there as an overflow in times of flood.

Via Giulia

Via Giulia runs parallel to the Tiber from the Ponte Sisto, and was laid out by Julius II to connect the bridge with the Vatican. The street was conceived as the centre of papal Rome, and Julius commissioned Bramante to line it with imposing palaces. Bramante didn't get very far with the plan, as Julius was shortly after succeeded by Leo X, but the street soon became a popular residence for wealthier Roman families. It is still packed full with stylish *palazzi* and antique shops and as such makes for a nice wander, with features such as the playful **Fontana del Mascherone**, right behind the Farnese palace and topped with the Farnese emblem, to tickle your interest along the way. Just beyond the fountain, behind the high wall of the Palazzo Farnese, the ivy-draped **arch** across the street connects to more French diplomatic offices, the remnant of a Renaissance plan to connect the Farnese palace with the Villa Farnesina across the river, while further along still, the **Palazzo Falconieri**, recognizable by the quizzical falcons crowning each end of the building, now the home of the Hungarian Academy, was largely the work of Borromini, who enlarged it in 1646–49.

On the corner of Via Gonfalone, the **Museo Criminologico** (Tues & Thurs 9am–1pm & 2.30–6.30pm, Wed, Fri & Sat 9am–1pm; €2; ⓦwww .museocriminologico.it) offers a small but intriguing look at crime in general and Italy's underworld in particular. There are some gruesome early instruments of torture – manacles, lashes, head braces – a display on the unfortunate Beatrice Cenci (see p.75) and a selection of guillotines, nooses and various articles worn by the condemned, although inevitably the most interesting stuff – if you can read Italian – is that most pertinent to the world of **Italian crime**: the Mafia, the *Brigate Rosse* and Italian prison life. All in all, it is a perfect antidote to the more effete Renaissance splendours of Via Giulia and around. You can continue to the end of Via Giulia for the church of **San Giovanni dei Fiorentini** (covered on p.63).

The Jewish Ghetto

By way of contrast, cross over to the far side of Via Arenula and you're in what was once the city's **Jewish Ghetto**, a crumbling area of narrow, confusing switchback streets and alleys with a lingering sense of age. There was a Jewish population in Rome as far back as the second century BC, and, as the empire expanded into the Middle East, their numbers eventually swelled to around 40,000. Revolts in the colonies led to a small tax on Jews and a special census, but they were never an especially persecuted group, and were only effectively ghettoized in the mid-sixteenth century when Pope Paul IV issued a series of punitive laws that forced them into what was then one of Rome's most squalid districts: a wall was built around the area and all Jews, in a chilling omen of things to come, were made to wear yellow caps and shawls when they left the district. Later, after Unification, the ghetto was opened up.

By the late 1930s, Jews were again being victimized – barred from certain professions and prohibited from marrying non-Jews under Mussolini's **racial legislation**. The subsequent Nazi occupation brought inevitable deportations but the majority of Rome's Jewish population survived, and currently numbers 16,000 (around half Italy's total). Nowadays, however, it is spread all over the city, and a handful of kosher restaurants, butchers and the like are pretty much all that remains to mark this out from any other quarter.

Via Portico d'Ottavia

The main artery of the Jewish area is **Via Portico d'Ottavia**, a short pedestrian street which leads southwest from Via Avernula to the **Portico d'Ottavia**, a not terribly well-preserved second-century BC gate, rebuilt by Augustus and dedicated to his sister in 23 BC, and then rebuilt again by Septimus Severus in 203 AD. It's next door to the **Teatro di Marcello**, and together (summer daily 9am–7pm, winter daily 9am–6pm; free) they form a site of mild interest and a short-cut through to Via del Teatro di Marcello and the Capitoline Hill. The theatre has served many purposes over the years: begun by Julius Caesar and finished by Augustus, it was pillaged in the fourth century and not properly restored until the Middle Ages, after which it became a formidable fortified palace for a succession of different rulers, including the Orsini family. It has been recently restored and provides a grand backdrop for classical concerts in the summer.

Piazza Mattei to Piazza di Campitelli

On the north side of Via Portico d'Ottavia, narrow Via della Reginella leads to **Piazza Mattei**, whose **Fontana delle Tartarughe**, or "turtle fountain", is a delightful late-sixteenth-century creation, perhaps restored by Bernini, who apparently added the tortoises. The **Palazzo Mattei** flanks one side of the square, and stretches down Via dei Funari ("Ropemakers' Street") to the corner of Via Caetani. The palace is now partly occupied by the Centro degli Studi Americani, but it's possible to wander into the courtyard, whose antique friezes and statues still give some sense of the power and grandeur of this once-great Roman family.

A few yards up Via Caetani on the right is a memorial to the former Italian prime minister **Aldo Moro**, whose dead body was left here in the boot of a car on the morning of May 9, 1978, 54 days after his kidnap by the *Brigate Rosse* or Red Brigades. It was a carefully chosen spot, not only for the impudence it showed on the part of the terrorists in that it was right in the centre of Rome, but also for its position midway between the headquarters of the Communist and Christian Democrat parties. A plaque (and sometimes a wreath) marks the spot, and tells part of the story of how Moro, a reform-minded Christian Democrat, was the first right-wing politician to attempt to build an alliance with the then popular Italian Communists. Whether it was really left-wing terrorists who kidnapped him, darker, right-wing forces allied to the establishment, or perhaps a combination of the two, there's no doubt that Moro's attempt to alleviate the Right's postwar monopoly of power found very little favour with others in power at the time – though that didn't make his death any less of a shock.

Given the "*Mani pulite*" years that have followed, during which corruption in both politics and business was supposed to have been exposed and to some extent ended, and the minuscule change and the political cynicism that resurfaced in the 1990s, it's a tragedy which carries a lot of resonance for Romans. The prime minister who took over after Moro's death was none other than elder statesman of Italian politics **Giulio Andreotti**, whose alleged involvement with the Mafia saw him twice tried – and acquitted – for collusion, most recently in 2003.

Via dei Funari continues towards Piazza Campitelli, where **Santa Maria in Campitelli** (daily 7am–7.30pm), opposite the Irish embassy, is a heavy, ornate church built by Carlo Reinaldi in 1667 to house an ancient enamel image of *The Virgin*, deemed to have miraculous powers following respite from a plague. It was originally housed in another church on Via Portico d'Ottavia but was moved here by Pope Alexander VII so as to be in more appropriately splendid surroundings. Everything in the church focuses on this small framed image, encased in an incredibly ornate golden altarpiece, which fills the entire space between the clustered columns of the transept. There's not much else to see, although the paintings, including a dramatic *Virgin with Saints* by Luca Giordano, in the second chapel on the right, represent Baroque at its most rampant, and in front a copy of the altar *Virgin* gives the opportunity for a close-up look of the miraculous image.

Piazza delle Cinque Scuole and the Synagogue

Just south of Via Portico d'Ottavia, **Piazza delle Cinque Scuole**, named for the five religious schools that once stood here, is overlooked by one side of the **Palazzo Cenci**, which huddles into the dark streets here, a reminder of the untimely death of one **Beatrice Cenci**, who was executed, with her stepmother, on the Ponte Sant'Angelo in 1599 for the murder of her incestuous father – a story immortalized in verse by Shelley and in paint by an unknown artist whose portrait of the unfortunate Beatrice still hangs in the Palazzo Barberini.

On the other side of the square is the area's principal Jewish sight: the huge **Synagogue** (Sun–Thurs 10am–5pm, Fri 9am–2pm; closed Sat & Jewish hol; €7.50; Ⓦwww.museoebraico.it), built in 1904 and dominating all around with its bulk. Carabinieri stand guard 24 hours a day outside, ever since a PLO attack on the building in 1982 killed a 2-year-old girl and injured many others. The only way to see the building is on one of the short guided tours, which run regularly in English – just turn up – taking in the small two-room **museum** afterwards. The impressive interior rises to a high, rainbow-hued dome, and the tours are excellent, giving good background on the building and Rome's Jewish community in general.

Isola Tiberina

Almost opposite the synagogue, the **Ponte Fabricio** crosses the Tiber to **Isola Tiberina**. Built in 62 BC, it's the only classical bridge to remain intact without help from the restorers (the Ponte Cestio, on the other side of the island, was partially rebuilt in the last century). As for the island, it's a calm respite from the city centre proper, and is mostly given over to Rome's oldest hospital, the **Fatebenefratelli**, founded in 1548 – appropriately, it would seem, as the island was originally home to a third century BC temple of Aesclapius, the Roman god of healing. Opposite the hospital entrance, the church of **San Bartolomeo** (Mon–Sat 9am–12.30pm & 3.30–6pm, Sun 9am–1pm) stands on the temple's original site, and is worth a peep inside for its ancient columns, probably rescued from the temple, and an ancient wellhead on the altar steps, carved with figures relating to the founding of the church, including St Bartholomew himself, who also features in the painting above the altar, hands tied above his head, on the point of being skinned alive – his famous and gruesome mode of martyrdom. Beyond the island, you can see the remains of **Ponte Rotto** (Broken Bridge) on the river, all that remains of the first stone bridge to span the Tiber. Built between 179 and 142 BC, it collapsed at the end of the sixteenth century.

Piazza Bocca della Verità and around

Back on the north bank, a little way down Via del Teatro di Marcello on the right, the church of **San Nicola in Carcere** (daily 7.30am–noon & 4.30–7.30pm; excavations €3) was built in the eighth century on the site of three Republican temples. It was later dedicated to St Nicholas, the patron saint of seafarers – this used to be the riverfront, and was the site of a lively fish market. The church is nice enough, but the real interest is in the ancient remnants it incorporates. The nave is formed by a wonderful mixture of ancient columns, both Ionic and Corinthian, while down below, informal guided tours of the excavations show how the church is supported by the central Temple of Juno and the columns of two temples either side. You can walk down the narrow Roman street that ran between the temples, squeezing between the massive blocks of the central temple and the column bases of the Temple of Janus that hold up one side of the church – columns that are clearly visible on the outside too.

Cross the road and walk up, keeping the Palatine Hill on your left, and you reach the church of **Santa Maria della Concezione** (daily 6am–noon & 3.30–6pm), where a chapel immediately to the right of the entrance has a wonderful series of frescoes by Zuccarri depicting scenes from the life of Christ, including a naturalistic and dynamic flagellation scene on the left. A little way beyond the church is one of the entrances to the **Roman Forum** (see p.93).

A few steps away from here, a little way down Via San Teodoro on the left, the round church of **San Teodoro**, Rome's Greek national church, is open only sporadically, usually in the morning, and in any case its ancient feel has been somewhat smoothed over inside by the paint and plaster of later years. St Theodore was martyred on this spot in the fourth century AD, and the church originally dates from the sixth century. If you're lucky enough to get in, you'll be able to see the apse mosaics, which are contemporary with the original church, showing Christ with saints, including a bearded Theodore, next to St Peter on the right.

Back towards the Tiber, Via di Teatro di Marcello meets the riverside main drag at the **Piazza della Bocca della Verità**, also known as the Forum Boarium due to its function as a cattle market in ancient times. There are two of the city's better-preserved Roman temples here, the **Temple of Portunus** and the **Temple of Hercules Victor** – the latter long known as the temple of Vesta because, like all vestal temples, it is circular. Both date from the end of the second century BC, and although you can't get inside, they're fine examples of Republican-era places of worship; the Temple of Hercules Victor is, for what it's worth, the oldest surviving marble structure in Rome.

Most people don't bother to go into the church of **Santa Maria in Cosmedin** (daily 10am–5pm), opposite, which is a shame because it's one of Rome's most beautiful – and typical – medieval basilicas, with a thirteenth-century baldachino over a pink ancient Roman bathtub that serves as the altar and a colourful and ingenious Cosmati mosaic floor – one of the city's finest. The sacristy acts as a rather dowdy giftshop, and also displays one of the church's greatest treasures – an eighth-century mosaic of the *Adoration of the Magi*. However, the church's fame rests on the so-called **Bocca della Verità** ("Mouth of Truth") in the portico outside, an ancient Roman drain cover in the shape of an enormous face that in medieval times would apparently swallow the hand of anyone who hadn't told the truth. It was particularly popular with husbands anxious to test the faithfulness of their wives; now it is one of the city's biggest tour-bus attractions, and there are day-long queues of people having their photograph taken with their hand inside.

On its northern side, Piazza Bocca della Verità peters out peacefully at the stolid **Arch of Janus**, perhaps Rome's most weathered triumphal arch, beyond which the campanile of the church of **San Giorgio in Velabro** (daily 10am– 12.30pm & 4–6.30pm) is a stunted echo of that of Santa Maria across the way. Inside is one of the city's barest and most beautiful ancient basilicas, an ancient-columned nave lit by bare stone windows carved with an intricate design. Only the late-twelfth-century fresco in the apse, the work of Pietro Cavallini, lightens the melancholy mood, showing Christ and the Virgin, and various saints, including St George on the left, to whom the church is dedicated – and whose cranial bones lie in the reliquary under the high altar canopy, placed here in 749 AD, shortly after the original basilica was built.

Immediately to the left of the church the building incorporates a small **arch**, erected by the Forum Boarium market traders in honour of Septimus Severus and his family – whose portraits you can see on the inside, apart from that of Geta which, like the version on Septimus Severus's arch in the main forum, was erased after his assassination by his brother Caracalla. Opposite the church, behind an iron gate, you can see the arches of the **Cloaca Maxima**, the ancient city's main sewer, which emerges on the Tiber just to the left of the nearby **Ponte Palatino**; look closely from the bridge itself and you should be able to spot the giant arch placed there to take the outflow, now overgrown with trees and bushes.

The Tridente

The northern part of Rome's city centre is sometimes known as the **Tridente**, due to the trident shape of the roads leading down from the apex of Piazza del Popolo – Via del Corso in the centre, Via di Ripetta on the left and Via del Babuino on the right. The area around **Piazza di Spagna**, especially, is travellers' Rome. Historically it was the **artistic quarter** of the capital, and wealthy young men and women on eighteenth- and nineteenth-century grand tours would come here in search of the colourful, exotic city. This part of Rome has always had a cultural feel: Keats and Giorgio de Chirico are just two of the many artists and writers who have lived on Piazza di Spagna, Goethe had lodgings along Via del Corso, and places such as *Caffè Greco* and *Babington's Tea Rooms* were the meeting-places of a local artistic and ex-pat community for almost two centuries. Today these institutions have been supplemented by latter-day traps for the tourist dollar: American Express and McDonald's have settled into the area, and the local residents are more likely to be investment bankers than artists or poets – **Via Condotti** and around is these days strictly international designer territory, with some of Rome's fanciest stores. But the air of a Rome being discovered, even colonized, by foreigners persists, even if most of those hanging out on the **Spanish Steps** are flying-visit teenagers.

Piazza di Spagna and around

At the southern end of Via del Babuino, **Piazza di Spagna** further underlines the area's international credentials, taking its name from the Spanish Embassy which has stood here since the seventeenth century – though oddly enough part of the square was once known as Piazza di Francia for the French church of Trinità dei Monti at the top of the Spanish Steps. It's a long, thin straggle of a square, almost entirely enclosed by buildings, and centring on the distinctive, boat-shaped **Fontana della Barcaccia**, the last work of Pietro Bernini, father of the more famous Gianlorenzo. It apparently commemorates the great flood of Christmas Day 1598, when a barge from the Tiber was washed up on the slopes of Pincio Hill close by. The square itself is fringed by high-end clothes and jewellery shops and is normally thronged with tourists, but for all that it's one of the city's most appealing open spaces. The large **Colonna dell' Immacolata** at the southern end commemorates Pius IX's official announcement, in 1854, of the dogma of the Immaculate Conception while, close by, hackles were raised when McDonald's unveiled plans to open a branch on the

THE TRIDENT

ACCOMMODATION

Condotti	F
Dei Borgognoni	J
Homs	I
D'Inghilterra	H
Manfredi	C
Margutta	B
Palazzetto	D
Piazza di Spagna	E
Plaza	G
De Russie	A

RESTAURANTS & CAFÉS

Antica Birreria Peroni	34
Antico Forno	33
Babington's Tea Rooms	17
La Baguette	24
Beltramme	18
Dal Bolognese	4
Caffé Greco	19
Casa de Chirico	21
Il Chianti	32
Ciampini al Café du Jardin	8
Defa	9
Dolce e Doni	23
Il Gelato di San Crispino	31
Gina	11
'Gusto	13
Hamasei	27
Herbier	30
Margutta	7
Matricianella	25
Da Michele	35
Museo-Atelier	10
Naturist Club	26
Osteria delle Frezze	12
Otello alla Concordia	15
Pizza Ciro	28
Pizza House	29
Pizza Re	6
Pizzeria-Tavola Calda	1
Recafé	20
Tadolini	10

BARS

Canova	2
L'Enoteca Antica	16
'Gusto	14
Lowenhaus	5
Rosati	3
Shakti	22

square in the early 1980s. Its presence here is proof that the American multinational won what turned out to be quite a battle. But it's to the city's credit that this is one of the most discreet examples you'll encounter, tucked into one end of the piazza, with thematically appropriate interior decor. Not surprisingly, you can now find branches of McDonald's all over the city – and most of them look much the same as they do anywhere else.

Keats-Shelley Memorial House

Facing directly onto the square, opposite the Barcaccia fountain at Piazza di Spagna 26, the house where the poet John Keats died in 1821 now serves as the **Keats-Shelley Memorial House** (Mon–Fri 9am–1pm & 3–6pm, Sat 11am–2pm & 3–6pm, Sun closed; €3.50; Ⓦ www.keats-shelley-house.org), an archive of English-language literary and historical works and a museum of manuscripts and literary mementoes relating to the Keats circle of the early nineteenth century – namely Keats himself, Shelley and Mary Shelley and Byron (who at one time lived across the square). Its four rooms contain manuscripts, letters and the like, and various personal effects of Keats, Shelley, Byron and associates, including an ancient silver scallop shell reliquary containing locks of Keats's, Shelley's, Milton's and Elizabeth Barrett Browning's hair – once owned by Pope Pius V – and an alabaster urn with Shelley's jawbone. Keats's death mask, stored in the corner room in which he died from tuberculosis, captures a resigned grimace, while the books that line the walls form the museum's library, which is devoted to the period and its literature.

Keats didn't really enjoy his time in Rome, referring to it as his "posthumous life": he came here only under pressure from doctors and friends when it was arguably already too late. He was also tormented by his love for Fanny Brawne, and he spent months in pain before he finally died, at the age of just 25, confined to the house with his artist friend Joseph Severn, to whom he remarked that he could already feel "the flowers growing over him". If you really want to get into the Romantic poet experience, there's a flat on the third floor available to rent through the UK-based Landmark Trust (Ⓣ 01628 825925, Ⓦ www.landmarktrust.org.uk).

Casa di Chirico

Almost next door to the Keats-Shelley House, the fourth-floor **Casa de Chirico** (open the first Sun of every month 10am–1pm, tours every 45min, or by appointment Tues–Sat 10am–5pm; €5) was the home of the Greek-Italian metaphysical artist Giorgio de Chirico for thirty years until his death in 1978 and is now a small, evocative museum. His wife, Isa, lived on here until 1990, when she too died, after which the apartment was donated to the city. It's kept pretty much as she left it, and gives a fantastic glimpse into how De Chirico lived, as well as having a great many of his paintings on display. There are works from his classic period in the entrance hall and first living area, including portraits of himself, often dressed up, and others of his wife, who modeled for him until he died. The chair in which he used to watch TV (only with the sound turned down, apparently) sits by the door, while the next-door living room is filled with paintings from his last few years, all harking back to his proto-surrealist heyday. Upstairs, in keeping with the untouched nature of the house, De Chirico's cell-like bedroom is left with his books and rather uncomfortable-looking single bed, while across the hall the **video player** in Isa's bedroom is marked with stickers placed there to remind her how it worked. At the end of the corridor, De Chirico's studio, lit by a skylight in the terrace above, has his brushes and canvases, more books and records, a portrait of his mother and a photo of his brother, Andrea Savigny, also a writer and artist.

The Spanish Steps

The **Spanish Steps** (or Scalinata di Spagna) sweep down in a cascade of balustrades and balconies beside Di Chirico's house, the hangout, during the nineteenth century, of young hopefuls waiting to be chosen as artists' models. The scene has not changed much; it is still a venue for international posing and fast pick-ups late into the summer nights. It was, in fact, a largely French initiative to build them – before their construction the French church of Trinità dei Monti

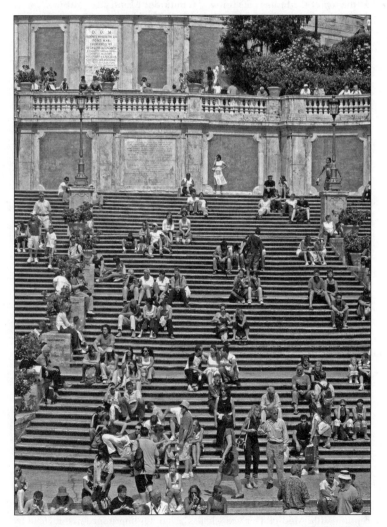

△ The Spanish steps

was accessible only by way of a rough path up the steep slope. After a few decades of haggling over the plans, the steps were finally laid in 1725, and now form one of the city's most distinctive attractions, built to a design, by one Francisco de Sanctis, that is deliberately showy, perfect for strollers to glide up and down while chatting and looking each other up and down. The steps also contain a religious message, the three flights and three landings an allusion to the Holy Trinity. If you don't think you can make it on foot, it's worth knowing that there's a lift in the entrance of the Spagna metro station – down Vicolo del Bottino.

Trinità dei Monti

At the top of the Spanish Steps is the **Trinità dei Monti** (daily 10am–noon & 4–6pm), a largely sixteenth-century church designed by Carlo Maderno and paid for by the French king. Its rose-coloured Baroque facade overlooks the rest of Rome from its hilltop site, and it's worth clambering up here just for the views. The church also has a couple of impressive works by Daniele da Volterra, notably a soft, beautifully composed fresco of *The Assumption* in the third chapel on the right, whose array of finely realized figures includes a portrait of his teacher Michelangelo (he's the greybeard on the far right), while a *Deposition*, across the nave in the second chapel on the left, has another ingenious arrangement, with Christ hauled down from the cross as his mother and other figures grieve below. The French seventeenth-century artist Poussin considered this painting, which was probably painted from a series of cartoons by Michelangelo, as the world's third-greatest painting (Raphael's *Transfiguration* was, he thought, the best).

Via Sistina

From the church you can either continue north along past the Villa Medici to the Pincio terrace and the gardens of the Villa Borghese, or head south along **Via Sistina** to Piazza Barberini. Via Sistina was the first of Pope Sixtus V's planning improvements to sixteenth-century Rome, a dead straight street designed to connect Santa Maria Maggiore to Trinità dei Monti, which it almost still does, under a variety of names, and in the other direction to Piazza del Popolo, which it never quite managed. Nowadays it's the quickest way of getting to the Via Veneto and Quirinale areas from the Spanish Steps.

Sant'Andrea del Fratte

Just off Via Sistina to the right, **Sant'Andrea del Fratte** is tucked into a tight spot – like so many churches by Borromini, who designed the characteristic campanile. This is another church in which the great men of the Baroque era came together: inside, the apse is flanked by two histrionic angels designed by Bernini, originally intended for the Ponte Sant'Angelo, the bridge which connects the centro storico and Prati. To the left of the north door, a plaque remembers Angelika Kauffmann, an accomplished late-eighteenth-century Swiss painter and great friend of the English artist Joshua Reynolds, who lived in Rome and was a good friend of Geothe (see p.84), while the door in the opposite aisle gives way to a very pleasant tree-filled cloister.

Villa Medici

Walking north from the top of the Spanish Steps, you reach the sixteenth-century **Villa Medici**. This was where Galileo was imprisoned in the 1630s by the Vatican's Holy Office for heretically claiming that the earth was not the centre of the universe but instead revolved around the sun. He was forced to recant his theory and say seven penitential psalms a week for his trouble. Nowadays, the villa is home to the French Academy, and its interior and sumptuous gardens can usually be visited only when they host concerts and art shows. Occasionally, they throw open their doors to the curious public; check the newspapers, the usual listings sources or the Academy's website (Ⓦwww .villamedici.it) to find out when.

The Pincio Gardens

Further along, on the edge of the Villa Borghese, the **Pincio Gardens**, laid out by Valadier in the early nineteenth century and fringed with dilapidated busts of classical and Italian heroes, give fine views over the roofs, domes and TV antennae of central Rome, right across to St Peter's and the Janiculum Hill. The view is the main event here, but the benches are pleasantly shaded and a good place to take some weight off your feet, and the nineteenth-century **water clock** at the back is a quirky attraction.

Via del Babuino

Leading south from Piazza del Popolo to the Piazza di Spagna, **Via del Babuino** and the narrow **Via Margutta,** where the film maker Federico Fellini once lived, set the tone for the area, which in the 1960s was the core of a thriving art community and home to the city's best galleries and a fair number of its artists. High rents forced out all but the most successful, and the neighbourhood now supports a prosperous trade in antiques and designer fashions. Via del Babuino – literally "Street of the Baboon" – gets its name from the statue of Silenus which reclines outside the Tadolini studio about halfway down on the right. In ancient times the wall behind was a focus for satirical graffiti, although it is now coated with graffiti-proof paint. Inside the studio, the **Museo-Atelier Canova-Tadolini** is really a café-restaurant, but a highly original one, littered as it is with the sculptural work of four generations of the Tadolini family. The nineteenth-century sculptor Canova donated the building to Adam Tadolini, his most promising student, in 1818, and the family occupied the building for the next 150 years. You can sip a drink outside, next to the baboon, or sit inside among the busts, friezes and disembodied limbs – an eccentric experience (see p.236 for more). A little further down on the right, the church of **All Saints** (daily 9am–1pm) is the official Anglican church of Rome, its solid steeple and brick construction, erected in the late nineteenth century, serving as a further reminder of the English connections in this part of town.

Piazza del Popolo and around

At the far end of Via del Babuino, the oval-shaped expanse of **Piazza del Popolo** is a dignified meeting of roads laid out in 1538 by Pope Paul III (Alessandro Farnese) to make an impressive entrance to the city; it owes its present symmetry to Valadier, who added the central fountain in 1814. The monumental **Porta del Popolo** went up in 1655, the work of Bernini, whose patron Alexander VII's Chigi family symbol – the heap of hills surmounted by a star – can clearly be seen above the main gateway.

During summer, the steps around the obelisk and fountain, and the cafés on either side of the square, are popular hangouts. But the piazza's real attraction is the unbroken view it gives all the way back down Via del Corso, between the perfectly paired churches of **Santa Maria dei Miracoli** and **Santa Maria in Montesanto**, to the central columns of the Vittorio Emanuele Monument. If you get to choose your first view of the centre of Rome, make it this one.

Santa Maria del Popolo

On the far side of the piazza, hard against the city walls, **Santa Maria del Popolo** (Mon–Sat 7am–noon & 4–7pm, Sun 8am–1.30pm & 4.30–7.30pm) holds some of the best Renaissance art of any Roman church, with works by Raphael, Bramante, Pinturicchio, Sansovino and Caravaggio. It was originally erected here in 1099 over the burial place of Nero, in order to sanctify what was believed to be an evil place (the emperor's ghost had appeared here several times), but took its present form in the fifteenth century. Inside, there are frescoes by Pinturicchio in the first chapel of the south aisle, including a lovely *Adoration of Christ*, full of tiny details receding into the distance. Pinturicchio also did some work in the next chapel but one – the altarpiece *Madonna and Child and Saints* – and in the Bramante-designed apse, which in turn boasts two fine tombs by Andrea Sansovino.

The **Chigi chapel**, the second from the entrance in the northern aisle, was designed by Raphael for Agostino Chigi in 1516 (he lies in the tomb on the right, his brother Sigismondo on the left), although most of the work was actually undertaken by other artists and not finished until the seventeenth century. The odd pyramid-shaped memorials on either side have come in for lots of recent speculation, due to Dan Brown's fictional conspiracy theories – in *Angels & Demons* its statues helped lead to the secretive Illuminati. Michelangelo's protégé, Sebastiano del Piombo, was responsible for the altarpiece; and two of the sculptures in the corner niches, of Daniel, with the lions, on the left as you enter, and Habakkuk, diagonally opposite, are by Bernini.

But it's two pictures by **Caravaggio**, in the left-hand Cerasi chapel of the north transept, that attract the most attention. These are typically dramatic works – one, the *Conversion of St Paul*, showing Paul and horse bathed in a beatific radiance, the other, the *Crucifixion of St Peter*, has Peter as an aged but strong figure, dominated by the musclebound figures hoisting him up. Like his paintings in the churches of San Luigi dei Francesi and Sant'Agostino (see p.57), both works were considered extremely risqué in their time, their heavy chiaroscuro and deliberate realism too much for the Church authorities; one contemporary critic referred to the *Conversion of St Paul*, a painting dominated by the exquisitely lit horse's hindquarters, as "an accident in a blacksmith's shop". In the middle, Carracci's boldly coloured altarpiece, with its golds and pinks, offers a massive contrast.

Casa di Goethe

A short way down Via del Corso from Piazza del Popolo, on the left at no. 18, the **Casa di Goethe** (Tues–Sun 10am–6pm; €3; Ⓦ www.casadigoethe.it) is a genuinely engaging small museum. There seem to be houses all over Italy that Goethe stayed in, but he did spend over two years in this one, and wrote much of his classic travelogue *Italian Journey* here – indeed, each room is decorated with a quote from the book. Goethe had long dreamed of travelling to Italy, inspired by a journey his father made years earlier, and he came here – incognito, as Filippo Miller – in 1786, after touring the north of the country. His routine here was a bohemian one, associating with ex-pat artists and writers, far removed from his life in Germany, where he was a celebrated writer.

The house has been restored as a modern exhibition space and houses books, letters, prints and drawings, plus a reconstruction of his study in Vienna. Among the objects on display are Piranesi prints of public spaces in Rome, watercolours by Goethe himself and drawings by the German artist **Tischbein**, with whom he shared the house, including a lovely one of Goethe leaning out of the window over Via del Corso and a more formal painting of him reclining in the foreground of an idealized Roman *campagna* landscape.

Mausoleum of Augustus

Leading from Piazza del Popolo to Piazza del Augusto Imperatore, **Via di Ripetta** was laid out by Pope Leo X to provide a straight route out of the city centre from the old river port area here. **Piazza del Augusto Imperatore** is an odd square – these days not much more than a peaceful ring of cypresses, circled by paths, flowering shrubs and the debris of tramps – of largely Mussolini-era buildings. Its focus is the massive **Mausoleum of Augustus**, the burial place of the emperor and his family. Augustus died in 14 AD, giving way to his son Tiberius, who ruled until 37 AD (the last ten years from the island of Capri), when his nephew's son Caligula took over and effectively signalled the end of the Augustan age, and the order, prosperity and expansion that defined it. As Augustus himself had it, according to Suetonius: "I found Rome built simply out of bricks: I left her clad in marble." The mausoleum has been transformed into many buildings over the years, including a medieval fortress, and is occasionally open to the public by appointment, but the passageways and central crypt, where the ashes of the members of the Augustan dynasty were kept, don't add much to the picture you get from the outside. The good news is that further excavations are due to start shortly with a view to opening the building up to the public in a revamped form by around 2009. Watch this space…

Ara Pacis Augustae

On the far side of the square, the **Ara Pacis Augustae** or "Altar of Augustan Peace" is now enclosed in a controversial purpose-built structure designed by the New York-based architect Richard Meier, its angular lines and sheer white surfaces dominating the river side of the square (daily 9am–7pm; €6.50, audio guide €3.50). A marble block enclosed by sculpted walls, the altar was built in 13 BC, probably to celebrate Augustus's victory over Spain and Gaul and the peace it heralded. Much of it had been dug up piecemeal over the years, but the bulk was uncovered in the middle of the last century, in the heart of the Campus Martius, a few hundred yards south, where it had originally stood. Putting it back together was no easy task: excavation involved digging down to a depth of 10m and freezing the water table, after which many other parts had to be retrieved from museums the world over, or plaster copies made.

The result, on the surrounding walls especially, is a superb example of imperial Roman sculpture, particularly in the victory procession itself, on the mausoleum side of the altar. This is a picture of a family at the height of its power, with little inkling of the scandal and tragedy that would afflict it in years to come. The first part is almost completely gone, but the head of Augustus is complete, as are the figures that follow: the priests with their skull-cap headgear, then, behind the figure carrying an axe, Augustus's great general, Marcus Agrippa, hooded, clutching a rolled piece of parchment, with his son Gaius pulling on his toga. Then, respectively, come Augustus's wife Livia, followed by her son (and Augustus's eventual successor) Tiberius and niece Antonia, the latter caught simply and realistically turning to her husband, Drusus, while holding the hand of her son Germanicus. Of the various other children clutching the togas of the elders, the last is said to be the young Claudius, while the old man towards the end may be Maecenas, Augustus's most trusted advisor during his heyday.

On the front of the altar is a frieze of Aeneas making a sacrifice, while on the back is a well-preserved representation of Mother Earth bestowing peace and prosperity on Rome, holding two babies in her arms – said by some to be Lucius and Gaius, Augustus's grandchildren and his planned successors. On the river side, the veiled figure is believed to be their mother, Julia, Augustus's daughter, with Lucius in front of her. Julia later married Tiberius and was constantly disgraced for her promiscuity about Rome, and both children died young, before they could take on the responsibility that Augustus had planned for them.

Fontana di Trevi and around

Back on the eastern side of Via del Corso, off the busy bus terminus by **Piazza San Silvestro**, nowhere illustrates better how history sits cheek-by-jowl with the modern world in Rome than the church of **San Silvestro in Capite**. The peaceful, plant-filled terracotta courtyard that you walk through to get in feels a million miles away from the fume-drenched traffic outside. Inside, the blackened skull of John the Baptist that gives the church the second half of its name is displayed in a small chapel that doubles as a side entrance. The church itself was at one point the centre of the Franciscan movement in Rome, home to Margherita Colonna who espoused the then left-field beliefs of St Francis and whipped up a storm in the Catholic hierarchy. Nowadays its interior is classic over-stuffed Roman Barqoue, although the dark, ancient feel suits its long and illustrious history well.

On the other side of the square, and Via del Tritone, the classic Y-shaped nineteenth-century shopping arcade of **Galleria Alberto Sordi** (daily 10am–10pm) has recently reopened after years of neglect. Renamed after an Italian film star (actors used to hang out here seeking work), it's as spruce and sleek as it was in its heyday, and provides a welcome escape from this ultra-busy part of central Rome, especially on a hot day

The tight web of narrow, apparently aimless streets beyond open out on one of Rome's more surprising sights – the **Fontana di Trevi**, a huge, very Baroque gush of water over statues and rocks built onto the backside of a Renaissance palace; it's fed by the same source that surfaces at the Barcaccia fountain in Piazza di Spagna. The original Trevi fountain, designed by Alberti, was around the corner in Via dei Crociferi, but Urban VIII decided to upgrade it in line with his other grandiose schemes of the time and employed Bernini, among others, to design an alternative. Work didn't begin until 1732, when Niccolò Salvi won a competition held by Clement XII to design the fountain, and even then it took thirty years to finish the project. Salvi died in the process, his lungs shot by the time spent in the dank waterworks of the fountain. The Trevi fountain is now, of course, the place you come to chuck in a coin if you want to guarantee your return to Rome, though you might remember Anita Ekberg throwing herself into it in *La Dolce Vita* (there are police here to discourage you from doing the same thing). Recently restored, it's one of the city's most vigorous outdoor spots to hang out.

Accademia di San Luca

A short walk from the fountain, towards Via del Tritone, the **Accademia di San Luca** is Rome's school of art first and foremost, but it has a small gallery of pictures that is normally open to the public but is currently closed for restoration. The building itself is worth visiting anyway for its Borromini ramp, which spirals up from the main lobby instead of a staircase. The collection includes a fresco by Raphael, a *Venus* by Guercino and a couple of pictures by Titian and Rubens.

Santi Vincenzo ed Anastasio

Directly opposite the Trevi fountain, the grubby little church of **Santi Vincenzo ed Anastasio** is the parish church of the Quirinal Palace, and, bizarrely, holds in marble urns the hearts and viscera of the 22 popes who used the palace as a **papal residence**. Two tablets – one either side of the high altar – record each of the popes whose bits and pieces lie downstairs, from Sixtus V, who died in 1590, to Leo XIII, who passed away in 1903.

Museo Nazionale delle Paste Alimentari

Two minutes' walk south and east from the Trevi fountain at Piazza Scanderberg 114–120, the **Museo Nazionale delle Paste Alimentari** (daily 9.30am– 5.30pm; €10; ⓦwww.pastainmuseum.com) is not nearly as grand as it sounds. The small, homely exhibition follows the history of **pasta** from its earliest mentions in twelfth-century Palermo to the present day, with displays of artisanal and industrial kneaders, presses, adverts, and lots of cartoons and photos of famous people eating pasta. It covers the various regional traditions of Italy, and gives us the lowdown on how pasta is the superfood to beat them all – high in carbohydrates, cheap and easy to cook, and easy to digest. But to be honest it's all a bit of a yawn, and given the high prices can presumably be here only to cash in on the Trevi tourist trade.

Galleria Colonna

A short stroll south brings you to the **Galleria Colonna**, Via della Pilotta 17 (Sat 9am–1pm, closed Aug; €7), part of the Palazzo Colonna complex, whose gardens (not open to the public) stretch up the hill from here, linked to the palace by bridges over the narrow street. The gallery is outranked by many of Rome's other palatial collections, but it's worth visiting not only for its small but high quality collection of art but also for the glimpse it gives you of the home of one of Rome's most powerful Renaissance families. The ceiling paintings in the chandelier-decked Great Hall glorify the deeds of Marcantonio Colonna, notably his great victory against the Turks at the Battle of Lepanto in 1589, while other rooms remember the Colonna pope, Martin V – the frescoes in the Room of the Apotheosis which show him being received into heaven. Of the paintings, the highlight is the gallery's collection of landscapes by

Dughet (Poussin's brother-in-law), housed in a room frescoed with more scenes of the Battle of Lepanto; but other works stand out too, including Annibale Carracci's early and unusually spontaneous *Bean Eater* (though its attribution to him has since been questioned), *Narcissus* by Tintoretto and *Portrait of a Venetian Gentleman*, caught in a supremely confident pose by Veronese.

❹ Santi Apostoli

The back of the Palazzo Colonna is taken up by the large church of **Santi Apostoli** (daily 7am–noon & 4–7pm), a sixth-century basilica whose ancient origins are hard to detect now, encased as it is in an eighteenth-century shell and Napoleonic facade, and completely done up with Baroque finery inside. It too was part of the Colonna estate and is a Franciscan church, thanks to the family's early embrace of the movement, its wide, airy interior still looked after by the friars, who pad silently around while you take in its clash of Byzantine, Renaissance and Baroque architectural styles. The ceiling paintings are by the Genoese painter Baciccia, more famous for his work in the Gesú (see p.70), and the north aisle contains the nineteenth-century Italian sculptor Canova's first work in Rome, the very grand mausoleum of Clement XIV. But the church's statue-encrusted portico is perhaps its most impressive feature, commissioned by Pope Julius II, who lived in the palace next door, and looking over to the equally grandiose **Palazzo Odelscalchi** opposite, which was renovated by none other than Bernini in the 1660s but is currently not open to the public.

Museo delle Cere

At the end of the street, the **Museo delle Cere** (daily 9am–8pm; €5) is a quirky first-floor museum of waxworks that hosts a diverse array of characters from history and Italian culture: not essential viewing by any means but certainly different from anything else you'll see in Rome. It starts with a room devoted to the Fascist Council of 1943, with Mussolini at its head, gloomily – and fairly spookily – giving up on the war, off to the right of which are various titans of the war and post-war era: Hitler and Himmler, the Yalta conference threesome of Churchill, Stalin and Roosevelt, and Mao and Kruschev. Things lighten up a bit in other rooms, with footballers Totti – captain of Roma - and Nesta – the former Lazio captain, who subsequently moved to AC Milan. Deeper into the museum you're treated to various ancient musicians and artists, the usual chamber of horrors suspects – murderers, electric chairs and the like – even some wax dinosaurs, although by far the most frightening exhibit shows a fairytale prince about to waken the sleeping princess; look at her long enough and you'll see that she's actually breathing.

Ancient Rome

T here are remnants of the era of ancient Rome all over the city but the most concentrated and central grouping, which we've called **Ancient Rome**, is the area that stretches southeast from the Capitoline Hill. It's a reasonably traffic-free, self-contained part of the city. But it wasn't always like this: Mussolini ploughed **Via dei Fori Imperiali** through here in the 1930s with the idea of turning it into one massive archeological park. To an extent, of course, that's exactly what it is, and you can easily spend a day or more lazily picking your way through the rubble of what was once the heart of the ancient world. The most obvious place to start is with the original **Forum**, immediately below the Capitoline Hill, taking in the later **Imperial Forums** that lie nearby before heading up to the greener heights of the **Palatine Hill** or continuing straight on for the **Colosseum**.

The Forums

Immediately beyond the Vittoriano, just south of Via dei Fori Imperiali, the original **Roman Forum** was the centre of republican-era Rome. Even in ancient times Rome was a very large city, in many places stretching out as far as the Aurelian Wall (see p.116) in a sprawl of apartment blocks or *insulae*. The Forum was home to its political and religious institutions, its shops and market stalls, and a meeting-place for all – which it remained until the imperial era, when Rome's increased importance as a world power led to the building of the **Imperial Forums** nearby. Julius Caesar began the expansion in around 50 BC, building a new Senate building, and, beyond it to the northeast, a series of basilicas and temples. After his assassination, work was continued by his nephew and successor Augustus, and later by the Flavian emperors – Vespasian, Nerva and Trajan.

The Forum never really recovered from its downgrading, and it's odd to think that during the time when the empire was at its height, neglect had already set in. A fire in the third century AD destroyed many of the buildings, and although the damage was repaired, Rome was by this time in a general state of decay, the coming of **Christianity** only serving to accelerate the process, particularly for its pagan temples and institutions. After the fall of the city to barbarian invaders, the whole area was left in ruin, its relics quarried for the construction of other parts of Rome during medieval and Renaissance times; the odd church or tower was built *in situ* out of the more viable piles. Excavation of the site didn't start until the beginning of the nineteenth century, and has continued pretty

ANCIENT ROME

ACCOMMODATION A
Richmond

The **Forum**, **Palatine** and **Colosseum** are open daily: summer 8.30am–6pm; winter 9am–4.30pm. Entry to the Forum is free, while entry to the Palatine and Colosseum costs € 11 for both.

much without stopping: you'll notice a fair part of the site, especially up on the Palatine Hill, closed off for further digs.

Via dei Fori Imperiali

From Piazza Venezia, **Via dei Fori Imperiali**, a soulless boulevard imposed on the area by Mussolini in 1932, cuts south through the heart of Rome's ancient sites. Before then this was a warren of medieval streets that wound around the ruins of the ancient city centre, but, as with the Via della Conciliazione up to St Peter's (see Chapter 11), the duce preferred to build something to his own glory rather than preserve that of another era. A long-standing plan (previously championed by Mussolini) to make the entire ancient part of the city into a huge archeological park stretching right down to the catacombs on the Via Appia Antica is still mooted, but although excavations have been undertaken in recent years, they are continuing slowly. It's a dilemma for the city planners: Via dei Fori Imperiali is a major traffic artery, a function which must be preserved. One way around this would be to dig a tunnel under the road – an expensive option but one that is apparently being considered. For the moment, if you want a tranquil stroll between the major sights, you'll have to settle for coming on a Sunday, when a long stretch from Piazza Venezia to Via Appia Antica is closed to traffic and pedestrians take to the streets to stroll past the ruins of the ancient city.

The Imperial Forums

Nowadays there's a lot of interest along Via dei Fori Imperiali itself, where several of the **Imperial Forums** have been excavated since work started in the mid-1990s and much is now open to the public. The Forum of Trajan and the Forum of Augustus on the north side are the most impressive and accessible, but those of Vespasian and Nerva next door and Caesar on the south side might also detain you before you move on to the Forum proper. A **Visitor Centre** (daily 9.30am–6.30pm) opposite the church of Santi Cosma e Damiano (see below), has more information, a bookshop, and a café to rest your aching feet, if you need to.

The Forum and Trajan's Markets

One of the major victims of Mussolini's plan for the area was the remains of the **Forum of Trajan** (Tues–Sun 9am–6pm; € 3), a complex of basilicas, monuments, apartments and shops that was in its day the most sumptuous of the Imperial Forums, built at what was probably the very pinnacle of Roman power and prestige, after Trajan returned from conquering Dacia (modern Romania) in 112 AD. It's currently fairly unrecognizable, the main section no more than a sunken area of scattered columns to the left of the road, fronting the semicircle of **Trajan's Markets**, a tiered ancient Roman shopping centre that's also accessible from Via IV Novembre but is currently under restoration. Below the markets, the Basilica Ulpia was a central part of the Forum of Trajan, an immense structure, with five aisles and a huge apse at either end, that measured 176m long by 59m wide; the central nave is discernible from the large paved area in the centre, and the column stumps give an idea of its former dimensions. At the head of the basilica, enclosed in what is probably a small courtyard, the enormous **Trajan's Column** was erected to celebrate the emperor's victories in Dacia, and is covered top to bottom with reliefs commemorating the highlights of the campaign. The carving on the base shows the trophies brought back and bears an inscription saying that the column was dedicated to Trajan by the Senate and People of Rome in 113 AD. The statue on the top is St Peter, placed here by Pope Sixtus V in the late sixteenth century, and made from the bronze doors of Sant'Agnese fuori le Mura on Via Nomentana (see p.138).

Behind the Forum of Trajan, the **Torre delle Milizie** is fondly imagined to be the tower from which Nero watched Rome burning, although it's actually a twelfth-century fortification left over from days when Rome was divided into warring factions within the city walls. The top was destroyed by a blast of lightning in the fifteenth century.

The Forum of Augustus

Back on Via dei Fori Imperiali, the round brick facade you can see to the left, across the field of ruins, now houses the Order of Malta but was once part of the **Forum of Augustus**. Just beyond, the monumental staircase and platform was Augustus's Temple of Mars the Avenger, put up by Augustus in memory of his uncle and adoptive father, Julius Caesar, after the last of his assassins had been killed. The temple is backed by a large wall of grey stone that was erected to prevent fire from spreading into the forums from the densely inhabited adjacent neighbourhood of Suburra up on the Esquiline Hill.

You can get up closer to the ruins here by way of a metal walkway, which also takes you through to the lower streets of the Monti district, or just continue on down past the various other imperial forums to the visitor centre and the church of Santi Cosma e Damiano opposite.

Santi Cosma e Damiano

Across the road from Augustus's Forum, the vestibule of the church of **Santi Cosma e Damiano** (daily 8am–1pm & 3–7pm) was originally created from the Temple of Romulus in the Forum, which you can look down into from the nave of the church. Turn around, and you'll see the mosaics in the apse, showing the naturalistically depicted figures of the two saints being presented to Christ by St Peter and St Paul, flanked by St Felix on the left and St Theodore on the right. Outside, the cloister is wonderfully peaceful compared to the busy roads around. For a €1 donation you can also visit the massive Neapolitan **presepio** or Christmas crib, displayed in a room in the corner here (April–Oct daily 10am–1pm & 3–6.30pm; Nov–March Tues–Thurs 10am–1pm, Fri–Sun 10am–1pm & 3–5.30pm), a huge piece of work with literally hundreds of figures spread amongst the ruins of ancient Rome.

The Roman Forum

Not far from the church is the main entrance to the **Roman Forum** – not surprisingly one of the city's top attractions, but for many also one of its most disappointing, since you need a good imagination and some grasp of history to really appreciate the place. Certainly it holds some of the most ruined ruins

THE ROMAN FORUM

you'll see: indeed it was abandoned (and looted) for so long that very little is anything like intact. But these five or so acres were once the heart of the Mediterranean world, and are a very real and potent testament to a power that held a large chunk of the earth in its thrall for close on five centuries, and whose influence reverberates right up to the present day – in language, in architecture, in political terms and systems, even in the romance that time has lent to its ruins.

The Via Sacra

Immediately inside the main entrance, take some time to get orientated. You can sit down on the three long steps that flank the other side of the **Via Sacra**, which runs directly through the core of the Forum, from below the Capitoline Hill in the west to the far eastern extent of the site and the Arch of Titus (where there's a handy exit/entrance for the Colosseum). This was the best-known street of ancient Rome, along which victorious emperors and generals would ride in procession to give thanks at the Capitoline's Temple of Jupiter. It's

The decline and fall of the Forum

In 667 AD, Costans II, ruler of the Eastern empire, paid a state visit to Rome. He came to the Forum, and, seeing all the temples and basilicas held together with bronze and iron cramps, decided that the metal would serve better in his war against encroaching Islam and ordered all the metal to be transported back home and forged into spearpoints, arrowheads and armour for his forces. It took just twelve days to dismantle the metal props, but the result was a disaster: everything was captured en route to Constantinople by Saracen raiders, and the columns and arches supporting all the buildings in the Forum fell down with the next earth tremor. By the early ninth century hardly anything remained standing – ripe for the looters of later years, and one reason why so little is left today.

VIA DEI FORI IMPERIALI

Basilica of
Maxentius

Antiquarium

VIA SACRA

Santa Maria
Nuova

II

Exit   VIA SACRA

Arch of
Titus

Arch of
Constantine

0   50 m

Palatine Hill

possible, however, that the modern street isn't the original Via Sacra, and was in fact only given the name in the 1550s, when the Holy Roman Emperor, Charles V, visited Pope Paul III and the only triumphal arch they could find to march under was the Arch of Septimius Severus, a couple of hundred metres to your left.

The Regia and around

The steps you're sitting on are part of the **Regia**, or house of the kings, an extremely ancient – and ruined – group of foundations that probably date from the reign of the second king of Rome, Numa, who ruled from 715 to 673 BC. There was a shrine of Mars here, housing the shields and spears of the god of war, which generals embarking on a campaign rattled before setting off. If the shields and spears rattled of their own accord it was a bad omen, requiring purification and repentance rites. The Regia later became the residence of Julius Caesar, who moved in here in 45 BC – an imperious act which contributed to his downfall.

On the other side of the road from the Regia, the **Temple of Antoninus and Faustina** is the best-preserved temple in the Forum, mainly because of its preservation since the seventh century as the church of **San Lorenzo in Miranda**. The six huge Corinthian columns across its front are still connected by an inscribed lintel, dedicating the temple by order of the Senate to the god Antonino and the goddess Faustina, the parents of Marcus Aurelius – Roman emperors were always considered to be deities. Above the inscription was the roof architrave, along whose sides the original frieze of griffins, candelabra and acanthus scrolls can be seen. Otherwise, the brick stairs leading up to the floor of the temple are a modern reconstruction, while the facade of the church dates from 1602.

Next to the Regia, the pile of rubble immersed in cement with the little green roof is all that remains of the grandeur and magnificence that comprised the **Temple of Julius Caesar** – the round brick stump under the roof marks

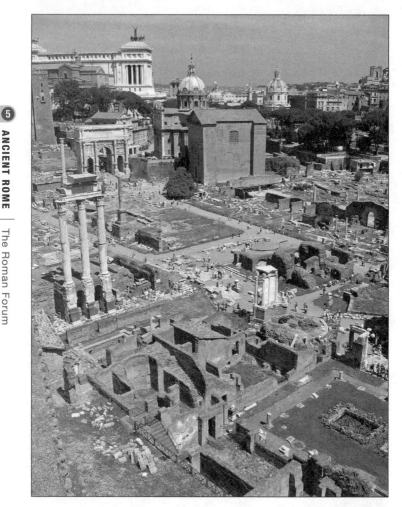

△ The Roman Forum

the spot where Caesar was cremated, and around which the temple was built. You may hear tour guides declaiming Mark Antony's "Friends, Romans, countrymen" speech from here; bear in mind that not only was the speech made up by Shakespeare, but also that apparently Mark Antony only read Caesar's will, and that he would have done it from the Rostra (see below).

The football pitch of broken columns across the street marks the site of the **Basilica Emilia**, built in the second century BC to house law courts, and, in the little booths and boutiques flanking it on the Via Sacra side, moneychangers. Close by, a little marble plaque dedicated to **Venus Cloacina** marks the site of a small shrine dedicated to Venus where the Cloaca Maxima canal drained the Forum, which was originally marshland. The Cloaca Maxima reaches all the way to the Tiber from here, and still keeps the area drained.

The Curia and around

A little way beyond, the large cube-shaped building on the right is the **Curia**, built on the orders of Julius Caesar as part of his programme for expanding the Forum – it connects up with the Forum of Caesar outside – although what you see now is a third-century AD reconstruction built during the era of the emperor Diocletian. The Senate met here during the republican period, and augurs would come to announce the wishes of the gods. For centuries the Curia served as a church, reverting to its original form only earlier this century, when it was restored, and its bronze doors – which had been removed in the seventeenth century to San Giovanni in Laterno, where they remain – were replaced with reproductions.

Inside, three wide stairs rise left and right, on which about three hundred senators on folding chairs could be accommodated. In the centre is the speaker's platform, with a porphyry statue of a togaed figure. Otherwise, apart from the floor, elegantly patterned in red, yellow, green and white marble, there's not much left of its ancient decor, only the grey and white marble facing each side of the speaker's platform, which would once have covered the entire hall. The ceiling is a modern replacement, and in Roman times would have been gilded. The large marble reliefs here, the *Plutei of Trajan* – found outside and brought here for safekeeping – show Trajan in the midst of public-spirited acts, forgiving the public debt owed by citizens to the state (porters carry large register books and place them before the seated emperor, where they will be burnt) and, on the right giving a woman a sack of money, a representation of the emperor's welfare plan for widows and orphans. Look closely at the reliefs and you can see how parts of the Forum would have looked at the time: in one, a fig tree, the columns and arches of the Basilica Julia, the facade of the Temple of Saturn, a triumphal arch and the Temple of Vespasian and Titus; in the other, the columns and eaves of the Temple of Castor and Pollux, and the Arch of Augustus.

In front of the Curia, the black, fenced-off paving of the **Lapis Niger** marks the traditional site of the tomb of Romulus, the steps beneath (usually closed) leading down to a monument that was considered sacred ground during classical times. Across the travertine pavement from here, the **Column of Phocas** is one of a few commemorative columns here that retains its dedicatory inscription. To the right, the **Arch of Septimius Severus** was constructed in the early third century AD by his sons Caracalla and Geta to mark their father's victories in what is now Iran. The friezes on it recall Severus and in particular Caracalla, who ruled Rome with undisciplined terror for seven years. There's a space where Geta was commemorated – Caracalla, who had inherited the empire jointly, had him executed in 213 AD, and his name expediently removed from the arch altogether.

The Rostra and around

To the left of the arch, the low brown wall of the **Rostra** faces the wide-open scatter of paving, dumped stones and beached columns that makes up the central portion of the Forum. In its heyday it would have been crowded with politicians, tribunes and traders. Facing the central part of the Forum, the Rostra was the place where important speeches were made, and it was probably from here that Mark Antony spoke about Caesar after his death. Left of the Rostra are the long steps of the **Basilica Julia**, built by Julius Caesar in the 50s BC after he returned from the Gallic Wars. All that remain are a few column bases and one nearly complete column, and you can't climb the stairs – although you can still see the gameboards scratched in the marble steps where idlers in the Forum played their pebble-toss games.

A bit further along, on the right, the guard rails lead into a kind of alcove in the pavement, which marks the site of the **Lacus Curtius** – the spot where, according to legend, a chasm opened in the city's earliest days and the sooth-sayers determined that it would be closed only when Rome had sacrificed its most valuable possession into it. Marcus Curtius, a Roman soldier who declared that Rome's most valuable possession was a loyal citizen, hurled himself and his horse into the void and it duly shut. Further on, towards the Capitoline, you reach the **Temple of Saturn** – the oldest temple in the Forum, dating origi-nally from 497 BC, although the base and eight columns you see today are the result of a series of restorations carried out between 42 BC and 380 AD. The temple was also the Roman treasury and mint. To the right of the temple, three columns still stand from the **Temple of Vespasian and Titus** of the 80s AD. Still further to the right, behind the Arch of Septimius Severus, the large pile of brick and cement rubble is all that remains of the **Temple of Concordia Augusta**, dedicated by Tiberius in 10 AD.

Santa Maria Antiqua and the Temple of Castor and Pollux

Retracing your steps past the Forum proper takes you to **Vicus Tuscus**, "Etruscan Street", at the end of which are public toilets and a water fountain, and the church of **Santa Maria Antiqua**, which formed the vestibule to the emperor Domitian's palace on the Palatine Hill, and was the first ancient building to be converted for Christian worship – recently open again after many years. Back around the corner to the right, the enormous pile of rubble topped by three graceful Corinthinan columns is the **Temple of Castor and Pollux**, dedicated in 484 BC to the divine twins or Dioscuri, the offspring of Jupiter by Leda, who appeared miraculously to ensure victory for the Romans in a key battle. The story goes that a group of Roman citizens were gathered around a water fountain on this spot fretting about the war when Castor and Pollux appeared and reassured them that the battle was won – hence the temple, and their adoption as the special protectors of Rome.

House of the Vestal Virgins

Beyond here, the **House of the Vestal Virgins** is a second-century AD recon-struction of a building originally by Nero. Vesta was the Roman goddess of the hearth and home, and her cult was an important one in ancient Rome. Her temple was in the charge of the so-called **Vestal Virgins**, who had the respon-sibility of keeping the sacred flame of Vesta alight, and were obliged to remain chaste for the thirty years that they served (they usually started at around age 10). If the flame should go out, the woman responsible was scourged; if she should lose her chastity, she was buried alive (her male partner-in-crime was flogged to death in front of the Curia). Because of the importance of their office, they were accorded special privileges: a choice section in the Colosseum was reserved for them; only they and the empress could ride in a wheeled vehicle within the confines of the city; and they had the right to pardon any criminal who managed to get close enough to one of them to beseech their mercy. A vestal virgin could resign her post if she wished, but she had the benefit of residing in a very comfortable palace: four floors of rooms around a central courtyard, with the round **Temple of Vesta** at the near end. The rooms are mainly ruins now, though they're fairly recognizable on the Palatine side, and you can get a good sense of the shape of the place from the remains of the courtyard, still with its pool in the centre and fringed by the statues or inscribed pedestals of the women themselves.

The Basilica of Maxentius

Opposite the vestals' house, the curved facade of the **Temple of Romulus** (the son of the emperor Maxentius, not the founder of Rome), dating from 309 AD, has been sanctified and serves as vestibule for the church of **Santi Cosma e Damiano** behind (see p.93). Just past the temple, a shady walkway to the left leads up to the **Basilica of Maxentius**, sometimes called the Basilica of Constantine, which rises up towards the main road – in terms of size and ingenuity probably the Forum's most impressive remains. By the early fourth century, when this structure was built, Roman architects and engineers were expert at building with poured cement. Begun by Maxentius, it was continued by his co-emperor and rival, Constantine, after he had defeated him at the Battle of the Milvian Bridge in 312 AD. It's said that Michelangelo studied the hexagonal coffered arches here when grappling with the dome of St Peter's and apparently Renaissance architects frequently used its apse and arches as a model.

The Antiquarium and Arch of Titus

Back on the Via Sacra, past the church of Santa Maria Nova, the **Antiquarium of the Forum** (free, but closed at the moment) houses a collection of statue fragments, capitals, tiles, mosaics and other bits and pieces found around the Forum – none of it very interesting, apart from a number of skeletons and wooden coffins exhumed from an Iron Age necropolis found to the right of the Temple of Antoninus and Faustina.

From the basilica the Via Sacra climbs more steeply, past a grassy series of ruins that no one has been able to positively identify, to the **Arch of Titus**, which stands commandingly on a low arm of the Palatine Hill, looking one way down the remainder of the Via Sacra to the Colosseum, and back over the Forum proper. The arch was built by Titus's brother, Domitian, after the emperor's death in 81 AD, to commemorate his victories in Judaea in 70 AD, and his triumphal return from that campaign, and it sets in stone the inauguration of the Vespasian dynasty and Rome's return to peace and stability following the disruption that ensued after Nero's death. It's a much restored structure, and you can see, in reliefs on the inside, scenes of Titus riding in a chariot with Nike, goddess of Victory, being escorted by representatives of the Senate and Plebs, and, on the opposite side, spoils being removed from the Temple in Jerusalem.

The Colosseum and the Palatine Hill

Beyond the Forum, a lake lay where the **Colosseum** stands now, drained by a small stream that wove between the **Palatine** and **Celian hills**, curving to empty into the Tiber close by. The slopes of the Palatine and Celian hills were inhabited by people living in shanties and huts until the great fire of 64 AD, when Nero incorporated the area into his grand design for the city, building a gigantic *nymphaeum* or courtyard to support his planned gardens on the Celian Hill, part of his Domus Aurea (see p.147), and cleaning up the slopes of the two hills. Eventually a temple to the deified Claudius was built on the Celian Hill, and the Palatine became the residence of the emperors, fed by water brought by the arched span of the Aqua Claudia.

The Palatine Hill

Turning right at the Arch of Titus takes you up to the ticket booth and main entrance to the **Palatine Hill** (daily 8.30am–6pm; €11, includes the Colosseum, valid the same day if bought before 1.30pm; guided tours in English at noon €3.50); there's another entrance on Via San Gregorio. The Palatine is supposedly where the city of Rome was founded, by Romulus and Remus, and holds some of its most ancient remnants. In a way it's a more pleasant site to tour than the Forum, larger, greener and more of a park – a good place to have a picnic and relax after the rigours of the ruins below. In the days of the Republic, the Palatine was the most desirable address in Rome (the word "palace" is derived from it), and the big names continued to colonize it during the imperial era, trying to outdo each other with ever larger and more magnificent dwellings.

Along the main path up from the Forum, the **Domus Flavia**, the work of the emperor Domitian, was once one of the most splendid residences, and, although it's now almost completely ruined, the peristyle is easy enough to identify, with its fountain and hexagonal brick arrangement in the centre. To the left, the top level of the gargantuan **Domus Augustana** spreads to the far brink of the hill – not the home of Augustus as its name suggests, but the private house of any emperor (or "Augustus"). From here, you can look down onto its vast central courtyard with maze-like fountain and wander to the brink of the deep trench of the **Stadium**. On the far side of the stadium, the ruins of the Domus and **Baths of Septimius Severus** cling to the side of the hill, the terrace giving good views over the Colosseum and the churches of the Celian Hill opposite.

The large grey building nearby houses the **Museo Palatino** (daily 9am–6pm), which contains an assortment of statues, pottery and architectural fragments that have been excavated on the Palatine during the last 150 years. The ground floor has finds from the early years of Rome and reconstructions of the original Iron Age village. The upper floor leaps ahead to the imperial age, and highlights include three beautifully preserved black marble *Herms*, statues of women that supposedly filled the niches in Augustus's Temple of Apollo (see below); a piece of terracotta frieze from the same temple showing Apollo and Hercules in dispute (a reference, perhaps to Augustus's rivalry with Mark Antony, who frequently identified himself with Hercules); and busts of various emperors: two of Nero, one old, one young, Hadrian, Antoninus Pius and very young Marcus Aurelius. There are nice details too – fragments of *intarsio*, a fragment of a relief showing Apollo playing the lyre; the bottom of a relief of a togaed figure carrying a brace of ducks – supposedly the personification of winter – from the fourth century AD.

In the opposite direction from the Domus Flavia is the **Cryptoporticus**, a long passage built by Nero to link the vestibule of his Domus Aurea (see p.147) with the Domus Augustana and other Palatine palaces, and decorated along with well-preserved Roman stucco-work at the far end, towards the **House of Livia**. This was originally believed to have been the residence of Livia, the wife of Augustus, and its courtyard and some of the inner rooms are decorated with scanty frescoes, though it's now identified as part of **House of Augustus** – the set of ruins beyond, next to which are the remains of the Palatine **Temple of Apollo**, dedicated by Augustus himself in 28 BC.

Climb up the steps by the entrance to the Cryptoporticus and you're in the bottom corner of the **Farnese Gardens**, one of the first botanical gardens in Europe, laid out by Cardinal Alessandro Farnese in the mid-sixteenth century and now a tidily planted, shady retreat from the exposed heat of the ruins. The gardens occupy the ruins of a palace built by Tiberius, the **Domus Tiberiana**, the most extant remains of which form a terrace which looks back over the Forum. A terrace at the opposite end looks down on the church of San Teodoro, across to St Peter's, and down on the new excavations immediately below – the traces of an **Iron Age village** that perhaps marks the real centre of Rome's ancient beginnings.

The Arch of Constantine

Leaving the Forum by way of the Via Sacra, under the Arch of Titus (see p.99), you see the huge **Arch of Constantine** to your right, placed here in the early decades of the fourth century AD after Constantine had consolidated his power as sole emperor. The deterioration of the arts during the late stages of the Roman Empire meant there were hardly any sculptors around who could produce original work, and most of the sculptural decoration here had to be removed from other monuments. The builders were probably quite ignorant of the significance of the pieces they borrowed: the round medallions are taken from a temple dedicated to the emperor Hadrian's lover, Antinous, and show Antinous and Hadrian engaged in the hunt. The other pieces, removed from the Forum of Trajan, show Dacian prisoners captured in Trajan's war there. The large inscription in the centre was made for the arch, and dedicates the arch to Constantine for his wisdom – presumably in making Christianity the official religion of the Empire, although no one really knows what this refers to.

Between the Arch of Constantine and the Colosseum, at a pivotal point in the Via Sacra, stood a monumental fountain or **Meta Sudans**, the outline of which can still be seen today in the form of a series of recently excavated low brick walls. A "Meta" was the marker in the centre of a racecourse, and was usually an obelisk or some other large, easily visible object. In this case it was a conical fountain that was probably dedicated to Apollo, and produced a slow supply of water that resembled sweat – hence its name the "Sweating Meta".

The Colosseum

Across the way from here, the **Colosseum** is perhaps Rome's most awe-inspiring ancient monument, and one which, unlike the Forum, needs little historical knowledge or imagination to deduce its function. This enormous structure was so solidly built that despite the depredations of nearly two thousand years – earthquakes, fires, riots, wars, and, not least, plundering for its seemingly inexhaustible supply of ready-cut travertine blocks (the Barberini and Cancelleria palaces, even St Peter's, all used stone from here) – it still stands relatively intact, a readily recognizable symbol not just of the city of Rome, but of the entire ancient world. It's not much more than a shell now, eaten away by pollution and cracked by the vibrations of cars and metro trains; around the outside, the arches would originally have held statues, and there are gaping holes where metal brackets linked the great blocks together. The basic structure of the place is easy to see, however, and has served as a model for stadiums around the world ever since: oddly enough, until Sydney 2000 it appeared on all winners' medals in the **Olympics**; and it still graces the (Italian) 5c coin. You'll not be alone in appreciating it, and during summer the combination of people and scaffolding can make a visit more like touring a

Visiting the Colosseum

The Colosseum is open every day between 8.30am and 5.30pm and entrance costs €11, which includes the Palatine Hill. Queues can be a problem: while they do move quickly, they're rarely less than 100m long and often stretch through the arcade on the metro station side of the stadium and into the scrum of touts outside. To avoid them, try turning up before the Colosseum opens, or buy an Archeocard or RomaPass (see p.30), which allow you to use a different queue. There are tours in English roughly every half an hour from 9.15am (€3.50), or you can rent your own audioguide (also €3.50). If you'd rather not take the stairs, there's a lift in the north-eastern corner – just keep walking from the ticket office.

Once inside, you're free to wander around most of the lower level, and all the way round the upper level, though even here you are still only about halfway up the original structure; all the higher parts of the stadium are closed these days. You can gaze down into the innards of the arena, but there's been no original arena floor since its excavation in the nineteenth century and as such it too is out of bounds to visitors. The upper floor on the northern side contains a decent bookshop and a space for regular temporary exhibitions; an area by the lifts is given over to a display of fragments of masonry from the Colosseum.

Beastly happenings at the Colosseum

The Romans flocked to the Colosseum for many things, but **gladiatorial contests** were the big attraction. Gladiatorial combat as a Roman tradition was a direct import from the Etruscans, who thought it seemly to sacrifice a few prisoners of war or slaves at the funeral games of an important person. By the second century BC gladiatorial games had become so institutionalized in Rome that a gladiatorial school, or Ludus, was installed in the city – a rather grim affair, consisting of a barracks for gladiators and a ring in which they could practise with blunt weapons under supervision.

Gladiatorial combat was probably the greatest and cruellest of all bloodsports. At the start of the games the gladiators would enter through the monumental door at the eastern end of the arena. They would make a procession around the ring and halt in front of the emperor's box, where they would make their famous greeting, "Hail Caesar, we who are about to die salute you." Gladiators were divided into several classes, each performing different types of combat. There was the heavily armed "Samnite", named after the type of arms the Romans had captured on the defeat of that tribe in 310 BC, equipped with heavy armour, an oblong bronze shield, a visored helmet with crest and plumes, and a sword (gladius). Usually a Samnite would be pitted against a combatant without armour, equipped only with a cast net and a trident, whose main protection was that he was unencumbered and thereby could be fleet of foot. He had, however, only one cast of his net in which to entangle the Samnite and kill him with his trident. Neither man was allowed to flee from the arena, and, once captured or disarmed, the roaring mob would be asked whether the loser should be killed or be allowed to live. If he had put up a good fight he would usually be spared; if he had not fought as valiantly as he should, he would be slaughtered on the spot. The advent of Christianity brought a gradual end to the gladiatorial games (contrary to popular opinion, Christians were never fed to the lions here), and in 404 AD the emperor Honorius abolished them altogether.

The other activities conducted in the Colosseum involved **animals**. In the hundred-day games that inaugurated the Colosseum, something like 9000 beasts were massacred – roughly twelve killings a minute – and during the 450 years of activity here several breeds of African elephant and lion were rendered extinct. There were also gladiatorial games which involved "hunting" wild animals, and sometimes creatures would be pitted against each other – bears would be tied to bulls and have to fight to the finish, lions would take on tigers, dogs would be set against wolves, and so on. The last games involving animals were conducted in the year 523 AD, after which the Colosseum gradually fell into disuse and disrepair.

modern building-site than an ancient monument. But visit late in the evening or early morning before the tour buses have arrived, go up a level to get a real sense of the size of the building, and the arena can seem more like the marvel it really is.

The Colosseum: past and present

Originally known as the Flavian Amphitheatre (the name Colosseum is a much later invention), it was begun around 72 AD by the emperor **Vespasian**, who was anxious to extinguish the memory of Nero, and so chose the site of Nero's outrageous Domus Aurea (see p.147) for the stadium. The gesture was meant to indicate that the days of Nero were over and the city was being given back to the people. The Colosseum is sited on a lake that lay in front of the vestibule of the palace, where Nero had erected a huge statue of himself as sun god. The lake was drained, and the Colosseum was – incredibly, given the size of the project – inaugurated by Vespasian's son Titus about eight years later, an event celebrated by a hundred days of continuous games; it was finally completed by Domitian, Titus's brother, the third of the Flavian emperors.

Up until this time gladiatorial and other bloody games had been conducted in a makeshift stadium in the Roman Forum, near the Curia. The stands were temporary and constructed of wood, and had to be erected and taken down every time there were games. It is said that seventy thousand Hebrew slaves did the heavy work at the Colosseum. Fifty thousand cartloads of pre-cut travertine stone was hauled from the quarries at Tivoli, a distance of 27km. In the depths of what must have been the muddy bottom of the lake, a **labyrinth** was laid out, walling in passages for the contestants and creating areas for assembling and storing sets, scenery and other requirements for gladiatorial contests.

The overall structure was tastefully designed, with close attention paid to decoration. On the outside, the arena's three **arcades** rose in strict classical fashion to a flat surface at the top punctuated only by windows, where there was a series of supports for masts that protruded at the upper limit. These masts, 240 in total, were used to array a canvas awning over the spectators inside the arena. Inside, beyond the corridors that led up to the seats, lavishly decorated with painted stuccoes, there was room for a total of around 60,000 people seated and 10,000 or so standing; the design was such that all 70,000 could enter and be seated in a matter of minutes – surely a lesson for designers of modern stadiums.

The seating was allocated on a strict basis, with the emperor and his attendants naturally occupying the best seats in the house, and the social class of the spectators diminishing further up the stands. There were no ticket sales as we conceive of them; rather, tickets were distributed through – and according to the social status of – Roman heads of households. These "tickets" were in fact wooden tags, with the entrance, row, aisle and seat number carved on them.

Inside the amphitheatre, the labyrinth below was covered over with a wooden floor, punctuated at various places for trap doors and lifts to raise and lower the animals that were to take part in the games. The floor was covered with canvas to make it waterproof and the canvas was covered with several centimetres of sand to absorb blood; in fact, our word "arena" is derived from the Latin word for sand.

The Celian and Aventine Hills and south central Rome

The area south of the Forum and Palatine has some of the city's most atmospheric and compelling Christian and ancient sights, from the relatively central **Circus Maximus** and **Baths of Caracalla** – one of the city's grandest ruins, and the venue of occasional, inspirational opera performances – to the **catacombs** on the ancient Via Appia on the outskirts, with quite a lot worth seeing in between. It also boasts some of the city's most pleasant corners, notably on the green and peaceful **Celian** and **Aventine** hills, while just below the Aventine **Via Ostiense** linked ancient Rome to its port of Ostia. It's home to a more recent, nineteenth-century attraction in the **Protestant Cemetery**, where the poets Keats and Shelley are buried. Around here are a couple of Rome's trendiest neighbourhoods, **Testaccio** – a working-class enclave that has become increasingly hip and gentrified over the past decade or so, and **Ostiense** itself, whose regeneration is more recent, spurred on by the conversion of the **Centrale Montemartini** electricity generating plant into an amazing new gallery. Beyond lies the magnificent rebuilt basilica of **Sant Paolo fuori le Mura** and Rome's futuristic 1930s experiment in extra-urban town planning, **EUR**.

The Circus Maximus

The southern side of the Palatine Hill drops down to the **Circus Maximus**, a long green expanse bordered by heavily trafficked roads that was the ancient city's main venue for chariot races. At one time this arena had a capacity of up to 400,000 spectators, and if it were still intact it would no doubt match the Colosseum for grandeur. As it is, a litter of stones at the Viale Aventino end is all that remains, together with a little medieval tower built by the Frangipani family at the southern end, and, behind a chain-link fence traced out in marble blocks, the outline of the **Septizodium**, an imperial structure designed to show off the glories of the city and its empire to those arriving on the Via Appia. The huge obelisk that now stands in front of the church of San Giovanni in

THE CELIAN AND AVENTINE HILLS AND SOUTH CENTRAL ROME

BARS

Oasi della Birra	3
On the Rox	9
Picasso	12

RESTAURANTS & CAFÉS

Aqua e Farina	11
Augustarello	2
Charro Café	10
Checchino dal 1887	13
Felice	7
Ketumbar	8
Da Remo	1
Caffé del Seme e	
La Foglia	6
Tuttifrutti	4
Volpetti Piu	5

San Paolo fuori le Mura (1km) ▼

0   100 m

San Bonaventura

VIA DEI SANTI QUATTRO CORONATI

S.Clemente

VIA CAPO D'AFRICA

VIA CELIO VIBENNA

VIALE DEL PARCO DEL CELIO

Parco
del Celio

VIA MARCO AURELIO

VIA ANNIA

SS. Quattro
Coronati

VIA DEI SANTI QUATTRO CORONATI

Santi Giovanni
e Paolo

VIA CLAUDIA

Ospedale
Militare
dei Celio

CLIVO DI SCAURO

PIAZZA CELIMONTANA

San Gregorio
Magno

VIA DI SANTO STEFANO ROTONDO

Sanatorio
Limberto I

VALLE VILLA CELIMO

S.Maria
in Domnica

Santo Stefano
Rotondo

Ospizo
D.Addolorata

VIA DI S. STEFANO ROTONDO

PIAZZA
DI PORTA CAPENA

VIA DI SAN GREGORIO

Villa
Celimontana

Ospedale
Britannico

VIA DI SANT ERASMO

VIA DELLA NAVICELLA

VIA DELL' AMBA ARADAM

VIA SANTI VALERIO

AVENTINO

Circo
Massimo

U.N. Food &
Agriculture
Organisation

VIA DI VALLE DELLE CAMENE

VIALE DELLE TERME DI CARACALLA

VIA DELLA FERRATELLA

PIAZZA
DI PORTA
METRONIA

VIA IPONINIO

PIAZZALE
METRONIO

VIA VALNERIO

VIA TRACIA

VIA GALLIA

VIA AVENTINA

Stadio delle
Terme

MONTE CAVARELLI

VIALE METRONIO

VIA PANNONIA

VIALE GUIDO BACCELLI

San Sisto
Vecchio

VIA DRUSO

Santi Nereo
e Achileo

PIAZZALE
NUMA
POPILIO

Parco
Egerio

BRAMANTE

Parco di
Porta Capena

VIA C. M.

LARGO
ENZO
FIORITTO

Baths of
Caracalla

VIA ANTONINA

VIALE DELLE TERME DI CARACALLA

VIA DI PORTA LATINA

VIA DI PORTA SEBASTIANO

S.GIOVANNI
PORTA LATINA

VIA DI VILLA PEPOLI

S.Cesareo

VIALE GIOTTO TATA

VIA GUERRIERI

Tomb of
the Scipios

Parco D.
Scipioni

VIALE GUIDO BACCELLI

VIA LUCIO FABIO CILONE

VIA DI PORTA

Aurelian Wall

VIA ODOARDO BECCARI

ARDEATINA

PORTA
S. SEBASTIANO

Museum of The Walls

LARGO
TERME DI
CARACALLA

VIA DI PORTA ARDEATINA

VIA APPIA ANTICA

N

PIAZZALE
12 OCTOBRE 1492

VIALE MARCO POLO

VIA CRISTOFORO COLOMBO

VIA CICILIA

PIGAFETTA

ACCOMMODATION
Sant'Anselmo A

**THE AVENTINE &
SOUTH CENTRAL ROME**

Domine Quovadis (300m) & Catacombs of San Callisto (1km) ▼

Laterno (see p.148) – at 385 tonnes and over 30m high the largest in the world – was once the central marker of the arena, and it's known that the obelisk now in Piazza del Popolo stood here too.

The Celian Hill

Via San Gregorio leads back towards the Roman Forum from the Circus Maximus. On the right, the **Celian Hill** is the most southerly of Rome's seven hills and one of its most peaceful, with few major roads and the park of Villa Celimontana at its heart, built on the site of an ancient zoo that was home to some of the animals that were to die in the nearby Colosseum.

San Stefano Rotondo

Ten minutes' walk from the Colosseum down Via Claudia, and not on the Celian Hill proper, the round church of **Santo Stefano Rotondo** is a truly ancient structure, built in the 460s AD and consecrated by Pope Simplicius to commemorate Christianity's first martyr. Recently open again after a lengthy restoration, its four chapels form the shape of a cross in a circle, atmospherically lit by the 22 windows of the clerestory. The interior is a magnificent and moody circular space, made up of two concentric rings, but the feature that will really stick in your mind is the series of stomach-turning frescoes on the walls of the outer ring, showing various saints being martyred in different ways: impalings, pinchings, drawings and quarterings, disembowelments, boilings in oil, hangings, beheadings – you name it.

Santa Maria in Domnica

On the opposite side of the main road, Via Claudia opens out into Piazza della Navicella, named after the "navicella" or Roman stone boat that sits outside the church of **Santa Maria in Domnica** (daily 8.30am–12.30pm & 4.30pm–7pm), a sixth-century church at the bottom of the Celian Hill. Above its apse is a ninth-century mosaic of Christ with some wonderfully individualised apostles and angels, while in the apse itself another mosaic shows Pachal I, who restored the church, kneeling at the feet of the Virgin.

Villa Celimontana

The **Villa Celimontana** park can be accessed via **Piazza della Navicella**, next door to the church, or Piazza Giovanni e Paolo (see below). These shady public gardens make a nice spot for a picnic, with lots of leafy walkways and grassy slopes, and you could do worse than take a stroll through before moving on to the other sights of the Celian Hill. There are also pony rides, worth considering if you're with kids (€3), as well as a small playground, and outdoor concerts on summer evenings.

Santi Giovanni e Paolo

On the other side of the park, at the Celian Hill's summit, the church of **Santi Giovanni e Paolo** (daily 8.30am–noon & 3.30–6.30pm), marked by its colourful campanile, is set in a peaceful **piazza** that makes it a popular location for weddings – despite the adolescent autograph hunters who occasionally throng outside the TV studios opposite. Originally founded by a Roman senator called Pammachius, the church acts as an unofficial memorial to conscientious objection, dedicated to two dignitaries in the court of Constantine who were beheaded here in 361 AD after refusing military service. The remants of what is believed to be their house are now open to the public (see below). Inside the church's dark interior, thronged with chandeliers, a railed-off tablet in mid-nave marks the shrine where the saints were martyred and buried, while outside in the far corner of the square, underneath the campanile, you can see the arches of part of a temple of Claudius, the remains of which extend far down the hill towards the Colosseum.

The Case Romane

The so-called **Case Romane** (daily except Tues & Wed 10am–1pm & 3–6pm; €6) are around the corner from – but actually situated underneath – Santi Giovanni e Paolo, on Clivio di Scauro, where the buttresses of the church arch over the street. It was believed to be the relatively lavish residence of Giovanni and Paolo – the two prominent citizens who were martyred during the third century AD and commemorated in the church (see above). The twenty or so rooms are in fact more likely to be a series of dwellings, separated by a narrow lane, rather than a single residence. Patchily frescoed with pagan and Christian subjects, most of the chambers are dark, poky affairs; you'll need some imagination to see them for the palatially-appointed living quarters they must have been.

However, there are standouts, including the Casa dei Genii, frescoed with winged youths and cupids, and the courtyard or nymphaeum, which has a marvellous fresco of a goddess being waited on, sandwiched between cupids in boats, fishing and loading supplies. The antiquarium, too, beautifully pulls together finds from the site, among them a *Christ with Saints* fresco, and ceramics, amphorae and fascinating small domestic artefacts – an intact imperial-age spoon, a bronze reel, bone sewing needles and almost perfect oil lamps.

San Gregorio Magno

The road descends from the church and Case Romane under a succession of brick arches to the originally medieval church of **San Gregorio Magno** on the left (daily 8.30am–12.30pm & 3–6.30pm; ring the bell marked "portinare" to gain admission), in a commanding position above the traffic drone of the road below, looking across to the lollipop pines of the Palatine Hill opposite. St Gregory founded a monastery here, and was a monk here before becoming pope in 590 AD. Stabilizing Rome after the fall of the empire, he effectively established the powerful papal role that would endure for the best part of the following 1500 years; he also dispatched St Augustine in the early seventh century to convert England to Christianity. Today's rather ordinary Baroque interior doesn't really do justice to the historical importance of the church, but the lovely Cosmati floor remains intact, and the chapel of the saint at the end of the south aisle has a beautifully carved bath showing scenes from St Gregory's life along with his marble throne, a beaten-up specimen that actually predates the saint by 500 years. More impressive is the structure to the left of the church entrance, where the original monastery stood, made up of three chapels and surrounded by cypress trees (Mon & Wed 3.30–5.30pm, Sat & Sun 9.30am–12.30pm; closed Aug). The churches of **Santa Silvia** and **Sant'Andrea** contain frescoes by Guido Reni, Domenichino and Pomarancio, while **Santa Barbara** treasures the table at which St Gregory apparently fed twelve paupers daily with his own hands for years.

The Aventine Hill

Beyond the Circus Maximus you can scale the **Aventine Hill** – the heart of plebeian Rome in ancient times. These days the working-class quarters of the city are further south, and the Aventine is one of the city's more upscale residential areas, covered with villas with large gardens that lend a leafy, suburban feel, and make it one of the few places in the city centre where you can escape the traffic.

Santa Sabina

A short way southwest along Via Santa Sabina, **Santa Sabina** (daily 6.30am–12.45pm & 4–7pm) is the principal church of the Dominicans in Rome, and a strong contender for the city's most beautiful basilica, a high and wide structure, its nave and portico restored back to their fifth-century appearance in the 1930s. In the portico, look at the main doors at the far end, which are contemporary with the church and boast eighteen panels carved with Christian scenes, forming an illustrated Bible that includes (top left) one of the oldest representations of the Crucifixion in existence. Inside, the windows above the arches of the nave are among the most beautiful features of the church, each one different, letting in light by way of lacy patterns carved into the stone. The mosaic inscription on the wall above the doors heralds the achievements of Celestino I, flanked by two female figures representing converted Jews and pagans. Immediately below, in the corner, a smooth piece of black marble, pitted with holes, was apparently thrown by the devil at St Dominic himself while at prayer, shattering the marble pavement but miraculously not harming the saint.

It's claimed that the orange trees in the garden behind the church (which you have to ask to see) are descendants of those planted by St Dominic himself. Whatever the truth of this, the views from the gardens are splendid – right across the Tiber to the centre of Rome and St Peter's – and beyond here you can also be taken up to see the room where the saint stayed: it's now a small, heavily decorated chapel, but the timbered far end hints at a more spartan authenticity. The cloister, accessible by way of a door off the portico, has been under restoration for some time but may be open again now.

Whether it is or not, take the time to wander into the **public gardens** next door to the church, which are a favourite with mothers and babies, and give wonderful views across the river towards the Vatican.

The Priorato di Malta

Follow the road south past the **Priorato dei Cavalieri di Malta** (℡06.6758.1234 to book tours – minimum 12 people), a priory that is one of several buildings in the city belonging to the Knights of Malta – now known simply as the "Order of Malta", which has a celebrated view of the dome of St Peter's through the keyhole of its main gate. The little piazza in front of the main gate has marble triumphal insignia designed and placed here by Piranesi to celebrate the knights' dramatic history. Piranesi also designed the church of **Santa Maria del Priorato** inside, which you can see along with the lovely **gardens**, if you organize your visit in advance. The gardens are quite formally planted, with roses and topiary, but lush too, with palms and sub-tropical plants that in combination with the high walls and entry restrictions give the feel of a secret, cloistered domain – in short, exactly what a city garden should be. They're beautifully tended, focusing on a small fountain and cage of doves in the centre, though to be honest the views are no better than the ones from the public gardens next to Santa Sabina. As for the church, it was rebuilt by Piranesi in 1765, the only thing the famous engraver built. Its elaborate decor is typical of Roman churches, but it differentiates itself with its monochromatic sculptural simplicity. Virtually all the decoration is in grey stone or marble, or covered in stucco, and the effect is impressively uniform – a fact that Piranesi, caught in thoughtful pose in a statue on the right, is no doubt contemplating.

Sant'Anselmo

Opposite the Priorato di Malta, spare five minutes or so for the church of **Sant'Anselmo** (daily 10am–noon & 4–7pm), a Benedictine complex containing a church and college, with pleasant gardens and a shop selling all manner of produce, Benedictine and otherwise: *limoncello*, *grappa*, *amaro*, as well as chocolate, beer, books, CDs and toiletries. The church is a plain basilica built in the last decade of the nineteenth century – not of much interest in itself, but known for its Gregorian chorus and reasonably regular concerts, usually held on Sunday evenings.

San Saba

Follow Via Sant'Anselmo through the leafy residential streets of the Aventine down to Piazza Albania, where there's a rare stretch of the so-called **Servian Wall** – the first wall to properly enclose Rome, built in the fourth century BC and named after the sixth-century Roman king Servius Tullius, who first planned it. Other stretches of the Servian Wall can be seen outside Termini. Cross the busy street and stroll up Via San Saba to the church of **San Saba** (daily 8am–noon & 4–7pm), built in the tenth century over a seventh-century structure constructed by monks who had fled here from the Middle East to escape the Arab advance. Topped with a fifteenth-century loggia and fronted by a pleasant if scruffy walled garden, it's worth visiting for its wonderful Cosmati-work door and floor, and an interior that feels very ancient, with a wonderful mixture of Roman pillars and thirteenth-century frescoes in a short additional left aisle and the beautifully proportioned apse.

The Baths of Caracalla and around

Southeast of the Aventine, beyond the large UN Food and Agriculture building, the **Baths of Caracalla** (Mon 9am–1pm, Tues–Sun 9am–sunset; €6, includes the Tomb of Cecilia Metella and the Villa dei Quintilli, valid 7 days), at Viale Terme di Caracalla 52, give a far better sense of the monumental scale of Roman architecture than most of the extant ruins in the city – so much so that Shelley was moved to write his Romantic play *Prometheus Unbound* here in 1819. The baths are no more than a shell now, but the walls still rise to very nearly their original height. There are many fragments of mosaics – none spectacular, but quite a few bright and well preserved – and it's easy to discern a floor plan. Set in extensive walled gardens, with numerous outbuildings, the baths were built around the long spine of the central hall, or frigidarium, at each end of which are vast courtyards – palestrae – which were used for sports before bathing. Off to the right of the frigidarium was the tepidarium – now hard to make out – and beyond this the domed chamber of the circular caldarium, which is easier to see outside the baths themselves. On the other side of the frigidarium was the piscine or swimming pool, a huge open space which would have been accessed by way of the apodytria, or changing rooms, on either side – you can get the best sense of this by following the route from the palestra at the far end.

As for Caracalla, he was one of Rome's most brutal and shortest-lived rulers, and it's no wonder there's nothing else in the city built by him. The baths were for many years used for occasional opera performances during the summer (one

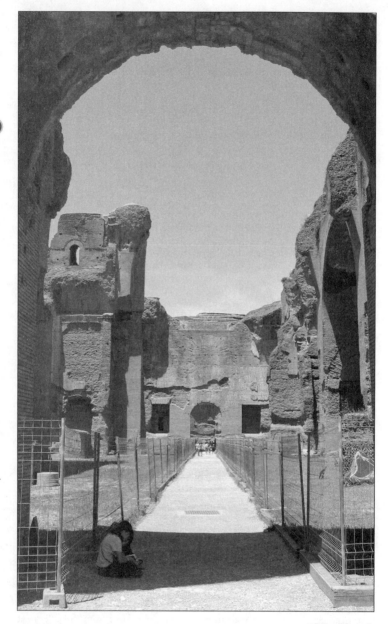

△ Baths of Caracalla

of Mussolini's better ideas), but these were stopped a few years ago due to damage to the site. Watch out for their re-emergence, though – it's a thrilling and inexpensive way to see the baths at their most atmospheric.

Santi Nereo ed Achille

Just outside the baths, the church of **Santi Nereo e Achille** (daily except Tues 10am–noon & 4–6pm) makes for a peaceful spot after the crowds at the baths, and is of interest for the ninth-century mosaic on the arch above its apse, which depicts Christ and three prostrate apostles, between a scene of the Annunciation on the left and a Virgin and Child on the right. The beautiful Cosmati work on the marble choir screen and the altar itself is also worth a look, as is the ornate throne sitting on two lions in the apse, said to have been preached from by Gregory the Great (see p.109) – a fact emphasized by the apse fresco showing St Gregory preaching to various cardinals. This is full of charming detail: you'll notice one of the cardinals – second from the right – has trouble hearing, while others confer as to what the great pope might be saying.

Back outside the church, on the far side of the Piazzale Numa Pompilio roundabout, Via di Porta San Sebastiano leads onto the **Via Appia Antica** which heads towards the catacombs and other archeological delights, a few kilometres south (see p.117).

Testaccio

Back towards the Tiber, across Via Marmorata, the working-class neighbourhood of **Testaccio** groups around a couple of main squares. For many years this tight-knit community was synonymous with the slaughterhouse that sprawls down to the Tiber just beyond. In the last couple of decades the area has become a trendy place to live, property prices have soared, and some uneasy contradictions have emerged, with vegetarian restaurants opening their doors in an area still known for the offal dishes served in its traditional trattorias, and gay and alternative clubs standing cheek-by-jowl with the car-repair shops gouged into Monte Testaccio.

The slaughterhouse, or **Mattatoio**, once the area's main employer, is now home to the centro sociali and "Villaggio Globale", a space used for concerts, raves and the like, along with stabling for the city's horse-and-carriage drivers, a gymnasium and a small Gypsy camp. For years there has been talk of sprucing it up into a chichi affair of shops and restaurants, but so far nothing has happened, and it's likely to remain as it is for some time to come. It also houses a branch of the **Museum of Contemporary Art of Rome** (MACRO; Tues–Sun 4pm–midnight), just inside the main gate, where a couple of large pavilions stage adventurous temporary exhibitions (for MACRO's main branch, see p.137).

Opposite the slaughterhouse, **Monte Testaccio**, a 50-metre-high mound of historic landfill, gives the area its name. The ancient Romans broke terracotta amphorae up into small shards and laid them down in an orderly manner over several centuries, sprinkling quicklime on them to dissolve the residual wine or oil. It's estimated that there are around 53 million amphorae here and it makes for an odd sight, the ceramic curls clearly visible through the tufts of grass that crown its higher reaches, the bottom layers hollowed out by the workshops of car and bike mechanics – and, now, clubs and bars.

The Protestant Cemetery

On the far side of Monte Testaccio, off Via Marmorata, on Via Caio Cestio X, the **Protestant Cemetery** (Mon–Sat 9am–5pm; donation expected) isn't in fact a Protestant cemetery at all, but is reserved for non-Roman Catholics of all nationalities, so you'll also find famous Italian atheists, Christians of the Orthodox persuasion, and the odd Jew or Muslim, buried here. It is nonetheless one of the shrines to the English in Rome, and a fitting conclusion to a visit to the Keats-Shelley Memorial House on Piazza di Spagna (see Chapter 4).

Most visitors come to see the grave of Keats, who lies next to his friend, the painter Joseph Severn, in the furthest corner of the less crowded, older part of the cemetery (turn left from the entrance), his stone inscribed as he wished with the words "here lies one whose name was writ in water". Severn died much later than Keats but asked to be laid here nonetheless, together with his brushes and palette. Just behind Severn and Keats lies Severn's one-year-old son, while behind there a plaque on the wall remembers the Swedish doctor and writer Axel Munthe, his wife Hilda and their two sons.

As for Shelley, his ashes were brought here at Mary Shelley's request and interred, after much obstruction by the papal authorities, in the newer part of the cemetery, at the top against the back wall – the Shelleys had visited several years earlier, the poet praising it as "the most beautiful and solemn cemetery I ever beheld". It had been intended that Shelley should rest with his young son, William, who died while they were in Rome and was also buried here, but his remains couldn't be found (although his small grave is nearby). Mary Shelley was so broken-hearted by the deaths of her son and husband that it was twenty years before she could bring herself to visit their graves.

Shelley's great friend, the writer and adventurer Edward Trelawny, lies next to him, while in front of Shelley's grave is a slab marking the final resting-spot of the American Beat poet Gregory Corso, who died in 2001 but was buried here, at his request, next to his hero Shelley. To the right of that a headless torso marked simply "Belinda" marks the grave of Belinda Lee – a little-known Hollywood starlet, who died in her mid-twenties in a car crash in Hollywood in 1961, just as her career was beginning to take off – and after a scandalous affair with one of the Orsini princes, hence her burial here. Among other famous internees, the political writer and activist Antonio Gramsci lies on the far right-hand side of the cemetery in the middle, and the Italian novelist Carlo Emilio Gadda is nearby. If you're at all interested in star-spotting you should either borrow or buy the booklet available at the entrance.

The Pyramid of Caius Cestius

Overlooking the cemetery, the most distinctive landmark in this part of town is the **Pyramid of Caius Cestius**, who died in 12 BC. Cestius had spent some time in Egypt, and part of his will decreed that all his slaves should be freed. The white pyramid you see today was thrown up by them in only 330 days of what must have been joyful building. It's open to the public on the second and fourth Saturday of each month, though you can visit the cats who live here, and the volunteers who care for them, any afternoon between 2.30 and 4.30pm.

The Museo della Via Ostiense

Right by the pyramid, the **Museo della Via Ostiense** (Tues & Thurs 9.30am–1.30pm & 2.30–4.30pm, Wed, Fri & Sat & 1st & 3rd Sun of each month 9.30am–1.30pm; free), housed in the old Porta San Paolo, is a museum devoted to the road that spears off on the far side of the intersection, originally built to join Rome to its Ostia and its port. There's not much here of interest unless you have half an hour to kill, but the model of Ostia is worth studying if you're on your way to catch a train to Ostia Antica from the Porta San Paolo station opposite (see p.209).

Ostiense and Garbatella

Immediately south of Testaccio, the industrial neighbourhood of **Ostiense** is one of the city's most up-and-coming areas, home to those who can no longer afford to live in already-gentrified Testaccio. There was until a few years ago no real reason to come here at all, unless you were on your way down the basilica of San Paolo (see below), but nowadays the Capitoline collections at **Centrale Montemartini** alone make it worth the trip, as well as the clubs, bars and restaurants that are beginning to spring up to serve the media types and companies that are moving in. There's also a project afoot to redevelop the large, currently derelict site of the **Mercati Generali**, Rome's vast former wholesale food market, on the left-hand side of Via Ostiense as you travel south into a brand-new retail, sport and cultural district. Scheduled for completion in 2008, and dubbed the "city of youth" this will likely bring both Ostiense – and neighbouring **Garbatella**, already worth visiting for its Mussolini-era residential architecture – further into Rome's mainstream.

Centrale Montemartini

For the moment it's the **Centrale Montemartini**, Via Ostiense 106 (Tues–Sun 9am–7pm; €4.50, €8.50 for joint ticket with Capitoline Museums, valid 7 days) that has done the most to put Ostiense on the map. A former electricity generating station, it was requisitioned to display the cream of the Capitoline Museums' sculpture while the main buildings were being renovated, and was so popular that it has become a permanent outpost of the venerable institution. Ten minutes' walk from Piramide metro station, or reachable Monday to Friday by bus #271 from Piazza Venezia, the huge rooms of the power station are ideally suited to showing off ancient sculpture, although checking out the massive turbines and furnaces has a fascination of its own.

The size of the building is the thing, most obviously in the **Machine Hall**, where there's the head, feet and an arm from a colossal statue, once 8m high, found in Largo Argentina. Elsewhere in the chamber are various heads, some of emperors (Claudius, Tiberius, Domitian), a large Roman *Athena*, and a fine statue of a Roman soldier from the Esquiline Hill, tucked away in a corner. In the adjacent **Furnace Hall**, the most obvious features are the furnace itself at the far end and a fragmented mosaic of hunting scenes that occupies half the floor; a walkway gives a good view of the latter's deer and boar, and figures on horseback or crouching to trap their prey in nets. Among the sculptures on display is an amazing third-century BC statue of a girl seated on a stool with legs crossed. Hercules stands next to the soft *Muse Polymnia*, the former braced for activity, the latter leaning on a rock and staring thoughtfully into the distance. Look out, too, for a wonderful pair of magistrates, one old, one young, but both holding the handkerchief they would use to herald the start of competitions and circuses.

San Paolo fuori le Mura

Two kilometres or so south of the Porta San Paolo, the basilica of **San Paolo fuori le Mura** or "St Paul's Outside-the-Walls" (summer daily 7am–6.30pm; winter 7am–6pm) is one of the four patriarchal basilicas of Rome (and thus not technically Italian territory), occupying the supposed site of St Paul's tomb, where he was laid to rest after being beheaded at Tre Fontane (see p.123). St Paul is joint patron saint of Rome, with St Peter. Of the four basilicas, this has probably fared the least well over the years. It was apparently once the grandest, connected to the Aurelian Wall by a colonnade over a kilometre in length, made up of eight hundred marble columns, but a ninth-century sacking by the Saracens and a devastating fire in 1823 (a couple of cack-handed roofers spilt burning tar, almost entirely destroying the church) means that the building you see now is largely a nineteenth-century reconstruction. You can reach the basilica by taking metro line B and walking two minutes to the eastern entrance, or bus #271 from Piazza Venezia – it stops outside the west entrance – though it doesn't run at weekends.

The church is a very successful – if somewhat clinical – rehash of the former building. Perhaps even more than St Peter's, it impresses with sheer size and grandeur, and whether you enter by way of the cloisters or the west door, it's impossible not to be awed by the space of the building inside, its crowds of columns topped by round-arched arcading, and the medallions of all the **popes** fringing the nave and transepts above, starting with St Peter to the right of the apse and ending with Benedict XVI at the top of the south aisle. Of all the basilicas of Rome, this gives you the feel of what an ancient Roman basilica must have been like: the huge, barn-like structure, with its clerestory windows and roof beams supported by enormous columns, has a powerful and authentic sense of occasion.

Some parts of the building did survive the fire. In the south transept, the **paschal candlestick** at the head of the nave, behind two large statues of St Peter (on the left) and St Paul (on the right) is a remarkable piece of Roman-esque carving, supported by half-human beasts and rising through entwined tendrils and strangely human limbs and bodies to scenes from Christ's life, the figures crowding in together as if for a photocall; it's inscribed by its makers, Nicolo di Angelo and Pietro Bassalletto. The bronze, eleventh-century **doors** at the end of the south aisle were also rescued from the old basilica, as was the thirteenth-century tabernacle by Arnolfo di Cambio, under which a slab from the time of Constantine, inscribed "Paolo Apostolo Mort", is supposed to lie – although it's hard to get a look at this. The arch across the apse is original, too, embellished with **mosaics** (donated by the Byzantine queen Galla Placidia in the sixth century) that show angels, saints Peter and Paul, the symbols of the Gospels, and Christ giving a blessing. The mosaics in the apse date from 1220 and show Luke, Paul, Peter and Andrew and the kneeling figure of Honorius III kissing the feet of Christ. The **cloister**, through the shop is probably Rome's finest piece of Cosmatesque work, its spiralling, mosaic-encrusted columns enclosing a peaceful rose garden. Just off here, the **Relics Chapel** houses a dustily kept set of artefacts, and the **Pinacoteca** shows engravings depicting San Paolo before and after the fire.

The Aurelian Wall

From Piazza di Porta San Paolo, you can make a long detour back into the city centre following the **Aurelian Wall**, built by the emperor Aurelian (and his successor Probus) in 275 AD to enclose Rome's seven hills and protect the city from invasion. The Aurelian Wall surrounds the city and, if you really are an enthusiast, you can walk its seventeen-kilometre circumference in an eight-hour day with a pause for lunch. However, for a taster, one of the best-preserved stretches runs between Porta San Paolo and Porta San Sebastiano, following Via Porta Ardeatina: cross the road from Piramide station and turn right and follow the walls, keeping them always on your left.

It is around two kilometres from Porta San Paolo to **Porta San Sebastiano**, built in the fifth century, where the **Museo delle Mura** (Tues–Sat 9am–2pm; €2.60), occupying a couple of floors of the gate, has displays of Aurelian's original plans and lots of photos of the past and present walls that are helpful in showing what is original and what medieval additions and how different structures have been incorporated into the walls over the years. The museum tells you more about the walls and the various gates than you really need to know, but you can climb up to the top of the gate for great views over the Roman *campagna* beyond, and walk a few hundred metres along the walls themselves – towards the east – before having to return to the museum.

From Porta San Sebastiano it is only a short walk up Via di Porta San Sebastiano to the Baths of Caracalla, past the **Tomb of the Scipios**. This stretch of the Via Appia was once lined with the tombs of rich families, and the Scipios were one of the great Republican dynasties, generals in the Punic Wars against Carthage. This family tomb was discovered in 1780 and its Etruscan-style sarcophagus transported to the Vatican, where it is on display (see p.191). These days the tomb is a rather sad sight, and you have to make do with peeking into the small entrance or looking down from the scruffy park just above.

Failing that, continue following the walls by walking along Via delle Mura Latine to Piazzale Metronio, from where you're just a short walk from San Giovanni in Laterano (see Chapter 8).

Via Appia Antica and the catacombs

Starting at the Porta San Sebastiano, the **Via Appia Antica** (or "Appian Way") is the most famous of the consular roads that used to strike out in each direction from the ancient city. The road, built by the censor Appio Claudio in 312 BC, is the only Roman landmark mentioned in the Bible. During classical times it was the most important of all the Roman trade routes, the so-called "Queen of Roads", carrying supplies right down through Campania to the port of Brindisi, some 500km southeast. It's no longer the main route south out of the city – that's Via Appia Nuova from nearby Porta San Giovanni – but it was an important part of early Christian Rome, its verges lined with numerous pagan and Christian sites, most famously the underground burial cemeteries or **catacombs** of the first Christians. Laws in ancient Rome forbade burial within the city walls, and most Romans were cremated. There are catacombs in other parts of the city – those attached to the church of Sant'Agnese on Via Nomentana (see p.138) are some of the best – but this is by far the largest concentration. There are five complexes in all, dating from the first century to the fourth century, almost entirely emptied of bodies now but still decorated with the primitive signs and frescoes that were the hallmark of the then-burgeoning Christian movement. Despite much speculation, no one really knows why the Christians decided to bury their dead in these tunnels: the rock here, tufa, is soft and easy to hollow out, but the digging involved must still have been phenomenal, and there is no real reason to suppose that the burial places had to be secret – they continued to bury their dead like this long after Christianity became the established religion. Whatever the reasons, they make intriguing viewing now. The three principal complexes are within walking distance of each other, though it's not really worth trying to see them all – the layers of shelves and drawers lose their fascination after a while. If you only go for one, you'd do best to focus on San Sebastiano (and maybe San Callisto) and explore the other attractions nearby.

Domine Quo Vadis

About 500m from Porta San Sebastiano, where the road forks, the church of **Domine Quo Vadis** is the first obvious sight, and signals the start of the catacomb stretch of road. Legend has this as the place where St Peter saw Christ

If you want to see a lot, including the Villa dei Quinilli and Parco degli Acquedotti, the **Archeobus** is probably the best choice for seeing Via Appia Antica: buses run from Termini and Piazza Venezia, among other city-centre locations, roughly every hour; tickets cost €8 for a return trip that lasts all day and you can hop on and off as you wish. If you're concentrating on Via Appia Antica proper, you might be better off saving your money and taking **public transport**: buses run south along Via Appia Antica and conveniently stop at or near to most of the main attractions. Bus #118 runs from Piazzale Ostiense almost as far as San Sebastiano; you can also take bus #218, which goes down Via Ardeatina, or bus #660, which goes from beyond the Tomb of Cecilia Metella to Colli Albani metro station. You could walk from Porta San Sebastiano and take everything in on foot, which allows you to stop off at the Parco Regionale dell'Appia Antica **information office** for the area – which is actually classified as a national park – at Via Appia Antica 58, on the right just before you get to Domine Quo Vadis (summer daily 9.30am–5.30pm, winter daily 9.30am–4.30pm; ☎06.512.6314; ⊛www.parcoappiaantica.org). You can rent **bikes** from here for €3 an hour or €10 a day, and pick up a good map and other information on the various Appia Antica sights. Much of the Via Appia Antica isn't particularly picturesque, at least until you get down to San Sebastiano (where you can also rent bikes), and a good option is to take a bus to San Callisto or San Sebastiano and double back or walk on further for the attractions you want to see. Bus #118 runs from Piazzale Ostiense almost as far as San Sebastiano; you can also take bus #218, which goes down Via Ardeatina, or bus #660, which goes from beyond the Tomb of Cecilia Metella to Colli Albini metro station. Finally there are a couple of handy – and decent – **restaurants** down by San Sebastiano too: *L'Archeologica*, just past the church, and the *Cecilia Metella*, right opposite; neither is especially cheap but both have nice gardens for alfresco eating in summer.

while fleeing from certain death in Rome and asked, "Where goest thou, Lord?", to which Christ replied that he was going to be crucified once more, leading Peter to turn around and accept his fate. The small church is ordinary enough inside, except for its replica of a piece of marble that is said to be marked with the footprints of Christ (the original is in the church of San Sebastiano).

Catacombs of San Callisto

A kilometre or so further on, down a walled and often traffic-choked stretch of road, you reach the **Catacombs of San Callisto** (daily except Wed 9am–noon & 2–5pm; €5; bus #118 or #218) – also accessible from Via Ardeatina), the largest of Rome's catacombs. The regular tours in English (around 45min) are usually run by priests, and take in a bit of preliminary explanation before heading into the high-vaulted passages, which stretch for some twenty miles and hold around half a million bodies. The catacombs were founded in the second century AD, and many of the early popes are buried here in the papal crypt, including Callisto himself. St Callisto was in fact the guardian of the cemetery before he became pope; he was later killed in a riot and buried here in 222 AD, along with Sixtus II and seven other early popes. The numerous passages and burial vaults are as atmospheric as you would expect and also feature some well-preserved seventh- and eighth-century frescoes, and the crypt of Santa Cecilia, who was buried here after her martyrdom, before being shifted to the church dedicated to her in Trastevere (see p.170) – a copy of Carlo Maderno's famous statue marks the spot.

Mausoleo delle Fosse Ardeatine

Close by the alternative entrance to the San Callisto catacombs, there's a catacomb of a different kind at the **Mausoleo delle Fosse Ardeatine** (Mon–Fri 8.15am–3.30pm, Sat & Sun 8.15am–5pm; free), where a site remembers the massacre of over 300 civilians during the Nazi occupation of Rome, after the resistance had ambushed and killed 32 soldiers on Via Rasella in the centre of the city (see p.128). The Nazis killed ten civilians for every dead German, burying the bodies here and then exploding mines to cover up their crime. The bodies were dug up after the war and reinterred in the mausoleum. Chapels have been installed in the so-called *Grotta del Eccido*, where the bodies were found, all of which have been interred in a nearby area under serried rows of stone slabs, itself under one huge stone slab. Just up from here there's a small museum with newspaper cuttings telling the story of the event, and various other artefacts relating to the tragedy.

Catacombs of San Domitilla

In the opposite direction from the San Callisto exit, up Via delle Sette Chiese on the left at no. 282, the **Catacombs of San Domitilla** (daily except Tues 8.30am–noon & 2.30–5pm; €5) are quieter than those of San Callisto; again you can take bus #218, or #714 down Via Cristoforo Colombo at the other end of Via delle Sette Chiese.

The catacombs adjoin the remains of a fourth-century basilica erected here to the martyrs Achilleus and Nereus, the servants of Domitilla, niece of Domitian. They fled south of Rome with her to escape the persecutions of Hadrian, but were killed and eventually buried here. The network itself is huge, stretching for around 17km in all, and contains more frescoes and early wall etchings, as well as the tombs of Nereus and Achilleus and a relief showing their martyrdom.

Catacombs of San Sebastiano

The **Catacombs of San Sebastiano** (daily except Sun 9am–noon & 2.30–5pm; €5), 500m further on from San Callisto on the right side of Via Appia Antica, are situated under a much renovated basilica that was originally built by Constantine on the spot where the bodies of the Apostles Peter and Paul are said to have been laid for a time. In the church, the first chapel on the left holds a statue of the saint as he lay dying, built above his original tomb, while opposite is the original slab of marble imprinted with the feet of Christ that you may have seen in the church of Domine Quo Vadis. Downstairs, half-hour tours wind around the catacombs, dark corridors showing signs of early Christian worship – paintings of doves and fish, a contemporary carved oil lamp and inscriptions dating the tombs themselves. The most striking features, however, are not Christian at all, but three pagan tombs (one painted, two stuccoed) discovered when archeologists were burrowing beneath the floor of the basilica upstairs. Just above here, Constantine is said to have raised his chapel to Peter and Paul, and although St Peter was later removed to the Vatican, and St Paul to San Paolo fuori le Mura, the graffiti above records the fact that this was indeed, albeit temporarily, where the two Apostles rested.

The Circus of Maxentius and Tomb of Romulus

A couple of hundred metres further on from the San Sebastiano catacombs, the group of brick ruins trailing off into the fields to the left are the remains of the **Villa and Circus of Maxentius** (daily 9am–1pm; €2.60), a large complex built by the emperor in the early fourth century AD before his defeat by

Constantine. It's a clear, long oval of grass, similar to the Circus Maximus (see p.105) back in town, but slightly better preserved and in a rather more bucolic location – making it a fantastic place to eat a picnic, lolling around in the grass or perching on the ruins. Clambering about in the remains, you can make out the twelve starting gates to the circus, or racetrack, the enormous towers that contained the mechanism for lifting the gates at the beginning of the races and the remains of a basilica. Other structures surround it, including, closer to the road, the ruins of what was once a magnificent mausoleum of an unknown person or persons, the so-called **Tomb of Romulus**, in the middle of a huge quadrangle of walls.

The Tomb of Cecilia Metella and beyond

Further along the Via Appia is the circular **Tomb of Cecilia Metella** (Tues–Sun 9am–4.30pm; €2, €6 including Terme di Caracalla and Villa dei Quintilli) from the Augustan period, converted into a castle in the fourteenth century. Known as "Capo di Bove" for the bulls on the frieze around it, the tomb itself, a huge brick-built drum, is little more than a large pigeon coop these days; various fragments and finds are littered around the adjacent later courtyards, and down below you can see what's left of a lava flow from thousands of years earlier.

Beyond Cecilia Metella the **Appia Antica** hits proper countryside, and the road heads straight south, its verges littered with ancient rubble, including tombs, shrines, gateposts and watchtowers, most of them excavated during the nineteenth century. There's no bus out here (although the Archeobus comes part of the way), but it's by far the most atmospheric stretch of the ancient Via Appia, and you should walk at least as far as the circular tomb of the **Casale Rotondo** – the largest of Via Appia's monuments, dating from the last decades of the first century BC – if you get the chance. Just past here, the road turns left towards the main entrance of the Villa dei Quintilli.

Villa dei Quintilli

The **Villa dei Quintilli** (daily except Mon: March 9am–4.30pm; April–Aug 9am–6.30pm; Sept 9am–6pm; Oct 9am–5.30pm; Nov–Feb 9am–3.30pm; €6, includes Cecilia Metella and Caracalla), reachable direct by taking the metro to Colli Albani and then a #663 or #664 bus, crowns the crest of a hill not far from the main road out to Ciampino. It's one of the largest and most complete suburban villas close to Rome, and dates from the mid-second century AD. As you might expect from the position of the place, the Quintilli were an influential Roman family; two brothers were consuls under Commodus, and subsequently executed by him in 182 AD.

The main building has a one-room **museum** with finds from the villa and surrounding area: a large statue of Zeus and three heads of Hermes, a lovely head of a woman and another of a man from the residential section of the villa, a fragment of a relief of Mithras slaying the Bull from the villa's baths, and three almost perfect wall designs of male nude figures in *opus sectile*.

The villa itself is up a track on the mound of the hill, enjoying panoramic views of the Roman countryside on all sides. On the northern side, the baths complex rears up, with steps leading down to its well-preserved caldarium, in which a rectangular pool is overlooked by massive windows designed to keep the temperature inside comfortably warm. A few rooms over, the frigidarium is perhaps the best-preserved room in the complex, with considerable traces of its mosaic floor and two columns at the far end. Retracing your steps, you can also walk the corridors of the residential part of the villa, though sadly many of the rooms and steps are closed off, while on the far side of the complex you wander into what must have been a hugely impressive main reception hall, whose large windows would have made the most of the countryside views.

Parci degli Acquedotti

A few minutes from the Villa dei Quintilli on the Archeobus, or a few minutes' walk from Subaugusta metro station, the **Parci degli Acquedotti** is a lovely spot, where two aqueducts snake between the pines of suburban Rome. Of the pair, the **Acqua Claudia** is unusually intact, its arches leading off south into the far distance. Looking north, along its more ruinous stretches, you can see central Rome, marked by the dome of St Peter's. The other, more sunken aqueduct is the **Acqua Felice**, which is supplemented by a modern pipe. Eleven major aqueducts supplied ancient Rome with water, built between the fourth century BC and third century AD. At its height the population of the city was around a million, and between them the aqueducts ensured that each member of the Roman populace had access to around 75 litres a day – more, in fact, than the people of many modern countries use. Designed to allow water to flow freely towards the city, they mostly consisted of tunnels bored underground, and it was only when they got closer to the city that the water would run along a conduit raised on arches, to help the water pressure when it got to the city itself. They're still an impressive sight, and make a nice place for a picnic.

EUR

From Piazza di Porta San Paolo and the Pyramide metro station, Via Ostiense leads south to join up with Via Cristoforo Colombo, which in turn runs down to **EUR** (pronounced "eh-oor") – the acronym for the district built for the "Esposizione Universale Roma". This was laid out to the designs of Marcello Piacentini for Mussolini and the aborted 1942 World's Fair, though it was not finished until well after the war. Reachable by bus #714 from Termini or taking metro line B, this is not so much a neighbourhood as a statement in stone, a rather soulless grid of square buildings, long vistas and wide processional boulevards linked tenuously to the rest of Rome by metro but light years away from the city in feel. Come here for its numerous museums, some of which – notably the exhaustive Museo della Civiltà – *are* worth the trip, or if you have a yen for modern city architecture and planning.

Exploring EUR

The great flaw in EUR is that it's not really built for people: the streets are wide thoroughfares designed for easy traffic flow and the shops and cafés are easily outnumbered by offices, although the columned buildings provide shade in numerous arcades. Of the main structures, it's the pre-war, Fascist-style constructions that are of most interest; the postwar development of the area threw up bland office blocks for the most part.

Piazza Marconi is the nominal centre of EUR, where the wide, classically inspired boulevards intersect to swerve around a friezed obelisk in the centre. A few minutes' walk from here, in the northwest corner of EUR, the **Palazzo della Civiltà del Lavoro** is a visual highlight – Mussolini-inspired architecture at its most assured, and chauvinistic: the inscription around the top reads "One Nation, of Poets, Artists, Heroes, Saints, Thinkers, Scientists, Navigators and Travellers." With a heroic statue on each corner, it's a successful and imposing structure, and far and away the best piece of architecture in EUR. Some have called it the "square Colosseum", which sums up its mixing of modern and classical styles perfectly. After undergoing a much-deserved restoration, it's due to re-open soon as Rome's new audiovisual museum.

All of EUR's other museums are within easy reach of here. On Piazza Marconi itself, the **Museo Nazionale delle Arti e delle Tradizioni Popolari** (Tues–Sat 9am–6pm; €4) is a run-through of applied arts, costumes and religious artefacts from the Italian regions, though everything is labelled in Italian; bring a dictionary. The **Museo Nazionale Preistorico ed Etnografico Luigi Pigorini**, Viale Lincoln 1 (Tues–Sat 9am–2pm; €4), is arranged in manageable and easily comprehensible order, but its prehistoric section is mind-numbingly exhaustive; the ethnographic collection does something to relieve things, however, with artefacts from South America, the Pacific and Africa. In the same building, further down the colonnade at Viale Lincoln 3, the **Museo dell'Alto Medioevo** (Tues–Sat 9am–8pm; €2) concentrates on artefacts from the fifth to the tenth centuries – local finds mainly, including some beautiful jewellery from the seventh century and a delicate fifth-century gold *fibula* found on the Palatine Hill.

But of all the museums, the most interesting is the **Museo della Civiltà Romana**, Piazza Agnelli 10 (Tues–Sat 9am–2pm, Sun 9am–1.30pm; €6.50,

€8.50 including planetarium). It's a very large museum, and amid the reconstructed statuary, tablets and inscriptions, the ordinary stuff impresses most – small bronze lamps, medical instruments, carved zodiac charts, musical instruments and the like. Among many reconstructions, the long corridor housing large casts of the reliefs from Trajan's Column is instructive, to say the least. The pièce de résistance is a room-filling model of Rome during the time of Constantine to a 1:250 scale that you can look down on from above – perfect for setting the rest of the city in context.

Part of the same complex, the city's new **Planetario e Museo Astronomico** (Tues–Fri 9am–2pm, Sat & Sun 9am–7pm; €6.50, €8.50 including the Museo della Civiltà Romana) has a small exhibition of astronomy and the planets and regular programmes in its domed planetarium, but they're in Italian only, and frankly not the most spectacular planetarium shows you'll see.

The Abbazia delle Tre Fontane

The perfect antidote to EUR is just a ten-minute walk from the Museo della Civiltà Romana. The **Abbazia delle Tre Fontane** (daily 6am–9pm) is a complex of churches founded on the spot where St Paul was martyred; it's said that when the saint was beheaded his head bounced and three springs erupted where it touched the ground. In those days this was a malarial area, and it was all but abandoned during the Middle Ages, but in the second half of the nineteenth century Trappist monks drained the swamp and planted eucalyptus trees in the vicinity; they still distil a eucalyptus-based chest remedy here, as well as an exquisite liqueur, chocolate bars, wine, toiletries and all manner of other monastic products – all sold at the small **shop and bar** by the entrance. Bus #761 from the Basilica di San Paolo goes right past, or it's a ten-minute walk from Laurentina metro on line B.

The abbey churches

As for the churches, they were rebuilt in the sixteenth century and restored by the Trappists. They're not particularly outstanding buildings, appealing more for their peaceful location, which is relatively undisturbed by visitors, than any architectural distinction.

The first and largest church, originally built in 625 and rebuilt and finally restored by the Trappists, is **Santi Vincenzo e Anastasio**. Its gloomy atmosphere is exacerbated by the fact that most of the windows are of a thick marble that admits little light – although the stained-glass ones, dating from the Renaissance with papal heraldry from that period, are beautiful. The three fountains in the floor, supposedly formed by the saint's bouncing head, have long since run dry.

To the right, the church of **Santa Maria Scala Coeli** owes its name to a vision St Bernard had here in which he saw the soul he was praying for ascend to heaven; the Cosmatesque altar where this is supposed to have happened is down the cramped stairs, in the crypt, where St Paul was allegedly kept prior to his beheading. Beyond, the church of **San Paolo alle Tre Fontane** (daily 8am–1pm & 3–6pm), holds the pillar to which St Paul was tied in the right transept and a couple of very well-preserved mosaic pavements from Ostia Antica. Try to be here, if you can, in the early morning or evening, when the monks come in to sing Mass in Gregorian chant – a moving experience.

On the way out, the **gatehouse** contains ceiling frescoes from the thirteenth century that show the possessions of the abbey at the time. They're in a pretty bad state, but the ones that remain have been restored and are still very interesting, showing a kind of picture map of Italy in the thirteenth century.

The Quirinale and East central Rome

The **Quirinale** is perhaps the most appealing of the hills that rise up on the eastern side of the centre of Rome, and was the first to be properly developed, when, in the seventeenth century, those who could afford it moved up to the higher ground from the city centre, and the popes made their home here in the **Palazzo del Quirinale**. Nowadays this is the residence of the president of Italy, and is only open for viewing on Sundays. The district holds some of the city's most compelling sights, such as the enormous **Palazzo Barberini**, home of some of the best of Rome's art, and, just beyond, the **Palazzo Massimo**, where a good deal of the city's ancient treasure is on display. This area, around **Stazione Termini**, is also where you might end up staying, home as it is to a good portion of the city's hotels. Beyond here, just outside the city centre, **Via Nomentana** hosts a couple of churches – Sant'Agnese fuori le Mura and Santa Costanza – that are well worth making the trip out to, while the district of **San Lorenzo** forms a hub for the city's students, and has some decent clubs and restaurants.

Piazza Barberini

Piazza Barberini is a traffic junction at the top end of the busy shopping street of Via del Tritone, named after Bernini's **Fontana del Tritone**, a sea-god gushing a high jet of water from a conch shell in the centre of the square. The recently restored fountain lends a unity to the square in more ways than one: traditionally, this quarter of the city was associated with the Barberini, a family who were the greatest patrons of Bernini, and the sculptor's works in their honour are thick on the ground around here. He finished the Tritone fountain in 1644, before designing the **Fontana delle Api** ("Fountain of the Bees"), which you can see at the bottom end of Via Veneto. Unlike the Tritone fountain you could walk right past this, a smaller, quirkier work, its broad scallop shell studded with the bees that were the symbol of the Barberinis.

Santa Maria della Concezione

A little way up Via Vittorio Veneto on the right, the Capuchin church of **Santa Maria della Concezione** (daily 9am–noon & 3–6pm) was another sponsored creation of the Barberini (founded in 1626), though it's not a particularly significant building in itself, and its only real treasure is Guido Reni's androgynous *St Michael Trampling on the Devil*, in the first chapel on the right. The devil in the picture is said to be a portrait of Innocent X, whom the artist despised and who was apparently a sworn enemy of the Barberini family. Take a look at the tomb slab of the founder of the church, Antonio Barberini, in front of the altar, which has an inscription – "Here lies dust, ashes, nothing" – that is quite at odds with the worldly, wealthy impression you get of the Barberinis elsewhere in the city.

The **Capuchin cemetery** (same times; donation expected), attached to the right of the church, continues the deathly theme, home as it is to the bones of 4000 monks who died between 1528 and 1870, set into the walls of a series of six chapels – a monument to "Our Sister of Bodily Death", in the words of St Francis, that was erected in 1793. Some bones and skulls are simply piled up, but others appear in abstract or Christian patterns or as fully clothed skeletons, their faces peering out of their cowls in twisted expressions of agony – the effect lies somewhere between chilling and ludicrous, and makes for one of the more macabre and bizarre sights of Rome.

Via Veneto

Via Veneto, which bends north from Piazza Barberini up to the southern edge of the Villa Borghese, is a cool, materialistic antidote to the murky atmosphere of the Capuchin grotto. The pricey bars and restaurants lining the street were once the haunt of Rome's beautiful people, made famous by Fellini's *La Dolce Vita*, but they left a long time ago, and Via Veneto, despite being home to some of the city's fanciest hotels, has never quite recovered the cachet it had in the Sixties and Seventies. Nonetheless, its pretty tree-lined aspect, pavement cafés, swanky stores and uniformed hotel bellmen lend it an upscale European air that is quite unlike anywhere else in the city, and there are any number of pricey café tables from which to soak up the atmosphere.

Palazzo Barberini

On the other side of Piazza Barberini, the **Palazzo Barberini**, Via Barberini 18, is home to a series of apartments that were once occupied by the Barberinis and, more importantly, the **Galleria Nazionale d'Arte Antica** (Tues–Sun 8.30am–7.30pm; €6; apartment tours – included in the ticket price – leave every 45min), a rich patchwork of mainly Italian art from the early Renaissance to late Baroque period. The gallery is still in the grip of a restoration that has been going on since 2004, and which will be continuing for some time yet, not least because the military, who have shared the building for decades, are due to move out, thus freeing up more gallery space. The result of the renovations is likely to be special, but it will be a while before you can safely predict what will be on display, and where.

It's an impressive collection, and highlights – which are likely to be on display whatever changes take place – include works by Titian, El Greco and Caravaggio. But perhaps the most impressive feature of the gallery is the building itself, worked on at different times by the most favoured architects of the day – Bernini, Borromini, Maderno – and the epitome of Baroque grandeur. The **first floor** Gran Salone, certainly, is guaranteed to impress, its ceiling frescoed by Pietro da Cortona in one of the best examples of exuberant Baroque trompe l'oeil work there is, a manic rendering of *The Triumph of Divine Providence* that almost crawls down the walls to meet you. Note the bees flying towards the figure of Providence

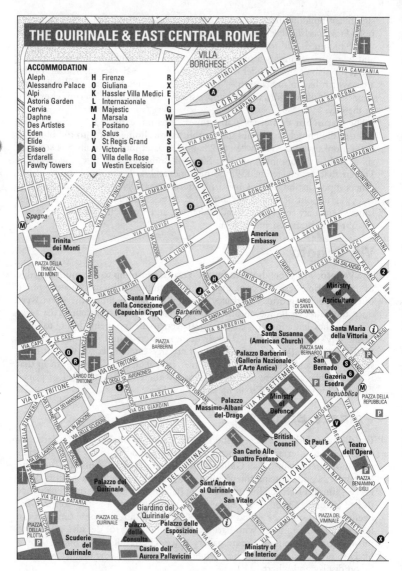

THE QUIRINALE & EAST CENTRAL ROME

ACCOMMODATION			
Aleph	H	Firenze	R
Alessandro Palace	O	Giuliana	X
Alpi	K	Hassler Villa Medici	E
Astoria Garden	L	Internazionale	I
Cervia	M	Majestic	G
Daphne	J	Marsala	W
Des Artistes	F	Positano	P
Eden	D	Salus	N
Elide	V	St Regis Grand	S
Eliseo	A	Victoria	B
Erdarelli	Q	Villa delle Rose	T
Fawlty Towers	U	Westin Excelsior	C

– the Barberini family symbol again. The displays here are mainly seventeenth-century works for the moment, with paintings by the Dutch Mannerists, Terbrugghen and Van Bronckhorst, Caravaggio's *Judith and Holofernes*, as well as a number of striking portraits of various saints: Spada's *St Jerome*, and another, more anguished depiction of the same saint by Guercino, Ribera's intense, staring *St James* and Saraceni's depictions of *St Gregory* and *St Francis*.

Next door there are later, frothier works by Boucher and Canaletto, among others, while across the hall a series of rooms displays early **Renaissance**

S. Agnese Fuori le Mura & S. Costanza (1km)

RESTAURANTS & CAFÉS

Africa	3
Colline Emiliane	5
Dagnino	6
New Orleans	2
Self-Service Luncheonette	4
Trimani	1

San Lorenzo, San Lorenzo fuori le Mura & Campo Verano

works, notably Fra' Filippo Lippi's warmly maternal *Madonna and Child*, painted in 1437 and introducing background details, notably architecture, into Italian religious painting for the first time. Next to it is a richly coloured and beautifully composed *Annunciation* by the same artist. In a further room on this floor, Raphael's beguiling *Fornarina* sits centre stage, a painting of a Trasteveran baker's daughter thought to have been the artist's mistress (Raphael's name appears clearly on the woman's bracelet), although some experts claim the painting to be the work of a pupil. Next to it is Sodoma's dark *Mystical Marriage* *of St Catherine*, while in the same room a beautifully composed *Pietà* by Giacomo Francia is one of the most overlooked works in the collection. Subsequent rooms hold a number of portraits, notably Bronzino's rendering of the marvellously erect *Stefano Colonna*, and a portrait of *Henry VIII* by Hans Holbein which feels almost as well known – probably because the painter produced so many of the monarch. Painted on the day of his marriage to his fourth wife, Anne of Cleves, he's depicted as a rather irritable but beautifully dressed middle-aged man – a stark contrast to the rather ascetic figure of *Erasmus of Rotterdam* by Quentin Matsys, which sometimes hangs nearby. Look out also, in the end room, for Tintoretto's *Christ taken in Adultery*, and two unusually small paintings by El Greco, *The Baptism of Christ* and *Adoration of the Shepherds*, as well as Titian's lively *Venus and Adonis*.

If you've still got the energy, you can take a tour of the Barberini apartments on the **second floor**. This is worth doing not so much for the dusty, painted Rococo rooms themselves (though the so-called Room of the Battles, showing various members of the Barberini and Colonna families engaged in glorious strife, is impressive) as for the circular staircase you climb to get there: the work of Borromini, and in sharp contrast to the huge and stately Bernini staircase you take to reach the paintings on the other side.

San Carlo alle Quattro Fontane

Continue on down Via delle Quattro Fontane, which heads southeast over the Quirinale from the palazzo, and you're at a seventeenth-century landmark, the church of **San Carlo alle Quattro Fontane** (Mon–Sat 10am–1pm & 3–6pm, Sat noon–1pm). This was Borromini's first real design commission, and in it he displays all the ingenuity he later became known for, elegantly cramming the church into a tiny and awkwardly shaped site that apparently covers roughly the same surface area as one of the main columns inside St Peter's. Tucked in beside the church, the cloister is squeezed into a tight but elegant oblong, topped with a charming balustrade.

Outside the church are the **four fountains** that give the street and church their name, each cut into a niche in a corner of the crossroads that marks the highest point on the Quirinal Hill. They were put here in 1593, and represent the Tiber and Aniene rivers and *Strength* and *Fidelity*, and they make a fine if busy spot to look back down towards the Trinità dei Monti obelisk in one direction and the Santa Maria Maggiore obelisk in the other – all part of Sixtus V's grand city plan.

Sant'Andrea al Quirinale

There's another piece of design ingenuity a few steps southwest of here, on Via del Quirinale, which is flanked on the left by public gardens and the domed

Via Rasella

More or less opposite Palazzo Barberini, **Via Rasella** was the scene of an ambush of a Nazi military patrol in 1944 that led to one of the worst Italian wartime atrocities – the reprisal massacre of 35 innocent Romans at the Ardeatine Caves outside the city walls (see p.119). A memorial now stands on the sight of the executions, and the event is commemorated every March 24. Oddly enough, Mussolini had a flat on Via Rasella in which he would entertain his mistresses.

church of **Sant'Andrea al Quirinale** (Mon–Sat 8.30am–noon & 3.30–7pm, Sun 9am–noon & 3.30–7.30pm), a flamboyant building that Bernini planned in a flat oval shape to fit into its wide but shallow site. Like San Carlo up the road, it's unusual and ingenious inside, and was apparently the church that Bernini himself was most pleased with, its wide, elliptical nave cleverly made into a grand space despite its relatively small size. Once you've taken this in, for a € 1 fee you can visit the sacristry, whose frescoes are similarly artful, with cherubs pulling aside painted drapery to let in light from mock windows, and the upstairs rooms of one St Stanislaus Kostka, where the Polish saint lived (and died) in 1568. The rooms have changed quite a lot since then, with paintings by the Jesuit artist Andrea Pozzo illustrating the life of the saint and culminating in a chapel that focuses on a disturbingly lifelike painted statue of Stanislaus lying on his deathbed.

Palazzo del Quirinale

Opposite the church is the featureless wall – the so-called "manica lunga" or "long sleeve" – of the **Palazzo del Quirinale** (Sun 8.30am–noon; € 5; Ⓦ www.quirinale.it), a sixteenth-century structure that was the official summer residence of the popes until Unification, when it became the royal palace. It's now the home of Italy's president (a largely ceremonial role), and it's worth braving the security for a glimpse of the style in which popes, despots, kings and now presidents like to live, with a fine set of state rooms and some very accomplished works of art – though note the limited opening hours, Sunday mornings only.

The first and perhaps most impressive of these is Melozzo da Forlí's fifteenth-century fresco of Christ, on the staircase off the courtyard, a fragment of a work that was painted for the apse of Santi Apostoli – the rest is in the Vatican (see p.202). Once inside, the spectacular first room, the Salone dei Corazzieri, was partly decorated by Carlo Maderno and essentially intended to glorify the life of Paul V, with frescoes interspersing the life of Moses with scenes showing the pope greeting various foreign emissaries and ambassadors. In case you were in any doubt of Paul V's achievements, Maderno throws in monochrome representations of some of his big building projects, including the Acqua Paola at one end of the room and St Peter's and the Quirinale itself at the other end. You can't always enter Maderno's Cappella Paolina, through the next door, but it's no great loss: its dimensions are precisely the same as the Sistine Chapel but it couldn't be more different, studded with a tasteless decorative ceiling, its walls covered in colourless nineteenth-century representations of the apostles. More grand rooms follow: the Salone del Balcone was where Pius IX gave his blessing on his election as pope; the room after contains a copy of Raphael's *John the Baptist* by Giulio Romano; while the three rooms beyond used to be one enormously long space but were remodeled during Napoleon's occupation of the place. Even now they cut quite a dash, frescoed under the direction of Pietro da Cortona in 1656 to a commission by Pope Alexander VII, with big Biblical moments depicted in accomplished and naturalistic style by a variety of artists, culminating in a dazzling *Adoration of the Shepherds* by Carlo Maratta. The last rooms are largely decorated in the style of the Savoy kings, who took over the palace in the nineteenth century, but the last room you see, the Salone delle Feste – originally the Sala Regia, where Paul V received foreign dignitaries – still packs quite a punch, its ceiling massively higher than the others at 16m and still decorated with Agostino Tassi's pseudo-oriental perspectives.

Piazza del Quirinale

If the Palazzo is closed, you can make do with appreciating the exceptional setting of the place in the **Piazza del Quirinale**, from which views stretch right across the centre of Rome. The main feature of the piazza is the huge statue of the **Dioscuri**, the name given to Castor and Pollux. These are massive five-metre-high Roman copies of classical Greek statues, showing the two godlike twins, the sons of Jupiter, who according to legend won victory for the Romans in an important battle (see also p.98). The statues originally stood at the entrance of the Baths of Constantine, the ruins of which lay nearby, and were brought here by Pope Sixtus V in the early sixteenth century to embellish the square – part of the pope's attempts to dignify and beautify the city with many large, vista-laden squares and long straight avenues. Nowadays it forms an odd concoction with the obelisk, originally from the Mausoleum of Augustus, which tops the arrangement, and the vast shallow bowl in front, which was apparently once resident at the Roman Forum – all in all a classic example of how Rome has most of its classical debris.

The Scuderie del Quirinale

The eighteenth-century **Scuderie del Quirinale** faces the palace from across the square, completing the triangle of buildings that make up the piazza. Originally the papal stables, it has been imaginatively restored as display space for some of the major travelling exhibitions that come to the city (opening times and prices vary; ⓦ www.scuderiequirinale.it). You'll probably want to visit only if there's something on that you specifically wish to see, but it costs nothing to call into the excellent art bookshop on the ground floor and see the equestrian spiral staircase that winds up from here to the main exhibition rooms. Plus, the modern glass staircase added to the side of the building gives the Quirinale's best view over Rome by far.

Casino dell'Aurora Pallavicini

Opposite the Scuderie, at Via XXIV Maggio 43 the **Palazzo Pallavicini-Rospigliosi** was originally commissioned by Cardinal Scipione Borghese in 1603 on the site of the baths of Constantine, specifically to be near the papal action at the Quirinale palace. There's a decent collection of Baroque painting in the gallery inside, but this can only be visited by appointment, and the only part you can turn up unannounced to see is the **Casino dell'Aurora Pallavicini** (open first day of every month 10am–noon & 3–5pm; free; ⓦ www .casinoaurorapallavicini.it), attached to the gardens on the left, where you can admire the Roman sarcophagi that frieze the facade, which is wonderfully well-preserved and full of tangled figures and exotic animals. It's a theme that is continued inside in the casino itself, with depictions of Roman triumphs at each end. However, the main focus is Guido Reni's ceiling fresco, *Aurora Scattering Flowers before the Sun* – a typically accomplished and smooth work, but somehow lacking in drama. In each corner, the poised and bucolic scenes of each season provide a nice counterpoint.

Via XX Settembre

Via XX Settembre spears out towards the Aurelian Wall from Via del Quirinale – not Rome's most appealing thoroughfare by any means, flanked by the deliberately faceless bureaucracies of the national government, erected after Unification in anticipation of Rome's ascension as a new world capital. It was, however, the route by which Italian troops entered the city on September 20, 1870, after the French troops defending the city had withdrawn, and the place where they breached the wall is marked with a column.

Halfway up, just north of Piazza della Repubblica, the church of **Santa Susanna** (daily 9am–noon & 4–7pm) is one of an elegant cluster of facades, although behind its well-proportioned Carlo Maderno frontage it isn't an especially notable building, except for some bright and soothing frescoes. The headquarters of American Catholics in Rome, it looks across the busy junction to the **Fontana dell'Acqua Felice**, which is playfully fronted by four basking lions, and focuses on a massive, bearded figure of Moses, in the central one of three arches. Marking the end of the Acqua Felice aqueduct, the fountain forms part of Pope Sixtus V's late-sixteenth-century attempts to spruce up the city centre with large-scale public works.

Opposite the church and fountain, the church of **San Bernardo alle Terme** (daily 7am–7pm) is so named (from *terme* – baths or springs) for the fact that it was once part of the vast complex of Diocletian's baths, and with its coffered ceiling and roof light, it's like a mini pantheon inside – although it is of course highly restored.

Santa Maria della Vittoria

Immediately opposite the Acqua Felice fountain, the church of **Santa Maria della Vittoria** (daily 7am–noon & 3.30–7pm) was, like Santa Susanna, built by Carlo Maderno. Its interior is one of the most elaborate examples of Baroque decoration in Rome: almost shockingly excessive to modern eyes, its ceiling and walls are pitted with carving, and statues are crammed into remote corners as in an over-stuffed attic. The church's best-known feature, Bernini's carving of the *Ecstasy of St Teresa*, the centrepiece of the sepulchral chapel of Cardinal Cornaro, continues the histrionics; a deliberately melodramatic work, it features a theatrically posed St Teresa of Avila against a backdrop of theatre-boxes on each side of the chapel, from which the Cornaro cardinals murmur and nudge each other as they watch the spectacle. St Teresa is one of the Catholic Church's most enduring mystics, and Bernini records the moment when, in 1537, she had a vision of an angel piercing her heart with a dart. It is a very Baroque piece of work in the most populist sense: not only is the event quite literally staged, but St Teresa's ecstasy verges on the worldly as she lays back in groaning submission beneath a mass of dishevelled garments and drapery.

Via Nazionale

A couple of minutes' walk downhill from the Quirinale Palace, **Via Nazionale** connects Piazza Venezia and the centre of town with the area around Stazione Termini and the eastern districts beyond. A focus for much development after Unification, its heavy, overbearing buildings were constructed to give Rome some semblance of modern sophistication when it became capital of the new country, but most are now occupied by hotels and mainstream shops and boutiques. At its bottom end, at the junction of Via XXIV Maggio, the palm-filled gardens of the **Villa Aldobrandini** are a nice respite from the traffic, high above the street and reached from the entrance on Via Mazzarino.

St Paul's-within-the-Walls

At the corner of Via Nazionale and Via Napoli is the American Episcopal church of **St Paul's-within-the-Walls** (daily 9am–1pm & 4–7pm), the first Protestant church to be built within the walls of the city after the Unification of Italy in 1870 and a peaceful and spiritual haven after the humdrum bustle of Via Nazionale. Dating from 1879, it was built in a neo-Gothic style by the British architect G.E. Street and is worth a quick peek inside for its works by English artists. The leaf-pattern ceramic tiles that line the walls of each side of the nave were designed by William Morris, and the apse mosaics, by the pre-Raphaelite artist Edward Burne-Jones, depict one of the church's founders, the American financier J.P. Morgan as St Paul, alongside his family, Garibaldi, General Ulysses Grant, and Abraham Lincoln. The 1913 mosaics on the western wall are by George Breck, who was director of the American Academy at the time.

Piazza della Repubblica

At the top of Via Nazionale, **Piazza della Repubblica** (formerly Piazza Esedra) is typical of Rome's nineteenth-century regeneration, a stern and dignified semicircle of buildings that was until recently rather dilapidated but is now – with the help of the new and very stylish *Hotel Exedra* – once again resurgent. The arcades make a fine place to stroll, despite the traffic, which roars ceaselessly around the **Fontana delle Naiadi**'s languishing nymphs and sea monsters.

Santa Maria degli Angeli

The piazza actually follows the semicircular outline of part of the Baths of Diocletian, built in 300 AD, the remains of which lie across the piazza and are partially contained in the church of **Santa Maria degli Angeli** (Mon–Sat 7am–6.30pm, Sun 7am–7.30pm). This is not Rome's most welcoming church by any means, but does give the best impression of the size and grandeur of Diocletian's bath complex, or at least of the tepidarium, whose structure it utilizes. It's a huge, open building, with an interior standardized by Vanvitelli into a rich eighteenth-century confection after a couple of centuries of piecemeal adaptation (started by an aged Michelangelo). The pink granite pillars, at three metres in diameter the largest in Rome, are original, and the main transept formed the main hall of the baths; only the crescent shape of the facade remains from the original caldarium (it had previously been hidden by a newer facing). The meridian that strikes diagonally across the floor in the south transept, flanked by representations of the twelve signs of the zodiac, was until 1846 the regulator of time for Romans (now a cannon shot fired daily at noon from the Janiculum Hill).

The exit channels you through the sacristry – and a small exhibition on the history of the baths and church – to Via Cernaia, behind another remnant of the baths, the **Aula Ottagona** (Octagonal Hall), formerly a planetarium and now part of the Museo Nazionale Romano (Mon–Sat 9am–2pm, Sun 9am–1pm; same ticket). The large domed room contains marble statues taken from the Baths of Caracalla and Diocletian, and two remarkable statues of a boxer and athlete from the Quirinal Hill. Excavations underground – accessible by stairs – show the furnaces for heating water for the baths and the foundations of another building from the time of Diocletian.

Museo delle Terme di Diocleziano

The buildings that surround Santa Maria degli Angeli are also recycled parts of Diocletian's baths – the complex was enormous, originally measuring 376m by 361m – and include the round church of San Bernardo alle Terme, off Via XX Settembre, and the round building, now an *albergo diurnale*, in the other direction, at the corner of Via Viminale and Via di Terme di Diocleziano. The rest of the baths – the huge halls and courtyards on the side towards Termini – have been renovated and, together with the Carthusian monastery attached to the church, now hold what is probably the least interesting part of the Museo Nazionale Romano (the better sections are across the street in Palazzo Massimo, see below, and in Palazzo Altemps, see p.65), the **Museo delle Terme di Diocleziano** (Tues–Sun 9am–7pm; €7, includes Palazzo Altemps, Palazzo Massimo, Crypta Balbi, valid 3 days).

Fronted by a fragrant garden, open to all, which centres on a large *krater* fountain with little cupids holding up its rim, the museum's most evocative part is the large cloister of the church whose sides are crammed with statuary, funerary monuments and sarcophagi and fragments from all over Rome. There's a lot to pick through, around three hundred bits and pieces in all, but standouts include the animal heads, found in the Forum of Trajan, a fine headless seated statue of Hercules from the second century AD, and a nice, if again damaged, statue of a husband and wife. Meanwhile there's an upstairs gallery that wraps around the cloister and includes finds dating back to the seventh century BC, and a downstairs section with more items – busts, terracotta statues, armour and weapons found in Roman tombs – all effectively, if rather academically, presented, but hardly compulsory viewing.

Palazzo Massimo

Across from Santa Maria degli Angeli, the snazzily restored **Palazzo Massimo**, Largo di Villa Perretti 1, is home to one of the two principal parts of the Museo Nazionale Romano (the other is in the Palazzo Altemps) – a superb collection of Greek and Roman antiquities, second only to the Vatican's, which has been entirely reorganized and features many pieces that have remained undisplayed for decades (Tues–Sun 9am–7pm; €7, includes Palazzo Altemps, Terme Diocletian, Crypta Balbi, valid 3 days, €4 for the audio guide).

Basement

This has displays of exquisite gold **jewellery** from the second century AD – necklaces, rings, brooches, all in immaculate condition – and some fine gold imperial hairnets. There's also – startlingly – the mummified remains of an eight-year-old girl, along with a fantastic **coin collection**, from the first bronze coinage of the fourth century BC to the surprisingly sophisticated coins of the Republic and imperial times, right up to the lira and concluding with a display devoted to the euro. It's all shown in glass cases equipped with magnifying glasses on runners, controlled by the buttons mounted on the front of each case.

The ground floor

The ground floor of the museum is devoted to statues from the **early empire**, including a gallery on the right with an unparalleled selection of unidentified busts found all over Rome. Their lack of clear identity is no barrier to appreciating them; they are amazing pieces of portraiture, and as vivid a representation of patrician Roman life as you'll find. Look out for the so-called *Statue of the*

△ Palazzo Massimo

Tivoli General, the face of an old man mounted on the body of a youthful athlete – sometimes believed to be a portrait of L. Munatius Plancus, the military officer who named Octavian "Augustus" (literally "Reverend") and so officially started the cult of the emperor. At the far end of the courtyard are more busts, this time identifiable as members of the imperial family: a bronze of Germanicus, a marvellous small bust of Caligula, several representations of Livia, Tiberius, Antonia and Drusus and a hooded statue of Augustus. You can find Greek sculpture on the far side of the courtyard, including bronzes of a Hellenistic prince holding a spear and a wounded pugilist at rest.

The first floor

The museum really gets going on the first-floor gallery, with groupings of the various **imperial dynasties** in roughly chronological order set around the courtyard, starting with the Flavian emperors, deliberately realistic and unidealised. The craggy determination of Vespasian and the pinched nobility of Nerva are in complete contrast to the next room, where Trajan appears next to his wife Plotina as Hercules, next to a bust of his cousin Hadrian, who is in turn next to his lover Antinous. These were some of the most successful years of the empire, and they continued with the Antonine emperors in the next room, which features Antonius Pius in a heroic nude pose and in several busts, flanked by likenesses of his daughter Faustina Minor. Faustina was the wife of Antonius's successor, Marcus Aurelius, who appears in the corridor outside. Also here is Commodus, the last and perhaps least successful of the Antonine emperors. Further on, past a room full of sarcophagi, including one showing the muses conversing with philosophers, are the Severans, with the fierce-looking Caracalla looking across past his father Septimius Severus to his brother Geta, whom he later murdered.

Just beyond the Severan emperors a hyper-realistic **sarcophagus** from 190 AD shows Roman victories over barbarians. Next door, at the back of the courtyard, there is an amazing sleeping hermaphrodite, an almost totally complete Dionysus that was fished out of the Tiber and bronzework from two imperial galleys found in southern Lazio, at Nemi, dating from the time of Caligula. A balustrade is studded with figures, each one different with a face on each side, handles are decorated with the faces of panthers, wolves and lions, and rudders come in the shape of forearms.

On the other side of the courtyard are more astonishing pieces, this time from various imperial villas outside Rome, many of them copies of **Greek originals**, including figures of Apollo and Dionysus, an Amazon and a barbarian, full of movement and vigour, as well as more dynastic busts discovered at Hadrian's villa in Tivoli, and a beautiful statue of a young girl holding a tray from Augustus's villa at Anzio.

The second floor

The second floor takes in some of the finest **Roman frescoes and mosaics** ever found and divides into three main parts. First there is a stunning set of **frescoes** from the Villa di Livia, depicting an orchard dense with fruit and flowers and patrolled by partridges, doves and other birds while beyond, on the same side of the courtyard, are floor **mosaics** showing naturalistic scenes – sea creatures, people boating – from the so-called Villa di Baccano on Via Cassia, a sumptuous mansion probably owned by the imperial Severi family. Four mosaic panels taken from a bedroom, featuring four chariot drivers and their horses, are so finely crafted that from a distance they look as if they've been painted, while in the adjoining room is a very rare example of *opus sectile*, a mosaic technique imported from the eastern provinces in the first century AD. Inlaid pieces of marble, mother-of-pearl, glass and hard stone are used instead of tesserae, the parts cut so as to enhance detail and give perspective depth.

More **mosaics** decorate the corridor outside, with floors showing Nile scenes, complete with crocodiles and hippos, while others come from Anzio, including one showing a reclining Hercules holding a cup and club while a wild boar emerges from a nearby cave,

The final section displays **wall paintings** rescued from what was believed to be the riverside villa of Augustus's daughter Julia and his trusted general Agrippa, built for their wedding. The villa wasn't lived in for long – Agrippa died of a fever nine years after their marriage – but the decoration was sumptuous in the extreme, including a room painted with garlands and an Egyptian-style frieze and two bedrooms painted deep red and covered with different figures.

Stazione Termini

Across the street from the museum is the low white facade of **Stazione Termini** (so named for its proximity to the Baths of Diocletian, nothing to do with being the terminus of Rome's rail lines) and the vast, bus-crammed hubbub that is Piazza dei Cinquecento in front. The station is a great building, an ambitious piece of modern architectural design that was completed in 1950 and still entirely dominates the streets around with its low, self-consciously futuristic lines – it's nicknamed "the dinosaur" for its curved front canopy. It has recently received a huge and sleek renovation that has converted part of its cavernous ticket hall to retail and restaurant space and upgraded the building in general – making it a nice spot for a browse and a wander, and a marvellous place to catch a train. It's got a good bookstore, a branch of the UPIM department store, even an exhibition space. **Piazza dei Cinquecento** is lined with a few stretches of Rome's original city wall, the Servian Wall, and is a good place to find buses and taxis. Like a lot of city railway stations, the streets around are low-life territory and, although not especially dangerous, are not a place to hang around for long.

San Lorenzo

A short walk east from Termini, the neighbourhood of **SAN LORENZO** spreads from the main campus of Rome's university, on the far side of Via Tiburtina, to the railway tracks – a working-class district, popular with students, that retains something of the air of a local neighbourhood, quite different from the rest of the city centre. It's home to some good and often inexpensive local restaurants (see p.243–245), and is also the location of the enormous **Campo Verano** cemetery (daily 7am–6pm) – since 1830 the largest Catholic burial-place in Rome. It's worth a visit for the grandiose tombs, such as the she-wolf-topped stone of the poet, journalist and activist Goffredo Mameli, just inside on the left. A contemporary of Garibaldi, he wrote the lyrics to the Italian National Anthem, *Il Canto degli Italiani*, in 1847, and fought on the side of Unification forces, receiving the bayonet wound that killed him in 1849, at the age of just 22.

San Lorenzo fuori le Mura

The area takes its name from the church of **San Lorenzo fuori le Mura** on Via Tiburtina right by the cemetery (daily: summer 7am–noon & 4–7.30pm; winter 7am–noon & 4–5.30pm), one of the seven great pilgrimage churches of Rome. It is a beautiful plain basilica, perhaps the city's best, and because of its relatively out-of-the-way location one of the most spiritual in feel, fronted by a columned portico and with a lovely twelfth-century cloister to its side. The original church here was built by Constantine over the site of St Lawrence's martyrdom – the saint was reputedly burned to death on a gridiron, halfway through his ordeal uttering the immortal words, "Turn me, I am done on this side." Where the San Lorenzo differs is that it's actually a combination of three churches – one a sixth-century reconstruction of Constantine's church by Pope Pelagius II, which now forms the chancel, another a fifth-century church from the time of Sixtus III, with a basilica from the thirteenth century by Honorius II joining the two.

Because of its proximity to Rome's railyards, the church was bombed heavily during World War II, but it has been rebuilt with sensitivity, and remains much as it was originally. Inside there are features from all periods: a Cosmati floor, again perhaps the city's most impressive, a thirteenth-century pulpit and a paschal candlestick with a twisted stem. The baldachino in the choir is dated 1147 and sits on its own colourful Cosmati floor, beyond which a thirteenth-century bishop's throne is perfectly placed to see the the sixth-century mosaic on the inside of the triumphal arch – a sixth-century depiction of St Lawrence with Pelagius II offering his church to Christ; the underneath of the arch is decorated with fruit and flowers. There are more mosaics below here, nineteenth century this time, adorning the tomb of Pope Pius IX. The body of the last papal ruler of Rome was carried here under cover of darkness in 1881, in a procession that was disrupted by a gang of Italian nationalists who attempted to throw his corpse into the river. Through the sacristy is the church's lovely small Romanesque cloister, one of Rome's simplest and most peaceful, with a well-tended garden and fish pond in the middle and a fragment of a bomb remembering the bombardment of the church in World War II. Downstairs, the catacombs (often closed) are where St Lawrence was apparently buried – a dank path leads to the pillars of Constantine's original structure.

Via Nomentana

At the north end of Via XX Settembre, the **Porta Pia** was one of the last works of Michelangelo, erected under Pope Pius IV in 1561. It's famous as the spot at which Italian troops first entered Rome on the 20 September, 1870 – hence the name of the street. Appropriately, it houses the small **Museo Storico dei Bersaglieri** (Tues & Thurs 9am–1pm; free), dedicated to a crack body of troops founded in 1836 (they're the ones with the large floppy feathers in their hats) and with displays on the founder, Alessandro La Marmora, along with sections on the Unification struggle, World War II and other conflicts.

To the right of the gate is the low-slung modern home of the **British Embassy**, while on the far side is the busy **Corso d'Italia** (in effect part of the central ring road that girdles the city centre). Straight on is the wide boulevard of **Via Nomentana**, lined with luxury villas that have long been home to some of the city's more illustrious names.

MACRO

The second turning on the left, Via Reggio Emilia, leads to the Museum of Contemporary Arts in Rome, or **MACRO,** at no. 54 (Tues–Sun 9am–7pm; €1), a former brewery whose complex of industrial buildings opened in 1999 as an arts and culture centre. There is a permanent collection of contemporary works here, mainly focusing on Italian artists since the 1960s, but its six large exhibition halls are mostly used to host temporary exhibitions, plus there's a library, bookstore and café.

Villa Torlonia

A kilometre down Via Nomentana on the right is the nineteenth-century **Villa Torlonia**, which the banker Prince Giovanni Torlonia turned over to Mussolini to use as long as he needed it. Mussolini lived in the **Casino dei Principi**, which remains closed, but the previously neglected grounds are now open to the public after a long period of restoration (daily 7am–1hr before sunset), as is the central **Casino Nobile**, which you can see by way of guided tours (€3 for this and the Casino delle Civette). Designed by Valadier in the early nineteenth century, this must have been a sumptuous place to live. Various rooms are decorated with cycles of frescoes whose unifying theme is frolicking and nakedness, alongside a general deference to bygone ages, with ancient Roman tableaux, including Antony and Cleopatra, hieroglyphics and portraits of great artists and thinkers. The tours whisk you around quickly enough, and it's worth taking a look – it's free – before moving on to the **Casina delle Civette** in the southeastern corner (March & Oct 9am–6pm; April–Sept Tues–Sun 9am–7pm; Nov–Feb 9am–4.30pm; €3), the "small house of the owls". This is something unusual in Rome – a Liberty-style dwelling full of art nouveau features, such as stained glass, flooring, wood panelling and inlays, that contribute to the kind of complete design vision that was common at the turn of the nineteenth century. Nowadays it doubles as a museum of stained glass.

Though originally designed in 1840, it was transformed in 1917 by one Vincenzo Fasoli into a comfortable residence for a Roman aristocrat – in this case **Prince Giovanni Torlonia** – in the fashionable style of the time. The house's name derives from the prince's love of owls, and their dominance in the decoration of the building (although much of this hasn't survived). Indeed, the prince was keen on all things of the night, as his upstairs bedroom shows, decorated as it is with a night sky and a bat-encrusted chandelier. The bird theme continues in the Room of the Swallows (with its stucco birds in each corner, and swallow-themed stained glass) and there are owls in the stained glass windows at the front of the house and the relief above the back door.

The rest of the park remains in restoration, and there are plans to return its other features, including an outdoor theatre, to their original splendour too. They have recently finished the so-called **Casino Medievale**, which has been turned into the comfy *La Limonaia* café-restaurant (Tues–Sun 10am–midnight; Mon 7pm–midnight), where you can sit outside in a lime-tree-filled garden. But whether they will ever get around to restoring the third-century AD **Jewish catacombs**, which are said to extend under the gardens for some ten kilometres, remains to be seen.

Sant'Agnese fuori le Mura

Further up Via Nomentana is the church of **Sant'Agnese fuori le Mura** (Mon 9am–noon, Tues–Sat 9am–noon & 4–6pm, Sun 4–6pm) dedicated to the 13-year-old saint who was martyred in Domitian's Stadium in 303 AD (see p.60). It's part of a small complex of early Christian monuments that also includes the catacombs underneath and the neighbouring church of Santa Costanza. To get into the church, walk down the hill and through the courtyard to the narthex or entrance hall of the building which, apart from some very out-of-place later fixtures, is much as it was built by Pope Honorius I in the seventh century, when he reworked Constantine's original structure – which had in turn been built over St Agnes's grave. Inside, the church proper has been updated in Baroque style, but the apse mosaic is contemporary with Honorius's building, showing Agnes next to the pope, who holds a model of his church, in typical Byzantine fashion.

Out of the narthex the custodian will lead you down into the **catacombs** (same hours as church; €5) that sprawl below the church, which are among the best-preserved and most crowd-free of all the city's catacombs. Indeed, if you have time for only one set of catacombs during your stay in Rome (and they really are all very much alike), these are perhaps the best. The custodian also sells little terracotta lamps in the shape of fish, or conventional Roman-style lamps with the "Chi-Rho" sign on – probably the most ancient symbol of Christianity. They are very reasonably priced and make a nice souvenir of the place.

Santa Costanza

After the catacombs the guide will show you the church of **Santa Costanza** (usually open the same hours as Sant'Agnese; free), whose decorative and architectural features illustrate the transition from the pagan to Christian city better than almost any other building in Rome. Built in 350 AD as a mausoleum for Constantia and Helena, the daughters of the emperor Constantine, it's a round structure which follows the traditional shape of the great pagan tombs (consider those of Hadrian and Augustus elsewhere in the city), and the mosaics on the vaulting of its circular ambulatory – fourth-century depictions of vines, leaves and birds – would have been as at home on the floor of a Roman *domus* as they were in a Christian church. Unfortunately, the porphyry sarcophagus of Santa Costanza herself has been moved to the Vatican, and what you see in the church is a plaster copy.

Monti and San Giovanni

mmediately north of the Colosseum and east of Via Cavour, the **Esquiline Hill** is the highest and largest of the city's seven hills. Formerly a sparsely populated area, with vineyards, orchards and olive groves stretching out to the Aurelian Wall, its most easterly reaches formed one of the most fashionable residential quarters of ancient Rome. In fact it consists of four separate summits: the *Oppian* (the part nearest the Colosseum, now a small park); the *Suburra*, which was ancient Rome's most notorious inner-city suburb; the *Fagutalis* and – the highest (65m) and largest – the *Cispius*, which is the site of the basilica of Santa Maria Maggiore. Immediately to the west, stretching over as far as the shopping street of Via Nazionale, the **Viminale Hill** is less rich in interest, the smallest of Rome's hills and known as the home of Italy's interior ministry and not much else. Together, the central parts of the two hills form a district known as "**Monti**", an appealing cobbled quarter with neighbourhood bars, restaurants, grocers and restorers' workshops. The nineteenth-century thoroughfare of **Via Cavour** is the spine of the area, a busy artery that ferries traffic from Termini down to the area around the Colosseum and the Roman Forums.

Overall this is a part of town that most travellers to Rome encounter at some point, partly because of key sights such as Nero's **Domus Aurea** and the basilica of **Santa Maria Maggiore**, but also because it's close to the lion's share of Rome's budget hotels, around Termini. Not far away to the east are other ancient churches: triple-layered **San Clemente**, a short walk from the Colosseum, the complex of **San Giovanni in Laterano**, which gives its name to the district – **San Giovanni** – and nearby **Santa Croce in Gerusalemme**.

Monti

Via Cavour is one of Rome's busiest thoroughfares, slashed through the Monti neighbourhood in the 1890s to connect the station district to the river. As you walk north, towards Santa Maria Maggiore, the streets off to the left are worth a wander and form Monti's most atmospheric quarter, focusing on the Via dei

PIAZZA DEL
VIMINALE

Ministry of
the Interior

S. Pudenziana

PIAZZA D.
ESQUILINO

VIMINALE
HILL

S. Maria
Maggiore

PIAZZA
S. MARIA
MAGGIORE

4

MONTI

A

5   S. Prassede

6
12

C

PIAZZA
D. ZINGARI

7

11

Cavour

PIAZZA
S. MARTINO
AI MONTI

LARGO
BRANCACCIO

13

M   VIA GIOVANNI LANZA

PIAZZA
MADONNA
D. MONTI

14

VIA IN SELCI

16

15

PIAZZA
FRANCESCO
DI PAOLA

S. Pietro
in Vincoli

S. Martino
ai Monti

Museo Nazionale
di Arte Orientale

17

CAVOUR

PIAZZA
S. PIETRO
IN VINCOLI

D. SETTE SALE

LARGO
LEOPARDI

LARGO D.
POLVERIERA

VIALE MONTE OPPIO

ESQUILINE
HILL

LARGO
G. AGNESI

Colosseo   M

Domus
Aurea

PARCO
DI COLLE
OPPIO

20

Colosseum

VIA LABICANA

PIAZZA
ISIDE

PIAZZA S.
CLEMENTE

21   22

S.Clemente

23

Ss. Quattro
Coronati

24

CELIAN HILL

PIAZZA
DI PORTA
METRONIA

0   200 m

RESTAURANTS & CAFÉS

Antico Caffé di Brasile	**6**
Arancia Blu	**3**
Baia Chiaia	**20**
Il Bocconcino	**23**
Alle Carrette	**16**
Enoteca Cavour	**17**
Charley's Sauciére	**24**
Il Dito e la Luna	**9**
Formula I	**8**
Il Guru	**4**
Luzzi	**22**
Monti D.O.C.	**13**
Le Naumacchie	**21**
Palazzo del Freddo di G. Fassi	**18**
Pommidoro	**1**
Tram Tram	**2**
Trattoria Monti	**11**
Birreria Moretti	**15**

MONTI & SAN GIOVANNI

N

Piazzale Sisto

Piazza dei Siculi

Piazzale Tiburtino

Piazzale Porta S. Lorenzo

Piazza dei Marsi Campani

Porta Magica

Vittorio Ⓜ
PIAZZA VITTORIO EMANUELE II

Porta Maggiore

Tomb of the Baker

Piazza di Porta Maggiore

Piazzale Labicano

Manzoni Ⓜ

SAN GIOVANNI

Museum of Musical Instruments

Piazza di Villa Wolkonsky

Piazza S. Croce in Gerusalemme

S. Croce in Gerusalemme

Scala Santa

Piazza S. Giovanni Laterano

Lateran Palace

Baptistery

San Giovanni in Laterano

Piazza di Porta S. Giovanni

⊠ Porta Asinaria

Largo Brindisi

Piazza Imola

San Giovanni Ⓜ

Piazzale Appio

Largo Magna Grecia

Prenestino & Pigneto

ACCOMMODATION

Grifo	C
Radisson SAS	B D
Rosetta	D
Sandy	A

BARS

Al Vino al Vino	12
Club Machiavelli	19
Druid's Den	7
Fiddler's Elbow	5
Finnegan	14
Rive Gauche 2	10

Serpenti and Via del Boschetto, and the narrow streets between them. The large building at the bottom of Via dei Serpenti is the church of **Madonna dei Monti**, whose high dome and generous proportions make it worth a peep. It's the work of Giacomo della Porta, who also contributed the fountains in the pleasant little piazza alongside.

San Pietro in Vincoli

On the other side of Via Cavour, steps lead up to the tranquil piazza in front of the recently restored church of **San Pietro in Vincoli** (daily 8am–12.30pm & 3–7pm) – one of Rome's most delightfully plain places of worship, built to house an important relic, the two sets of chains ("vincoli") that held St Peter when he was in Jerusalem and in Rome, which miraculously joined together. During the papacy of Sixtus IV, it was the cardinal seat of the pope's nephew, Giuliano della Rovere, who became Pope Julius II, of Sistine Chapel ceiling fame.

The chains of St Peter can still be seen in the confessio beneath the high altar, in a beautiful gold and rock crystal reliquary, but most people come for the **tomb** of Pope Julius II at the far end of the southern aisle, which occupied Michelangelo on and off for much of his career. Michelangelo reluctantly gave it up to paint the Sistine Chapel, and was never able to return to it for very long, being always at the beck and call of successive popes, who understandably had little interest in promoting the glory of one of their predecessors.

No one knows how the tomb would have looked had it been finished – it's generally assumed that Moses would have been on one end and the risen Christ on the other, with a statue of Julius himself surmounting the whole thing – and the only statues Michelangelo completed are the *Moses*, *Leah* and *Rachel*, which are still in the church, and two *Dying Slaves*, which are now in the Louvre. Moses, pictured as descended from Sinai to find the Israelites worshipping the golden calf, and flanked by the gentle figures of Leah and Rachel, is one of the artist's most captivating works and the rest of the composition – completed by later artists – seems dull and static by comparison. Because of a medieval mistranslation of scripture, Moses is depicted with satyr's horns instead of the "radiance of the Lord" that Exodus tells us shone around his head. Nonetheless, this powerful statue is so lifelike that Michelangelo is alleged to have struck its knee with his hammer and shouted, "Speak, damn you!". The rest of the group was finished by Michelangelo's pupils, while the statue of Julius II at the top, by Maso del Bosco, modelled on an Etruscan coffin lid, sadly fails to evoke the character of this apparently active, courageous and violent man – who was in fact laid to rest in St Peter's.

There's not much else to see in the church, but during the summer months it can be a bit of a scrum to see the tomb, and it's nice to wander around the building's less congested areas. In the north aisle there's a seventh-century mosaic of St Sebastian and to the right of the door is the tomb of the Pollaiolo brothers, Antonio and Piero, the fifteenth-century Tuscan sculptors who were responsible for Sixtus IV's elaborate tomb in St Peter's (see p.187).

Santa Pudenziana

Left off the end of Via Cavour, the church of **Santa Pudenziana**, down below street level on Via Urbana (daily 8am–noon & 4–6pm), has equally ancient origins. It was dedicated to St Prassede's supposed sister and was for many years believed to have been built on the site where St Peter lived and worshipped, though this has since been entirely discredited, and it's now thought to have simply been the site of a Roman bathhouse. The two relics the church used to house – the chair that St Peter used as his throne and the table at which he said Mass – have both long gone, to the Vatican and the Lateran, respectively. But the church still has one feature of ancient origin, the superb fifth-century apse mosaics – some of the oldest Christian figurative mosaics in Rome, though they've been tampered with and restored over the years. They're still fluid and beautiful works, centring on a golden enthroned Christ surrounded by the Apostles – not quite all of them, you'll notice, due to the fact that the mosaic was reduced in size when the church was restored in the sixteenth century and they cut off one from either side. Nonetheless, the mosaic is marvellous, not least the graphic arrangement of the Apostles that remain, and the expressiveness of their faces, each one of which is purposefully different from the next.

Behind the church, the **Ministero dell'Interno** marks the top of the Viminale hill. Piazza del Viminale, just in front, gives way to Via Viminale, and, on the left, Rome's **Teatro dell'Opera**, an unassuming building, but one which until the completion of the new Auditorium, was the city's main venue for opera.

San Martino ai Monti

On the other side of Via Cavour, the church of **San Martino ai Monti**, along Via Giovanni Lanza, is another place of worship that dates back to the earliest days of Christianity. It was dedicated to the saints Sylvester and Martin in the sixth century and incorporates an ancient Roman structure, but it was almost entirely rebuilt in the 1650s, and sports a ceiling from that time that is strangely modern in appearance, parts of it reminiscent of 1920s brushed stainless steel. The ceiling also shows the arms of the Medicis, specifically the family's last pope, Leo XI, who ruled briefly in 1605, and has a series of frescoes depicting scenes of the Roman Campagna and the interiors of the old Roman basilicas of St Peter and San Giovanni before they were gussied up in their present Baroque splendour – St Peter's is at the far end of the north aisle, San Giovanni near the door.

Santa Prassede

Follow Via San Martino ai Monti from here to the ninth-century church of **Santa Prassede** (daily 7am–noon & 4–6.30pm), which occupies an ancient site where it's claimed St Prassede harboured Christians on the run from persecution. She apparently collected the blood and remains of the martyrs and placed them in a well where she herself was later buried; a red marble disc in the floor of the nave marks the spot. In the southern aisle, the chapel of St Zeno was built by Pope Paschal I as a mausoleum for his mother, Theodora, and is decorated with marvellous ninth-century mosaics that make it glitter like a jewel-encrusted box. You'll need €0.50 to light them; Theodora is depicted on the left-hand arch. The chapel also contains a fragment of a column that Christ was supposedly tied to when he was scourged. In the apse are more ninth-century mosaics, showing Christ between saints Peter, Pudenziana and Zeno (on the right) and saints Paul, Praxedes and Paschal I (on the left). Note that Paschal's halo (like Theodora's) is in a rectangular form, indicating that he was alive when the mosaics were placed here.

Santa Maria Maggiore

Via Cavour opens out at Piazza Esquilino, behind the basilica of **Santa Maria Maggiore** (daily 7am–7pm). This is one of the city's five great basilicas, and has one of Rome's best-preserved Byzantine interiors – a fact belied by its dull eighteenth-century exterior. Unlike the other great places of pilgrimage in Rome, it was not built on any special Constantinian site, but instead went up during the fifth century after the Council of Ephesus recognized the **cult of the Virgin** and churches venerating Our Lady began to spring up all over the Christian world. According to legend, the Virgin Mary appeared to Pope Liberius in a dream on the night of August 4, 352 AD, telling him to build a church on the Esquiline Hill, on a spot where he would find a patch of newly fallen **snow** the next morning. The snow would outline exactly the plan of the church that should be built there in her honour – which, of course, is exactly what happened, and the first church here was called Santa Maria della Neve ("of

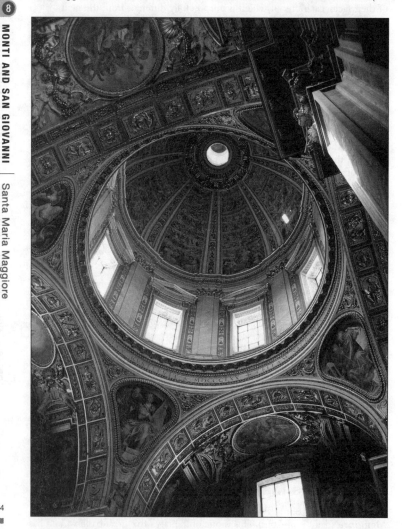

△ The Dome of Santa Maria Maggiore

the snow"). The present structure dates from about 420 AD, and was completed under the reign of St Sixtus III, who was pope between 432 AD and 440 AD.

Santa Maria Maggiore is noted for two special ceremonies. One, on August 5, celebrates the miraculous snowfall: at midday Mass white rose petals are showered on the congregation from the ceiling, and at night the fire department operates an artificial snow machine in the piazza in front and showers the area in snow that, naturally, melts immediately. The other takes place on Christmas morning, when the reliquary containing the crib is processed around the church and then displayed on the high altar.

The basilica

The **basilica** was encased in its eighteenth-century shell during the papacy of Benedict XIV, although the campanile, the highest in Rome, is older than this – built in 1377 under Pope Gregory XI. Inside, however, the original building survives intact, its broad nave fringed on both sides with strikingly well-kept mosaics (binoculars help), most of which date from the time of Pope Sixtus III and recount, in comic-strip form, incidents from the Old Testament. The ceiling, which shows the arms of the Spanish Borgia popes, Calixtus III and Alexander VI, was gilded in 1493 with gold sent by Queen Isabella as part payment of a loan from Innocent VIII to finance the voyage of Columbus to the New World.

The large chapel in the right transept holds the elaborate tomb of Sixtus V – another, less famous, **Sistine Chapel**, decorated with marble taken from the Roman Septizodium, and with frescoes and reliefs portraying events from his reign. In the middle, a bronze baldachino carried by four angels covers another small chapel. The chapel also contains the tomb of another zealous and reforming pope, Pius V, whose statue faces that of Sixtus; he's probably best known for excommunicating Queen Elizabeth I of England, in 1570.

Outside the Sistine Chapel is the modest tomb slab of the Bernini family, including Gian Lorenzo himself, to the right by the sanctuary steps, while opposite, the sumptuous **Pauline Chapel** is home to the tombs of the Borghese pope, Paul V, on the left, and his immediate predecessor Clement VIII, opposite. The floor is decorated with the Borghese arms, an eagle and dragon, and the magnificently gilded ceiling shows glimpses of heaven. The altar, of lapis lazuli and agate, contains a *Madonna and Child* dating from the twelfth or thirteenth century.

Between the two chapels, the **confessio** contains a kneeling statue of the dogmatic Pope Pius IX, the longest-serving pope in history, and the last one to hold real power – he was kicked out with Italian Unification in 1870, after 31 years. The reliquary here is said to contain fragments of the crib of Christ, in rock crystal and silver, while the high altar, above it, contains the relics of St Matthew, among other Christian martyrs. But it's the **mosaics** of the arch that really dazzle, a vivid representation of scenes from the life of Christ – *The Annunciation*, *The Adoration of the Magi* (in which Christ is depicted not as a child, unusually, but as a king himself) plus *The Massacre of the Innocents* on the left and *The Presentation in the Temple* and *Herod receiving the Magi* on the right. The central apse mosaics are later, but are no less impressive, commissioned by the late-thirteenth-century pope, Nicholas IV, and showing *The Coronation of the Virgin*, with angels, saints and the pope himself.

The museum and loggia

There's a **museum** underneath the basilica (daily 9am–6.30pm; €4), which sports what even by Roman standards is a wide variety of relics – a hair of the

Virgin and the arms of saints Luke and Matthew – as well as the usual liturgical garments and so on. The sporadically open nativity scene, or *Presepio*, the work of Arnolfo di Cambio, was originally created to decorate a chapel to hold the basilica's holy crib relics, and is well worth catching. You might prefer to save your money for the **loggia** above the main entrance (tours daily at 9am & 1pm, bookable in advance; €3), which has some magnificent mosaics showing Christ among various saints, sitting above four scenes that tell the story of the miracle of the snow: the one on the far left shows Mary appearing to Pope Liberius, the one on the far right scene shows the pope, and others trace the outline of the building in the miraculous snowfall.

Museo Nazionale di Arte Orientale

It's a short walk south from Santa Maria Maggiore to busy Largo Brancaccio, where the imposing Palazzo Brancaccio houses the **Museo Nazionale di Arte Orientale**, Via Merulana 248 (Mon, Wed, Fri & Sat 8.30am–2pm, Tues, Thurs & Sun 8.30am–7.30pm, closed 1st & 3rd Mon of every month; €4) – a first-rate collection of oriental art (the best in Italy) that has recently been restored. Beginning with Marco Polo in the thirteenth century, the Italians have always had connections with the east, and the quality of this collection of Islamic, Chinese, Indian and Southeast Asian art reflects this fact – not to mention making a refreshing break from the multiple ages of Western art you are exposed to in Rome. There are finds dating back to 1500 BC from a necropolis in Pakistan; architectural fragments, art works and jewellery from Tibet, Nepal and Pakistan; a solid collection from China, with predictable Buddhas and vases alongside curiosities such as Han dynasty figures and a large Wei dynasty Buddha with two boddhisatvas; and coins from twelfth-century Iran and northwest India.

Piazza Vittorio Emanuele II

Outside the museum, Largo Leopardi is home to the remains of the so-called **Auditorium of Maecenas,** the sole remnant of a villa that was home to the trusted friend and advisor of Augustus; the rest was swept up and incorporated into Nero's Domus Aurea (see opposite) long after Maecenas's death.

A few metres from here, up Via Leopardi, **Piazza Vittorio Emanuele II** was the centre of a district which became known as the "quartiere piemontese" when the government located many of its major ministries here after Unification. The arcades of the square, certainly, recall central Turin, as do the solid palatial buildings that surround it. It's more recently become the immigrant quarter of Rome, with a heavy concentration of African, Asian and Middle Eastern shops and restaurants. You'll easily hear a dozen different languages spoken as you pass through, although sadly the open-air **market** that used to surround the piazza has moved a few blocks east to Via Giolitti, between Via Ricasoli and Via Lamarmora, where there are two covered halls, one selling clothes, the other food.

Close to the northern end of the piazza, an eighteen-metre-high pile of Roman bricks is all that is left of a monumental public fountain known as the **Nymphaeum of Alexander Severus** (emperor from 222 to 235 AD) – a distribution point for water arriving in the city by a branch of the Aqua Claudia aqueduct and now home to a prosperous colony of cats.

The Domus Aurea

A short walk south from Piazza Vittorio Emanuele II, the **Parco di Colle Oppio** is a fairly unsavoury spot, a gathering place for street people and fascist youths, and as such not particularly safe after dark. It's dotted with remnants of the various Roman structures that once stood here: piles of rubble, the imposing fenced-off remains of **Trajan's Baths** on the far side, and a number of round brick stumps – well-heads that led down into the Esquiline's other most visited sight, after Santa Maria Maggiore, Nero's **Domus Aurea** or "Golden House", down towards Via Labicana and the Colosseum.

Currently closed for restoration following flooding, but one of the city's most intriguing sights, the "house" was a vast undertaking built on the summit of the Oppian and into its sides after a fire of 64 AD (allegedly started by Nero) devastated this part of Rome. It was not intended to be a residence at all; rather it was a series of banqueting rooms, nymphaeums, small baths, terraces and gardens, facing what at the time was a small lake fed by the underground springs and streams that drained from the surrounding hills. Rome was used to Nero's excesses, but it had never seen anything like the Golden House before. The facade was supposed to have been coated in solid gold, there was hot and cold running water in the baths, one of the dining rooms was rigged up to shower flower petals and natural scent on guests, and the grounds – which covered over two square kilometres – held vineyards and game. Nero didn't get to enjoy his palace for long – he died a couple of years after it was finished, and Vespasian tore a lot of the exposed facade down in disgust, draining its lake and building the Colosseum on top. Later, Trajan built his baths on top of the rest of the complex, and it was pretty much forgotten until its wall paintings were discovered by Renaissance artists, including Raphael. When these artists first visited these rooms, they had to descend ladders into what they first believed was some kind of mystical cave, or **grotto**; their attempts to imitate what they found here gave us the word "*grotesque*".

Inside the Domus Aurea

Tours start by taking you down a long corridor into the excavated rooms of the palace. The temperature always hovers at around 10°C and this, and the almost 100 percent humidity, makes it necessary to wear a sweater or jacket even in the middle of the Roman summer. The house can at first be confusing – Trajan's attempts to obliterate the palace with his baths complex mean that the baths' foundations merge into parts of the palace, and vice versa – but a free plan, not to mention the guide, helps you sort it out.

There are various covered fountains, service corridors, terraces and, most spectacularly, the **Octagonal Room**, domed, with a hole in the middle, which is supposed to have rotated as the day progressed to emulate the passage of the sun. Most of the rooms are decorated in the so-called Third Pompeiian style, with garlands of flowers, fruit, vines and foliage, interspersed with mythical animals and fanciful depictions of people looking back through windows at the viewer. Perhaps the best preserved frescoes are in the **Room of Achilles at Skyros**, and illustrate Homer's story of Achilles being sent to the island of Skyros disguised as a woman to prevent him being drawn into the Trojan Wars. In one fresco, Achilles is in drag at the Skyros court; another shows him putting his female clothes aside and picking up a shield, brought to him by Ulysses (in the crested helmet) to catch him out and betray his disguise.

San Giovanni in Laterano and around

The area immediately south and east of the Esquiline and the Colosseum is known as **San Giovanni**, after the basilica complex that lies at the end of Via Merulana, which was, before the creation of the separate Vatican city state, the headquarters of the Catholic Church. It's a mixed area, mainly residential, but it has some compelling sights in the basilica of San Giovanni itself, the church of Santa Croce in Gerusalemme just beyond; and, back towards the Colosseum, the amazing church of San Clemente.

San Giovanni in Laterano

The basilica of **San Giovanni in Laterano** (daily 7am–6.30pm; guided tours of the basilica ☎06.6988.6392) is officially Rome's cathedral and the seat of the pope as bishop of Rome, and was for centuries the main papal residence. However, when the papacy returned from Avignon at the end of the fourteenth century, the Lateran palaces were in ruins and uninhabitable, and the pope moved across town to the Vatican, where he has remained ever since. The Lateran Treaty of 1929 accorded this and the other patriarchal basilicas extraterritorial status.

There has been a church on this site since the fourth century, the first established by Constantine, and the present building, reworked by Borromini in the mid-seventeenth century, evokes – like San Clemente or San Stefano – Rome's staggering wealth of history with a host of features from different periods; the statue of Constantine in the porch was found on the Quirinale Hill while the doors of the church itself were taken from the Curia, or Senate House, of the Roman Forum. The obelisk that stands on the north side of the church is the oldest in Rome, dating from the fifteenth century BC and brought here from Thebes by Constantine, originally for the Circus Maximus, but raised here by Sixtus V.

The basilica

The **interior** of San Giovanni has been extensively reworked over the centuries. Much of what you see today dates from the seventeenth century, when the

Aldobrandini family pope, Clement VIII, had the church remodelled for Holy Year. The gilded ceiling of the nave has as its centrepiece the papal arms of Pope Pius VI, from the late 1700s, while the ceiling in the crossing bears, on the left, the Aldobrandini insignia, and on the right the tomb of Pope Innocent III, who died in 1216 and was buried here in the late 1800s at the behest of Pope Leo XIII, when he had this wing of the crossing remodelled. Leo XIII himself, who died in 1903, is buried opposite. The first pillar on the left of the right-hand aisle shows a fragment of Giotto's fresco of Boniface VIII, proclaiming the first Holy Year in 1300, a gentle work with gorgeous colours that is at odds with the immensity and grandeur of the rest of the building. On the next pillar along, a more recent monument commemorates Sylvester I – "the magician pope", bishop of Rome during much of Constantine's reign – and incorporates part of his original tomb, said to sweat and rattle its bones when a pope is about to die.

As for the nave itself, it's lined with eighteenth-century statues of the apostles in flashy and dramatic Rococo style, each one of which gives a clue as to their identity or manner of death: St Matthew, the tax collector, is shown with coins falling out of a sack; St Bartholomew holds a knife and his own skin (he was flayed alive); St Thomas holds a set square (he's the patron saint of architects) and St Simon a saw (he was, apparently, sawn to death). At the head of the nave, the heads of St Peter and St Paul, the church's prize relics, are kept secure behind the papal altar, while a museum holds assorted treasures through the bookshop (daily 9am–6pm; €1). The mosaics in the apse are undeniably impressive, but fake – they were added in the later nineteenth century to replace the lost originals; but the baldachino just in front is most definitely genuine, a splash of Gothic grandeur made by the Tuscan sculptor Giovanni di Stefano in the fourteenth century that shelters the glassed-over bronze tomb of Martin V – the Colonna pope who was responsible for returning the papacy to Rome from Avignon in 1419.

The cloisters

Outside the church, the **cloisters** (daily 9am–6pm; €2), reachable from a door by the north transept, are one of the most pleasing parts of the complex, decorated with early thirteenth-century Cosmati work and with fragments of the original basilica arranged around. Rooms off to the side form a small museum, with, in no particular order, the papal throne of Pius V and various papal artefacts (including the vestments of Boniface VIII).

The Lateran Palace and Baptistry

Adjoining the basilica is the **Lateran Palace**, home of the popes in the Middle Ages and also formally part of Vatican territory. Next door, the **Baptistry** (daily 7am–12.30pm & 4–7.30pm; free) has been carefully restored, along with the side of the church itself, after a car bombing in 1993. It is the oldest surviving baptistry in the Christian world, an octagonal structure built during the fifth century that has been the model for many such buildings since. Oddly, it doesn't really feel its age, although the mosaics in the side chapels and the bronze doors to the chapel on the right, brought here from the Baths of Caracalla, quickly remind you where you are.

The Scala Santa and Sancta Sanctorum

There are more ancient remains on the other side of the church, on Piazza di Porta San Giovanni, foremost of which is the **Scala Santa** (April–Sept daily

6.15am–noon & 3.30–6.45pm; Oct–March daily 6.15am–noon & 3–6.15pm), claimed to be the staircase from Pontius Pilate's house down which Christ walked after his trial. It was said to have been brought to Rome by St Helena and was placed here by Pope Sixtus V, who also moved the chapel here – it was formerly the pope's private place of worship. The 28 steps are protected by boards, and the only way you're allowed to climb them is on your knees, which pilgrims do regularly – although there are staircases either side for the less penitent. At the top, **Sancta Sanctorum**, or chapel of San Lorenzo, holds an ancient (sixth- or seventh-century) painting of Christ that is attributed to an angel, hence its name – *acheiropoeton*, or "not done by human hands". You can't enter the chapel, and, fittingly perhaps, you can only really get a view of it by kneeling and peering through the grilles.

Santi Quattro Coronati

Between San Giovanni in Laterano and the Colosseum, the church of **Santi Quattro Coronati** (daily 6.15am–8pm; cloister and San Silvestro chapel Mon–Sat 9.30am–noon & 4.30–6pm, Sun 9am–10.40am & 4–5.45pm), up the steps off Via Santi Quattro Coronati, is dedicated to four soldier martyrs who died because they refused to worship a statue of Aesclapius during the persecutions of Diocletian. Originally built in 1110 by Pope Paschal II, it's a fortified, somewhat dishevelled building whose interior feels quiet and ancient, a world away from the crowds around the Colosseum below. The feel is intensified by the pretty cloister, accessed through a door in the north aisle, which is elegantly proportioned and contains a small, neat garden. The church itself has an extra-wide apse and some very old frescoes on the south and west walls, as well as giant series of apse paintings showing the martyrdom of the soldiers and a *matroneum*, or women's gallery – something rarely seen nowadays. A convent of Augustinian nuns lives here now, and it's them you sometimes have to ask for the key to get into the chapel of St Sylvester, which contains the oldest extant frescoes in Rome – painted in 1248 and relating the story of how the fourth-century pope cured the emperor Constantine of leprosy and then baptized him. Constantine is shown giving his crown to the pope in a symbolic transfer of power.

San Clemente

Back on Via San Giovanni in Laterano, the church of **San Clemente** (Mon–Sat 9am–12.30pm & 3–6pm, Sun 10am–12.30pm & 3–6pm; €5 for the lower church and temple) is a cream-coloured twelfth-century basilica that brilliantly encapsulates continuity of history in the city – it is in fact a conglomeration of three places of worship from three very different eras in the history of Rome. Pope St Clement I, to whom the church is dedicated, was the third pope after St Peter (and in fact is said to have been ordained by him), and he reigned from 90 AD until 99 AD, when he was exiled and martyred in the Crimea. His relics are kept in this church, and have been venerated here from the very earliest times.

The basilica

The **ground-floor church** is a superb example of a medieval basilica: its facade and courtyard face east in the archaic fashion, and there are some fine, warm mosaics in the apse. The choir is partitioned off with beautiful white marble slabs bearing the earliest papal insignia in the city, the monogram of Pope John II, who reigned from 533 to 535 AD. The gilded ceiling bears the arms of Pope Clement XI, from the early years of the eighteenth century, during whose papacy the church was remodelled. Perhaps the highlights of the main church, though, are the fifteenth-century frescoes in the chapel of St Catherine by Masolino, whose soft yet vivid colours show scenes from the life of St Catherine on the left: at the top, the saint – in the blue dress – attempts (in vain) to convert the emperor Maxentius to Christianity, and in fact succeeds in converting his wife (in green) – for which the wife is beheaded. In the centre St Catherine is shown being pulled apart by two wheels – hence the famous firework – until an angel intervenes and she too is beheaded (a scene shown in the far right panel).

The early church and Mithraic temple

Downstairs there's the nave of an **earlier church**, dating back to 392 AD, with a frescoed narthex depicting, among other things, the *Miracle of San Clemente* and the transferral of his body from St Peter's to San Clemente. And at the eastern end of this church, steps lead down to the labyrinthine third level, which contains a dank **Mithraic temple** of the late second century, alongside several rooms of a Roman house built after the fire of 64 AD. In the temple is a statue of Mithras slaying the Bull and the seats upon which the worshippers sat during their ceremonies. The underground river that formerly fed the lake in front of the Domus Aurea can be heard rushing to its destination in the Tiber, behind the Circo Massimo, a reminder that Rome is built on very shaky foundations indeed.

Next door to the Roman house, across a narrow alleyway, are the ground-floor **rooms** of a first-century imperial building, all of which can be explored by the spooky light of fluorescent tubes set in the ceiling and along the mossy brick walls.

Porta Asinaria and the Aurelian Wall

In the opposite direction from San Giovanni in Laterano, across the far side of the square in front of the church, the **Porta Asinaria**, one of the city's grander gateways, marks the Aurelian Wall. If you're here in the morning, you could visit the new and second-hand clothing market on **Via Sannio** (Mon–Sat until about 1.30pm). Once you've seen the market, you could continue on for five minutes to **Piazzale Metronio**, from where you can follow the line of the **Aurelian Wall** as far as **Porta San Sebastiano** and the Aurelian Wall museum (see p.116) – a twenty-minute walk.

Santa Croce in Gerusalemme

Otherwise, follow the wall on the city side by way of Viale Carlo Felice for five minutes to another key Roman church, **Santa Croce in Gerusalemme** (daily 6.45am–7.30pm), one of the seven pilgrimage churches of Rome. Santa Croce, despite its Renaissaance and Baroque adornments, feels a very ancient church – parts of it date from the fourth century AD. It is supposed to stand on the site of the palace of Constantine's mother St Helena, and houses the relics of the true cross she had brought back from Jerusalem, stored in a surreal Mussolini-era chapel up some steps at the end of the left aisle. The Renaissance apse frescoes show the discovery of the fragments, under a seated Christ, and are very fine indeed – a beautiful, technicolour, naturalistic scene showing trees and mountains and the saint at the centre, with the true cross and a kneeling cardinal. Steps behind lead down to the original level of Helena's house – now a chapel dedicated to the saint and decorated with Renaissance mosaics; the tiles on the stairs down are an inscription relating to the true cross discovery and were done at the same time as the apse frescoes.

National Museum of Musical Instruments

The first floor of the palace next door to Santa Croce is the home of the **National Museum of Musical Instruments** (Tues–Sun 8.30am–7.30pm; €4), an interesting display of Italian and European instruments with good information, much of it in English. There are early Roman and Etruscan pieces, lots of stringed instruments, and others divided into mechanical instruments, instruments used by travelling musicans, church instruments and early piano-fortes. Not what you came to Rome for, perhaps, but worth a look if you're in this part of town.

Porta Maggiore and beyond

North of here towards the rail tracks, the **Porta Maggiore** is probably the most impressive of all the city gates, built in the first century AD to carry water into Rome from the aqueducts outside, and incorporated into the Aurelian walls. The **aqueducts** that converge here are the **Aqua Claudia**, which dates from 45 AD, and the **Aqua Marcia**, from 200 BC. The Roman engineers built them one on top of the other to channel the water of the Aqua Claudia into the city in a way that did not interfere with the pre-existing Aqua Marcia – a feat recounted in the monumental tablet over the central arches.

The famous **Tomb of the Baker**, in white travertine, just outside the gate, is a monument from about 30 AD. The baker in question was a public contractor who made a fortune selling bread to the imperial government. The round holes in the tomb represent the openings of the baker's ovens – a style that strangely enough was picked up in the Mussolini era and can be seen time and again in Fascist architecture.

Beyond Porta Maggiore lie residential areas of little interest if you're in Rome for a short while, although the **Prenestino** and **Pigneto** areas are becoming increasingly gentrified and home to some trendy bars and clubs.

The Villa Borghese and north central Rome

The area outside the Aurelian walls, to the north and northeast of the city, was once a district of market gardens, olive groves and patrician villas, trailing off into open country. During the Renaissance, these vast tracts of land were appropriated as summer estates by the city's wealthy, particularly those affiliated in some way to the papal court. One of the most notable estates, the **Villa Borghese**, was the summer playground of the Borghese family and is now a public park, home to the city's most significant concentration of museums, including the **Galleria Borghese**, which houses the resplendent art collection of the aristocratic family – a Roman must-see in anyone's book – and the **Villa Giulia**, built by Pope Julius III for his summer repose and now the National Etruscan Museum. North of Villa Borghese stretch Rome's post-Unification residential districts – not of much interest in themselves, except perhaps for **Foro Italico**, which is worth visiting either to see Roma or Lazio play at its Olympic Stadium, or simply to admire Mussolini's stylish, of-its-time sports complex.

Villa Borghese

Immediately above Piazza del Popolo, the hill known as the Pincio (see p.83) marks the edge of the city's core and the beginning of a collection of parks and gardens that forms Rome's largest central open space – the **Villa Borghese**. This is made up of the grounds of the seventeenth-century palace of Scipione Borghese, which were bought by the city at the turn of the twentieth century; it celebrated its centenary in 2003 with lots of events and renovation work, and has an informative website worth checking at ⓦ www.villaborghese.it. It's a huge area, and its woods, lake and grass, criss-crossed by roads, are about as near as you can get to peace in the city centre. There are any number of attractions

RESTAURANTS & CAFÉS

La Maremma	2
Red	1
La Scala	3

ACCOMMODATION

Ostello del Foro Italico	A

for those who want to do more than just stroll or sunbathe: a tiny boating lake, a zoo – renamed the "Bioparco" in an attempt to re-brand a previously poor image (see Chapter 21, "Kids' Rome") – and some of the city's finest museums. The equestrian ring of the Galoppatoio, just beyond the Pincio Gardens, is home to a large hot-air balloon that gives twenty minutes' worth of one of the best views of the city centre you'll find (daily 9.30am–dusk).

▶ Catacombe Di Priscilla (750m)

The Museo e Galleria Borghese

The best place to make for first, if you want some focus to your wanderings, is the Casino Borghese itself, on the far eastern side, which was built in the early seventeenth century and turned over to the state when the gardens became city property in 1902 as the **Museo e Galleria Borghese**, Piazza le Scipione

Borghese 5 (Tues–Sun 9am–7pm; €8.50; pre-booked visits are obligatory, as a limited number of people are allowed in every 2hr; ☎06.32.810, ⊛www.galleriaborghese.it). Reopened several years ago after a lengthy restoration, the Borghese has taken its place as one of Rome's great treasure houses and should not be missed.

Some history

When Camillo Borghese was elected pope and took the papal name Paul V in 1605, he elevated his favourite nephew, Scipione Caffarelli Borghese, to the cardinalate and put him in charge of diplomatic, ceremonial and cultural matters at the papal court. Scipione possessed an infallible instinct for recognizing artistic quality, and, driven by ruthless passion, used fair means or foul to acquire prized works of art. He was also shrewd enough to patronize outstanding talents such as Gian Lorenzo Bernini, Caravaggio, Domenichino, Guido Reni and Peter Paul Rubens. To house the works of these artists, as well as his collection of antique sculpture and other pieces, he built the casino, or summer house, and predictably

Villa Borghese vehicle rentals

Available from the corner of Viale Obelisco and Viale Orologio and other places in the Pincio Gardens.
Bike rental €4.50 an hour, 2 hours €8, 3 hours €11.
Go Karts €2.50 for half an hour, €4 an hour.
Rollerblades €4 an hour.

he spared no expense. The palace, which was built in the early 1600s, is a celebration of the ancient splendour of the Roman Empire: over the years its art collection has been added to, and its rooms redecorated – most notably during the last quarter of the eighteenth century, when the ceilings were re-done to match the artworks in each room. The recent restoration of the sumptuous interior seemed to go on forever, but now the gallery's Roman-era mosaics, rich stucco decorations and trompe l'oeil ceilings provide the perfect surroundings in which to enjoy the artworks that Cardinal Scipione Borghese collected so voraciously.

The porch and entrance hall

Entrance is through a **porch**, which displays classical sculpture, notably several large statues of Dacian prisoners from the time of the emperor Trajan. Inside, the **entrance hall** has a splendid ceiling by Marino Rossi, painted in 1775–78, depicting the foundation and early history of Rome – Jupiter is in the centre, surrounded by various moral and spiritual attributes and historical and mythological characters such as Romulus, Remus and the she-wolf. On the floor, a series of Roman mosaics from about 320 AD depict gladiators fighting and killing various animals and each other – a circle with a line drawn through it next to the name indicates the deceased, and blood gushes gruesomely from the pierced throats and hearts of the animals. Among a number of notable statues, there's a *Bacchus* from the second century AD, a *Fighting Satyr*, and, on the wall facing the entrance door, a melodramatic piece in marble of Marcus Curtius flinging himself into the chasm (see p.98) – his horse is a Roman sculpture and the figure is by Bernini's father. There are also colossal heads of the emperors Hadrian and Antoninus Pius on the right, and a female head of the Antonine period, with a lotus flower to represent Isis, on the left.

The ground floor: the Museo Borghese

The **ground floor** beyond the entrance hall contains sculpture, a mixture of ancient Roman items and seventeenth-century works, roughly linked together with late-eighteenth-century ceiling paintings showing scenes from the Trojan War. The first room off the entrance hall, whose paintings depict the *Judgement of Paris*, has as its centrepiece Canova's famous statue of *Pauline Borghese* posed as Venus, with flimsy drapery that leaves little to the imagination.

The second ground-floor room, the **Room of the Sun**, has a marvellous statue of *David* by Bernini, finished in 1624, when the sculptor was just 25. The face is a self-portrait, said to have been carved with the help of a mirror held for him by Scipione Borghese himself, and its expression of grim determination is perfect. There's more work by Bernini in the next room, where his statue of *Apollo and Daphne* is a dramatic, poised work that captures the split second when Daphne is transformed into a laurel tree, with her fingers becoming leaves and her legs tree trunks. Mocked by Apollo, Cupid had taken revenge by firing a golden arrow which infected the god with immediate and ardent love, and shooting Daphne with a leaden one designed to hasten the rejection of amorous advances. Daphne, the daughter of a river god, called on her father to help her avoid being trapped by Apollo, who was in hot pursuit; her father changed her into a laurel tree just as Apollo took her into his arms – a desperately sad piece of drama to which Bernini's statue does full justice. This statue also caused a great scandal when it was unveiled. The poet and playwright, Maffeo Barberini, who later became Pope Urban VIII, wrote a couplet in Latin, which is inscribed on the base, claiming that all who pursue fleshly lusts are doomed to end up holding only ashes and dust.

Pauline Borghese

Pauline Borghese, the sister of Napoleon and married (reluctantly) to the reigning Prince Borghese, was a shocking woman in her day, with grand habits. There are tales of jewels and clothes, of the Negro who used to carry her from her bath, of the servants she used as footstools, and, of course, of her long line of lovers. The statue of her in the Villa Borghese was considered outrageous by everyone but herself: when asked how she could have posed almost naked, she simply replied, "Oh, there was a stove in the studio." Interestingly, the couch on which she reposes originally had a kind of clockwork mechanism inside, which allowed the statue to rotate while the viewer remained stationary.

Next door, the walls of the large **Room of the Emperors** are flanked by red porphyry seventeenth- and eighteenth-century busts of Roman emperors, facing another Bernini sculpture, *The Rape of Proserpine*, dating from 1622, a coolly virtuosic work that shows the story of the carrying off to the underworld of the beautiful nymph Proserpine, daughter of Gaia, goddess of the earth. The brutal Pluto grasps the girl in his arms, his fingers digging into the flesh of her thigh as she fights off his advances, while the three-headed form of Cerberus snaps at their feet.

In the small room next door, there's a marvellous statue of a sleeping hermaphrodite, from the first century AD, and a large porphyry Roman bathtub whose feline feet are almost modern in style. But it's back to the Berninis in the following **Aeneas Room**, where a larger-than-life statue of Aeneas, carrying his father, Anchises, out of the burning city of Troy, was sculpted by both father Pietro and his then 15-year-old son Gian Lorenzo in 1613. The statue portrays a crucial event in Roman myth when, after the defeat of the Trojans, Aeneas escaped with his family and went on a long voyage that ended up on the shores of what became Latium – his descendants eventually founding the city of Rome. The old man carries the statues representing their family household gods; the small boy carrying a flaming pot with what became the Vestal Fire is Aeneas's son Ascanius. Also here, in the far corner, is a late, in fact unfinished work by Bernini, *Truth Revealed in Time*, done late in his career when he had been accused of faulty architectural work in part of St Peter's. Truth, with a sappy look on her face, clutches the sun, representing time, to her breast.

The **Egyptian Room**, beyond, contains artefacts, friezes and paintings with an Egyptian theme, Roman floor mosaics, and a statue of a satyr on a dolphin dating from the first century AD. Further on, the **Room of Silenus** contains a variety of paintings by Cardinal Scipione's protégé Caravaggio, including the *Madonna of the Grooms* from 1605 on the right wall, a painting that at the time was considered to have depicted Christ far too realistically to hang in a central Rome church – Cardinal Scipione happily bought it for his collection. Take note also of Caravaggio's self-portrait as Bacchus as you enter, gazing lasciviously at the coy boy with the basket of fruit opposite. *St Jerome* on the far wall is captured writing at a table illuminated only by a source of light that streams in from the upper left of the picture, while *David holding the Head of Goliath* on the right wall, sent by Caravaggio to Cardinal Scipione from exile in Malta, where he had fled to escape capital punishment for various crimes, is perhaps the last painting he ever did; the head of Goliath is believed to be a self-portrait. The cardinal managed to get the artist off, but Caravaggio died of malaria after landing in Italy at Porto Ercole, north of Rome, in 1610.

The first floor: Galleria Borghese

Upstairs – reachable by a spiral staircase out of the Room of the Emperors – houses one of the richest small collections of paintings in the world. Turn left for a room with several important works by **Raphael**, his teacher Perugino and other masters of the Umbrian School from the late fifteenth and early sixteenth centuries, not least Raphael's *Deposition* over the fireplace, produced in 1507 for a noble of Perugia in memory of her son, and pillaged from Perugia cathedral by associates of Cardinal Scipione. Look also for the *Lady With a Unicorn* and *Portrait of a Man*, by Perugino, and, over the door, a copy of the artist's portrait of a tired-out Julius II, painted in the last year of the pope's life, 1513. The room also contains a beautiful, sensitive *Virgin with Child* by Guiliano Romano, while

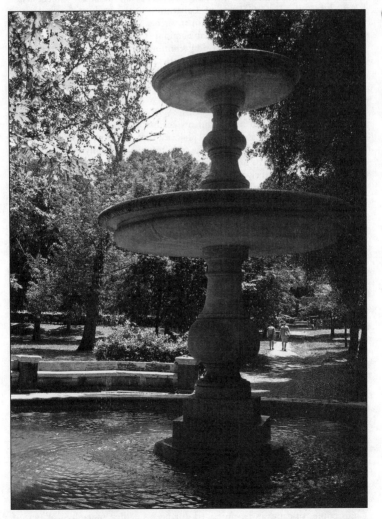

△ Villa Borghese

nearby Andrea del Sarto tackles the same subject with slightly more gusto. The next room contains more early-sixteenth-century paintings, prominent among which are Cranach's *Venus and Cupid with a Honeycomb*, from 1531, and Brescianino's *Venus and Two Cupids*, from about 1520 – both remarkable at the time for their departure from classical models in their treatment of their subjects. The Cranach *Venus*, dressed in a diaphanous robe, shows Cupid carrying a honeycomb, demonstrating the dangers of carnal love. Opposite, they are complemented perfectly by Corregio's saucy *Danae*.

Retracing your steps, look out for two early-sixteenth-century copies of Leonardo's *Leda and the Swan* (the original has been lost), Lorenzo Lotto's touching *Portrait of a Man*, a soulful study that hints at grief over a wife lost in childbirth, symbolized by the tiny skull and rose petals under the subject's right hand, and, in the large **Gallery of Lanfranco** at the back of the building, a series of self-portraits done by Bernini at various stages of his long life. Next to these are a lifelike bust of Cardinal Scipione executed by Bernini in 1632, accurately portraying him as a worldly connoisseur of fine art and fine living, and a smaller bust of Pope Paul V, also by Bernini. Next door's *Young Man and Faun* is the sculptor's earliest-known work, from 1615.

Beyond here a small room has Dosso Dossi's *SS Cosma e Damiano* and Jacopo Bassano's lively and naturalistic *Last Supper*, while further on there are two paintings by Domenichino: the *Cuman Sibyl* and a large *Diana*, the latter showing the goddess and her attendants celebrating and doing a bit of target practice – one of them has just shot a pheasant through the head and everybody else is jumping with enthusiasm; in the foreground a young nymph, lasciviously bathing, looks out with a lustful expression. Scipione was so keen on the work that he apparently imprisoned the artist until he agreed to sell it. Next, the **Room of Psyche** has, along with works by Bellini and the other Venetians of the early 1500s, Titian's *Sacred and Profane Love*, painted in 1514 when he was about 25 years old, to celebrate the marriage of the Venetian noble Nicolo Aurelio (whose coat of arms is on the sarcophagus). It shows his bride, Laura Bagarotto, dressed in white representing Sacred Love, and Venus, representing Profane Love, carrying a lamp symbolizing the eternal Love of God. The bride cradles a bowl of jewels that refer to the fleeting happiness of life on earth.

Museo Carlo Bilotti

Recently opened in the orangery of the Villa Borghese, the **Museo Carlo Bilotti** (Tues–Sun 9am–7pm; €6) is, like the Galleria Borghese, made up of a family bequest, this time of Carlo Bilotti – a perfume and cosmetics baron who, until his death in 2006, collected art and hobnobbed with the brightest and best in the international art world. Portraits of him by Larry Rivers, and of his wife and daughter by Andy Warhol, open the exhibition and add to the slightly self-congratulatory air of the place. However, the paintings are beautifully displayed, and act as a nice adjunct to the Modern Art Museum ten minutes' walk away, since most of the 22 works exhibited here are by the great modern Italian painter Giorgio de Chirico. It's a small but varied collection of his work, and you get a good sense of de Chirico's versatility, from the impressionistic *Nude Woman from Behind* to his almost perversely traditional *Self-Portrait with the Head of Minerva* and the pastiche Canaletto scene that hangs next to it. The weird stuff with which he made his name is here too, including *Metaphysics with Biscuits* and *Melancholy of a Street*, and plays on the *Archeologists* theme you might have seen in the modern art museum, although these are 1960s copies of canvases he produced during his earlier 'metaphysical' period.

Eating and drinking, Roman style

Rome is rightly proud of its own cuisine, and has a large number of great, well-established restaurants serving local specialities to a clientele that would be satisfied with nothing less. Roman cooking is dominated by the earthy preferences of the working classes, with a little influence from the city's millennia-old Jewish population thrown in. Pasta is a staple, and sauces are hearty and satisfying, while Roman meat choices famously lean towards various unspeakable parts of cows and lambs.

Pasta

Although you'll find all sorts of **pasta** served in Roman restaurants, spaghetti is probably the most popular, as it stands up well to the coarse, gutsy sauces the Romans prefer: *aglio e olio* (oil and garlic), *cacio e pepe* (pecorino and ground black pepper), *alla carbonara* (with beaten eggs, cubes of pan-fried *guanciale* – cured pork jowl – or bacon, and pecorino cheese), *alla*

▲ A plateful of pasta

gricia (with pecorino and *guanciale*) and *all'amatriciana* (with tomato and *guanciale*). *Spaghetti alle vongole* (with baby clams) is common and always good, best when a little peperoncino is added to give the clams an extra kick, and there's also *maccheroni alla ciociara*, with slices of sausage, prosciutto and tomato. *Pasta al pajata* (with calf's intestines) is an old Roman standard, as are *gnocchi*, in Rome usually served with a meat sauce and traditionally eaten on Thursdays.

Main courses

Perhaps the most common Roman **meat** dish is *abbacchio*, milk-fed lamb roasted to melting tenderness with rosemary, sage and garlic. You'll also find *scottadito*, grilled lamb chops eaten with the fingers, and *saltimbocca alla romana*, thin slices of veal

Top five restaurants serving Roman specialities

Checchino dal 1887 Via Monte Testaccio 30 ⓣ06.574.6318. See p.247.
Da Giggetto Via del Portico d'Ottavia 21a–22 ⓣ06.686.1105. See p.240.
Matricianella Via del Leone 4 ⓣ06.683.2100. See p.243.
Da Paris Piazza San Calisto 7a ⓣ06.581.5378. See p.246.
Al Pompiere Via Santa Maria dei Calderari 38 ⓣ06.686.8377. See p.241.

cooked with a slice of prosciutto and sage on top, served plain or with a Marsala sauce. But to the rest of Italy Rome means offal, and although it has been ousted from many of the more refined city-centre restaurants, you'll still find it on the menus of traditional places, especially those in the old slaughterhouse district of Testaccio. One of the most common – and palatable – dishes is *coda alla vaccinara*, oxtail stewed in a rich sauce of tomato and celery. You'll also come across *pajata*, the intestines of an unweaned calf, often with pasta, as well as *lingua* (tongue), *rognone* (kidney), *milza* (spleen – delicious as a pâté on toasted bread) and *trippa* (tripe). Look out too for *testerelle d'abbacchio*, lamb's head baked in the oven with herbs and oil; and *coratella*, lamb's heart, liver, lungs and spleen cooked in olive oil with lots of black pepper and onions. More conventionally, fish also features, almost always as cod or *baccala* and best eaten Jewish-style, deep-fried in batter: like British fish and chips without the chips.

Pizza, snacks and *fritti*

Rome is surpassed only by Naples in the quality of its **pizzas** – and even this is arguable if you prefer the thin and crispy Roman variety. There are many traditional pizzerias in the city centre, most of them open evenings only and serving the thin-crust Roman pizza – best when baked in a wood-burning oven (*cotta a legna*). As with most Italian pizza, it's tastiest at its simplest; just a cheese and tomato topping with a bit of sausage or mushroom added, or with that most Roman of ingredients, *fiori di zucca* (courgette flowers). You can also find great pizza by the slice (*pizza al taglio*), always sold by weight, and either *pizza rossa* – with some sort of tomato-based sauce – or *pizza bianca*: unadulterated by anything other than a drizzle of oil and some rosemary. A lot of places sell *pizza al taglio* alongside other Roman streetfood and basic treats, including various deep-fried specialities, or **fritti**, like *suppli* (fried rice balls with mozzarella) and *arancini* (fried rice balls also with cheese but with added tomato), as well as spit-roast chicken and *porchetta* – pork stuffed with herbs and roasted on a spit – which you'll find most commonly outside the city (for example Frascati), where it's munched between thick hunks of rustic bread.

◀ Preparing pizza

Vegetables

Artichokes (*carciofi*) are the quintessential Roman **vegetable**, best in spring but served all year – "alla romana" (stuffed with garlic and roman mint and stewed) and in all their unadulterated glory as *alla giudea*, flattened and deep fried in olive oil. Another not-to-be-missed side dish is batter-fried squash or courgette blossom, stuffed with mozzarella and a sliver of anchovy. Among other vegetables, you can find heavenly roast potatoes, cooked with lots of rosemary and usually served with lamb or roast chicken, great fresh asparagus in spring, broccoli in winter and various haricot and borlotti bean dishes year-round.

Cheese and desserts

The king of Roman **cheeses** is pecorino Romano, sharp, salty and crumbly and used in cooking instead of Parmesan. The very best mozzarella from Campania has also become more common in Rome. Made from the milk of the buffalo that roam around Naples, it's best eaten when fresh, and Rome is lucky to be near enough for it to be rushed up here to be enjoyed as soon as possible. As for desserts, you may want to try a **tartufo** – chocolate ice cream covered in chocolate, basically – or just have an ice cream. The city centre's *gelaterie* are among Italy's best, and there's nothing like enjoying your dessert Italian-style, strolling through the streets after the sun has gone down.

Vintage Rome

Much of the **wine** served in Rome comes from the Castelli Romani just south of the city. The best known is **Frascati**, a light, easy-drinking white made from a blend of Malvasia and Trebbiano grapes – like many Italian wines it's much better than the exported varieties would have you believe. The small town of Marino (p.214) has a great **wine festival** on the first Sunday of October, at which you can sample Castelli Romani wines to your heart's content. Elsewhere in Lazio, the big wine is called **Est! Est! Est!**, another drinkable white that hails from Montefiascione. The story goes that in the twelfth century a bishop's servant was sent to find the best wines of the region, and to indicate the ones he liked by daubing the word "Est" on the door of the producer. He liked the wines of Montefiascione so much he daubed the word three times for emphasis. Hopefully you'll feel the same.

If you're a fan, the Casa de Chirico (see p.80) is a kilometre or so southwest of here, near the Spanish Steps.

Museo Pietro Canonica

Another newly opened Villa Borghese museum, the **Museo Pietro Canonica** occupies the house and studio of the nineteenth-century Italian sculptor (daily 9am–7pm; €3). Canonica was an establishment artist and as such not only did the city bequeath him this impressive, castellated bolt-hole to live in, but the museum devoted to him is virtually a roll-call of European historical names. Canonica seemingly knew everyone and sculpted everybody, and one room alone contains busts of a king of England (Edward VII), the man who took Turkey to independence (Mustafa Kemal Atatürk), numerous Italian royals and nineteenth-century dignitaries, and Pope Benedict XV (a supplement to the artist's memorial to him in St Peter's). Other rooms document nineteenth-century world history – Simon Bolivar astride a stallion (1954), Atatürk again, this time leading the Turkish charge, and an equestrian statue of King Faisal of Iraq (1933) – to name only the most prominent examples of an epic collection.

The museum also includes Canonica's studio on the ground floor, still with his tools and the piece he was working on when he died in 1959, along with a couple of portraits of the great man and some of his own botched attempts at landscapes – which show that he was probably right to stick to sculpture. Upstairs are the apartments he occupied with his wife, who continued to live here until she died in 1987. The rooms are left much as they were then, with original furniture, the living room with a piano and a score of music on it (Canonica was also an accomplished musician and composer) and family photographs. Oddly, there is only one that shows Canonica himself, a holiday snap taken in the mountains, on the right side of the dining room.

The Galleria Nazionale d'Arte Moderna

The Villa Borghese's two other major museums are situated on the northwestern side of the park, along the Viale delle Belle Arti, in the so-called "Academy Ghetto" – the Romanian, British, Dutch, Danish, Egyptian and other cultural academies are all situated here. The **Galleria Nazionale d'Arte Moderna**, Via delle Belle Arti 131 (Tues–Sun 8.30am–7.30pm; €6.50; ⓦ www.gnam.arti.beniculturali.it) is probably the least obviously appealing building here, a huge, lumbering, Neoclassical construction housing a wide selection of nineteenth- and twentieth-century Italian (and a few foreign) names. However, the museum's compact and suprisingly engaging collection is beautifully displayed – and can make a refreshing change after several days of having the senses bombarded with Etruscan, Roman and Renaissance art. There is also a reasonably priced café, the *Caffè delle Arti*, out the back door at Via Gramsci 73, which is part of the gallery complex and is the best place to grab something to eat and drink if you're wilting.

The **ground floor** is given over to nineteenth-century works, with the left side concentrating on works up to 1883, including early pieces by the so-called Macchiaioli School of Tuscany – Fattori, Lega, Cecioni, Nino Costa – with a giant statue of Hercules by Canova in the large central hall. Rooms on the right side are devoted to later nineteenth-century paintings, including more work from Fattori and other like-minded Italian impressionists, while the large hall is dominated by Ettore Ferrari's 1886 model for his statue of Bruno Giordano on

Campo de' Fiori (see p.71) and some mighty battle scenes promoting the glory and sacrifice of the Italian Unification, including Fattori's *Battle of Custoza*. The rooms beyond contain a handful of paintings by Courbet, Degas, Van Gogh and Cézanne, as well as the Dutchman Mesdag, amongst Italian works of the same period, although the peculiar mystic paintings of the 'divisionist' Gaetano Previati stand out – indeed they're so odd they get an entire room to themselves.

The museum's twentieth-century collection on the upper level has sculptural works by Rodin and the Croatian Ivan Mestrovic, but the most significant parts of the collections are Italian. These include early works by Giacomo Balla, with a view of the Villa Borghese, divided into fifteen different panels, and some painterly portraits from everyday life – *La Pazza* and *Il Mendicante*. The swirling, Futurist abstract works he painted five years later hang in the next room, alongside paintings by his student Boccioni. There are also pieces by Carlo Carrá and Giorgio Morandi, while Giorgio de Chirico (see p.80) dominates one room. Later rooms focus on the art of the 1930s, some of it – like Libero Andreotti's *Affrico e Mensola* and Sironi's *The Constructor* – iconic and fascistic in look and intent, before leading on to the totally abstract paintings of Jackson Pollock, Mark Rothko and Cy Twombly, Rome's own American artist, who lived in the city for most of his life.

Museo Nazionale Etrusco di Villa Giulia

The **Villa Giulia**, five minutes' walk away towards Via Flaminia, is a harmonious collection of courtyards, loggias, gardens and temples put together in a playful Mannerist style for Pope Julius III in the mid-sixteenth century, and arguably a more essential stop than the Modern Art Museum. It's home to the **Museo Nazionale Etrusco di Villa Giulia**, Piazzale Villa Giulia 9 (Tues–Sun 8.30am–7.30pm; €4), which, along with the Etruscan collection in the Vatican, is the world's primary collection of Etruscan treasures, and a good introduction – or conclusion – to the Etruscan sites in Lazio, which between them contributed most of the artefacts on display here. It's not an especially large collection, but it's worth taking the trouble to see the whole.

The east wing

The entrance room of the **east wing** houses two pieces of Etruscan sculpture, one showing a man astride a seahorse, a recurring theme in ancient Mediterranean art,

---

The Etruscans

The **Etruscans** remain something of a historical mystery. We know that they lived in central Italy – in Etruria – from around 900 BC until their incorporation into the Roman world in 88 BC. However, whether they were native to the region, or whether they had originally migrated here from overseas, specifically from Asia Minor, remains a matter of debate. The Romans borrowed heavily from their civilization, and thus in many ways the influence of the Etruscans is still felt today: our alphabet, for example, is based on the Etruscan system, and bishops' crooks and the "fasces" symbol (a bundle of rods with an axe that is found, among other places, behind the speaker's rostrum in the US House of Representatives) are just two other Etruscan symbols that endure. The Etruscans were also masters of working in terracotta, gold and bronze, and accomplished carvers in stone, and it is these skills – together with their obvious sensuality and the ease with which they appeared to enjoy life – that make a visit to the Villa Giulia so beguiling.

and an oddly amateurish centaur – basically a man pasted to the hindquarters of a horse – both from Vulci and dating from the sixth century BC. The next rooms contain bronze objects from the seventh and sixth centuries BC – urns used to contain the ashes of cremated persons, among which a beautiful bronze example, in the shape of a finely detailed dwelling hut, stands out – and a number of terra-cotta votive offerings of anatomical parts of the human body, their detail alluding to the Etruscans' accomplishments in medicine. A gold dental bridge shows their skill at dentistry too.

The next room displays items found in Veio – among them Hercules and Apollo disputing over the sacred hind which Apollo had shot and Hercules claimed. Next door, in the octagonal room, the remarkable *Sarcophagus of the Married Couple* (dating from the sixth century BC, and actually containing the ashes of the deceased rather than the bodies), is from Cerveteri, and is one of the most famous pieces in the museum – a touchingly lifelike portrayal of a husband and wife lying on a couch. He has his right arm around her; she is offering him something from her right hand, probably an egg – a recurring theme in Etruscan art. Their clothes are modelled down to the finest detail, including the laces and soles of their shoes, and the pleats of the linen and lacy pillowcases. In case you're wondering, the holes in the backs of their heads, and at other spots, are ventilation holes to prevent the terracotta from exploding when the hollow piece was fired. Beyond are more finds from Cerveteri: hundreds of vases, pots, drinking vessels and other items, and, among a number of busts and images, clearly portraits of real people, a depiction of a man, complete with cauliflower right ear, and a finely stitched cut to the right of his mouth – clearly a tough customer.

Upstairs, in the balcony over the married couple sarcophagus, there are displays on the Etruscan language, and the *cistae* recovered from tombs around Praeneste – drum-like objects, engraved and adorned with figures, that were supposed to hold everything the body needed after death – including a special area devoted to the beautiful and justifiably famous *Ficorini Cista*, made by an Etruscan craftsman named Novios Plautios for a lady named Dindia Malconia and probably a wedding present. In the same room, marvellously intricate pieces of gold jewellery have been worked into tiny horses, birds, camels and other animals. Further on you'll find mostly bronzes, mirrors, candelabra, religious statues and tools used in everyday life. Notice, particularly, the elongated statues of priests and priestesses, some of whom hold eels in their hands and are engaged in some kind of rite. There is also a realistic bronze statuette of a ploughman at work, plodding along behind his oxen.

After this hall you are at the bottom of the "U" curve that forms the building's outline, and holds an enormous collection of **jewellery** – all of it fascinating. Branching off are items and reconstructions from the enormous temple excavated at Pyrgi, Cerveteri's seaport, in the 1960s, including replicas of gold foil plates thought at one time to offer a Rosetta Stone-like key to the Etruscan language – the plates are in three different languages, Etruscan, Punic and Greek, and represent some of the oldest pre-Roman inscriptions ever found. In the rooms to the west of here are items from the very earliest Etruscan collections, together with the story of how everything was brought together, a model of the villa, and original architectural drawings by, among others, Michelangelo.

The atrium and beyond

Exiting the U-shaped room you will find several hundred examples of Etruscan pottery, terracottas and bronze items, including charcoal braziers and pieces of armour, and, remarkably, a trumpet that has not sounded for two thousand years. This gallery will lead you to the steps down to the upper floor of the west wing, which is devoted to the **Faliscians**, a people from northeast Lazio who spoke a dialect of Latin but were culturally Etruscans. This part of the museum was reorganized relatively recently and is clearly labelled in English, with good information in each room from the excavations at Narce, Falerii Nuovi, Civita Castellana and other sites in the Faliscian area. The displays include a drinking horn in the shape of a dog's head that is so lifelike you almost expect it to bark; a *holmos*, or small table, to which the maker attached 24 little pendants; and a bronze disc breastplate from the seventh century BC decorated with a weird, almost modern abstract pattern of galloping creatures.

In the **atrium**, two storeys high, are finds from the temples at Sassi Caduti and the Sanctuary of Apollo in Civita Castellana – Etruscan artistry at its best, with gaudily coloured terracotta figures that leer, run, jump and climb; a beautiful, lifelike torso of Apollo, dating from around the turn of the fourth century BC; and a bust of Juno which has the air of a dignified matron, the flower pattern on her dress still visible, as are her earrings, necklace and crown. Further are display cases containing articles found outside Etruria but obviously of Etruscan origin or influence.

The west wing ground floor

The ground floor of the **west wing** displays more artefacts with obvious connections to the Etruscans, including North African ostrich eggs, an Etruscan symbol of resurrection and rebirth, and mirrors, some of which have mythological events etched on their backs. The next series of galleries has items from Lake Nemi and the Alban Hills in southern Lazio, with an oak log that was used as a coffin and cases of terracotta votive offerings – anatomical parts, babies in swaddling clothes and models of temples and houses. There are also more *cistae*, gold breastplates and belt buckles, bronze pots with griffins' heads looking in to see what's cooking, and a wonderful bronze throne with elaborately worked scenes of hunting, military parades and horse racing.

Parioli and north

The area north of Villa Borghese is the **PARIOLI** district, whose quiet, winding streets, large villas and lush, leafy gardens make up one of Rome's wealthier neighbourhoods. However, it's not of that much interest to anyone who doesn't live there, and unless you're dining at one of its top restaurants, the main reason you might visit is to attend a concert at the city's new Auditorium complex.

Villa Ada

Immediately east of Parioli stretches the enormous public park of the **Villa Ada**, connected with Villa Borghese by Via Salaria – the old trading route between the Romans and Sabines, so called because the main product transported along here was salt. The Villa Ada was once the estate of King Vittorio Emanuele III and is a nice enough place in which to while away an afternoon, with a bucolic atmosphere that is a world away from the busy streets of the city centre. But otherwise it's not really worth the special journey from the centre of town, unless you want to visit the catacombs, the Egyptian embassy or Rome's only mosque, housed in its grounds.

The Catacombe di Priscilla

The **Catacombe di Priscilla** (Tues–Sun 8.30am–noon & 2.30–5pm; €5), which you can reach from Via Salaria, are a frescoed labyrinth of tunnels that can be visited on regular (obligatory) guided tours. No one quite knows why these catacombs are here, or whether they are Christian or pagan in origin. The so-called **Greek Chapel** has a number of obviously Christian frescoes – Daniel in the lions' den, the resurrection of Lazarus, Noah, the sacrifice of Isaac – painted between the second and fourth centuries AD. However, other paintings are harder to pin down – one that is claimed as the earliest known depiction of the *Virgin and Child* could simply be a picture of a mother and child, both of whom were probably buried here.

The Auditorium

Ten minutes' walk from the western end of Viale dei Parioli, on the far side of the Villa Glori park, Rome's new **Auditorium** (daily 10am–6pm; free; ☏06.80.242; ⓦ www.auditoriumroma.com) is in fact three auditoriums built in one complex, their large bulbous shapes making them look like three giant, lead-skinned armadillos crouched together. Designed by everyone's favourite Italian architect, Renzo Piano, and opened in spring 2006, it's a clever building: the foyers all join up and, above, the three buildings make a large amphitheatre, used for outdoor performances given in the piazza below. It's clever, too, in the way it has incorporated the remains of a Republican-era villa between two of the concert halls, which was discovered when building began, and actually halted the project for two years while it was excavated.

Each concert hall is conceived and designed for a different kind of musical performance: the smallest, the *Sala Petrassi* on the right side, accommodates 700 people and is designed for chamber concerts, the middle *Sala Sinopoli* holds 1200, while the largest of the three, the eastern *Sala Santa Cecilia*, can seat 2700 listening to big symphonic works, and is now home to Rome's flagship orchestra, the Academy of Santa Cecilia. You can walk right around the building outside, exploring the Parco della Musica, as it's known. The main entrance is on Via Pietro de Coubertin, where there's a great book and CD shop and decent café, or you can cut through to the park from Viale Maresciallo Pilsudksi, where there's a children's playground.

Ponte Milvio

To the west of the Parioli district the Tiber sweeps around in a wide hook-shaped bend. These northern outskirts of Rome aren't particularly enticing, though the **Ponte Milvio**, the old, originally Roman, footbridge where the emperor Constantine defeated Maxentius in 312 AD, still stands and provides wonderful views of the meandering Tiber, with the city springing up green on the hills to both sides and the silty river running fast below. Inside a **guardhouse** on the right (northern) bank of the Tiber, a marble plaque bears the arms of the Borgia family – including the papal badge in the centre, the shield of Callisto III – featuring a bull – on the right and the arms of Rodrigio Borgia, who later became Pope Alexander VI but was at the time his father's secretary of state, on the left. On the northern side of the river, **Piazzale di Ponte Milvio** has a cheap and cheerful market (Mon–Sat 8am–1.30pm) and a handful of bars and restaurants.

Foro Italico

It's just ten minutes' walk from the Ponte Milvio – past the huge Italian Foreign Ministry building – to the **Foro Italico** sports centre, one of the few parts of Rome to survive intact pretty much the way Mussolini planned it. This is still used as a sports centre, but it's worth visiting as much for its period feel and architecture as anything else. Its centrepiece is the **Ponte Duca di' Aosta**, which connects Foro Italico to the town side of the river, and is headed by a white marble obelisk capped with a gold pyramid that is engraved MUSSOLINI DUX in beautiful 1930s calligraphy. The marble finials at the side of each end of the bridge show soldiers in various heroic acts, loading machine guns and cannons, charging into the face of enemy fire, carrying the wounded and so forth, each bearing the face of Mussolini himself – a very eerie sight indeed.

Beyond the bridge, an avenue patched with more mosaics revering the *Duce* leads up to a fountain surrounded by images of muscle-bound figures revelling in sporting activities. Either side of the fountain are the two main stadiums: the larger of the two, the **Stadio Olimpico** on the left, was used for the Olympic Games in 1960 and is still the venue for Rome's two football teams on alternate Sundays (see Chapter 20, "Sports and Outdoor Activities"). The smaller **Stadio dei Marmi** ("stadium of marbles") is ringed by sixty great male statues, groins modestly hidden by fig leaves, in a variety of elegantly macho poses – each representing both a sport and a province of Italy. It's a typically Fascist monument in many ways, but a rather ironic choice for what was a notoriously homophobic government.

10

Trastevere and the Janiculum Hill

Across the river from the centre of town, on the right bank of the Tiber, **TRASTEVERE** is a smallish district, sheltered under the heights of the Janiculum Hill. It was the artisan area of the city in classical times, neatly placed for the trade that came upriver from Ostia and was unloaded nearby. Located outside the city walls, Trastevere (the name means literally "across the Tiber") was for centuries heavily populated by immigrants, and this uniqueness and separation lent the neighbourhood a strong identity that lasted well into this century. It has moved from its working-class roots, and the many bars and restaurants can at night be thronged with tourists, lured by the charm of its narrow streets and closeted squares. However, even if the local Festa de' Noantri ("celebration of we others"), held every July, seems to symbolize the slow decline of local spirit rather than celebrate its existence, there is good reason to come to Trastevere. It is among the more pleasant places to stroll in Rome, peaceful in the morning, lively come the evening, as dozens of trattorias set tables out along the cobblestone streets, and still buzzing late at night, when its bars and clubs provide a focus for one of Rome's most dyanamic night-time scenes: see Chapters 14–16 for details.

East of Viale di Trastevere

The quietest part of Trastevere lies on the southeastern side of **Viale di Trastevere**, the wide boulevard that cuts through the centre of the district. Just the other side of the Tiber from the Aventine Hill and Testaccio, it feels oddly cut off from the city centre, a small knot of peeling streets and echoing squares that are a peaceful contrast to the relatively spruced-up Trastevere proper. You can get here either by walking across the Ponte Garibaldi and turning left off Viale di Trastevere, by way of Isola Tiberina or Ponte Palatino, or from Testaccio, from where a short stroll over the Ponte Sublico leaves you right by the Porta Portese.

ACCOMMODATION
Antico Borgo
  di Trastevere   E
Artù   D J
Carmel   J
Casa Di Santa
  Francesca Romana   H G
Cisterna   F
Domus Tiberina   G
Grand Hotel del
  Gianicolo   L M K C A I B
Ripa
San Francesco
Santa Maria
Suore Pallotine
Trastevere
Villa della Fonte

Sant'Onofrio

Villa Lante

Puppet Shows

Monument to
Giuseppe
Garibaldi

PIAZZALE
GIUSEPPE
GARIBALDI

Orte
Botanico

Palazzo
Corsini

Villa
Farnesina

Casa della
Fornarina

VIA CORSINI

Santa Maria
della Scala

Sant'
Egidio

Santa
Maria in Trastevere

JANICULUM HILL

VIA DI PORTA S.PANCRAZIO

San Pietro
in Montorio

LARGO DI
PORTA SAN
PANCRAZIO

Fontana
Paola

Memorial

VIA DI SAN PANCRAZIO

PIAZZALE
PURELIO

VIA ANGELO MASINA

American
Academy

PIAZZA
FRANCESCO
CUCCHI

LARGO
MINUTILLI

VIA CALANDRELLI

Ministero
della Pubblica
Istruzione

TRASTEVERE & THE JANICULUM HILL

BARS

Art Café Friends	9
Blue Knight	2
Enoteca Ferrara	12
Enoteca Trastevere	31
Gianicolo	28
Ombre Rosse	16
Mr Brown	11
San Calisto	22
Stardust	13

RESTAURANTS & CAFÉS

Akropolis	34
Anita Garibaldi	4
Antico Arco	26
ATM Sushi Bar	3
Da Augusto	15
Bibli	29
Cassetta de' Trastevere	17
Ci-Lin	19
Ferrara	12
Fidelio	23
Frontoni Dal 1921	33
Ivo	30
Da Lucia	18
Ai Marmi	27
Di Marzio	20
Da Olindo	6
La Renella	14
Da Paris	24
Dar Poeta	7
Il Ponentino	21
Romolo	5
Pizzeria San Callisto	25
Alla Scala	8
La Scala	10
Sisini	32
Tasso's Oak	1

TRASTEVERE AND THE JANICULUM HILL

10

169

Via Portese

Porta Portese

Trastevere at its most disreputable but also at its traditional best can be witnessed on Sunday, when the **Porta Portese** flea market stretches from the Porta Portese gate down Via Portuense to Trastevere train station in a congested medley of antiques, old motor spares, cheap clothing, trendy clothing, cheap *and* trendy clothing, household goods, bric-a-brac and assorted junk. Haggling is the rule, and keep a good hold of your wallet or purse. Come early if you want to buy, or even move – most of the bargains, not to mention the stolen goods, have gone by 10am, by which time the crush of people can be intense.

San Francesco a Ripa

Not far from Piazza di Porta Portese, the fairly ordinary church of **San Francesco a Ripa** (Mon–Sat 7am–1pm & 4–7.30pm, Sun 7am–noon & 4–7pm) is best known for the fact that St Francis himself once stayed here. You can see the actual room he slept in (through the sacristy and up some steep stairs), which includes the rock he used as a pillow and embroidery that is apparently the work of Santa Chiara. It's also the burial place of the twentieth-century Italian artist Giorgio di Chirico (see p.80), who lived in Rome until his death in the 1970s and is buried behind the first chapel on the left, in a simple white room named after the painter. But perhaps the most visually memorable item in the church is the writhing, orgasmic statue of a minor saint, the Blessed Ludovica Albertoni, that Bernini sculpted towards the end of his career. As a work of Baroque sauciness, it bears comparison with his more famous *Ecstasy of St Teresa* in the church of Santa Maria in Vittoria; indeed it's perhaps even more shameless in its depiction of an earthily realized divine ecstasy – the woman is actually kneading her breasts.

Santa Cecilia in Trastevere

Five minutes north of San Francesco, on its own quiet piazza off Via dei Genovesi, is the church of **Santa Cecilia in Trastevere** (daily 9.30am–12.30pm & 4–6.30pm), a cream, rather sterile church – apart from a pretty front courtyard – whose antiseptic eighteenth-century appearance belies its historical associations. A church was originally built here over the site of the second-century home of St Cecilia, whose husband Valerian was executed for refusing to worship Roman gods and who herself was subsequently persecuted for her Christian beliefs. The story has it that Cecilia was locked in the caldarium (hot room) of her own baths for several days but refused to die, singing her way through the ordeal (Cecilia is the patron saint of music). Her head was finally half hacked off with an axe, though it took several blows before she finally succumbed. Below the high altar, under a Gothic baldachino, Stefano Maderno's limp, almost modern statue of the saint shows her incorruptible body as it was found when exhumed in 1599, with three deep cuts in her neck – a fragile, intensely human piece of work that has helped make Cecilia one of the most revered Roman saints. Behind all this presides an apse mosaic from the ninth century showing Paschal I, who founded the current church, being presented to Christ by St Cecilia flanked by various saints.

The excavations of the baths and the rest of the Roman house are on view in the crypt below (€2.50) – a series of dank rooms with some fragments of mosaic and a gaudily decorated chapel at the far end. More alluring by far is the singing gallery above the nave of the church (Mon–Sat 10.15am–12.15pm, Sun 11.15am–12.15pm; €2.50, ring the bell to the left of the church door to get in), where Pietro Cavallini's late-thirteenth-century fresco of the Last Judgement is all that remains of the decoration that once covered the entire church. It's a powerful painting, an amazingly fluid, naturalistic piece of work for the time, with each of the Apostles, ranked six each side of Christ, captured as an individual portrait, while Christ sits in quiet, meditative majesty in the centre, flanked by angels.

Following Via dei Genovesi back towards Viale Trastevere, you pass the church and ancient hospital of **San Giovanni dei Genovesi** on the left, set up to care for sailors from Genova in the fifteenth century, from which the street takes its name. This in itself isn't of much interest and in any case is rarely open. But just past the church on the right its **cloister** (Tues, Thurs & Sun 3–6pm; closed Aug; ring the bell marked "sposi magnanti") is a lovely and very peaceful spot, a two-tiered quadrangle filled with orange and lime trees.

West of Viale Trastevere

The most obvious way to approach Trastevere is to cross over from Isola Tiberina or from the pedestrian Ponte Sisto at the end of Via Giulia, both of which leave you five minutes from the heart of the neighbourhood. There's a bit more life on this west side of **Viale Trastevere**, centred on the **Piazza Santa Maria in Trastevere**, the heart of old Trastevere, named after the church in its northwest corner.

Piazza Belli

Right by the river, the traffic junction of **Piazza Belli** marks the beginning of Viale Trastevere. The brick building with the crenellations and tower is known as the **Casa di Dante**, although it's doubtful that the poet ever stayed here, and the top-hatted statue opposite is of the Roman poet Giuseppe Giocachino Belli – "the poet of the people of Rome", according to the inscription – who in the nineteenth century produced thousands of sonnets recording life in the city in dialect.

San Crisogono

On Viale di Trastevere itself, 100m or so from the river, the church of **San Crisogono** (daily 7.30–11.30am & 4–7pm; excavations €2) is a large, typically Roman basilica, with a nave lined with ancient columns and one of the city's finest Cosmati mosaic floors. The church itself is relatively feature-less apart from a beautiful thirteenth-century apse mosaic showing the church's saint and St James, and it's the remains of the earlier buildings below that mark the church out – two buildings really, an early Christian structure from the third century AD and a later fifth-century basilica whose substantial remnants cover almost the entire footprint of the main church. There are some very worn frescoes – San Crisogono himself in the centre of the apse, and a saint healing a sick man (covered in spots) in the north aisle, as well as various bits of Roman stonework, including a couple of impressively carved sarcophagi.

Santa Maria in Trastevere

The church of **Santa Maria in Trastevere** (daily 7am–9pm) is held to be the first Christian place of worship in Rome, built on a site where a fountain of oil is said to have sprung on the day of Christ's birth. The greater part of the structure now dates from 1140, after a rebuilding by Innocent II, a pope from Trastevere. These days many people come here for the church's mosaics, which are among the city's most impressive: those on the cornice were completed a century or so after the rebuilding and show the Madonna surrounded by ten female figures with lamps – once thought to represent *The Wise and Foolish Virgins*. Inside, there's a nineteenth-century copy of a Cosmatesque pavement of spirals and circles, and more twelfth-century mosaics in the apse, Byzantine-inspired works which depict a solemn yet sensitive parade of saints thronged around Christ and Mary, while underneath a series of panels shows scenes from the life of the Virgin by the painter Pietro Cavallini. Beneath the high altar on the right, an inscription – "FONS OLEI" – marks the spot where the oil is supposed to have sprung up, to the right of which there is a chapel crowned with the crest of the British monarchy – placed here by Henry, cardinal of York, when he and his family, the Stuarts, lived in exile in Rome.

Museo di Roma in Trastevere

A short walk from Santa Maria in Trastevere, the long triangle of Piazza di Sant'Egidio is home to the small **Museo di Roma in Trastevere** (Tues–Sun 10am–8pm; €3), a small collection of artefacts illustrating Roman folklore – paintings of nineteenth-century life, models of popular Roman sights, and, best of all, life-sized tableaux showing scenes of nineteenth-century Roman life – an *osteria*, a pharmacy, a saltarello dance and the like. There is also a permanent display of the watercolours of one Ettore Roesler Franz, which capture a rustic Rome – when the countryside started beyond the Aurelian Walls – that almost entirely disappeared with the turn of the century developments of the city centre. All in all, the museum is much more accessible and engaging than the displays of its counterpart in the centre (see p.60), and it has decent regular temporary exhibitions too.

Pizza Trilussa

Facing the pedestrian Ponte Sisto (see p.72), **Piazza Trilussa** is a busy open space that focuses on the steps up to its grand 1613 fountain, where the waters of the **Acqua Paola** emerge. On the other side, the upper torso of the poet **Trilussa**, after whom the square is named, casually leans on a marble plinth as if declaiming his poems – one of which is printed beneath him. Trilussa is actually the pen-name (and an anagram) of Carlo Alberto Salustri, who, like the nineteenth-century Roman poet Belli (see p.171), wrote in dialect – often for humorous effect.

Palazzo Corsini

Cutting northwest through the backstreets towards the Tiber, you'll come across the **Palazzo Corsini**, Via della Lungara 10, built originally for Cardinal Riario in the fifteenth century, and totally renovated between 1732 and 1736 by Ferdinando Fuga for the cardinal and art collector Neri Maria Corsini. He collected most of the paintings on display in the **Galleria Nazionale d'Arte** di **Palazzo Corsini** (Tues–Sun 8.30am–2pm; €4), a relatively small collection that only takes up a few rooms of the giant palace. This sets out to dwarf everything with its size – a fitting final home for Queen Christina of Sweden, who renounced Protestantism and with it the Swedish throne in 1655, bringing her library and fortune to Rome, to the delight of the Chigi pope, Alexander VII. She lived first in Palazzo Farnese and then here for a number of years, dying in the palace in 1689. She is one of only three women to be buried in St Peter's, not withstanding the fact that her life left quite a lot to be desired by the papal standards of the time: she was an affirmed lesbian, murdered one of her own servants, and enjoyed a notoriously wild lifestyle.

It's not hard to imagine the queen roaming the lofty rooms and drafty corridors of the palace – such is its haunting grandeur – and there are echoes of northern Europe in the first room of the gallery, where a number of Netherlandish paintings introduce the collection – a *Village Fete* by Maarten van Cleve, *Butcher's Shop* by David Teniers and Rubens' *St Sebastian tended by Angels*. There is also a depiction of *St George and the Dragon* by Francesco Raibolini, a *Madonna and Child* by Murillo and the sensitive *Straw Madonna* by Van Dyck, and in the next room a *St John the Baptist* by Caravaggio and *Madonna and Child* by Gentileschi. Beyond here there's a room full of landscapes, including lush scenes by Dughet and a depiction of the Pantheon by Charles Clérisseau, when there was a market held in the piazza outside – though it's a rather fanciful interpretation, squeezing the Pyramid of Cestius and Arch of Janus into the background.

Queen Christina's **bedchamber** is decorated with frescoes by an unknown artist – grotesques with scenes of the miracles of Moses as well as the Riario coat of arms, and on the wall a portrait of the queen by Justus van Egmont. Next door, look out for the curious Corsini Throne, thought to be a Roman copy of an Etruscan throne from the second or first century BC. Cut out of marble, its back is carved with warriors in armour and helmets, below which wild boars the size of horses are pursued by hunters. The base is decorated with scenes of a sacrifice, notably the minotaur devouring a human being – only discernible by the kicking legs that protrude from the feasting beast. The final rooms are chock-full of more paintings from the seventeeth and eighteenth centuries, best of which are a famous portrayal of *Salome With the Head of St John the Baptist* by Guido Reni, and *Ecce Homo* by Guercino. Following the corridor back to the entrance takes you past a painting of *Prometheus* by Salvatore Rosa – one of the most vivid and detailed expositions of human internal anatomy you'll see – and Luca Giordano's *Entry of Christ into Jerusalem*.

The Orto Botanico

The grounds of the Palazzo Corsini are now the site of the **Orto Botanico** (Tues–Sat 9.30am–6.30pm; €4), which, after Padua's botanical gardens, is the most important in Italy – and a good example of eighteenth-century garden design. It's a pleasantly neglected expanse these days, a low-key bucolic treat clasping the side of the Janiculum Hill. You can clamber up to high stands of bamboo and ferns cut by rivulets of water and stroll through a wood of century-old oaks, cedars and conifers. A grove of acclimatized palm trees stands in front of the so-called Fountain of the Tritons, a rather grand name for the relatively small-scale fountain that forms the centrepiece of the lower part of the gardens. There's a herbal garden with medicinal plants, greenhouses holding succulents and cacti and a collection of orchids that bloom in springtime and early summer – and, a nice touch, a garden of aromatic herbs put together for the blind; the plants can be identified by their smell or touch, and are accompanied by signs in

Braille. The garden also has the distinction of being home to one of the oldest plane trees in Rome, between 350 and 400 years old, situated by the recently restored monumental staircase.

Villa Farnesina

The **Villa Farnesina** (Mon–Sat 9am–1pm; €5), across the road from the Palazzo Corsini, is more interesting than its larger neighbour. Built during the early sixteenth century by Baldassare Peruzzi for the Renaissance banker Agostino Chigi, it is a unique building, known for its Renaissance frescoes and contributed to by some of the masters of the Renaissance. Chigi situated his villa here to be close to the papal court and away from his business cronies. Most people come to view the Raphael-designed painting of *Cupid and Psyche* in the now glassed-in loggia (at the original front of the building, which is now at the back), completed in 1517 by the artist's assistants, Giulio Romano, Francesco Penni and Giovanni da Udine. The painter and art historian Vasari claims Raphael didn't complete the work because his infatuation with his mistress – "La Fornarina", whose father's bakery was situated nearby – was making it difficult to concentrate, and says that Chigi arranged for her to live with the painter in the palace while he worked on the loggia. More likely he was simply so overloaded with commissions that he couldn't possibly finish them all.

Whoever was responsible, it's mightily impressive, a flowing, animated work bursting with muscular men and bare-bosomed women. Actually it would have made even more of an impact if completed as planned because the blue would have been much brighter – what you see is just the preparatory colour. The only part Raphael is said to have completed is the female figure with her back turned on the lunette to the right of the door leading out to the east. He did, however, apparently manage to finish the *Galatea* in the room next door, which he fitted in between his Vatican commissions for Julius II. Kenneth Clark called it "the greatest evocation of paganism of the Renaissance", although Vasari claims that Michelangelo, passing by one day while Raphael was canoodling with La Fornarina, finished the painting for him. It's more of a mixed bag thematically, with bucolic country scenes interspersed with Galatea on her scallop-shell chariot and a giant head once said to have been painted by Michelangelo in one of the lunettes – which otherwise feature scenes from Ovid's *Metamorphoses* by Sebastiano del Piombo. The ceiling shows Chigi's horoscope constellations, frescoed by the architect of the building, Peruzzi, who also decorated the upstairs *Salone delle Prospettive*, where trompe l'oeil balconies give views onto contemporary Rome – one of the earliest examples of the technique. This room leads through to Chigi's bedroom, decorated with Sodoma's bold and colourful scenes from the life of Alexander the Great.

The Janiculum Hill

It's about a fifteen-minute walk up Via Giuseppe Garibaldi to the summit of the **Janiculum Hill** – not one of the original seven hills of Rome, but the one with the best and most accessible views of the centre. If you don't want to take the main road, follow Vicolo del Cedro from Via della Scala and take the steps up from the end, cross the main road, and continue on the steps that lead up to San Pietro in Montorio. Failing that, bus #115 crosses the hill from Viale Trastevere to the Gianicolo terminal on the Vatican side, although the walk from Piazzale Garibaldi down to the Vatican only takes a further twenty minutes or so.

San Pietro in Montorio

Now part of a complex that includes the Spanish Academy and Spanish ambassador's residence, the church of **San Pietro in Montorio** (daily 9am–noon & 4–6pm) was built on a site once believed to have been the place of the saint's crucifixion. The compact interior is particularly intimate – it's a favourite for weddings – and features some first-rate paintings, among them Sebastiano del Piombo's graceful *Flagellation*. Don't miss Bramante's little **Tempietto** (daily 9am–noon & 4–6pm) in the courtyard on the right, one of the seminal works of the Renaissance, built on what was supposed to have been the precise spot of St Peter's martyrdom. The small circular building is like a classical temple in miniature, perfectly proportioned and neatly executed.

Up to Porta San Pancrazio

The Janiculum was the scene of a fierce 1849 set-to between Garibaldi's troops and the French, and the white marble **memorial** around the corner from the church is dedicated to all those who died in the battle. A little further on, the **Fontana di Acqua Paola** – constructed for Paul V in 1612 with marble from the Roman Forum – gushes water at a bend in the road, a recently restored and very grandiose affair whose ancient water supply is provided by Lake Bracciano way to the north of Rome, and in turn goes on to feed the fountain down below on Piazza Trilussa as well as those on Piazza Farnese across the river.

At the top of the hill, the city gate of **Porta San Pancrazio** was built during the reign of Urban VIII, destroyed by the French in 1849, and rebuilt by Pope Pius IX five years later. It has recently been restored and will house the new Museum of the Roman Republic 1848–49 – yet to open at the time of writing. On the far side is **Piazzale Aurelio**, the start of the old Roman Via Aurelia, and close by the numerous buildings of the **American Academy in Rome**. By the time you get up here you might also be ready for a drink, in which case the American Academy's local **bar**, *Gianicolo*, on the square, is a perfect spot for a drink and a bite to eat.

Villa Doria Pamphilj

Just beyond the Porta, down Via di San Pancrazio, is the rather grand entrance to the grounds of the **Villa Doria Pamphilj**, the largest and most recent of Rome's parks, laid out in the mid-seventeenth century for Prince Camillo Pamphilj and acquired for the city in the 1970s. The stately white Baroque villa is not open to the public, but the sprawling greenery that surrounds it is an enchanting mix of formal parterres and shady lawns and glades, dotted with fountains and statues, and wilder, more bucolic tracts. From the main gate, a path leads downhill and round to the right for around 250m, emerging at the villa. From here, follow the path southwest past the house for around 500m to reach the tree-fringed lake, fed at its northern end by a once-grand cascade of tiny waterfalls and grottoes, and inhabited by scores of turtles that bask photo-genically on its banks. It all makes for a delightful wander (beware, signposting is minimal), though it's best to bring a picnic as there's no café.

△ Garibaldi Monument, Janiculum Hill

The Passeggiata del Gianicolo

Most people turn right before they reach the crest of the hill, however following the **Passeggiata del Gianicolo** along the ridge to **Piazzale Guiseppe Garibaldi**, where there's an equestrian monument to Garibaldi – an ostentatious work from 1895. Just below is the spot from which a cannon is fired at noon each day for Romans to check their watches, leaving a whiff of powder in the air and setting all the car alarms off, although most people bring their kids up here for the weekend puppet shows or the nearby carousel.

Further on, the statue of **Anita Garibaldi** is a fiery, melodramatic work (she cradles a baby in one arm, brandishes a pistol with the other, and is galloping full speed on a horse) that recalls the important part she played in the 1849 battle and also marks her grave – she died later in the campaign. Spread out before her are some of the best views over the city. Immediately opposite, the Renaissance **Villa Lante** is a jewel of a place that is now the home of the Finnish Academy in Rome and gives a panoramic view of the city, although you can only visit on official business or for an exhibition or performance of some kind. Descending from here towards the Vatican and St Peter's, follow some steps off to the right and, next to a small amphitheatre, you'll find the gnarled old oak tree where the sixteenth-century Italian poet **Torquato Tasso**, friend of Cellini and author of *La Gerusalemme Deliverata* ("Jerusalem Delivered"), is said to have whiled away his last days. Further down the hill, next to the Jesuit children's hospital, the church of **Sant'Onofrio** (Sun 10am–noon) sits on the road's bend, with an L-shaped portico and one of the city's most delightful small cloisters, to the right. Tasso moved into the church in the last weeks of his life and died while living here; if you're lucky and it's open you can visit the poet's cell, which holds some manuscripts, his chair, his death mask and personal effects.

⑪

The Vatican and around

On the west bank of the Tiber, directly across from Rome's historic centre, the **VATICAN CITY** was established as an independent sovereign state in 1929. It's a tiny territory, with a population of around a thousand, surrounded by high walls on its western side, while its eastern side opens its doors to the rest of the city in the form of St Peter's and its colonnaded piazza.

The Latin name *Mons Vaticanus* (Vatican Hill) is a corruption of an Etruscan term, indicating a good place for observing the flights of birds and lightning on the horizon – believed to prophesy the future. It's believed that later **St Peter** himself was buried in a pagan cemetery nearby, giving rise to the building of a basilica to venerate his name and the later siting of the headquarters of the

Vatican practicalities

The **Vatican Museums** and the **Basilica of San Pietro (St Peter's)** are open to visitors (no shorts or bare shoulders for St Peter's), and it's also possible to visit the **Vatican Gardens,** though only on one guided tour a day (March–Oct Tues, Thurs & Sat 10am, Nov–Feb Sat only at 10am; €13.50); garden visits last about two hours and tickets must be booked in advance on ☏06.6988.4466; ⊛www.vatican.va; you pay when you pick your tickets up on the day and the dress code is as for St Peter's. The gardens are lovely and offer great views of St Peter's. You can also, if you wish, attend a **papal audience**: these happen once a week, usually on Wednesdays at 10.30am in the Audiences Hall of Paul VI on the south side of St Peter's, and are by no means one-to-one affairs – you'll be with hundreds of others. During the summer months they are occasionally held in the square or at the pope's country residence in Castel Gandolfo (see p.216). They're free, you don't have to be a Catholic to attend and it's often possible to get a place on one if you apply in advance, either in person, to the office of the Prefettura della Casa Pontificia, 00120 Citta del Vaticano (☏06.6988.3114, ☏06.6988.5378), or by sending a letter or fax with your name, your home address, your Rome address, and your preferred date of audience. The office is on the right side of St Peter's Square (Mon–Fri 9am–1pm). Bear in mind that the pope also appears each Sunday at noon to bless the crowds on St Peter's Square – or, in late July and throughout August, in Castel Gandolfo. Finally, if you want to send a postcard with a Vatican postmark, there are Vatican **post offices** on the north side of Piazza San Pietro and inside the Vatican Museums.

Roman Catholic Church here. The Vatican ruled Rome until 1870, when Italian Unification led to an impasse, and a period of over fifty years when the pope didn't leave the Vatican. After reaching an uneasy agreement with Mussolini, the Vatican became a sovereign state in 1929, and nowadays has its own radio station, daily newspaper (*L'Osservatore Romano*), its own version of the euro complete with the pope's head (collector's items, incidentally, should you be given one), postal service, and security service in the colourfully dressed Swiss Guards. Its relationship with the Italian state is, not surprisingly, anything but straightforward.

Apart from entering St Peter's or the museums, you wouldn't know at any point that you had left Rome and entered the Vatican; indeed the area around it, known as the **Borgo**, holds one or two sights that are technically part of the Vatican (like Castel Sant'Angelo), but is one of the most cosmopolitan districts of Rome, full of hotels, restaurants and scurrying tourists and pilgrims – as indeed it always has been since the king of Wessex founded the first hotel for pilgrims here in the eighth century. You may find yourself staying in one of the many mid-range hotels, or in the neighbouring nineteenth-century district of **Prati** (named after the pastures that used to lie here) just to the north, although unless you're a pilgrim it's a better idea to base yourself in the more atmospheric city centre and travel back and forth on the useful #64 bus. However much you try, one visit is never anywhere near enough.

Castel Sant'Angelo and around

The best route to the Vatican and St Peter's is across **Ponte Sant'Angelo**, flanked by angels carved to designs by Bernini and known as his "breezy maniacs". On the far side is the great circular hulk of the **Castel Sant'Angelo** (Tues–Sun 9am–7.30pm; €8, free guided tours in English Sat & Sun 4.30pm), designed and built by the emperor Hadrian as his own mausoleum (his ashes were interred here until a twelfth-century pope appropriated the sarcophagus, which was later destroyed in a fire). The original building was a grand monument, faced with white marble and surrounded with statues and topped with cypresses, similar in style to Augustus's mausoleum across the river. It was renamed in the sixth century, when Pope Gregory the Great witnessed a vision of St Michael here that ended a terrible plague. The mausoleum's position near the Vatican was not lost on the papal authorities, who converted the building for use as a fortress and built a passageway to link it with the Vatican as a refuge in times of siege or invasion – a route utilized on a number of occasions, most notably when the Medici pope, Clement VII, sheltered here for several months during the Sack of Rome in 1527.

Inside, from the monumental entrance hall, a spiral ramp leads up into the centre of the mausoleum itself, passing through the chamber where the emperor was entombed and over a drawbridge, one of the defensive modifications made by the Borgia pope, Alexander VI, in the late fifteenth century. It continues to the main level at the top, where a small palace was built to house the papal residents in appropriate splendour. After the Sack of Rome, Pope Paul III had some especially fine renovations made, including the beautiful *Sala Paolina*, which features frescoes by **Pierno del Vaga**, among others. The gilded ceiling here displays the Farnese family arms, and on the wall is a trompe-l'oeil fresco of one of the family's old retainers coming through a door from a darkened

RESTAURANTS & CAFÉS

Borgo Antico	15
Del Frate	5
Les Etoiles	13
Fonclea	11
Gran Caffè Borgo	14
La Grotta Azzurra	10
Lingua Lunga	8
L'Insalateria	1
Non Solo Pizza	4
Osteria dell' Angelo	3
Ragno d'Oro	7
Senza Fondo	6
Dal Toscano	9

BARS

Four Green Fields	2
Fonclea	11
Simposio di P.Constantini	12

ACCOMMODATION

Amalia	F
Arcangelo	J
Atlante Star	L
Bramante	M
Colors	I
Davos	E
Dei Consoli	K
Domus Mazzini	A
Farnese	B
Giulio Cesare	C
Gerber	D
ISA	G
Ottaviano	H
La Rovere	N

room. You'll also notice Paul III's personal motto, *Festina Lente* ("make haste slowly"), scattered throughout the ceilings and in various corners of all his rooms. Elsewhere, some rooms hold swords, armour, guns and the like, while others are lavishly decorated with grotesques and paintings (don't miss the bathroom of Clement VII on the second floor, with its prototype hot and cold water taps and mildly erotic frescoes). Below are dungeons and storerooms (not visitable), which can be glimpsed from the spiralling ramp, testament to the castle's grisly past as the city's most notorious Renaissance prison – Benvenuto Cellini and Cesare Borgia are just two of its more famous detainees. The quiet bar upstairs offers one of the best views of Rome and excellent coffee.

Ospedale di Santo Spirito

One of the cornerstones of the Borgo neighbourhood is the **Ospedale di Santo Spirito** (tours all year except Aug; Mon 10am & 3.30pm; €7.50), the oldest hospital in Rome, founded in the eight century by Pope Innocent III, who, as legend has it, was moved after dreaming of dead and unwanted babies being tossed into the Tiber. It was later developed by Sixtus IV as a hospital for pilgrims, and the oldest buildings date from this time and have recently been opened to the public. These two giant halls, each 60 metres long and joined by an octagonal hall that used to serve as the main entrance, served as wards until 2000. Frescoes illustrating the lives and deeds of Innocent III and Sixtus IV, twelve of whose building projects around Rome are illustrated, line the main walls, while outside the main door a window contains a barrel in which *proietti* or abandoned babies were left anonymously – alongside a slot for donations. Behind the two wards the hospital still functions, and tours take in two cloisters – one originally designated for nuns, the other for monks – and the main courtyard of the later Palazzo Commendatore; you can in fact peek into the latter – an elegant courtyard that's now used as car parking space by the hospital officials –without going on a tour.

If you're in the mood for more hospital history, walk around the corner to the river side of the complex, where, just before the modern entrance, the **Museo Storico dell'Art Sanitaire** (Mon, Wed & Fri 10am–noon; €3), houses a rather macabre jumble of ancient medical artefacts. There's a model of the original hospital, anatomical models of body parts and casts, horrible pickled babies in jars, vile-looking scalpels, forceps and syringes as well as the inevitable old-style pharmacy – not for the squeamish.

Piazza San Pietro and the Basilica di San Pietro

The approach to St Peter's from the Castel Sant'Angelo is disappointing, and has been so since Mussolini created the approach of **Via della Conciliazione**, when he realized the earlier plan of Pope Nicholas V and swept away the houses of the previously narrow streets and replaced them with this wide, sweeping avenue. Nowadays St Peter's somehow looms too near as you get closer, and the vastness of Bernini's **Piazza San Pietro** is not really apparent until you're right on top of it. In fact, in tune with the spirit of the Baroque, the church was supposed to be even better hidden than it is now: Bernini planned to complete its colonnade with a triumphal arch linking the two arms, so obscuring the view until you were well inside the square, but this was never carried out and the arms of the piazza remain open, symbolically welcoming the world into the lap of the Catholic Church. The obelisk in the centre was brought to Rome by Caligula in 36 AD, and it stood for many years in the centre of Nero's Circus on the Vatican Hill (to the left of the church); according to legend, it marked the site of St Peter's martyrdom. It was moved here in 1586, when Sixtus V ordered that it be erected in front of the basilica, a task that took four months and was apparently done in silence, on pain of death.

The matching **fountains** on either side are the work of Carlo Maderno (on the right) and Bernini (on the left). In between the obelisk and each fountain, a circular stone set into the pavement marks the focal points of an ellipse, from which the four rows of columns on the perimeter of the piazza line up perfectly, making the colonnade appear to be supported by a single line of columns.

Basilica di San Pietro

The piazza is so grand that you can't help but feel a little let down by the sight of the **Basilica di San Pietro** (daily: April–Sept 7am–7pm; Oct–March 7am–6pm), better known to many as **St Peter's**. From here, its facade – by no means the church's best feature – obscures the dome that signals the building from just about everywhere else in the city. Amid a controversy similar to that surrounding the restoration of the Sistine Chapel a few years ago, the facade has also recently been restored, leaving the previously sober travertine facade a decidedly yellowish grey.

The experience of visiting St Peter's has changed quite a bit over recent years. Not so long ago you could freely stroll around the piazza and wander into the basilica when you felt like it. Now much of the square is fenced off, and you can only enter St Peter's from the right-hand side (exiting to the left); you also have to go through security first, and the queues can be horrendous unless you get here early in the morning. Once you get close to the basilica, you're channeled through various entrances depending on what you want to see first – all of which is strictly enforced by the unsmiling suited functionaries that appear at every turn. A carefree experience it is not.

Some history

Built to a plan initially conceived at the turn of the fifteenth century by Bramante and finished off, heavily modified, over a century later by Carlo Maderno, **St Peter's** is a strange hotchpotch of styles, bridging the gap between the Renaissance and Baroque eras with varying levels of success. It is, however, the principal shrine of the Catholic Church, built as a replacement for the rundown structure erected here by Constantine in the early fourth century on the site of St Peter's tomb. As such it cannot fail to impress: worked on by the greatest Italian architects of the sixteenth and seventeenth centuries, it occupies a site rich with historical significance. In size, meanwhile, St Peter's beats most other churches hands down (although it's not officially the largest in terms of area – that honour belongs to the Basilica of Our Lady of Peace, Côte d'Ivoire).

Bramante had originally conceived a Greek cross plan rising to a high central dome, but this design was altered after his death and revived only with the elderly Michelangelo's accession as chief architect. Michelangelo was largely responsible for the dome, but he too died (in 1564) before its completion. He was succeeded by Vignola, and the dome was eventually finished in 1590 by Giacomo della Porta. Carlo Maderno, under orders from the Borghese Pope

Paul V, took over in 1605, and stretched the church into a Latin cross plan, which had the practical advantage of accommodating more people and followed more directly the plan of Constantine's original basilica. But in so doing he completely unbalanced all the previous designs, not least by obscuring the dome (which he also modified) from view in the piazza. The inside, too, is very much of the Baroque era, largely the work of Bernini, who created many of the most important fixtures. The church was finally completed and reconsecrated on November 18, 1626, exactly 1300 years to the day after the original basilica was first consecrated. At least the inscription on the façade leaves no doubt who was responsible for getting the job finished: as Pasquino commented at the time – 'I thought it was dedicated to St Peter!'

Inside St Peter's

One of the channels on the right side of the piazza funnels you into the basilica, with the other two leading to the underground grottoes and the ascent to the dome – both the latter have exits into the main church, allowing you to visit the three sights in an order of your choice. Bear in mind that whichever you

ST PETER'S

0   20 m

Tomb of Paul III
Tomb of Urban VIII
Cattedra of St Peter

Bernini's Baldacchino
Monument to Alexander VII   St Veronica   St Helena
Entrance to the Treasury   St Andrew   Confessio   St Longinus
Exit from the Grottoes
John XXIII

St Peter
Countess Mathilda of Tuscany
Tomb of Innocent VIII   Chapel of the Blessed Sacrament

Monument to Clementina Sobieska   Monument to Queen Christina of Sweden
Benedict XV
Exit from the Dome

Statue of Charlemagne   Monument to the Stuarts   Michelangelo's Pietà   Statue of Constantine

Holy Door

N

opt for first, you need to be properly dressed to enter, which means no bare knees or shoulders – a rule that is very strictly enforced.

Entering the basilica, to the left of the Holy Door, which is only opened every fifty years and was last kept open during the jubilee year 2000 by John Paul II, the first thing you see on the right is Michelangelo's **Pietà**, completed when he was just 24. Following an attack by a vandal a few years back, it sits behind glass, strangely remote from the life of the rest of the building. When you look at the piece, its fame comes as no surprise: it's a sensitive and individual work, and an adept one too, draping the limp body of a grown man across the legs of a woman with grace and ease. Though you're much too far away to read it, etched into the strap across Mary's chest are words proclaiming the work as Michelangelo's – the only piece ever signed by the sculptor and apparently done after he heard his work, which had been placed in Constantine's basilica, had been misattributed by onlookers. You can see the inscription properly on the plaster cast of the statue in the Pinacoteca of the Vatican Museums.

Women dominate the north aisle. Just after the *Pietà*, on a pillar, is a monument to the controversial **Queen Christina of Sweden** (see p.173), in the shape of a huge medallion (she's buried in the grottoes downstairs), while on the next pier along is Bernini's statue of **Countess Mathilda of Tuscany**. At the end of the aisle, the remains of **John XXIII** lie under a wax effigy, and get a lot of attention from pilgrims. It's a suitably humble memorial to a humble pope.

John is remembered with more pomp by a modern relief in a chapel on the other side of the basilica in the south aisle, opposite a kneeling rendering of an equally pious pope, **Benedict XV**, the work of Pietro Canonica (see p.161). On a pillar to the right of here is Antonio Pollaiuolo's tomb of the late-fifteenth-century pope, **Innocent VIII** – banker to Queen Isabella of Spain and the financier of Columbus's voyage to the New World – the only tomb to survive from the Constantinian basilica. In the upper statue of the monument the pope holds what looks like a mason's trowel – in fact the spearpoint of Longinus, given to him by the Ottoman sultan Bajazet II to persuade him to keep the sultan's brother and rival in exile in Rome. On the last pillar of the south transept is an austere monument by Canova depicting the last of the **Stuart pretenders** to the English throne, while opposite, over the exit from the dome, is a monument to **Clementina Sobieska**, the wife of James III (the Stuart pretender to the English throne) – the third of the three women buried in St Peter's.

As you walk down the **nave**, the size of the building becomes more apparent – and not just because of the bronze plaques set in the floor that make comparisons with the sizes of other churches. For the record, the length of the nave is 186m from the door to the back of the apse, while the width at the crossing is 137m; even at its narrowest part, the nave is 60m wide. Off the north transept, the wonderful gilded Baroque **Chapel of the Blessed Sacrament** was designed by Borromini, with work by Pietro da Cortona, Domenichino and Bernini. It's not open to the casual sightseer, but it is worthy of a visit, which can be managed if you go there to pray along with the clergy, who maintain a vigil there during the time the basilica is open.

The **dome** is breathtakingly imposing, rising high above the supposed site of St Peter's tomb. With a diameter of 44m, it is only 1.5m smaller than the Pantheon, and the letters of the inscription inside its lower level are nearly 2m high. It's supported by four enormous piers, decorated with reliefs depicting the basilica's "**major relics**": St Veronica's handkerchief, which was used to wipe the face of Christ and is adorned with his miraculous image; the lance of St Longinus, which pierced Christ's side; and a piece of the True Cross, in the pier of St Helen (the head of St Andrew, which was returned to the Eastern Church by Pope Paul VI in 1966, was also formerly kept here). On the right side of the nave, near the pier of St Longinus, the bronze statue of **St Peter** is another of the basilica's most venerated monuments, carved in the thirteenth century by Arnolfo di Cambio; its right foot has been polished smooth by the attentions of pilgrims. On holy days the statue is dressed in papal tiara and vestments.

Bronze was also used in Bernini's **baldachino**, the centrepiece of the sculptor's Baroque embellishment of the interior, a massive 26m high (the height, apparently, of Palazzo Farnese), cast out of 927 tonnes of metal removed from the Pantheon roof in 1633. To modern eyes, it's an almost grotesque piece of work, with its wild spiralling columns copied from columns in the Constantine basilica. But it has the odd personal touch, with female faces expressing the agony of childbirth on each corner except the front right one, where there's a beaming baby – said to have been commissioned by a niece of Bernini's patron (Urban VIII), who gave birth at the same time as the sculptor was finishing the piece. You'll also notice the bees that adorn just about anything to do with the Barberini family – in this case Bernini's patron Urban VIII.

Bernini's feverish sculpture decorates the apse, too, his bronze **Cattedra** enclosing the supposed chair of St Peter in a curvy marble and stucco throne, surrounded by the doctors of the Church (the two with bishops' mitres are St Augustine of Hippo and St Ambrose, representing the Western Church; the two to the rear are portraits of St John Chrysostom and St Athanasius of the Eastern Church). Puffs of cloud surrounding the alabaster window displaying the dove of the Holy Spirit (whose wingspan, incidentally, is 2m) burst through brilliant gilded sunbeams. On the right, the **tomb of Urban VIII**, also by Bernini, is less grand but more dignified, while on the left, the **tomb of Paul III**, by Giacomo della Porta, was moved up and down the nave of the church before it was finally placed here to balance that of Urban. More interesting is Bernini's **monument to Alexander VII** in the south transept, its winged skeleton struggling underneath the heavy marble drapes, upon which the Chigi pope is kneeling in prayer. The grim reaper clutches an hourglass: the Baroque at its most melodramatic, and symbolic. On the left sits *Charity*, on the right, *Truth Revealed in Time*; to the rear are *Hope* and *Faith*.

The Treasury

An entrance off the south aisle, under a giant monument to Pius VIII, leads to the steeply priced **Treasury** (daily: summer 9am–6pm; winter 9am–5pm; €6), where

The Vatican necropolis

The baldachino and confessio just in front are supposed to mark the exact spot of the **tomb of St Peter**, and excavations earlier this century did indeed turn up – directly beneath the baldachino and the remains of Constantine's basilica – a row of Roman tombs with inscriptions confirming that the Vatican Hill was a well-known burial ground in classical times. Whether the tomb of St Peter was found is less clear: a shrine was discovered, badly damaged, that agrees with some historical descriptions of the saint's marker, with a space in it through which ancient pilgrims placed their heads in prayer. Close by, the bones of an elderly but physically fit man were discovered and later claimed as the relics of the Apostle, although speculation ever since has been rife. It is possible to take an English-language tour of the Vatican necropolis, but you need to fill in a form and book two or three months in advance to be sure of getting a place. The Scavi office is through the arch to the left of St Peter's (Mon–Sat 9am–3.30pm; ☏06.6988.5318; ℻06.6987.5518; ✉scavi@fsp.va).

a wall tablet records the names of all the popes buried in St Peter's. Along with more recent additions, this holds artefacts from the earlier church: a spiral marble column (the other survivors form part of the colonnade around the interior of the dome), once thought to be from the old temple of Jerusalem; a wall-mounted tabernacle by Donatello showing the dead Christ being revealed by angels (the latter carved by Michelozzo); a rich blue-and-gold dalmatic that is said once to have belonged to Charlemagne (though this has since been called into question); the vestments and tiara for the bronze statue of St Peter in the nave of the basilica; and the massive though fairly ghastly late-fifteenth-century bronze tomb of Sixtus IV by Pollaiuolo, viewable from above – said to be a very accurate portrait.

The Grottoes

The middle channel outside leads to the Vatican **Grottoes** (daily: summer 8am–6pm; winter 7am–5pm), which extend right under the main footprint of the main church and hold some column bases from Constantine's original basilica as well as a number of beautiful mosaics. The majority of the popes are buried here, with the more significant honoured by monuments. Canova's statue of Pius VI hogs the central aisle, while the tombs in the south aisle include a plain slab commemorating Paul VI, John Paul I, who reigned for just 33 days and whose death has been clouded by numerous (mostly disproved) conspiracy theories, and a little further down on the left, John Paul II – whose plain tomb perhaps unsurprisingly receives by far the most attention. The last pope specifically requested that he should rest down here, and perhaps not entirely accidentally he lies in the space previously occupied by the revered John XXIII. Across the aisle the supposed tomb of St Peter sits immediately beneath Bernini's baldachino and is marked by two lions. Leaving, you emerge in the main basilica, by Bernini's statue of St Longinus.

Ascending to the roof and dome

You can make the **ascent to the roof and dome** (daily: May–Sept 8am–6pm; Oct–April 8am–5pm; €7 via lift, €4 using the stairs) by taking the furthest right of the three entrances to the basilica complex, through the northern courtyard between the church and the Vatican Palace. You'll probably need to queue when you get here, and, even with the lift, there's a long climb via a narrow stairway that spirals up the dome. The views from the gallery around the interior of the dome give you a sense of the enormity of the church. From there, the roof grants views from behind the huge statues onto the piazza below, before the ascent to the lantern at the top of the dome, from which the views over the city are as glorious as you'd expect. Remember that it is over three hundred fairly claustrophobic steps through the double shell of the dome to reach the lantern; you should probably give it a miss if you're either in ill health or uneasy with heights or confined spaces. The exit leads you back into the north aisle of the church itself.

The Vatican Museums

A fifteen-minute walk out of the northern side of the piazza takes you up to the only part of the Vatican Palace you can visit independently, the **Vatican Museums**, at Viale Vaticano 13 – quite simply, the largest, richest, most

THE VATICAN MUSEUMS

UPPER FLOOR

- Museo Gregoriano Etrusco
- Galleria dei Candelabri
- Galleria degli Arazzi
- Galleria delle Carte Geografiche
- Hall of the Immaculate Conception
- Sala Sobieski
- Raphael Stanze (Raphael Rooms)
- Raphael's Loggia
- Chapel of Nicholas V

LOWER FLOOR

- Museo Gregoriano Profano; Museo Pio Christiano; Museo Missionario Etnoligico
- Entrance
- Sala Rotonda
- Animal Room
- Mask Room
- Museo Pio-Clementino
- Gallery of Statues
- Gallery of Busts
- Hall of Muses
- Octagonal Courtyard
- Bramante Staircase
- Vestibule
- Greek Cross Room
- Museo Gregoriano Egizio
- Pinacoteca
- Cortile della Pigna
- Museo Chiaramonti
- Braccio Nuovo
- Vatican Library
- Cortile della Biblioteca
- Library of Sixtus V
- Cortile del Belvedere
- Museum of Christian Art
- Aldobrandini Marriage Room
- Appartamento Borgia
- Sistine Chapel

N

0   50 m

compelling and perhaps most exhausting museum complex in the world (March–Oct Mon–Fri 8.45am–3.20pm, Sat 8.45am–1.20pm; Nov–Feb Mon–Sat 8.45am–12.30pm, last exit 1.45pm; €12, audioguides €6. Closed Sun, holidays and religious holidays, except the last Sun of each month when admission is free; @www.vatican.va provides up-to-date info). If you have found any of Rome's other museums disappointing, the Vatican is probably the reason why: so much booty from the city's history has ended up here, and so many of the Renaissance's finest artists were in the employ of the pope, that not surprisingly the result is a set of museums so stuffed with antiquities as to put most other European collections to shame.

As its name suggests, the complex actually holds a collection of museums on very diverse subjects, with displays of classical statuary, Renaissance painting, Etruscan relics and Egyptian artefacts, not to mention the furnishings and decoration of the palace itself. There's no point in trying to see everything in one visit.

Once inside, you have a choice of routes, but the only features you really shouldn't miss are the Raphael Rooms and the Sistine Chapel – and there are plenty of signs to make sure you don't. Above all, decide how long you want to spend here, and what you want to see, before you start; you could spend anything from an hour to the better part of a day here, and it's easy to collapse from museum fatigue before you've even got to your most important target of

The Palace – and the Museums' layout

The Vatican Palace complex was built piecemeal over the years, and in fact the two long corridors that make up most of the 'museum' space were built to join the original palace next to St Peter's, constructed around 1450, with a newer building, the Belvedere, built on the higher ground to the north by Innocent VIII in 1490 as a summer casino. Bramante oversaw the connection of the two buildings in the 1500s, creating a vast courtyard that during the early sixteenth century was used for festivals and banquets, until Sixtus V divided it into separate quadrangles. It was divided again by the construction of the nineteenth-century Braccio Nuovo, resulting in its current form.

The museums occupy four principal structures: the **original Palace** at the end nearest St Peter's; the **Belvedere Palace** to the north, and the two long **galleries**. In the middle of all are the three **courtyards**: the **Cortile del Belvedere** at the southern end, the small **Cortile della Biblioteca** in the middle, created by the construction of the Vatican Library and Braccio Nuovo, and, the northernmost of the three, the **Cortile della Pigna** – named after the huge bronze pine cone (*pigna* in Italian) mounted in the niche at the end, an ancient Roman artefact that was found close to the Pantheon. In classical times this was a fountain with water pouring out of each of its points. Also in this courtyard is a large modern bronze sculpture of a sphere within a sphere, which occasionally rotates – though to an erratic schedule. If you're on a guided tour, you'll stop here to be talked through the Sistine Chapel paintings before going in, as it's forbidden to speak inside. Even if you're not, it can be worth listening in if there's one being given in English, but be discreet.

The old main entrance to the museums was created by Pope Pius XI, in 1932, and its huge bronze spiral staircase, the work of one Giuseppe Momo, provides a dignified exit to the museums. On it are displayed the heraldic arms of all the popes from 1447 (Nicholas II) to Pius XI's predecessor (Benedict XV), while the staircase is in the form of a double helix, one half ascending, the other descending – an idea that Frank Lloyd Wright copied when designing the Guggenheim in New York. The museum entrance has since been modernized, and you now enter through a door in the bastion wall to the left of the monumental entrance, through a large hall and a new monumental marble staircase. An escalator carries you up to the actual museum.

Finally, bear in mind that the collections of the Vatican Museums are in a constant state of restoration, and are often closed and shifted around with little or no notice. The most important departments are usually open but don't be surprised if some things are off limits or in a different position to the one given in our account; again, the website can help with this.

interest. Be conservative – the distances between different sections alone can be vast and very tiring.

One further thing: on any given day there will be a **queue** to get into the museums, and even getting here before opening will mean you have to stand in line for a while. During the summer months don't count on waiting in line for much less than an hour, and probably much longer. Finally, avoid Mondays, when the rest of the city's museums are closed and everyone flocks to the Vatican and St Peter's.

Museo Pio-Clementino

To the left of the entrance, the small **Museo Pio-Clementino** is home to some of the Vatican's best classical statuary, including the fourth-century BC statue of *Apoxmenos* in the **vestibule**, in which an athelete is shown scraping dirt from his body. The adjoining **Octagon Courtyard** holds two statues that proved a huge influence on Renaissance artists; the serene *Apollo Belvedere*, a Roman copy of a fourth-century BC original, and the first-century BC *Laocoön*. The latter was discovered near Nero's Golden House in 1506 by a ploughman who had inadvertently dug through the roof of a buried part of Trajan's Baths, and depicts the prophetic Trojan priest being crushed with his sons by serpents sent by the gods to punish him for warning his fellow citizens of the danger of the Trojan horse. It is perhaps the most famous classical statue ever, referred to by Pliny who thought it carved from a single piece of marble, and written about by Byron – who described its contorted realism as "dignifying pain". Some scholars theorize that the statue is in fact a sixteenth-century fake by Michelangelo, which isn't as mad is it sounds – Michelangelo did design a substitute arm for the statue, and this was found to be an almost exact match for the "original". Diagonally opposite the *Apollo Belvedere* is a statue of Hermes that Poussin thought the greatest male nude he'd ever seen, while diagonally opposite the *Laocoön* is a group of nineteenth-century classical figures by Canova. In between the two stands a statue of Venus from the second century AD, said to be a portrait of Marcus Aurelius's wife Faustina.

Leave the courtyard between the two braying dogs and you're in the **Animal Room**, named for its animal sculptures, although only a few are of ancient provenance and perhaps the most impressive features are the floor and wall mosaics, all from Hadrian's villa at Tivoli. There are more mosaics from Hadrian's villa through the Gallery of Statues in the small **Gallery of Masks**. This room is often closed but you can still peer in to see these, an ancient Roman toilet, and the statue of *Venus of Cnidos*, the first known representation of the goddess, with towel and pitcher, and full of grace and movement. As for the **Gallery of Statues**, its long corridor has an impressive array of ancient statuary, including two seated Roman nobles that mark its far end, from the first and third century BC. Beyond, the most interesting part of the **Gallery of Busts** is on your immediate right, where the shelves groan with great emperors, from Julius Caesar and Augustus (as a young man and also as a God, crowned with wheat) right up to Trajan at the other end. On the upper shelves you'll see how in subsequent centuries it became fashionable to sport a beard, starting with Antoninus Pius and Marcus Aurelius right up to the intense gaze of Caracalla.

Back past the Animal Room, the frescoed **Hall of the Muses**, so called for the statues that line its central section, has as its centrepiece the so-called *Belvedere Torso*, which was found in the Campo de' Fiori during the reign of Julius II. It's signed by Apollonius, a Greek sculptor of the first century BC, and is generally thought to be a near-perfect example of male anatomy. Its portrayal, either of Hercules sitting on his lion skin or Ajax resting, was studied by most key Renaissance artists, including Michelangelo, who incorporated its turning pose into his portrait of Christ in the *Last Judgement* in the Sistine Chapel.

A short corridor leads to the **Sala Rotonda**, centring on a vast bowl from the Domus Aurea and with a floor paved with a second-century AD Roman mosaic from the town of Otricoli, north of Rome, depicting battles between men and sea monsters. There is more classical statuary around the room, notably a huge gilded bronze statue of a rather dim-witted-looking Hercules, also from the second century AD and the only surviving gilded bronze statue on display in the Vatican Museums. On each side of the statue are busts of the emperor Hadrian and his lover, Antinous – who is also depicted in the same room, to the right of the entrance, as a huge statue dressed as Bacchus. Opposite this is a beautiful white marble statue of Claudius, in the guise of Jupiter, with his oak leaf crown and an eagle at his feet.

Beyond here, the **Greek Cross Room** is decorated in Egyptian style, although the pharaonic statues flanking the entry door are nineteenth-century imitations. Another Roman mosaic, from the second century AD, shows Minerva and the phases of the moon, while the two huge porphyry boxes are the sarcophagi of queens Helen and Costanza. On Helen's, soldiers vanquish their enemies, a reference to the fact that she was the mother of Constantine, while that of Costanza, the daughter of the emperor, shows *putti* carrying grapes, loaves of bread and lambs – a reference to the eucharist, as she was a devout Christian.

Museo Gregoriano Egizio

The **Museo Gregoriano Egizio**, founded in the nineteenth century by Gregory XVI, isn't one of the Vatican's main highlights. But this says more about the rest of the Vatican than the museum, which has a distinguished collection of ancient Egyptian artefacts. It holds some vividly painted mummy cases (and two mummies), along with *canopi*, the alabaster vessels in which the entrails of the deceased were placed. There is also a partial reconstruction of the Temple of Serapis from Hadrian's Villa near Tivoli, along with another statue of his lover Antinous, who drowned close to the original temple in Egypt and so inspired Hadrian to build his replica – dressed here as Osiris. The Egyptian-style statues in shiny black basalt next door are also Roman imitations, as is the reclining figure of the Nile river god, complete with crocodile, next door. Hadrian collected some original Egyptian bits and pieces, too, some of which are housed in the room which curves around the niche containing the pine cone, including various Egyptian deities – look out for the laughing dwarf god Bes. The next rooms contain Egyptian bronzes from the late pharaonic period and early days of the Roman Empire, including a group of items from the cult of Isis, which became popular in Rome itself. Beyond, are a couple of rooms with clay tablets inscribed in cuneiform writing from Mesopotamia; Assyrian, Sumerian and Persian bas-reliefs on stone tablets; and, in the last room, a lovely relief of a kneeling winged god from 850 BC.

Museo Gregoriano Etrusco

Past the entrance to the Egyptian Museum a grand staircase, the Simonetti Stairs, leads up to the **Museo Gregoriano Etrusco**, which holds sculpture, funerary art and applied art from the sites of southern Etruria – a good complement to Rome's specialist Etruscan collection in the Villa Giulia, although you have to be keen on the Etruscans to visit both.

The first exhibits on display are finds from the seventh-century BC **Regolini-Galassi tomb**, which was discovered near Cerveteri, and contained the remains of three Etruscan nobles, two men and a woman; the breastplate of the woman and her huge *fibula* (clasp) are of gold. Take a look at the small ducks and lions with which they are decorated, fashioned in the almost microscopic beadwork for which Etruscan goldsmiths were famous. There's also armour, a bronze bedstead, a funeral chariot and a wagon, as well as a great number of enormous storage jars, in which food, oil and wine were contained for use in the afterlife.

Beyond here are **Etruscan bronzes**, including weapons, candelabra, barbecue sets (skewers and braziers); women's beautiful makeup cases known as *cistae* and, most notably, the so-called *Mars of Todi*, a three-quarter-size votive statue found in the Umbrian town of Todi. On a flap of the figure's armour an inscription gives the name of the donor. Further on, there is a large collection of Etruscan sarcophagi and stone statuary from Vulci, Tarquinia and Tuscania in northern Lazio. Particularly interesting here are the finely carved horses' heads from Vulci and the sarcophagus of a magistrate from Tarquinia which still bears traces of the paint its reliefs were coloured with. There is also Etruscan jewellery, with exquisite goldsmith work, crowns of golden oak and laurel leaves, necklaces, earrings and rings set with semiprecious stones and a *fibula* complete with the owner's name etched on it in such small writing that a magnifying glass is provided for you to read it.

Heading up some stairs from this room you come to a series of large rooms which look out from the north side of the Belvedere Palace and offer stunning **views** of the hill of Monte Mario. Inside, you'll find lots of vases, assorted weapons and items of everyday household use, as well as a magnificent terracotta statue of Adonis lying on a lacy couch, found near the town of Tuscania in the 1950s. Finally, don't miss the Greek *krater*, among a lot of Greek pottery found in Etruscan tombs, which shows Menelaus and Ulysses asking the Trojans for the return of Helen. It's housed in a special display case and can be rotated by pressing the electrical switch on the bottom of the case.

The Galleria dei Candelabri and Galleria degli Arazzi

Outside the Etruscan Museum, the staircase leads back down to the main – and consequently crowded – Sistine route, taking you first through the **Galleria dei Candelabri**, the niches of which are adorned with huge candelabra taken from imperial Roman villas. This gallery is also stuffed with ancient sculpture, its most memorable piece a copy of the famous statue of *Diana of Ephesus*, on the right, whose multiple breasts are, according to the Vatican official line, bees' eggs. Beyond here the deliberately darkened **Galleria degli Arazzi** has, on the left, Belgian tapestries to designs by the school of Raphael which show scenes from the life of Christ and, on the right, tapestries made in Rome at the Barberini workshops during the 1600s, showing scenes from the life of Maffeo Barberini, who became Pope Urban VIII.

The Galleria delle Carte Geografiche and Hall of the Immaculate Conception

Next, the **Galleria delle Carte Geografiche** (Gallery of the Maps), which is as long (175m) as the previous two galleries put together, was decorated in the late sixteenth century at the behest of Pope Gregory XIII, the reformer of the calendar, to show all of Italy, the major islands in the Mediterranean and the papal possessions in France, as well as large-scale maps of the maritime republics of Venice and Genoa. The maps are fantastic, illustrative yet precise, and this gallery, with its ceiling frescoes, illustrating scenes that took place in the area depicted in each adjacent map, is considered by many to be the most beautiful in the entire museum complex.

After the Gallery of the Maps, there is a hall with more tapestries and, to the left, after one more room, the **Hall of the Immaculate Conception**, which sports nineteenth-century frescoes of Pope Pius IX declaring the Doctrine of the Immaculate Conception of the Blessed Virgin Mary on December 8, 1854. From here all visitors are directed to a covered walkway suspended over the palace courtyard of the Belvedere, which leads through to the Raphael Rooms.

Raphael Stanze (Raphael Rooms)

The **Raphael Stanze (Raphael Stanze** or **Stanze di Raffaelo)** are, apart perhaps from the Sistine Chapel, the Vatican's greatest work of art. This set of rooms formed the private apartments of Pope Julius II, and when he moved in here he commissioned Raphael to redecorate them in a style more in tune with the times. Raphael died before the scheme was complete, but the two rooms that were completed by him, as well as others completed by pupils, are among the highlights of the Renaissance.

The Stanza di Constantino

The first of the Raphael Rooms that you come to, the **Stanza di Constantino**, was not in fact done by Raphael at all, but painted partly to his designs about five years after he died by his pupils Giulio Romano, Francesco Penni and Raffello del Colle, between 1525 and 1531. It shows scenes from the life of the emperor Constantine, who made Christianity the official religion of the Roman Empire. The enormous painting on the wall opposite the entrance is the *Battle of the Milvian Bridge* by Giulio Romano and Francesco Penni – a depiction of a decisive battle in 312 AD between the warring co-emperors of the West, Constantine and Maxentius. With due regard to the laws of propaganda, the victorious emperor is in the centre of the painting mounted on his white horse while the vanquished Maxentius drowns in the river to the right, clinging to his black horse. The painting to your left as you enter, the *Vision of Constantine* by Giulio Romano, shows Constantine telling his troops of his dream-vision of the Holy Cross inscribed with the legend "In this sign you will conquer". Opposite, the *Baptism of Constantine*, by Francesco Penni, is a flight of fancy – Constantine was baptized on his deathbed about thirty years after the battle of the Milvian Bridge.

The Sala dei Chiaroscuri and Capella di Niccolo V

Beyond the Stanza di Constantine, the **Sala dei Chiaroscuri** was originally painted by Raphael, but curiously Pope Gregory XIII had his paintings removed and the room repainted in the rather gloomy style you see today – although there is a magnificent gilded and painted ceiling which bears the arms of the Medici. Through the windows you can glimpse a covered balcony known as **Raphael's loggia**, which was built by Bramante in 1513 and decorated by Raphael and his pupils, but there's usually no entry to it. A small door on the other side of the room leads into the little **Capella di Niccolo V**, with wonderful frescoes by Fra Angelico painted between 1448 and 1450, showing scenes in the lives of saints Stephen and Lawrence.

The Stanza di Eliodoro

From here head straight through the souvenir shop to the **Stanza di Eliodoro**, the first of the Raphael rooms proper. The fresco on the right of the entrance, *The Expulsion of Heliodorus from the Temple*, tells the story of Heliodorus, the agent of the eastern king Seleucus IV, who was slain by a mysterious rider on a white horse while trying to steal the treasure of Jerusalem's Temple. It's an exciting piece of work, painted in the years 1512–14 for Pope Julius II, and the figures of Heliodorus, the horseman and the fleeing men are adeptly done, the figures almost jumping out of the painting into the room. The group of figures on the left, however, is more interesting – Pope Julius II, in his papal robes, Giulio Romano, the pupil of Raphael, and, to his left, Raphael himself in a self-portrait.

On the left wall as you enter, the *Mass of Bolsena* is a bit of anti-Lutheran propaganda, and relates a miracle that occurred in the town in northern Lazio in the 1260s, when a German priest who doubted the transubstantiation of Christ found the wafer bleeding when he broke it during a service – the napkin onto which it bled can be seen in the cathedral at Orvieto, 90km north of Rome. The pope facing the priest is another portrait of Julius II. The composition is a neat affair, the colouring rich, the onlookers kneeling, turning and gasping as the miracle is realized. On the window wall opposite, the *Deliverance of St Peter* shows the saint being assisted in a jail-break by the Angel of the Lord – a night scene, whose clever chiaroscuro predates Caravaggio by nearly one hundred years. It was painted by order of Pope Leo X, as an allegory of his imprisonment after a battle that took place in Ravenna a few years earlier. Finally, on the large wall opposite *The Expulsion of Heliodorus from the Temple*, *Leo I Repulsing Attila the Hun* is an allegory of the difficulties the papacy was going through in the early 1500s and shows the chubby cardinal Giovanni de' Medici, who succeeded Julius II and became Leo X in 1513. Leo later had Raphael's pupils paint a portrait of himself as Leo I, so, confusingly, he appears twice in this fresco, as pope and as the equally portly Medici cardinal just behind.

The Stanza della Segnatura

The next room, the **Stanza della Segnatura** or Pope's study, is probably the best known – and with good reason. Painted in the years 1508–11, when Raphael first came to Rome, the subjects were again the choice of Julius II, and, composed with careful balance and harmony, it comes close to the peak of the painter's art. *The School of Athens*, on the near wall as you come in, steals the show, a representation of the triumph of scientific truth in which all the great minds of antiquity are represented. Plato and Aristotle discuss philosophy at the centre of the painting: Aristotle, the father of scientific method, motions downwards; Plato, pointing upward, indicating his philosophy of otherworldly spirituality, is believed to be a portrait of Leonardo da Vinci. On the far right, the crowned figure holding a globe was meant to represent the Egyptian geographer, Ptolemy; to his right the young man in the black beret is Raphael, while in front, demonstrating a theorem to his pupils on a slate, the figure of Euclid is a portrait of Bramante. Spread across the steps is Diogenes, lazily ignorant of all that is happening around him, while to the left Raphael added a solitary, sullen portrait of Michelangelo as Heraclitus writing – a homage to the artist, apparently painted after Raphael saw the first stage of the Sistine Chapel almost next door. Other identifiable figures include the beautiful youth with blonde hair on the left looking out of the painting, Francesco Maria della Rovere, placed here by order of Julius II. Della Rovere, the Duke of Urbino, also appears as the good-looking young man to the left of the seated dignitaries, in the painting opposite, the *Disputation over the Sacrament*, an allegory of the Christian religion and the main element of the Mass, the Blessed Sacrament – which stands at the centre of the painting being discussed by all manner of popes, cardinals, bishops, doctors, even the poet Dante.

The Stanza Incendio

The last room, the **Stanza Incendio**, was the last to be decorated, to the orders (and the general glorification) of Pope Leo X, and in a sense it brings together three generations of work. The ceiling was painted by Perugino, Raphael's teacher, and the frescoes completed to Raphael's designs by his pupils (notably Giulio Romano). The most striking of them is the *Fire in the Borgo*, facing the main window – an oblique reference to Leo X restoring peace to Italy after Julius II's reign but in fact describing an event that took place during the reign of Leo IV, when the pope stood in the loggia of the old St Peter's and made the sign of the cross to extinguish a fire. As with so many of these paintings, the chronology is deliberately crazy: Leo IV is in fact a portrait of Leo X, while on the left, Aeneas carries his aged father Anchises out of the burning city of Troy, two thousand years earlier. This last Raphael Room is connected to the **Sala Sobieski**, with its nineteenth-century painting of the Polish king driving Turks out of Europe, by the small **Chapel of Urban VI**, with frescoes and stuccoes by Pietro da Cortona.

The Appartamento Borgia

Outside the Raphael Rooms, you can either proceed direct to the Sistine Chapel, or take the stairs down to the **Appartamento Borgia**, which was inhabited by Julius II's hated predecessor, Alexander VI – a fact which persuaded Julius to move into the new set of rooms he called upon Raphael to decorate. Nowadays host to a large collection of modern religious art (see below), the Borgia rooms were almost exclusively decorated by Pinturicchio in the years 1492–95, on the orders of Alexander VI, though sadly the lighting is poor – more focused on the modern art than it is on the ceilings. The first room is named after its ceiling decorations of the twelve sybils, and the next shows Euclid kneeling at Geometry's throne above the fireplace, but it's the frescoes in the third, the **Sala dei Santi** that are especially worth seeing, typically rich in colour and detail and depicting the legend of Osiris and the Apis bull – a reference to the Borgia family symbol. Among other images is a scene showing St Catherine of Alexandria disputing with the emperor Maximilian, in which Pinturicchio has placed his self-portrait behind the emperor. The Arch of Constantine is clearly visible in the background. The figure of St Catherine is said to be a portrait of Lucrezia Borgia, and the room was reputedly the scene of a decidedly un-papal party to celebrate the first of Lucrezia's three marriages, which ended up with men tossing sweets down the fronts of the women's dresses.

The religious collection is spread throughout the main apartments and the forty or so rooms include works by some of the most famous names in the **modern art** world: a typically tortured Van Gogh *Pietà*; an exquisite pastel drawing of Joan of Arc by Redon; liturgical vestments designed by Matisse; a fascinating *Landscape with Angels* by Salvador Dalí, donated by King Juan Carlos of Spain; and one of Francis Bacon's studies of Innocent X after Velázquez.

The Capella Sistina (Sistine Chapel)

Steps lead up from the the Appartamento Borgio to the **Capella Sistina (Sistine Chapel)**, a huge barn-like structure built for Pope Sixtus IV between 1473 and 1481. It serves as the pope's official private chapel and the scene of the conclaves of cardinals for the election of each new pontiff. The ceiling

THE SISTINE CHAPEL

paintings here, and the *Last Judgement* on the wall behind the altar, together make up arguably the greatest masterpiece in Western art, and the largest body of painting ever planned and executed by one man – Michelangelo. They are also probably the most viewed paintings in the world: it's estimated that on an average day about 15,000 people trudge through here to take a look; and during the summer and on special occasions the number of visitors can exceed 20,000.

WALL PAINTINGS

1 Perugino
Moses' Journey into Egypt

2 Botticelli
The Trials of Moses

3 Rosselli
Crossing of the Red Sea

4 Rosselli
Moses and the Law

5 Botticelli
Punishment of the Rebels

6 Signorelli
Testament and Death of Moses

7 Matteo da Lecce
Fight over the Body of Moses

8 Arrigo Palludano
Resurrection of Christ

9 Rosselli
Last Supper

10 Perugino
Jesus giving St Peter the Keys of Heaven

11 Roselli
Sermon on the Mount

12 Ghirlandaio
Calling of St Peter and St Andrew

13 Botticelli
Cleansing of the Leper

14 Perugino
Baptism of Christ

15 Michelangelo
The Last Judgement

CEILING PAINTINGS

1   The Creation of Light
2   The Creation of the Sun and the Moon
3   The Separation of Land and Water
4   The Creation of Adam
5   The Creation of Eve
6   The Temptation and Expulsion from the Garden of Eden
7   The Sacrifice of Noah
8   The Story of the Flood
9   The Drunkenness of Noah

10   David and Goliath
11   Judith and Holofernes
12   The Punishment of Haman
13   The Brazen Serpent

14   Jeremiah
15   Daniel
16   Ezekiel
17   Isaiah
18   The Delphic Sibyl
19   Zachariah

20   Joel
21   The Erythraean Sibyl
22   The Cumaean Sibyl
23   The Persian Sibyl
24   The Libyan Sibyl
25   Jonah

26   Aminadab
27   Salmon, Booz, Obed
28   Roboam, Abia
29   Ozias, Joatham, Achaz
30   Zorobabel, Abiud, Elichiam
31   Achim, Eliud
32   Jacob, Joseph
33   Eleazar, Matthan
34   Azor, Sadoch
35   Josias, Jechonias, Salathiel
36   Ezekias, Manasses, Amon
37   Asa, Josophat, Joram
38   Jesse, David, Solomon
39   Naasson

It's useful to carry a pair of binoculars with you in order to see the paintings better, but bear in mind that it is strictly forbidden to take pictures of any kind in the chapel, including video, and it is also officially forbidden to speak – although this is something that is rampantly ignored.

The wall paintings

Upon completion of the structure, Sixtus brought in several prominent painters of the Renaissance to decorate the walls. The overall project was under the management of Pinturicchio and comprised a series of paintings showing (on the left as you face the altar) scenes from the life of **Moses** and, on the right, scenes from the life of **Christ**. There are paintings by, among others, Perugino, who painted the marvellously composed cityscape of *Jesus giving St Peter the Keys to Heaven*, Botticelli, with *The Trials of Moses* and *Cleansing of the Leper*, and Ghirlandaio, whose *Calling of St Peter and St Andrew* shows Christ calling the two fishermen to be disciples, surrounded by onlookers, against a fictitious medieval landscape of boats, birds, turrets and mountains. Some of the paintings were in fact collaborative efforts, and it's known that Ghirlandaio and Botticelli in particular contributed to each other's work. Anywhere else they would be pored over very closely indeed. As it is, they are entirely overshadowed by Michelangelo's more famous work.

The ceiling paintings

Michelangelo's **frescoes** depict scenes from the Old Testament, from the *Creation of Light* at the altar end to the *Drunkenness of Noah* over the door. The sides are decorated with prophets and sibyls and the ancestors of Jesus. Julius II

Julius II and the origins of the Sistine Chapel frescoes

When construction was completed in 1483 during the reign of Pope Sixtus IV, the Sistine Chapel ceiling was painted as a blue background with gold stars to resemble the night sky. Over the altar there were two additional paintings by Perugino and a large picture of the Virgin Mary. Sixtus IV was succeeded by Innocent VIII, who was followed by Alexander VI, the Borgia pope who, after the brief reign of Pius III, was succeeded in 1503 by Giuliano della Rovere, who took the name **Julius II**. Though a Franciscan friar, he was a violent man with a short temper; his immediate objective as pope was to try to regain the lands that had been taken away from the papacy during the reigns of Innocent VIII and Alexander VI by the French, Germans and Spanish. For this purpose he started a series of wars and secret alliances.

Julius II was also an avid collector and patron of the arts, and he summoned to Rome the best artists and architects of the day. Among these was **Michelangelo**, who, through a series of political intrigues orchestrated by Bramante and Raphael, was assigned the task of decorating the Sistine Chapel. Work commenced in 1508. Oddly enough, Michelangelo hadn't wanted to do the work at all: he considered himself a sculptor, not a painter, and was more eager to get on with carving Julius II's tomb (now in San Pietro in Vincoli, see p.142) than the ceiling, which he regarded as a chore. Pope Julius II, however, had other plans, drawing up a design of the twelve Apostles for the vault and hiring Bramante to design a scaffold for the artist to work from. Michelangelo was apparently an awkward, solitary character: he had barely begun painting when he rejected Bramante's scaffold as unusable, fired all his staff, and dumped the pope's scheme for the ceiling in favour of his own. But the pope was easily his match, and there are tales of the two men clashing while the work was going on – Michelangelo would lock the doors at crucial points, ignoring the pope's demands to see how it was progressing, and legend has the two men at loggerheads at the top of the scaffold one day, resulting in the pope striking the artist in frustration.

△ Ceiling, the Sistine Chapel

lived only a few months after the Sistine Chapel ceiling was finished, but the fame of the work he had commissioned soon spread far and wide. Certainly, it's staggeringly impressive, all the more so for its recent restoration (financed by a Japanese TV company to the tune of $3 million in return for three years' world TV rights), which has lifted centuries of accumulated soot and candle grime off the ceilings to reveal a much brighter, more vivid painting than anyone thought existed. The restorers have also been able to chart the progress of Michelangelo as he moved across the vault. Images on fresco were completed before the plaster dried, and each day a fresh layer of plaster would have been laid, on which Michelangelo would have had around eight hours or so before having to finish for the day. Comparing the different areas of plaster, it seems the figure of Adam, in the key *Creation of Adam* scene, took four days; God, in the same fresco, took three. You can also see the development of Michelangelo as a painter when you look at the paintings in reverse order. The first painting, over the door, the *Drunkenness of Noah*, is done in a stiff and formal style, and is vastly different from the last painting, the *Creation of Light*, over the altar, which shows the artist at his best, the perfect master of the technique of fresco painting.

Entering from behind the altar, you are supposed, as you look up, to imagine that you are peering into heaven through the arches of the imaginary architecture that springs from the sides of the chapel, supported by little putti caryatids and *ignudi* or nudes, bearing shields and the oakleaf garlands of the della Rovere family of Julius II. Look at the pagan sibyls and biblical prophets which Michelangelo also incorporated in his scheme – some of the most dramatic figures in the entire work, and all clearly labelled by the painter, from the sensitive figure of the Delphic Sibyl to the hag-like Cumaean Sibyl, whose biceps would put a Bulgarian shotputter to shame. Look out, too, for the figure of the prophet Jeremiah – a brooding self-portrait of an exhausted-looking Michelangelo.

We've detailed the paintings of the central panels in the chart (see pp.196–197), but, specifically, they start with a large portrait of *Jonah and the Whale* and move on, consecutively, to *God Separating Light from Darkness* – his arms bowed, beard flowing, as he pushes the two qualities apart; *God Creating the Sun, the Moon and the Planets* – in which Michelangelo has painted God twice, once with his back to us hurling the moon into existence and simultaneously displaying another moon to the audience; *God Separating Land from Water*; and, in the fourth panel, probably most famous of all these paintings, the *Creation of Adam*, in which God sparks Adam into life with the touch of his finger. God's cape billows behind him, where a number of figures stand – representatives of all the unborn genera-tions to come after Adam. The startled young woman looking at Adam is either Eve or the Virgin Mary, here as a witness to the first events in human history.

The fifth panel from the altar shows the *Creation of Eve*, in which Adam is knocked out under the stump of a Della Rovere oak tree and God summons Eve from his side as he sleeps. She comes out in a half-crouch position with her hands clasped in a prayer of thanksgiving and awe. The sixth panel is the powerful *Temptation and Expulsion from the Garden of Eden*, with an evil spirit, depicted as a serpent, leaning out from the tree of knowledge and handing the fruit to Adam. On the right of this painting the Angel of the Lord, in swirling red robes, is brandishing his sword of original sin at the nape of Adam's neck as he tries to fend the angel off, motioning with both hands. The eighth panel continues the story, with the *Story of the Flood*, the unrighteous bulk of mankind taking shelter under tents from the rain while Noah and his kin make off for the Ark in the distance. Panel seven shows Noah and his family making a *Sacrifice of Thanksgiving* to the Lord for their safe arrival after the flood; one of the sons of Noah kneels to blow on the fire to make it hotter, while his wife brings armloads of wood. Lastly, there's the *Drunkenness of Noah*, in which Noah is shown getting drunk after harvesting the vines and exposing his genitals to his sons – it is strictly prohibited in the Hebrew canon for a father to show his reproductive organs to his children. Oddly enough, Noah's sons are naked too.

The Last Judgement

The **Last Judgement**, on the altar wall of the chapel, was painted by Michelangelo more than twenty years later, between 1535 and 1541. Michelangelo wasn't especially keen to work on this either – he was still engaged on Julius II's tomb, under threat of legal action from the late pope's family – but Pope Paul III, an old acquaintance of the artist, was keen to complete the decoration of the chapel. Michelangelo tried to delay by making demands that were likely to cause the pope to give up entirely, insisting on the removal of two paintings by Perugino and the closing of a window that pierced the end of the chapel. Furthermore, he insisted that the wall be replastered, with the top 15cm out of the perpendicular to prevent the accumulation of soot and dust. Surprisingly, the pope agreed.

The painting took five years, again single-handed, and is probably the most inspired and most homogeneous large-scale painting you'll ever see, Michelangelo's technical virtuosity taking a back seat to the sheer exuberance of the work. The human body is fashioned into a finely captured set of exquisite poses, in which even the damned can be seen as a celebration of the human form. Perhaps unsurprisingly, the painting offended some, and even before it was complete Rome was divided as to its merits, especially regarding the etiquette of introducing a display of nudity into the pope's private chapel. But Michelangelo's response to this was unequivocal, lampooning one of his fiercer critics, the pope's master of ceremonies at the time, **Biago di Cesena**, as Minos, the doorkeeper of hell, with ass's ears and an entwined serpent in the bottom right-hand corner of the picture. Later the pope's zealous successor, Pius IV, objected to the painting and would have had it removed entirely had not Michelangelo's pupil, Daniele da Volterra, appeased him by carefully – and selectively – adding coverings to some of the more obviously naked figures, forever earning himself the nickname of the "breeches-maker". During the recent work, most of the remaining breeches have been discreetly removed, restoring the painting to its former glory.

Briefly, the painting shows the **last day of existence**, when the bodily resurrection of the dead takes place and the human race is brought before Christ to be either sent to eternity in Paradise or condemned to suffer in Hell. The centre is occupied by Christ, turning angrily as he gestures the condemned to the underworld. St Peter, carrying his gold and silver keys, looks on in astonishment at his Lord filled with rage, while Mary averts her eyes from the scene. Below Christ a group of angels blasts their trumpets to summon the dead from their sleep. Somewhat amusingly, one angel holds a large book, the book of the damned, while another carries a much smaller one, the book of the saved. On the left, the dead awaken from their graves, tombs and sarcophagi (one apparently has the likeness of Martin Luther) and levitate into the heavens or are pulled by ropes and the napes of their necks by angels who take them before Christ. At the bottom right, Charon, keeper of the underworld, swings his oar at the damned souls as they fall off the boat into the waiting gates of hell. Among other characters portrayed are many martyred saints, the Apostles, Adam, and, peeking out between the legs of the saint on the left of Christ, Julius II, with a look of fear and astonishment.

Museum of Christian Art and the Vatican Library

After the Sistine Chapel, you're channelled all the way to the exit by way of the **Museum of Christian Art**, which is not of great interest in itself, but does give access to a small room off to the left that contains a number of ancient Roman frescoes and mosaics, among them the celebrated *Aldobrandini Wedding*, a first-century BC Roman fresco that shows the preparations for a wedding in touching detail. Other items in a room that is extremely rich in interest include frescoes showing scenes from the Odyssey, and another, later piece from Ostia depicting a ship being loaded with grain, as well as some fantastic mosaics of wild beasts.

Back down the main corridor, the **Vatican Library**, home to around a million books and manuscripts (you can't touch any of them) is decorated with scenes of Rome and the Vatican as it was during his reign. Over one of the doors of the corridor you can see the facade of St Peter's as it was in the late 1500s, before Maderno's extension of the nave; over the facing door you can see the erection of the obelisk outside in the Piazza San Pietro, showing the men, ropes, animals and a primitive derrick, with the obelisk being drawn forward on a sled, while beyond the corridor opens out into the dramatic **Library of Sixtus V** on the right, a vast hall built across the courtyard in the late sixteenth century to glorify literature – and of course Sixtus V himself.

Braccio Nuovo and Museo Chiaramonti

The **Braccio Nuovo** and **Museo Chiaramonti** both hold classical sculpture, although be warned that they are the Vatican at its most overwhelming – close on a thousand statues crammed into two long galleries – and you need a keen eye and much perseverance to make any sense of it all. The **Braccio Nuovo** was built in the early 1800s to display classical statuary that was particularly prized, and it contains, among other things, probably the most famous extant image of Augustus, and a bizarre-looking statue depicting the Nile, whose yearly flooding was essential to the fertility of the Egyptian soil. It is this aspect of the river that is represented here: crawling over the hefty river god are sixteen babies, thought to allude to the number of cubits the river needed to rise to fertilize the land.

The 300-metre-long **Chiaramonti gallery** is especially unnerving, lined with the chill marble busts of hundreds of nameless, blank-eyed ancient Romans, along with the odd deity. It pays to have a leisurely wander, for there are some real characters here: sour, thin-lipped matrons with their hair tortured into pleats, curls and spirals; kids, caught in a sulk or mid-chortle; and ancient old men with flesh sagging and wrinkling to reveal the skull beneath. Many of these heads are ancestral portraits, kept by the Romans in special shrines in their houses to venerate their familial predecessors, and in some cases family resemblances can be picked out. The fine head of Athena, on the left as you exit, has kept her glass eyes, a reminder that most of these statues were originally painted to resemble life, with eyeballs where now a blank space stares out.

The Pinacoteca

The **Pinacoteca**, housed in a separate building on the far side of the Vatican's main spine, ranks possibly as Rome's best picture gallery, with works from the early primitives right up to the nineteenth century.

The display is chronological, and starts with a beautiful collection of works from the **Gothic period**, among them an amazing, almost mosaic-like *Last Judgement* by Nicolo and Giovanni from the second half of the twelfth century in the first room, and the stunning Simoneschi triptych by Giotto in the next room, depicting the *Martyrdom of SS Peter and Paul* and painted in the early 1300s for the old St Peter's, where it remained until 1506 when it was removed for the rebuilding of the new church. In the rooms that follow are lovely pieces by Masolino, Fra Angelico and Filippo Lippi, while the next room has the naturalistic works of Palmezzano and Melozzo de Forlí's musical angels – fragments of a fresco commissioned for the family church of Santi Apostoli by Giuliano delle Rovere, the future Pope Julius II. Another part of the same fresco resides in the Palazzo Quirinale (p.129). Julius II also makes an appearance in

⑪

de Forlí's *Sixtus IV opening the Vatican Library* in the same room – he's the large figure in red, and the painting is as much a family scene as anything, also showing the pope's brother Raffaele Riario (Giuliano's father) behind him (in blue), another nephew, Girolamo, also in blue, and on the far left Giuliano's brother Giovanni, then the prefect of Rome.

The next room holds Carlo Crivelli's magnificently angst-ridden *Pietà*, while beyond here lie the rich backdrops and elegantly clad figures of the **Umbrian School painters**, Perugino and Pinturicchio. Raphael has a room to himself, with three very important oil paintings, and, in climate-controlled glass cases, the tapestries that were made to his designs to be hung in the Sistine Chapel during conclave. The cartoons from which these tapestries were made are now in the Victoria and Albert Museum in London. Of the three paintings, the *Coronation of the Virgin*, on the right, was done when he was only 19 years old; the *Transfiguration*, in the middle, was interrupted by his death in 1520 and finished by his pupils; and the *Madonna of Foglino*, on the left, shows saints John the Baptist, Francis of Assisi and Jerome, and was painted as an offering after a cannonball (in the centre of the painting) struck his house.

Leonardo's *St Jerome*, in the next room, is unfinished, too, but it's a remarkable piece of work, with Jerome a rake-like ascetic torn between suffering and a good meal. Look closely at this painting and you can see that a 25-centimetre square, the saint's head, has been reglued to the canvas after the painting was used as upholstery for a stool in a cobbler's shop in Rome for a number of years. Caravaggio's *Descent from the Cross*, two rooms on, however, gets more attention, a warts 'n' all canvas that unusually shows the **Virgin Mary** as a middle-aged mother grieving over her dead son, while the men placing Christ's body on the bier are models that the artist recruited from the city streets – a realism that is imitated successfully in Reni's *Crucifixion of St Peter* in the same room: the Baroque at full throttle. Take a look, too, at the most gruesome painting in the collection, Poussin's *Martyrdom of St Erasmus*, which shows the saint stretched out on a table with his hands bound above his head in the process of having his small intestine wound onto a drum – basically being "drawn" prior to "quartering". The views over the Vatican Gardens nearby, with the dome of St Peter's in the background, provides a suitable antidote if you need it.

The Musei Gregoriano Profano, Pio Cristiano and Missionario Etnologico

Leaving the Pinacoteca, you're well placed for the further grouping of museums in the modern building next door. The **Museo Gregoriano Profano** holds more classical sculpture, mounted on scaffolds for all-round viewing, including mosaics of athletes from the Baths of Caracalla and Roman funerary work, notably the Haterii tomb friezes, which show backdrops of ancient Rome and realistic portrayals of contemporary life. It's thought the Haterii were a family of construction workers and that they grabbed the opportunity to advertise their services by incorporating reliefs of the buildings they had worked on (including the Colosseum), along with a natty little crane, on the funeral monument of one of their female members.

The adjacent **Museo Pio Cristiano** has intricate early Christian sarcophagi and, most famously, an expressive third-century AD statue of the *Good Shepherd*. And the **Museo Missionario Etnologico** displays art and artefacts from all over the world, collected by Catholic missionaries, and seems to be inspired by the Vatican's desire to poke fun at non-Christian cults – as well as pat itself on the back for its own evangelical successes.

⑫

Out from the city

You may find there's quite enough of interest in Rome to keep you occupied during your stay. But it can be a hot, oppressive city, its surfeit of churches and museums sometimes seem intensely wearying, and if you're around long enough you really shouldn't feel any guilt about freeing yourself from its weighty history to see something of the countryside around. Two of the main attractions visitable on a day-trip are, admittedly, ancient Roman sites, but just the process of getting to them can be energizing. And there are other attractions further afield that may even tempt you to stay overnight – though to visit the places we've included here this isn't necessary. **Tivoli**, about an hour by bus east of Rome, is a small provincial town famous for the travertine quarries nearby and for two villas – one Renaissance, one Roman, both of them complete with landscaped gardens and parks. **Ostia**, southwest of the city near the sea, and similarly easy to reach on public transport, is the city's main seaside resort (though one worth avoiding), and was also the site of the port of ancient Rome, the ruins of which – **Ostia Antica** – are well preserved and worth seeing. North of Rome, the Etruscan site of **Cerveteri** is an atmospheric alternative to the archeology of the city itself, while **Bracciano** has the airy location on its lake and the appeal of an Italian provincial town. South of Rome, the **Castelli Romani** provide the closest and most appealing stretch of countryside close to Rome; and the coastal towns of **Anzio and Nettuno** its most accessible seaside resorts.

Tivoli

Just 40km from Rome, perched high on a hill and looking back over the plain, **TIVOLI** has always been something of a retreat from the city, due to its fresh mountain air and pleasant position on the Aniene River. In classical days it was a retirement town for wealthy Romans; later, during the Renaissance, it again became the playground of the moneyed classes, attracting some of the city's most well-to-do families out here to build villas. Nowadays the leisured classes have mostly gone, but Tivoli does very nicely on the fruits of its still-thriving travertine business, exporting the precious stone worldwide (the quarries line the main road into town from Rome), and supports a small airy centre that preserves a number of relics from its ritzier days. To do justice to the gardens and villas – especially if Villa Adriana is on your list – you'll need time; set out early, and try to be in Tivoli mid-morning at the latest.

Villa d'Este

Most people head first for **Villa d'Este** (summer daily 9am–1hr before sunset; winter Tues–Sun 9am–1hr before sunset; €6.50), across the main square of Largo Garibaldi. Once a convent, it was transformed into a country villa by Pirro Ligorio in 1550 for Cardinal Ippolito d'Este, and is now often thronged with visitors even outside peak season. The villa itself is worth a visit. It has been recently restored to its original state, with beautiful Mannerist frescoes in its seven rooms showing scenes from the history of the d'Este family in Tivoli. But most people come here to see the **garden**, which peels away down the hill in a succession of terraces; it's probably the most contrived garden in Italy, but also the most ingenious, almost completely symmetrical, its carefully tended lawns, shrubs and hedges interrupted at decent intervals by one playful fountain after another. In their day some of these were quite amazing – one was a water organ, the air for the pipes being forced by water valves, another imitated the call of birds – though nowadays the emphasis is on the quieter creations. Newly restored and once again fully open to the public, they're collectively unique and a must-see if you're in Tivoli; just make sure that you don't *touch or drink* the water in the fountains – it comes directly from the operating sewers of Tivoli.

Among the fountains, the central, almost Gaudí-like Fontana del Bicchierone, by Bernini, is one of the simplest and most elegant; on the far left, the Rometta or "Little Rome" has reproductions of the city's major buildings and a boat holding an obelisk; while perhaps the best is the **Fontana dell'Ovato** on the opposite side of the garden, fringed with statues, behind which is a rather dank arcade, in which you can walk.

Villa Gregoriana

Tivoli's other main attraction, the **Villa Gregoriana** (April–Oct daily 10am– 6.30pm; €4), recently reopened after restoration, was created when Pope Gregory XVI diverted the flow of the river here to ease the periodic flooding of the town in 1831. At least as interesting and beautiful as the d'Este estate, it remains less well known and less visited, and has none of the latter's conceits – its vegetation is lush and overgrown, descending into a gorge over 60m deep.

There are two main waterfalls – the larger Grande Cascata on the far side, and a small Bernini-designed one at the neck of the gorge. The path winds down to the bottom of the canyon, passing ruined Roman resting pavilions and scaling the drop on the other side past two grottoes, where you can get right up to the roaring falls. The dark, torn shapes of the rock glower overhead. It's harder work than the Villa d'Este – if you blithely saunter down to the bottom

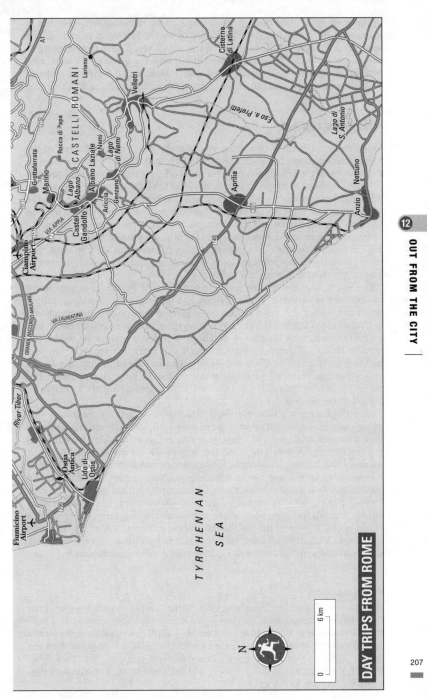

TYRRHENIAN
SEA

N

0   6 km

DAY TRIPS FROM ROME

of the gorge, you'll find that it's a long way back up the other side – but it is in many ways more rewarding; the path leads up on the far side to an exit and the substantial remains of a **Temple of Vesta**, which you'll have seen clinging to the side of the hill. This is now incorporated into the gardens of a restaurant, but it's all right to walk through and take a look, and the view is probably Tivoli's best – down into the chasm and across to the high green hills that ring the town.

Villa Adriana

Once you've seen these two sights you've really seen Tivoli – the rest of the town is nice enough but there's not that much to it. But just outside town, at the bottom of the hill, fifteen minutes' walk off the main Rome road (ask the Rome–Tivoli bus to drop you or take the local CAT #4 from Largo Garibaldi), **Villa Adriana**, or Hadrian's Villa (daily 9am–1hr before sunset; €6.50), puts the achievements of the Tivoli popes and cardinals very much into the shade. This was probably the largest and most sumptuous villa in the Roman Empire, the retirement home of the emperor Hadrian for a short while between 135 AD and his death three years later, and it occupies an enormous site. You need time to see it all; there's no point in doing it at a gallop and, taken with the rest of Tivoli, it makes for a long day's sightseeing.

The site is one of the most soothing spots around Rome, its stones almost the epitome of romantic, civilized ruins. The imperial palace buildings proper are in fact one of the least well preserved parts of the complex, but much else is clearly recognizable. Hadrian was a great traveller and a keen architect, and parts of the villa were inspired by buildings he had seen around the world. The massive Pecile, for instance, through which you enter, is a reproduction of a building in Athens. The Canopus, on the opposite side of the site, is a liberal copy of the sanctuary of Serapis near Alexandria, its long, elegant channel of water fringed by sporadic columns and statues leading up to a temple of Serapis at the far end.

Near the Canopus a museum displays the latest finds from the usually on-going excavations, though most of the extensive original discoveries have found their way back to Rome and many museums in Europe. Walking back towards the entrance, make your way across the upper storey of the so-called Pretorio, a former warehouse, and down to the remains of two bath complexes. Beyond is a fishpond with a *cryptoporticus* (underground passageway) winding around underneath. It is great to walk through the cryptoporticus and look up at its ceiling, picking out the names of the seventeenth- and eighteenth-century artists (Bernini, for one) who visited and wrote their signatures here using a smoking candle. Behind this are the relics of the emperor's imperial apartments. The Teatro Maríttimo, adjacent, with its island in the middle of a circular pond, is the place to which it's believed Hadrian would retire at siesta time to be sure of being alone.

Practicalities

Buses leave Rome for Tivoli and Villa Adriana every twenty minutes from Ponte Mammolo metro station (line B) – journey time fifty minutes. In Tivoli, the bus station is in Piazza Massimo near the Villa Gregoriana, though you can get off earlier, on the main square of Largo Garibaldi, where you'll find the tourist office (Mon 9am–3pm, Tues–Fri 9am–6.30pm, Sat 9am–3pm; ☏0774.334.522), which has free maps and information on **accommodation** if you're planning to stay over.

Ostia

There are two Ostias: one an over-visited seaside resort, the **Lido di Ostia**, which is well worth avoiding; the other, one of the finest ancient Roman sites – the excavations of the port of **Ostia Antica** – which are on a par with anything you'll see in Rome itself and easily merit a half-day journey out. Both Lido di Ostia and Ostia Antica are reachable by overground train from Porta San Paolo station, next to Piramide metro station on line B, or from Basilica San Paolo or Magliana metro stations, further down line B. All you need is a regular €1 ATAC ticket.

Lido di Ostia

The **LIDO DI OSTIA** has for many years been the number one, or at any rate the closest, seaside resort for Romans. The beaches are OK, and have recently been cleaned up, but the town is on the whole a poor outpost of the city, with little, if anything, to recommend it – you're probably better off making the slightly longer journey to Anzio or Nettuno if you want to swim (see p.217). If you do come here, the water is most inviting along the coastal road between Ostia and Torvaianica, and there are nudist areas around the 8 or 9km marker.

Ostia Antica

Two stops before Lido di Ostia on the train from Rome, the site of **OSTIA ANTICA** marked the coastline in classical times, and the town which grew up here was the port of ancient Rome, a thriving place whose commercial activities were vital to the city further upstream – until they were curtailed by the silting up of the harbour. The **excavations** (Tues–Sun April–Oct 8.30am–6pm, March 8.30am–5pm, Nov–Feb 8.30am–4pm; €4) remain relatively unvisited; indeed until the 1970s the site was only open one day a week and few people realized how well the port had been preserved by the Tiber's mud. Still relatively free of the bustle of tourists, it's an evocative site, and it's much easier to reconstruct a Roman town from this than from any amount of pottering around the Forum – or even Pompeii. It's very spread out, so be prepared for a fair amount of walking; and carry some water, to avoid the rather pricey snack bar in the back of the museum.

The site

From the entrance, the **Decumanus Maximus**, the main street of Ostia, leads west, past the the **Baths Complex** on the right, where there's an interesting mosaic of seahorses and other creatures. A little way down on the right, at the corner of **Via della Fontana**, a pavement inscription of a cup marks what would have been a bar. Via della Fontana itself is a wonderfully preserved street, and gives a good idea of a typical Roman urban layout, with its ground floor shops and upper floor apartments. The fountain that gives the street its name is on the right, a long coffin-shaped thing that would have been a source of fresh water for the homes and businesses nearby. Right past here takes you to **Caserma dei Vigili**, whose courtyard focuses on a shrine to the cult of Fortuna.

The Decumanus Maximus continues to the town's commercial centre, **Piazzale delle Corporazioni**, where the remains of shops and trading offices

OSTIA ANTICA

River Tiber

Museo Ostiense

P

Baths of Mithras

Terme dei Sette Sapienti

Casa degli Aurighi

House of Cupid and Psyche

Casa Dei Dipinti

Horrea

Casa Copadino

House of Diana

Thermopolium

Forum

Republican Temples

Porta Occidentale

Mithraeum

Casa delle Mese

House of Apulius

Horrea

Caserma Dei Vigili

Baths of Neptune

Baths Complex

Horrea

Porta Romana

PIAZZALE DELLA VITTORIA

PIAZZALE DELLE CORPORAZIONI

Theatre

Horrea di Hortensius

Collegio Degli Augustali

C. Fortuna Annonaria

Baths

Capitol

Fish Shop

Domus delle Colonne

Caupona di Alexander

Porta Marina

Terme della Marciana

Synagogue

Entrance

CINTA SILIANA

Porta Laurentina

Necropoli di Porta Laurentina

Porta Romana

N

Lido di Ostia

Fiumicino Airport

still fringe the central square. These represented commercial enterprises from all over the ancient world, and the mosaics of boats and fish and suchlike just in front denote their trade (grain merchants, ship fitters, ropemakers and so on) as well as their origin (Carthage, for example). Flanking the southern side of the square, the **theatre**, with its comic and tragic masks, has been much restored but is nonetheless impressive, enlarged by Septimius Severus in the second century AD to hold up to four thousand people; it sometimes hosts performances of classical drama during summer. On the left of the square, the **House of Apulius** preserves mosaic floors and, beyond, a dark-aisled **mithraeum** with more mosaiced benches illustrating the practices of the cult of Mithras.

Behind here – past the substantial remains of the *horrea* or warehouses that once stood all over the city – the **House of Diana** is probably the best-preserved private house in Ostia, with a dark, mysterious set of rooms around a central courtyard, and again with a mithraeum at the back. Across the road, the **Thermopolium** is an ancient Roman café, complete with seats outside, a high counter, display shelves and even wall paintings of parts of the menu. At the back is a marble wall slab which once held hooks for hanging coats, beyond which is what would have been a peaceful small courtyard with a fountain. Opposite the Thermopolium, steps lead to the top of the **Casa dei Dipinti**, giving a fine view over the site. The house itself is sometimes locked but if you can get in you'll be rewarded with a wonderful mosaic fragment showing birds and people.

North of here, the half a dozen rooms of the **Museo Ostiense** are full of sculptural finds from the site and well worth seeing. In a room to the left as you enter is a wall painting of *Mithras Slaying the Bull* from one of Ostia's mithraeums. The central room has a fine headless male figure in repose, foot resting on a column base, and a figure of Trajan in full battle dress, between two busts of him and another of Hadrian, along with a likeness of Commodus as a young boy. The room beyond has a statue of Septimus Severius next to his wife, Julia Donna, as the goddess Ceres, while opposite a beautifully preserved figure of Maxentius and his sister Fausta look on. In a room off here are various carved sarcophagi found on Via Ostiense, all amazingly well preserved, including one of a young boy, decorated with cupids, while off to the other side are various representations of Venus and a wall painting of the Three Graces from the second century AD.

Left from here, the **Forum** centres on the **Capitol** building, reached by a wide flight of steps, and is fringed by the remains of baths and a basilica. Continuing on down the main street, more **horrea**, superbly preserved and complete with pediment over the entrance and names inscribed on the marble, merit a detour off to the right (although you can't enter, you can peer into the courtyard), before reaching the **Porta Occidentale** or western gate a few yards further on. On the left here is what may have been a **fish shop**, judging by its floor mosaics, still with its shelves and marble table, across from which Via delle Foce leads off right. To the left of here a long alley leads to another **mithraeum**, this time painted with scenes of mithraic rites. On the other side of Via delle Foce is a complex of **Republican temples**, possibly dating back to the time of Sulla, behind which is the **House of Cupid and Psyche**, which has a courtyard you can walk into with a copy of the statue of Cupid and Psyche that you can see in the museum, its rooms clearly discernible on one side, a colourful marbled floor at the top, and a columned nymphaeum, with marble niches, on the right.

Keep on down Via delle Foce from here and you soon reach the **Terme dei Sette Sapienti** on the left, with its round arcaded courtyard and wonderfully intact floor mosaic. Steps lead up to the roof for good views over this part of the site and the fragments of wall paintings below. The atmpospheric arcaded passageways of the complex lead to the **Casa degli Aurighi**, which you can ascend for more excellent views, beyond which Via degli Aurighi takes you back to the main Decumanus Maximus. A right turn takes you down to the **Porta Marina**, or sea gate. This is marked by the **Caupona di Alexander** on the left, a wine shop with flower mosaics identifying the owner and showing various forms of combat. Beyond here the road continues on for a little way to what was once the sea – but is now just the main road.

Cerveteri

CERVETERI provides the most accessible Etruscan taster from Rome, travelling from Rome's Lepanto station by COTRAL **bus** (line A; every 40min; 80min) to Piazza Aldo Moro. The same Roma–Cerverteri bus also links to the train station 7km away at **LADISPOLI**, incidentally the best of the uninspiring seaside resorts just outside the capital. Swimming spots exist about ten minutes' walk from the station, although the best is further north, around half an hour away at the **Torre Flavia** – a medieval construction restored in 1565 by an Orsini cardinal, now collapsing elegantly into the water in four equal parts.

The settlement here dates back to the tenth century BC and was once a trading heavyweight, one of the Mediterranean's largest centres. Cerveteri, also known as Caere, ranked among the top three cities in the twelve-strong Etruscan federation, its wealth derived largely from the mineral-rich **Tolfa hills** to the northeast – a gentle range that gives the plain a much-needed touch of scenic colour. In its heyday, the town spread over 8km (something like thirty times its present size), controlling territory 50km up the coast. Rot set in from 351 BC, when the Romans assumed control without granting full citizenship rights.

The present town is a thirteenth-century creation, dismissed by D.H. Lawrence – and you really can't blame him – as "forlorn beyond words". On arrival, make straight for the Etruscan **necropolis** (May–Sept Tues–Sun 9am–7pm; Oct–April Tues–Sun 9am–4pm; €4, €6.50 including museum), just 1km away in Banditaccia and signposted from the central piazza. From the seventh to first century BC, the Etruscans constructed a literal city of the dead here, weird and fantastically well preserved, with complete streets and homes. Some tombs are strange round pillboxes carved from cliffs; others are covered in earth to create the barrows that ripple the surrounding plateau. Archeologists speculate that women were buried in separate small chambers within each "house" – easy to distinguish – while the men were laid on deathbeds (occasionally in sarcophagi) hewn directly from the stone. Indeed archeological evidence suggests that the position of women in Etruscan society was roughly on a par with that of men. Cremated slaves lie in urns alongside their masters – civilized by comparison with the Romans, who simply threw them into mass burial pits. The twelve or so show-tombs, lying between the two main roads, open and close in random rotation. If possible, don't miss the **Tomba Bella** (Tomb of the Bas-Reliefs), **Tomba dei Letti Funebri** (Tomb of the Funeral Beds) and the **Tomba dei Capitelli**.

You could spend several hours wandering about, but you might be better off heading back into town to the **Museo Nazionale di Cerveteri**, at the top of the old quarter in the sixteenth-century **Castello Ruspoli** (Tues–Sun 9am–7pm;

€ 4). This has two large rooms containing a fraction of the huge wealth that was buried with the Etruscan dead – vases, terracottas and a run of miscellaneous day-to-day objects; most of the best stuff though has been whisked away to Villa Giulia in Rome (see p.162). En route, quench your appetite at the little **trattoria**, *Tukulcha*, on the necropolis road, which serves hearty country-style food and crisp Cerveteri white wines (no credit cards; closed Mon).

Bracciano

The closest of northern Lazio's lakes to Rome, the smooth, roughly circular expanse of **Lago di Bracciano** fills an enormous volcanic crater. It's nothing spectacular, with few real sights and a landscape of rather plain, rolling country-side and, while popular with Romans escaping the heat of the city, its shores are fairly peaceful even on summer Sundays, and you can eat excellent lake fish in its restaurants.

The lake's main settlement is **BRACCIANO**, on the western shore, about half an hour by train from Rome San Pietro (direction Viterbo), a small town that was catapulted into the news when Tom Cruise and Katy Holmes got married there in 2006. The couple tied the knot at the imposing **Castello Orsini-Odelscalchi** (April–Sept Tues–Sat 10am–12.30pm & 3–6pm, Sun 9am–12.30pm & 3–6.30pm; Oct–March Tues–Sat 10am–noon & 3–5pm, Sun 9am–noon & 3–5.30pm; tours every 30min; € 6), which dominates the town, a late-fifteenth-century structure privately owned by the Odelscalchi family. The outer walls, now mostly disappeared, contained the rectangular piazza of the medieval town; nowadays the castle is a little rundown, its interior home to rusting suits of armour and faded frescoes, but the view from the ramparts, over the broad blue oval of the lake, is worth the admission price alone.

The best place to **swim** in the lake is from the beach at Lungolago Argenti, below Bracciano town. You can rent a boat and picnic on the beach, and the nearby trattorias are good and inexpensive – try *Da Tonino* at no. 18, which serves good pasta and fish right on the water's edge. The shore between Trevig-nano and Anguillara also boasts fine swimming spots, and there are good **restaurants** in both towns. One of the best is the *Casina Bianca*, Via della Rena 100 (closed Mon), Trevignano, which serves fresh fish on a terrace overlooking the lake.

The Castelli Romani and Alban Hills

Just free of the sprawling southern suburbs of Rome, the thirteen towns that make up the **Castelli Romani** date back to medieval times. These hills – the **Colli Albani** – have long cooled rich and powerful urbanites, and their rich volcanic soil produces some extraordinary white wines. The region is now pretty heavily built-up, with most of the historic centres ringed by unprepos-sessing suburbs, and summer weekends see traffic jams of Romans trooping out to local trattorias. But off-peak, it's worth the journey, either as an excursion from Rome or a stop on the way south. By car, there are two obvious routes, both starting with Frascati and Grottaferrata and then spearing off at Marino along either the eastern or western side of Lago Albano. COTRAL **buses** serve the area (every 30min; 35min) from Rome's Anagnina metro station (line A).

Frascati and around

Just 20km away from Rome, **FRASCATI** is the nearest of the Castelli towns and also the most striking, dominated by the majestic **Villa Aldobrandini**, designed by Giacomo della Porta at the turn of the sixteenth century (1598–1603). The Baroque *palazzo* is off-limits, but the **gardens** are open (Mon–Fri: summer 9am–1pm & 3–6pm; winter 9am–1pm & 3–5pm; €2). Sadly the elaborate water theatre, where statues once played flutes, no longer spouts as well as it used to, but the view from the front terrace is superb, with Rome visible on a clear day.

Frascati's main square, **Piazza Marconi**, is right beneath the Aldobrandini villa, and home to a **tourist office** (Tues–Fri 8am–2pm & 4–7pm, Sat 8am–2pm; ℡06.942.0331). Just beyond here is the pedestrianized old centre, which revolves around the two squares of **Piazza San Pietro** and **Piazza del Mercato** just beyond. Frascati is also about the most famous of the Colli Albani wine towns: ask at the tourist office for details of winery tours and tastings, or simply indulge at one of the many trattorias in town. Better yet, pick up a *porchetta* (roast pork) sandwich from one of the stands on **Piazza del Mercato** and take the greasy bundle into a *cantine*, where wine is sold from giant wooden barrels for just 50c a glass. Try the *Antica Osteria di Castello*, just off Piazza del Mercato, or *Grappolo d'Oro*, just off Piazza del Gesú. For **accommodation**, *The Pinocchio*, Piazza del Mercato 21, has affordable, stylish rooms, its warm tones offsetting all the black lacquer (℡06.941.7883, www.hotelpinocchio.it; ❷), and its **restaurant** specializes in porcini mushrooms and duck.

Tusculum, beautifully sited on a nearby hill, was an Etruscan centre that became overrun by Roman patricians. The Emperor Tiberius and orator Cicero both had villas here, but Pope Celestine III destroyed the resort in 1191 and the inhabitants moved down to modern-day Frascati. Undergrowth has submerged most of the Roman remains, but there's a small theatre, and the views are fine.

North of Lago Albano

Three kilometres or so down the road, **GROTTAFERRATA** is known for its wine and its eleventh-century **abbey** – a fortified Basilian (Greek Orthodox) monastery surrounded by high defensive walls and a now-empty moat (daily: summer 6am–12.30pm & 3.30–7pm; winter 6am–12.30pm & 3.30pm–sunset; free). It's a timeless spot; the little **church of Santa Maria** inside has a Byzantine-style interior decorated with thirteenth-century mosaics and the **chapel of St Nilo** off the right aisle has frescoes by Domenichino. Through the inner courtyard there's a small museum (closed for restoration) displaying classical and medieval sculptures.

MARINO, another 4km further on, is a pleasant little town set around a pretty main square, Piazza Matteoti, and its wine is perhaps the region's best after Frascati. On Piazza Matteoti, the Fontana dei Mori has mermaids and manacled Moors commemorating the Battle of Lepanto, and spouts *vino* on special occasions such as the first Sunday of October during its Sagra dell'Uva festival, while at other times of the year you can sample the local wine in the *For de Porta* vineria in the corner of the square or the food at the *Rotonda* restaurant in the opposite corner.

East of Lago Albano

The scenic Via dei Laghi skirts the eastern rim of **Lago Albano** until a winding road leads up to **Monte Cavo** (949m), the second highest of the Colli Albani and topped with the masts and satellite dishes of the Italian

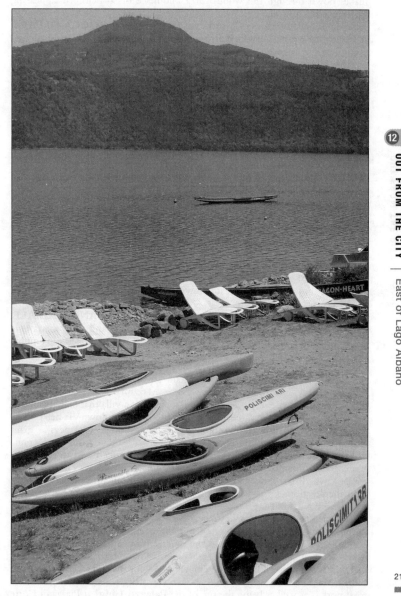

△ Lago Albano

military – who operate from nearby Ciampino airport. There used to be a hotel here, a former Passionist convent, but the building is now derelict, and the summit is much less of a tourist attraction than it used to be. A temple to Jupiter once stood here, but now the only extant antiquity is the Via Sacra, which, about 1000m from the top, emerges from dense undergrowth, and snakes down through the woods for a kilometre or so before disappearing again into thick bush.

On the far side of Monte Cavo, the road bears right for **ROCCA DI PAPA**, at 680m the loftiest Castelli Romani town. It's also one of the most picturesque, with a medieval quarter that tumbles down the hill in haphazard terraces, and motor traffic kept to a strictly enforced minimum. Make for the small Piazza Garibaldi, a lively place in summer, with a bar and restaurant, and soak up the views.

West of Lago Albano

Leaving Marino, the road joins up with the ancient Roman Via Appia, which travels straight as an arrow down the west side of Lago Albano. **CASTEL GANDOLFO** is the first significant stop, best known as the pope's summer retreat. Set four hundred metres above the lake, it's a pleasantly airy place, and enjoys great views over the entire lake from its terraces close by the main Piazza della Libertá, a bustling oblong of cafés and papal souvenir shops, at the end of which is the imposing bulk of the Papal Palace itself. Inevitably Vatican business predominates, especially on Sundays between July and September when the pope traditionally gives a midday address from the palace. If it's hot, you can take good advantage of the lake here: there's a pleasant lido just below town, with lots of restaurants and pizzerias and a small stretch of grey beach from where you can stroll the whole shoreline in about two hours. The road leads down from the main road, just north of Castel Gandolfo's old centre.

From Castel Gandolfo a panoramic road leads to **ALBANO LAZIALE**, one of the larger towns along the ancient Via Appia, and with a strategic position that has left it with lots of Roman remnants: a crumbled old amphitheatre, once with room for 15,000 spectators, fragments of a gate right in the town centre, and the the foundations of the Roman garrison's baths behind the church of **San Pietro**, on the main street, Corso Matteotti. In one direction on Corso Matteotti, busy Piazza Mazzini looks south over Villa Comunale park, where there are sketchy remains of a villa that once belonged to Pompey, while in the other direction, off to the right down Via della Stella, the **Tomb of Horatii and the Curiatii**, whose strange "chimneys" – giant truncated cones resembling Etruscan funerary urns – date from the Republican era. You can get the lowdown on all this in the nearby **Museo Civico**, Viale Risorgimento 3 (Mon–Sun 9am–1pm, also Wed & Thurs 4–7pm; €2.50), which has lots of information and a small but high-quality archeological collection.

There are much nicer places to stay than Albano, but if you're hungry, *Sesto*, a bar and *tavola calda* on the main street at no. 40, is a good place for either a snack or full lunch, with outdoor seating out the back. Otherwise the Via Appia continues on to **ARICCIA**, across the nineteenth-century **Ponte di Ariccia** – whose Roman viaduct arches are visible below – into the town's central piazza, a well-proportioned square embellished with Bernini's round church of **Santa Maria dell'Assunzione**. Ariccia, incidentally, is famous for *porchetta* – roast pork – as well as being the site of the **Palazzo Chigi** at Piazza di Corte

14 (Tues–Fri guided tours at 11am, 4pm & 5.30pm, Sat & Sun hourly 10.30am–6pm; €7), built by Bernini for Pope Alexander VII.

Lago di Nemi

Just beyond Ariccia, **GENZANO** was once the seat of the Sforzas, an aristocratic Renaissance family, and is still dominated by the **Castello Sforza-Cesarini** at the top of the town, a decrepit building whose grounds now form the pleasantly bucolic **Parco Sforza** (daily 10am–1pm & 3–8pm; free), whose wooded paths and ponds give wonderful views over the Lago di Nemi. There's a great **restaurant** here, right opposite the castle, *La Scuderia*, Piazza Sforza Cesarini 1 (☏06.939.0521; closed Mon), whose impeccable service and superb, moderately priced local food is worth stopping for.

A detour east will take you to **NEMI**, built high above the tiny crater lake of the same name. The village itself isn't much to write home about, but a cobbled road leads down to fields of strawberries that lie between the steep walls of the crater and the shores of the lake and make a good place to picnic. The town is known for its year-round strawberry harvest, and celebrates this on the first Sunday in June in the Sagra delle Fragole. On the northern shore of the lake you'll notice the large, hangar-like local museum (daily 9am–6pm; €2). This re-opened recently, and contains the scanty remains of two Roman pleasure boats said to have been built by Caligula, which caught fire and sank in ancient times. They were raised in the 1930s by the Mussolini government and placed in the specially constructed hangars, prime examples of reinforced concrete engineering and Fascist architecture. In the last days of the German occupation in 1944 they were set on fire again, so what you see is the ruins of a ruin. Many of the bronze fittings of these boats have been transferred to Palazzo Massimo in Rome but there are always interesting exhibitions of recent local archeological finds on display.

Anzio and Nettuno

About 40km south of Rome, and easily seen on a day-trip, **ANZIO** is the first town of any note, the centre of a lengthy spread of settlement that focuses on a lively central square and a busy fishing industry. Much of the town was damaged during a difficult Allied landing here on January 22, 1944, to which two military cemeteries (one British, on the road to Aprilia, and another American, just outside nearby Nettuno) bear testimony, as does a small museum. Despite thorough rebuilding, it's a likeable resort, still depending as much on fish as tourists for its livelihood.

In town, the seafood **restaurants** that crowd together along the harbour are reasonably priced: *La Cicala*, right by the water at Riviera Zanardelli 11 (☏06.984.6747; closed Wed) is as good as any, with outside seating and decent food and service; *Pierino*, a couple of blocks inland at Piazza C. Battisti 3 (☏06.984.5683; closed Mon), is a cut above the rest. The **beaches**, which edge the coast on either side, are sandy and not unbearably thronged outside of August, and stretch right up to the ruins of the **Villa di Nerone** to the north. Anzio is also a possible route to the island of Ponza; **hydrofoils** leave daily from April to August from Via Porto Innocenziano (☏06.984.5083; �🌐www.vetor.it). For timings and other information, ask at the **tourist**

office at Piazza Pia 19 (Tues–Sat 9am–1pm, Wed & Thurs also 3–6pm; ℡06.984.5147).

NETTUNO, a couple of kilometres down the coast, and walkable by the shoreline road, is more of the same, but with slightly smaller beaches, and less clear and calm water. Again, it's a mostly modern town, but there's a well-preserved old quarter, still walled, with a couple of decent **trattorias** on the main square – information is available from the **tourist office** at the port (Mon–Fri 10am–12.30pm & 5–7.30pm, Sat 10am–12.30pm & 5.30–7pm; ℡06.980.3335).

Listings

Listings

Accommodation

A s you might expect, there is plenty of **accommodation** in Rome, and for much of the year you can usually find something without too much trouble. However, it's always worth booking in advance if you want to snag a bargain, especially when the city is at its busiest – from Easter to the end of October, and during the Christmas and New Year period. Rome's ongoing makeover since Jubilee year 2000 seems to have dramatically enhanced the city's allure for all sorts of visitors, not just pilgrims, and the amount of accommodation at all levels has increased significantly. You're sure to find something to suit within your budget, but don't leave it too late.

The hotel booking site Ⓦ www.venere.com is a good last-minute option if you do; you can also call them on ☎00800.8363.7300 (Mon–Sat 10am–8pm). Or, if you arrive in Rome without booking and can't find anywhere, the tourist office or **Enjoy Rome** may be able to help you (see p.31). The rooms offered by the touts at Termini are rarely a good deal, and can often be rather dodgy; if you do take the bait, be sure to establish the (full) price beforehand, in writing if necessary, and use them only as a last resort.

Overall, **hotel rates** have like everything else in Rome increased over the last few years, despite the increase in capacity. Nonetheless it's still possible to pick up a bargain, especially during low season and during the heat of August, when many places, especially the higher-grade hotels, drop their prices by up to fifty percent. You may find, however, that a number of hotels in the lower categories ask for payment in full upfront, not just a credit card.

Hotels and pensions

You'll enjoy Rome the most if you **stay** right in the heart of things – in the **centro storico** or around **Campo de' Fiori**. There are plenty of hotels in these areas, and plenty too that aren't all that expensive, but they fill quickly so book well in advance if you can. The **Tridente** and the area east of Via del Corso, towards **Via Veneto** and around the **Spanish Steps**, is the city's prime hunting-ground for upscale accommodation, but there are more affordable options too. Consider also staying across the river: in **Prati**, the pleasant nineteenth-century neighbourhood close to the Vatican and nicely distanced from the hubbub of the city centre, or in lively **Trastevere**, which boasts plenty of relatively new lodging options, all located within easy walking distance of the centre of town and the sights, and lots of places to eat.

Many of the city's cheaper hotels are located conveniently close to **Termini**, and you could do worse than hole up in one of these, so long as you can tolerate the relative seediness of this district. The streets on both sides of the station – Via

Short-term apartment rentals and bed and breakfast

Renting an **apartment** in Rome has many advantages; for families with children or small groups, it can be a cheaper option than a hotel, and much more flexible. Short-term rentals are becoming very popular, however, so you must book well in advance. All of the places listed below have helpful websites, with pictures of their accommodation in Rome, which ranges from small city-centre apartments to grand villas outside the city. You can also find a good array of freelance options in the magazine *Wanted in Rome*. If you really want to do things in style, you can rent one of two apartments in the Keats-Shelley House on Piazza di Spagna, either through the museum itself or the UK's **Landmark Trust** (see p.80). **Bed and breakfast** is also a viable alternative these days: various agencies rent rooms in people's apartments and the tourist office has a long list of addresses you could try. Many options are out of the city centre, but to some extent this is real Rome, away from the tourists, and has its own appeal; prices are also relatively low – usually around €50–60 for a double room.

At Home Via del Babuino 56 ☎06.3212.0102, ⓦwww.at-home-italy.com. Katia and Sabrina have perhaps the city's best choice of short-let apartments, and the best service too. If you're considering renting an apartment for anything from a week to six months, they should be the first people you call.

City Apartments Viale Opito Oppio 78 ☎06.7698.3140, ⓦwww.roma.cityapartments .it. A great selection of apartments all over the city, from around €140 a night. The same people also run the *City Guesthouse*, which has excellent double rooms for €85–120 a night, and although you might not want to be this far out, they are within walking distance of the Porta Furba metro stop on line A.

The Tourist Friend ☎06.6821.0410, ⓦwww.bandbinrome.com. Bed and breakfast rooms and a few apartments in the city centre – from around €80 a night for a double room.

Welcome in Rome Via Ottaviano 73 Rome 00192 ☎06.3975.1474, ⓦwww .homesinrome.com. Apartments in the city and villas outside Rome too.

Amendola, Via Principe Amedeo, Via Marghera, Via Magenta, Via Palestro – are stacked full of bargain hotels, and some buildings have several pensions to choose from. It's far from Rome's most attractive quarter, but the area has improved dramatically since Termini itself and nearby Piazza Vittorio have been spruced up. However, especially if you're a woman travelling alone, use your common sense and avoid the more obvious dives.

Centro Storico

See the map on p.53.

Abruzzi Piazza della Rotonda 69 ☎06.9784.1351, ⓦwww.hotelabruzzi.it. This hotel used to be a very old-fashioned *pensione* right in the heart of the centro storico, but it's been updated into something a bit more comfortable. The knockout views of the Pantheon are still the main reason to stay here though. Doubles from €195.

Cesàri Via di Pietra 89a ☎06.674.9701, ⓦwww .albergocesari.it. In a perfect position close to the Pantheon, this has been a hotel since 1787 – as they will be sure to tell you – and it has also been very recently

renovated. The rooms are quiet and comfortable, and are elegant enough while having all the modern touches. Doubles €160–220.

Due Torri Vicolo del Leonetto 23 ☎06.6880.6956, 06.687.6983 or 06.687.5765, ⓦwww .hotelduetorriroma.com. Quietly elegant, this little hotel was once a residence for cardinals, following which it served as a brothel. Completely remodelled, it retains a homely feel and some rooms have private terraces with rooftop views. A good location just north of Piazza Navona. €150–200 for a double.

Genio Via G. Zanardelli 28 ☎06.683.3781, ☏06.6830.7246, ⓦwww.leonardihotels.com/ **Genio**. Perfectly located for Piazza Navona and the rest of the centro storico, as well as for the Vatican sights, this comfortable, recently redone hotel draws tourist groups as well as individual travellers. The view from the rooftop terrace is superb, and there are also a few rooms available with the same view. Doubles €240.

Mimosa Via Santa Chiara 61 ⓣ 06.6880.1753, ⓦ www.hotelmimosa.net. Clean, if slightly scruffy rooms, most without bathrooms. In a good position, on a quiet street, close to Santa Maria sopra Minerva and the Pantheon, and popular with groups of visiting students. Rooms are charged per person, not per room. No credit cards. Doubles for €75 without bath, €100+ with bath.

Navona Via dei Sediari 8 ⓣ 06.686.4203, ⓦ www.hotelnavona.com. Completely renovated *pensione*-turned-hotel housed in a building that dates back to the first century AD, built on the ancient Roman baths of Agrippa. Very close to Piazza Navona, although standards of cleanliness – and friendliness – are prone to be patchy, and you might be better off staying at their more upscale sister hotel, the *Zanardelli* (see below). Doubles €130–160.

Nazionale Piazza Montecitorio 131 ⓣ 06.695.001, ⓦ www.nazionaleroma.it. This luxury hotel is housed in a sixteenth-century *palazzo* in peaceful Piazza Montecitorio, perfectly located halfway between Piazza Navona and Piazza di Spagna. Inevitably, given its position next door to the Italian parliament, it's popular with visiting politicians and dignitaries, and the rooms are accordingly well fitted out, with every modern convenience. Doubles go for €340, except during Aug when they drop to around €200.

Pantheon Via Pastini 131 ⓣ 06.678.7746, ⓦ www.hotelpantheon.com. This comfortable four-star is, as you might expect from the name, a stone's throw from the Pantheon. The well-equipped rooms range from the functional, with beamed wooden ceilings, to deluxe affairs on two levels with skylighted sitting rooms. From €200 for a double.

Portoghesi Via dei Portoghesi 1 ⓣ 06.686.4231, ⓦ www.hotelportoghesiroma.com. Decent, well-equipped modern rooms, five minutes from the heart of the centro storico. Breakfast is included and is served on the roof terrace upstairs. Doubles €190.

Santa Chiara Via Santa Chiara 21 ⓣ 06.687.2979, ⓦ www .albergosantachiara.com. A friendly, family-run

hotel in a great location, on a quiet piazza behind the Pantheon. Nice rooms too, some of which overlook the church of Santa Maria sopra Minerva, and the price includes breakfast. Doubles €200–250.

Zanardelli Via G. Zanardelli 7 ⓣ 06.6821.1392, ⓦ www.hotelnavona.com. The more lavish alternative to the *Navona* and run by the same family. Located just north of Piazza Navona, the building used to be a papal residence and has many original fixtures and furnishings. The rooms are elegant, with antique iron beds, silk-lined walls, and modern amenities, but are still decently priced. Doubles €150–180.

Campo de' Fiori and the Ghetto

See the map on pp.68–69.

Arenula Via S. Maria de' Calderari 47 ⓣ 06.687.9454, ⓦ www.hotelarenula.com. Simple, clean rooms, each with its own bath, television and telephone. No lift, and top-floor rooms are quite a climb, but it's in a good location. Doubles €125.

Campo de' Fiori Via del Biscione 6 ⓣ 06.6880.6865, ⓦ www.hotelcampodefiori.com. A friendly place in a nice location with clean and pleasant rooms that come in all shapes and colours. The large roof terrace has some great views, and the hotel also owns a number of nearby small apartments if you're keen to self-cater. Doubles vary quite a lot in price, but you should be able to find something for around €150. Apartments go for around €180 a night for two.

🏃 **Residenza Farnese** Via del Mascherone 59 ⓣ 06.6889.1388, ⓕ 06.6821.0980. Situated on a quiet side street right by the massive Palazzo Farnese (French Embassy), the rooms here are large and tastefully appointed and the staff very helpful; and the location can't be bettered – great for both the centro storico and Trastevere, just across the water by way of the Ponte Sisto footbridge. Good value at €180 a night for a double.

Della Lunetta Piazza del Paradiso 68 ⓣ 06.6686.1080, ⓕ 06.689.2028, ⓦ www .albergodellalunetta.it. An unspectacular hotel, but in a nice location close to Campo de' Fiori. Simple, smallish rooms surround a green courtyard, and if you look up you will see the dome of San Andrea della Valle looming above – also viewable from a nice roof terrace. Doubles without baths cost from €90, breakfast not included.

In Parione Via dei Chiavari 32 ☎ 06.6880.2560, Ⓦ www.inparione.com. In a nice part of town, close to the Campo de' Fiori but very quiet, many of the rooms here look down to a bakery and enjoy the smell of freshly baked bread. The clean if basic rooms are kept to a high standard. Doubles for around €100.

Pomezia Via dei Chiavari 13 ☎ & Ⓕ 06.686.1371, Ⓦ www.hotelpomezia.it. Slightly more upscale – and expensive – than its budget neighbours, but still a low-priced choice. A small bar occupies half of the reception area, and Maurizio, the owner, keeps it open all night for those who want it. Doubles cost €100–150.

Smeraldo Vicolo dei Chiodaroli 9 ☎ 06.687.5929, Ⓦ www.smeraldoroma.com. Clean and comfortable hotel with a modern if rather bland interior and rooms with shiny new baths, televisions and a/c. The terrace and some rooms have lovely views over Rome's rooftops. Breakfast is not included in the price. Doubles €125–150.

Sole Via del Biscione 76 ☎ 06.6880.6873, Ⓦ www.solealbiscione.it. This place enjoys one of the best locations in the centre, and has reasonable rooms with televisions and phones, and a small roof terrace with a spectacular view of the nearby domes. No breakfast, no credit cards. Doubles cost €130–160, although there are a few with shared bathrooms for around €100.

Teatro di Pompeo Largo del Pallaro 8 ☎ 06.687.2812, Ⓦ www.hotelteatrodipompeo.it. Built above the remains of Pompey's ancient Roman theatre, the rooms here are comfortable, with high-beamed wooden ceilings, marble-topped furniture, satellite TV and (in some) great views – breakfast included. Doubles €180–200.

The Tridente

See the map on p.79.

Dei Borgognoni Via del Bufalo 126 ☎ 06.6994.1505, Ⓦ www.hotelborgognoni.it. Nicely situated four-star that has pleasant large rooms that have been well renovated. A surprisingly big hotel, considering its location tucked down a side street not far from Piazza di Spagna, and handy for this part of town and the centro storico. From about €280 a night.

Condotti Via Mario de' Fiori 37 ☎ 06.679.4661, Ⓦ www.hotelcondotti.com. A cosy and inviting hotel, with comfortable rooms with satellite TV and minibars, if a bit devoid of personality – although this is somewhat compensated for by the cheerful and welcoming staff. Not a bad price for the location, with doubles from €175.

Erdarelli Via due Macelli 28 ☎ 06.679.1265, Ⓦ www.erdarelliromehotel.com. A rather plain hotel with no-frills rooms, but it's welcoming enough and for its location, just around the corner from the Spanish Steps, the prices can't be beaten, with doubles for around €125 with en-suite facilities, less without.

Firenze Via due Macelli 106 ☎ 06.679.7240, Ⓦ www.hotelfirenzeroma.it. A decent three-star, a bit more characterful than its neighbours, and recently renovated, with large rooms with TVs and minibars that are good value for money. €100–160 for a double.

Hassler Villa Medici Trinità dei Monti 6 ☎ 06.699.340, Ⓦ www.hotelhasslerroma.com. Location, location, location – at the top of the Spanish Steps, you can't get much closer to the heart of Rome than this. A luxury hotel, with simple, elegant rooms and every convenience a guest could possibly require, including a health club, but what you are paying for above all is the reputation and of course its view. The so-called "classic" rooms – the cheapest – start at €550 and go up to about €700.

Homs Via della Vite 71–72 ☎ 06.679.2976, Ⓦ www.hotelhoms.it. In the heart of the Spanish Steps neighbourhood, this small four-star has recently refurbished rooms and a very friendly atmosphere – something that's not always guaranteed in the hotels of this ritzy area. Doubles start at about €180, and they also have a two-bedroom rooftop apartment for around €250 a night.

Internazionale Via Sistina 79 ☎ 06.6994.1823 or 06.678.4686, Ⓦ www.hotelinternazionale.com. In the first century AD this site was part of Lucullus's villa, and original elements can still be seen in the present hotel. Since Lucullus's day it has been home to nuns, an abbot, artists and musicians – and most recently has been thoroughly updated while retaining its ancient grace and atmosphere. Very good value for this level of style and comfort, with satellite TV, wi-fi, minibar. etc. Don't overlook the fourth-floor terrace views. Doubles €180–260.

D'Inghilterra Via Bocca di Leone 14 ☎ 06.699.811, Ⓦ www.hotel dinghilterraroma.it. Billing itself as one of the world's finest 100 hotels, this old favourite, formerly the apartments of the princes of Torlonia, does not disappoint, and is reasonable value compared to the cost of a similar level of pampering elsewhere in the city. Intimacy, opulence, exquisite antiques, frescoed rooms, and all the delights of the ancient city centre on your doorstep. Doubles from €400.

Manfredi Via Margutta 61 ☎06.320.7676, ⓦwww.hotelmanfredi.com. Occupying a sixteenth-century building, this is a first-class budget hotel with an ideal location on Via Margutta, moments from the Spanish Steps. Doubles start at about €150.

Margutta Via Laurina 34 ☎06.322.3674, ⓦwww.hotelmargutta.it. Popular hotel, handily located in the Corso/Piazza del Popolo shopping area. Three rooms have tiny private balconies. Reserve well ahead. Doubles go for €125–150.

Palazzetto Vicolo del Bottino 8 ☎06.699.0878, ⓦwww.wineacademyroma.com. The International Wine Academy is a project of the owners of the *Hassler* hotel at the top of the Spanish Steps, and as well as running courses on wine and hosting a distinguished restaurant and rooftop bar (Aug & Sept 7.30pm–1am), it rents out some of its sumptuously decorated rooms. Not especially quiet (the rooms open onto the Steps), but the location just off Piazza di Spagna is great, and it fully merits the (highish) prices. Doubles €200–300 – breakfast included.

Piazza di Spagna Via Mario de' Fiori 61 ☎06.679.3061, ⓦwww.hotelpiazzadispagna.it. A small hotel just a few minutes' walk from the Spanish Steps that is a good alternative to the sumptuous palaces that characterize this area. Family owned and run, its rooms are comfortable, all have a/c, minibar, phone and TV, and some have Jacuzzis. Friendly staff, too. Doubles go for around €200.

🏃 **Plaza** Via del Corso 126 ☎06.6992.1111, ⓦwww.grandhotelplaza.com. One of the most sumptuous hotels in Rome, with huge rooms furnished with antiques and a fantastic lobby that's worth dropping into even if you're not staying here. The rooms have been updated and have everything you might need, including WiFi. Rates have increased with modernization, but doubles still go for around €360 – not bad for the atmosphere alone, and you couldn't be more central, bang on Via del Corso, and just around the corner from the shops and restaurants of the Spanish Steps district.

🏃 **De Russie** Via del Babuino 9 ☎06.328.881, ⓦwww.roccofortehotels.com. Since opening in 2000, the *Russie* has quickly become the abode of choice for visiting movie stars in-the-know and hip travellers spending someone else's money, with doubles that are among the city's most expensive at €650 a night. If you can't afford that, just pop in for a drink in the lovely enclosed garden.

Via Veneto, the Quirinale and Termini

See the map on pp.126–127.

Aleph Via San Basilio 15 ☎06.422.901, ⓦwww.boscolohotels.com. One of the newest of the city's upscale options, done up in the most opulent Roman tradition. The work of an American architect, the decor was loosely inspired by Dante's Divine Comedy – with evocations of Heaven, Purgatory and Hell, the latter most particularly by the hotel's restaurant, called simply *Sin*. Doubles from €330.

Alpi Via Castelfidardo 84 ☎06.444.1235, ⓦwww.hotelalpi.com. One of the more peaceful yet convenient options close to Termini, recently renovated, and within easy walking distance of the station. Pleasant if somewhat small double rooms with bathrooms for around €150, and a good buffet breakfast – much better than you would normally expect in a hotel of this category.

🏃 **Des Artistes** Via Villafranca 20 ☎06.445.4365, ⓦwww.hoteldesartistes.com. One of the better hotels in the Termini area. Exceptionally good value, spotlessly clean, and with a wide range of rooms, including dorm beds for around €25. Eat breakfast or recover from a long day of sightseeing on the breezy roof terrace. Doubles go for around €150, with en-suite facilities.

Astoria Garden Via Bachelet 8 ☎06.446.9908, ⓦwww.hotelastoriagarden.it. In a peaceful area east of Termini, this recently renovated hotel was once the home of an Italian count. Rooms are pleasant, quiet and some have balconies that look onto the large garden below. Doubles cost about €200, however, which is quite a lot for the location.

Cervia Via Palestro 55 ☎06.491.057, ⓦwww.hotelcerviaroma.com. Pleasant rooms in a lively and very friendly *pensione*. If you don't mind lugging your bags a few more steps, ask for the discounted rooms on the third floor. Great value at €50–80 for a double.

⑬

Daphne Via di San Basilio 55, Via degli Avignonesi 20, ☎06.8745.0087, ⓦwww .daphne-rome.com. Two wonderfully welcoming *pensioni* run by an American woman and her Roman husband. Bright, beautifully renovated modern rooms in two great locations close to Piazza Barberini, and as much advice as you need on how to spend your time in Rome. Some rooms have shared bathrooms (€90–130), some en suite, (€130–200).

Eden Via Ludovisi 49 ☎06.478.121, ⓦwww .hotel-eden.it. Just off Via Veneto, this former private residence, on a quiet tree-lined street, is one of Rome's most enchanting hotels, with a lobby decorated with understated elegance and rooms that have everything you would expect from a luxury hotel. Those on the fifth floor are a bit more special, with private balconies offering spectacular views of the city. Even if you can't get one of these, the rooftop bar or restaurant is good compensation. Doubles from around €480.

Eliseo Via di Porta Pinciana 30 ☎06.487.0456 or 06.481.5474, ⓦwww.leonardihotels.com/Eliseo. This hotel's gracious facade looks out onto the ancient city walls and Villa Borghese, yet is only steps away from swanky Via Veneto. Inside, the decor is decidedly Rococo, with the emphasis on peaceful comfort. Great views of the city from the breakfast room. Doubles cost around €240.

Fawlty Towers Via Magenta 39 ☎06.445.4802, ⓦwww.fawltytowers.org. Playfully named accommodation, this place has both dorm beds for around €25 and clean and comfortable hotel rooms, some with private bath, for €45–55. There's a communal kitchen, Internet access, and a pleasant roof terrace, but you should check where in fact you are going to be – occasionally they try to move you to accommodation on a different site if the main building is full.

Majestic Via Veneto 50 ☎06.421.441, ⓦwww .hotelmajestic.com. Opened in 1889, this is Via Veneto's oldest hotel, and, with its precious antiques and sumptuous furnishings, it set, the standard for hotels that would follow on Rome's most fashionable street. The reception is as ostentatious as you would expect, with ceiling frescoes, silk hangings, and big, comfy couches. Each room is a bit different, but all are elegant and roomy, with huge marble baths.

Doubles start at about €350, which isn't bad value for this kind of hotel.

Marsala Via Marsala 36 ☎06.444.1315, ⓦwww .hotelmarsala.com. Handily situated two-star, 50m east of the station, with clean, if fairly basic rooms and a friendly English-speaking staff. Doubles with en-suite facilities go for around €150.

Positano Via Palestro 49 ☎06.490.360, ⓦwww .hotelpositano.it. Not glamorous, but reasonably priced convenient, with comfortable rooms two minutes' walk from Termini. Helpful management too. Doubles €100.

Salus Piazza Indipendenza 13 ☎06.444.0330, ⓦwww.hotelsalus.crimar.it. This modest establishment has the virtues of being attractive, clean, efficiently run and friendly – things that can't always be said for the hotels in this neighbourhood – and it also has an internal garden for guests' use. Doubles €75–130 depending on season and facilities.

Victoria Via Campania 41 ☎06.473.701, ⓦwww.hotelvictoriaroma.com. Newly remodelled in imperial Roman style, this Swiss-managed hotel is situated between the super-deluxe grandeur of Via Veneto and the verdant freedom of Villa Borghese. Many rooms enjoy views of the ancient walls and beyond. Doubles cost around €300.

Villa delle Rose Via Vicenza 5 ☎06.445.1788, ⓦwww.villadellerose.it. This centuries-old aristocratic villa sits amidst its own tranquil rose gardens, belying the fact that it's only a block from Termini Station. Newly done up, it's quiet, pleasant and appealingly decorated, with a very friendly staff, and doubles start at €100.

Westin Excelsior Via Veneto 125 ☎06.47.081, ⓦwww.starwoodhotels.com. This grand white palace on Via Veneto was recently renovated to its original turn-of-the-century Empire style and is once again the choice of royalty when they visit Rome, who favour the antiques, crystal chandeliers and tapestries that decorate each room – along with, of course, every modern-day convenience. Doubles for around €750 make it perhaps Rome's priciest hotel.

Monti and San Giovanni

See the map on pp.140–141.

Elide Via Firenze 50 ☎06.488.3977, ⓦwww .hotelelide.com. A *pensione* for over fifty years, and one of the cheapest private beds you'll find in the city, with clean, simple rooms and friendly staff. Several of the rooms are right on a busy street, though; if noise bothers you, ask for a room at the back. Doubles cost €35–80 with shared facilities, €50–100 with en-suite bath or shower. Breakfast extra.

Giuliana Via A. Depretis 70 ☎06.488.0795, ⊛www.hotelgiuliana.com. Newly renovated Termini area hotel that has a loyal following, and a friendly and helpful owner. Very simple rooms, but the hotel is excellently maintained, and the €140–165 high-season price for doubles includes a rudimentary breakfast.

Grifo Via del Boschetto 144 ☎06.487.1395, ⊛www.hotelgrifo.com. A new addition to the Monti district, the decor is crisply functional and modern, but the roof terrace overlooks a timeless scene of medieval Rome at its most picturesque. Doubles cost between €140 and 150.

Radisson SAS Via F. Turati 171 ☎06.444.841, ⊛www.rome.radissonsas.com. Launched a few years ago as one of Rome's new designer hotels, and also the flagship for the radical makeover of the area around Termini, this hotel is now part of the Radisson SAS chain, but still sports starkly aesthetic rooms and a state-of-the-art rooftop bar and spa. It's within walking distance of Termini, and the rates aren't bad, at around €200 for a double.

Richmond Largo Corrado Ricci 36 ☎06.6994.1256, ⊛www.hotelrichmondroma .com. For devotees of Rome's most ancient splendours, this is the perfect choice; with a location right across the way from the Forums and the Colosseum, and a roof terrace for taking in the views of the ancient city. Rooms are small, but well planned and newly freshened. Doubles from €190.

Rosetta Via Cavour 295 ☎ & ℻06.4782.3069. Family-run *pensione* in a nice location very close to the Colosseum. The small rooms are a bit shabby, but they're comfortable enough, and have private baths, TV, and telephone. No breakfast. Doubles start at €85.

St Regis Grand Via V.E. Orlando 3 ☎06.47.09, ⊛www.stregis.com/grandrome. Originally the brainchild of legendary hotelier Caesar Ritz, a few years ago this truly grand property was fully restored to its glimmering gilded glory, all done up in Empire and Regency style with no luxury appointment omitted. Doubles from €530.

Trastevere

See the map on pp.168–169.

Antico Borgo di Trastevere Vicolo del Buco 7, ☎06.588.3774, ⊛www.trasterehouse.it. This small seventeenth-century palace is home to one of Trastevere's newest lodging options, and it's been neatly done up, although some of the rooms can be a bit cramped. It's located in a quiet corner of this bustling district, but is just seconds away from all the action. €100–140 for a double room.

Carmel Via G. Mameli 11 ☎06.580.9921, ⊛www.hotelcarmel.it. Pleasant, simply furnished rooms, with private bathrooms and two with their own terrace, on the western side of Trastevere. There's also a leafy roof terrace for all guests. If you arrange it ahead of time they can provide a kosher kitchen for your personal use. Doubles €100–120.

Cisterna Via della Cisterna 7–9 ☎06.581.7212, ⊛www.cisternahotel.it. Friendly two-star with a homely feel, bang in the middle of Trastevere. Twenty rooms, some with colourful tiled floors and wooden beamed ceilings, and all with private bathrooms. The peaceful terrace garden out the back is a treat when the weather is nice. Doubles from €100.

Domus Tiberina Via in Piscinula 37 ☎06.580.3033, ⊛www.domustiberina.com. Located on the quiet side of the popular Trastevere quarter, this boutique hotel nevertheless lies within a few minutes' walk of everything you might want to see. Rooms are small, but newly refurbished, and cost €100–140 for a double.

Grand Hotel del Gianicolo Viale delle Mura Gianicolensi 107 ☎06.5833.3405, ⊛www .grandhotelgianicolo.it. Commanding the heights of the Janiculum Hill above Trastevere and with views of the entire city, this former convent is just a few blocks away from the American Academy and the joys of Villa Pamphilj. In addition to the understated elegance of the hotel itself, the grounds sport a large swimming pool set amidst subtropical gardens. A wonderful choice if you want somewhere that feels far from the hubbub of the city centre. Doubles from €150.

Ripa Via degli Orti di Trastevere 3 ☎06.58.611, ⊛www.ripahotel.com. One of the latest additions to Rome's burgeoning bevy of designer hotels, the *Ripa* is situated in Trastevere's lower and less attractive reaches but makes up for it with the effort-less style of its rooms and lobby. Whether you want to pay €200–270 a double to stay down here, though, is another matter.

San Francesco Via Jacopa de' Settesoli 7 ⊤**06.5830.0051,** ⓦ**www.hotelsanfrancesco.net.** This fairly new Trastevere option is well located – close enough to everything but discreet enough to be restful; and its location just across the river from Testaccio makes it an ideal base if you want to be close to some of the best of Rome's nightlife. Rooms are comfortable, if a little uninspired. Doubles €135–175.

Santa Maria Vicolo dei Piede 2 ⊤**06.5894626,** ⓦ**www.hotelsantamaria.info.** A few yards off Piazza Santa Maria in the heart of Traste-vere, the rooms of this small three-star surround an orange-tree-filled garden, giving the feel of a place far removed from the noise of the city. Doubles €180–250.

Trastevere Via Luciano Manara 24/25 ⊤**06.581.4713.** Another good place to stay if you want to be in the heart of Trastevere, with nicely renovated doubles for around €100 and quads for €150, and apartments to rent that can house up to five people.

Villa della Fonte Via della Fonte d'Olio 8, ⊤**06.580.3797,** ⓦ**www.villafonte.com.** This attractive place also has a hidden-away, almost secret feel to it, yet is just a few steps from the district's main square, Piazza Santa Maria in Trastevere. Rooms are cosy and newly renovated, maintaining traditional medieval style. Doubles €130–160.

The Aventine

See the map on pp.106–107.

Sant'Anselmo Piazza Sant'Anselmo 2 ⊤**06.570.057,** ⓦ**www.aventinohotels.com.** One of a few hotels on the Aventine Hill that make up a small chain and have the advantage of being fairly central while feeling a million miles away from the city centre. Its nicely furnished doubles cost from €180 a night.

Prati

See the map on pp.180–181.

Amalia Via Germanico 66 ⊤**06.3972.2356,** ⓦ**www.hotelamalia.com.** Located on an attractive corner of this busy shopping area close to the Vatican, this place provides four-star amenities at three-star prices, including double-glazing on all windows for maximum

peace and security, and nicely renovated double rooms for €150–200. There's a branch of Castroni next door, for stocking up on provisions (see p.275). Don't be misled by the claims of its website, though – it's nowhere near the Spanish Steps!

Arcangelo Via Boezio 15 ⊤**06.687.4143,** ⓦ**www.travel.it/roma/arcangelo.** A clean and reliable hotel, with comfortable, elegant rooms in a quiet street not far from the Vatican. The lounges have a warm, clubby feel. Doubles from €165.

Atlante Star Via Vitelleschi 34 ⊤**06.687.3233,** ⓦ**www.atlantehotels.com.** Just steps away from the Vatican, this is the neighbourhood's most luxurious option, with lovely antique-filled rooms with marble bathrooms for €230–290. Perhaps its most impressive feature is the rooftop terrace, which offers a 360-degree view of Rome, and the very popular *Les Etoiles* restaurant. There are free airport pick-ups, and a nearby annexe, the *Atlante Garden* (Via Crescenzio 78 ⊤06.687.2361), offers similar luxury at slightly lower rates – around €175–240.

Bramante Vicolo delle Palline 24 ⊤**06.6880.6426,** ⓦ**www.hotelbramante.com.** This little hotel, located right next to the ancient wall running from the Vatican to Castel Sant'Angelo, was once home to the sixteenth-century architect Domenico and later became an inn. Recently restored, its rooms are charmingly decorated with original wood-beam ceilings and antique furniture and fittings. Doubles are a reason-able €150–220.

Colors Via Boezio 31 ⊤**06.687.4030,** ⓦ**www.colorshotel.com.** Run by the friendly people from Enjoy Rome, this is a smaller version of their popular *Fawlty Towers* (see p.226), a hostel/hotel in a quiet neighbourhood near the Vatican. Dorm beds cost €25 a night, and private rooms from €80 without bath, from €100 with bath. There are kitchen facilities, a lounge with satellite TV, and a small terrace, and the same organization rents out self-catering apartments for €80–120 a night with two people sharing.

Dei Consoli Via Varrone 2d ⊤**06.6889.2972,** ⓦ**www.hoteldeiconsoli.com.** From the elegantly welcoming entrance, just around the corner from all the splendours of the Vatican, to the thoughtfully designed rooms, where every comfort is included, this is an excellent choice. The decor on each floor is thematically inspired by old masters; and the top floor, curiously adorned with battle scenes, is where honeymooners are usually lodged. Doubles from €260.

Davos Via degli Scipioni 239 ⊕ 06.321.7012, ℗ 06.323.0367. Simple, affordable *pensione* on a quiet street. Rooms are clean and quite basic, but all except one have a private bath. No credit cards. Doubles from around €60.

Domus Mazzini Via Monte Zeblo 9 ⊕ 06.4542.1592. Small *pensione* with just four nicely decorated double rooms for around €80 a night, including breakfast. A bit of a hike from the Vatican and St Peter's, but the neighbourhood is nice, and the place has the feel of staying in someone's home – which in a sense you are.

Farnese Via Alessandro Farnese 30 ⊕ 06.321.1953, ℗ www.farnese.hotelinroma .com. Another grand aristocratic residence that has been turned into an upscale hotel. All the rooms have recently been renovated, adding touches such as soundproof windows and doors, handmade walnut furniture, and marble bathrooms. Some rooms have private balconies, and there is a rooftop terrace with a great view of the Vatican. Doubles cost around €280.

Gerber Via degli Scipioni 241 ⊕ 06.321.9986, ℗ www.hotelgerber.it. A friendly staff and elegant comfortable rooms make this hotel great value for its convenient location on a quiet street not far from the Vatican. Doubles cost a decent €110–150.

Giulio Cesare Via degli Scipioni 287 ⊕ 06.321.0751, ℗ www.hotelgiuliocesare.com. This charming hotel is no longer the Villa Patricia, home of an Italian countess, but you may feel like royalty once you step into the foyer, with its glistening golden ceiling. An attentive staff will lead you down mirror-lined hallways to elegantly decorated rooms with marble baths – all very handsome, for rates of around €330 a double.

Isa Via Cicerone 39 ⊕ 06.321.2610, ℗ www .hotelisa.com. Metro A Lepanto or bus #30, #70, #280, #913. A fairly short walk from the Vatican, the grim exterior of this hotel is deceptive, hiding moderately large rooms that have been nicely renovated with warm wooden panelling, brightly coloured beds and shiny marble basins. Excellent value for the €140–220 double room prices.

La Rovere Vicolo San Onofrio 4–5 ⊕ 06.6880.6739, ℗ www.hotellarovere.com. Just round the corner from St Peter's and across the bridge from Piazza Navona, this attractive boutique hotel is tucked quietly away from all the bustle and offers a terrace garden and antique-filled setting for its guests to relax in. Good value, with doubles from €130 to 230.

Hostels and convents

If you're on a tight budget, or just travelling on your own and eager to meet people, staying in a **hostel** can make a lot of sense, and Rome has plenty of options, although they can get pretty crowded during peak season. Rome also has lots of accommodation run by **religious organisations**, and these can prove an excellent alternative since they are usually cheap and can often be found in central locations. We've listed a few, but there are loads, all over the city. Bear in mind most have strict rules about curfews and often a single-gender policy. One thing to remember generally is that most hostels, both secular and religious, usually have a few private rooms as well.

Alessandro Palace Hostel Via Vicenza 42 ⊕ 06.4938.0534, ℗ www.hostelsalessandro .com. See the map on pp.126–127. This place has been voted one of the top hostels in Europe, and it sparkles with creative style. Pluses include no lock-out or curfew, a good bar with free pizza every night, Internet access and satellite TV. Beds €22–30, doubles €70, with bath €90. A few blocks away, on the city-centre side of Termini, you'll also find *Alessandro Downtown*, Via C. Cattaneo 23 (⊕ 06.4434.0147).

Casa di Santa Brigida Piazza Farnese 96 ⊕ 06.6889.2596, ℗ www.brigidine.org. See the map on pp.68–69. Located right on this sublime Renaissance square, this place is hard to beat – clean and comfortable, with no curfew; all rooms have their own facilities, and breakfast is included. If they're full then

Camping

For those determined to sleep outdoors, it's no surprise that all Rome's **campsites** are some way out of the city. However they are easy enough to get to. The closest site is **Camping Flaminio**, 8km north of the centre at Via Flaminia Nuova 821 (March–Oct; ☎06.333.2604, ⊛www.villageflaminio.it); it also has bungalows for rent and a swimming pool, restaurant and lots of facilities. To get there from the city centre, either take the Roma-Nord service from Piazzale Flaminio to Due Ponti, or take bus #910 to Piazza Mancini and transfer to bus #200 (ask the driver to drop you at the "fermata pi" *vicina al campeggio*). **Camping Tiber**, on Via Tiberina at Km1400 (March–Oct; ☎06.3361.0733, ⊛www.campingtiber.com), is another good bet – right beside the Tiber, quiet, spacious and friendly, with a bar/pizzeria, a swimming pool and really hot showers; and it too has bungalows as well as camping spaces. It has a free shuttle service (8am–11pm every 30min) to and from the nearby Prima Porta station, where you can catch the Roma-Nord train service to Piazzale Flaminio (about 20min).

the same order has other locations in Rome.
Casa di Santa Francesca Romana Via dei Vascellari 61 ☎06.581.2125, ⊛web.tiscali.it/sfromana. See the map on pp.168–169. This former medieval palace and then convent has been newly restructured as a refined and cheerful accommodation option in Trastevere. Although the rooms are fairly institutional, the central courtyard is very inviting, and the curfew is not until 2am, with no lock-out during the day. Breakfast included. Singles €70, doubles €100.
Ostello del Foro Italico Viale delle Olimpiadi 61 ☎06.323.6267, ⊛www.ostellionline.org. Rome's official HI hostel, though not particularly central or easy to get to from Termini – take bus #32, #69, #224 or #280 and ask the driver for the "ostello". Facilities include a bar, restauraunt and laundry. You can call ahead to check out availability, but they won't take phone bookings. Costs €18 including breakfast, and you can join here if you're not an HI member already.
Ottaviano Via Ottaviano 6 ☎06.3973.8138, ⊛www.pensioneottaviano.com. See the map on pp.180–181. A simple *pensione*-cum-hostel near to the Vatican that is very popular with the backpacking crowd; book well in advance, fluent English spoken. Dorm beds for around €20; doubles €50 with shared bath.
Sandy Via Cavour 136 ☎06.488.4585, ⊛www .sandyhostel.com. See the map on pp.140–141. Run by the same folk as the

Ottaviano, and with main dormitory beds for €14–18 but with a few private rooms as well for €35.
Suore Pallottine Viale della Mura Aurelie 7b ☎06.393.6351, ⊛www.procuramissionariepallot-tine.it. Simple, clean accommodation near the Vatican, run by nuns, but open to both women and men. Midnight curfew April–Sept, 11pm in winter. Singles cost €47 for a room without bath, €62 with bath, doubles are €69–94. Breakfast is included.
Villa Santa Cecilia Via Argeleto 54–58 ☎06.5237.1688, ⊛http://151.1.140.34/vsc/. Metro B Magliana, where you change for Lido and the overground train to Vitinia. Thirty minutes by metro from Termini, a hostel/hotel run by religious organization (no curfew) with singles, doubles, triples and four-bedded rooms, all with private bathrooms, for €32 per person. All include breakfast.
YWCA Via C. Balbo 4 ☎06.488.0460, ☏06.487.1028. Open to women and men, and conveniently situated just ten minutes' walk from Termini, although the market outside may get you up earlier than you might want. There is a range of singles (from €50), doubles (from €80), triples and quads (€26 per person) – without bath, but including breakfast. Curfew 11pm.

Eating

Although Rome is undeniably a major-league cultural and historic city, it just doesn't compare to London or Paris for cutting-edge sophistication and trendiness. In many ways it's like an overgrown village. This can be bad news for nightlife, but it's great news for **food**. Romans, as a group, are still very much in touch with the land – many even have small farms of their own in the countryside nearby, or they return to their home villages regularly. So the city's denizens know a good deal about freshness and authenticity, and can be very demanding when it comes to the quality of the dishes they are served.

Consequently, eating out is a major, often hours-long, activity in Rome, and the meals you'll enjoy generally range from good to truly remarkable. You'll find that most city-centre **restaurants** offer standard Italian dishes, and some specialize purely in Roman fare, but there have been a few more adventurous places cropping up of late. At the geographical centre of the country, the capital also has numerous establishments dedicated to a variety of **regional cuisines**, and a reasonable number of excellent **ethnic restaurants**, although many of these are in outlying areas. Rome is also blessed with an abundance of good, honest **pizzerias**, churning out thin, crispy-baked pizza from wood-fired ovens. House wine is usually drinkable, if rarely memorable, but there are also any number of *enoteche* – **wine bars** – which really know their business (we've listed some of the best of these in this chapter and also in Chapter 15). We've also listed a range of places serving snacks and the best of the city's cafés, **gelaterie** and **pasticcerie**. **Vegetarians** will find plenty of options in virtually all Italian eateries. Many pasta dishes and pizzas, of course, are made entirely without meat; lentils and other beans and pulses are a part of traditional cookery; and wonderful fresh vegetables and cheeses are always available. Even so, there are a number of restaurants that specialize in vegetarian cuisine, and some of them are among the most appealing places in Rome.

One final caveat: generally speaking it's hard to find truly bad food and rip-off prices in Rome. However, it may be wise to **avoid places** that are adjacent to some major monuments, such as the Pantheon, Piazza Navona, or the Vatican. The food in these places can be poor, and the prices truly outlandish, sometimes as much as three times the going rate. Near major sights, use the guide!

Note, that many places are closed during August.

Coffee, pastries, sandwiches and snacks

All Roman bars and cafés serve **coffee** of course, and most sell **pastries** to go with them in the morning and **panini**, *tramezzini* and sometimes other snacks like pizza the rest of the day. Other places for snacks include wine bars, which

Most Italians start their day in a bar, their breakfast consisting of a coffee with hot milk (a cappuccino) and a *cornetto* – a jam-, custard- or chocolate-filled croissant, sweeter than the French variety. At other times of the day, **sandwiches** (panini) can be pretty substantial, and cost €2–3; bars also offer *tramezzini*, ready-made sliced white bread with mixed fillings – less appetizing than the average panino but still tasty and slightly cheaper at around €1.50 a time. If you want hot takeaway food, it's possible to find slices of **pizza** (*pizza rustica* or *pizza al taglio*) pretty much every-where, and you can get most things, plus spit-roast chicken, pasta, and hot meals, in a *rosticceria*. Italian **ice cream** (*gelato*) is justifiably famous; reckon on paying upwards of €2 for a cone (*un cono*) with one scoop (*gusto*), with the price rising by each scoop you have – two is the most common choice. Most bars have a fairly good selection, but for real choice go to a *gelateria*, where the range is a tribute to the Italian imagination and flair for display; we've listed our favourites at the end of this chapter.

Restaurants

An Italian meal traditionally starts with **antipasto** (literally "before the meal"), consisting of various cold cuts of meat, seafood and various vegetable dishes. A plateful of various antipasti from a self-service buffet will set you back €5–10 a head, an item chosen from the menu slightly less. Bear in mind that if you're moving onto pasta, let alone a main course, you may need quite an appetite to tackle this. The next course, **il primo**, consists of a soup or pasta dish, and it's fine to eat just this and nothing else; pasta dishes go for around €8–12. This is followed by **il secondo** – the meat or fish course, usually served alone, except for perhaps a wedge of lemon or tomato, a garnish of salad, or a potato or two. Watch out when ordering fish, which will either be served whole or by weight: 250g is usually plenty for one person, or ask to have a look at the fish before it's cooked; main fish or meat courses will normally be anything between €10 and about €20 (more only in truly gourmet restaurants). Vegetables or salads – **contorni** – are ordered and served separately, and sometimes there won't be much choice: potatoes will usually come as chips (*patatine fritte*); salads are either green (*verde*) or mixed (*mista*). Afterwards you nearly always get a choice of fresh fruit (*frutta*) and a selection of **desserts** (*dolci*) – sometimes just ice cream, but often more elaborate items, such as *zuppa inglese* (spongecake or trifle).

Many Italians wouldn't dream of going out to eat and not ordering a full **five-course meal** – starter, first, second, vegetable, dessert or fruit, plus wine, mineral water, coffee and a *digestivo*, such as an *amaro* (home-made herb liqueur) – but don't feel you have to follow the pattern; you can order as little or as much as you want, and no one will raise an eyebrow. Roman restaurants keep pretty rigid **opening hours**, generally from noon to 3pm and from 7.30 to 11pm, although some stay open later, especially in summer. Early in the week tends to be quieter, and many places are closed in August. It's always a good idea to make a reservation, particularly towards the weekend. Getting the **bill** (*il conto*) can sometimes be a struggle – nothing moves fast in Rome when it comes to mealtimes – but, when you do, service of 10–15 percent will occasionally be included, and if so it will be clearly indicated. Otherwise a small **tip** is fine, rounding the bill up €2–3 or so, as waiters in Italy are paid well. Almost everywhere they add a cover charge of around €2 a head; on your bill it will either be labelled as **"coperto"** or **"pane"**, as it is technically for the bread, which they bring automatically.

Bars and cafés

It's important to be aware of the procedure when you enter an Italian **bar**. It's cheapest to drink standing at the counter (there's often nowhere to sit anyway), in which case you pay first at the cash desk (*la cassa*), present your receipt (*scontrino*) to the barperson and give your order. It's customary to leave an extra 10c or 20c coin on the counter for the barperson, although no one will object if you don't. If there's waiter service, just sit where you like, though bear in mind that this will cost perhaps twice as much, especially if you sit outside (*fuori*) – the difference is usually shown on the price list as *tavola* (table) or *terrazzo* (any outside seating area).

Coffee and soft drinks

Coffee is always excellent, drunk small and black (espresso, or just *caffè*), which costs 80c to €1 a cup, or as a cappuccino (about €1.50). If you want your espresso watered down ask for a *caffè americano* or *caffè lungo*. Coffee with a shot of alcohol is *caffè corretto*; with a drop of milk it's *caffè macchiato*, a full small cup of the same is *caffè macchiato lungo*. Many places also now sell decaffeinated coffee (ask for "Hag", even when it isn't), while in summer you might want to have your coffee cold (*caffè freddo*). For a real treat ask for *caffè granitá* – cold coffee with crushed ice, usually topped with cream. In summer you can drink iced tea (*tè freddo*) – excellent for taking the heat off; hot tea (*tè caldo*) comes with lemon (*con limone*) unless you ask for milk (*con latte*). Milk itself is drunk hot as often as cold, or you can get it with a dash of coffee (*latte macchiato* or *caffè latte*) and sometimes as milk shakes – *frappe* or *frullati*.

Among **soft drinks**, a *spremuta* is a fresh fruit juice, squeezed at the bar, usually orange, lemon or grapefruit. There are also crushed-ice *granitas*, offered in several flavours, and available with or without whipped cream (*panna*) on top. Otherwise there's the usual range of fizzy drinks and concentrated juices: Coke is as prevalent as it is everywhere; the home-grown Italian version, Chinotto, is less sweet – good with a slice of lemon. Tap water (*acqua semplice*) is quite drinkable, and you won't pay for it in a bar. Mineral water (*acqua minerale*) is a more common choice, either still (*senza gas* or *naturale*) or sparkling (*con gas* or *frizzante*) – about 50c a glass.

Alcohol

Beer (*birra*) is always a lager-type brew which usually comes in one-third or two-third litre bottles, or on draught (*alla spina*), measure for measure more expensive than the bottled variety. A small beer is a *piccola* (20cl or 25cl), a larger one (usually 40cl) a *media* (pronounced "maydia"). If you want Italian beer, or lager, ask for *birra chiara*. You may also come across darker beers (*birra nera* or *birra rossa*). Prices start at €3–4 for a *media*, but anywhere remotely fancy won't charge any less than about €6.

All the usual **spirits** are on sale and known mostly by their generic names. There are also Italian brands of the main varieties: the best Italian brandies are Stock and Vecchia Romagna. A generous shot of these costs about €3, imported stuff much more. The home-grown Italian firewater is *grappa*, available just about everywhere. It's made from the leftovers from the winemaking process (skins, stalks and the like) and is something of an acquired taste; should you acquire it, it's probably the cheapest way of getting plastered. You'll also find **fortified wines** such as Campari; ask for a Campari-soda and you'll get a ready-mixed version from a bottle; a slice of lemon is a *spicchio di limone*, ice is *ghiaccio*. You might also try Cynar – believe it or not, an artichoke-based sherry often drunk as an aperitif. There's also a daunting selection of **liqueurs**. *Amaro* is a bitter after-dinner drink: it has a base of pure alcohol in which various herbs are steeped, according to various family traditions. It's highly regarded as a digestive aid to cap a substantial meal. *Amaretto* is much sweeter with a strong taste of almond; *sambuca,* a sticky-sweet aniseed concoction, traditionally served with a coffee bean in it and set on fire (though, increasingly, this is something put on to impress tourists); Strega – yellow, herb-and-saffron-based stuff in tall, elongated bottles – is about as sweet as it looks but not unpleasant.

△ Diners in the *centro storico*

always serve some sort of food, usually cold cuts and cheese, and *tavola calde* and *rosticcerie*, which have a range of Roman specialities – *suppli* (deep-fried rice balls) and other traditionally Roman deep-fried delights, roast chicken and potatoes, and even green vegetables. A complete meal for two at one of these places can cost less than €10, and although they're usually standing-room only, some have a counter and few chairs, Expect to pay €3–4 for a decent-sized **pizza** slice from one of the many *pizza al taglio* or *pizza rustica* outlets scattered throughout the city.

Centro Storico

See map on p.53.

Camilloni Piazza Sant'Eustachio 54 ℡06.686.4995. Tues–Sun 8.30am–midnight. A contender for Rome's best coffee, larger than its rival *Sant'Eustachio* across the square, with inside seating and great cakes.

Enoteca Corsi Via del Gesù 87–88 ℡06.679.0821. Lunch only, closed Sun. Tucked away between Piazza Venezia and the Pantheon, this is an old-fashioned Roman trattoria and wine shop where you eat what they happen to have cooked that morning. They do a menu that changes each day, and it gets very busy at lunchtimes – so much so that you may have to wait for a table at the height of the midday rush. Very cheap – €8 or so for a main course, €5 for a primo.

Enoteca del Corso Corso Vittorio Emanuele 293 ℡06.6880.1594. Closes at 9.30pm. Long-established wine shop that not only has a great selection of wines but also sells chocolate and does focaccia sandwiches and other snacks at lunchtime and early evening.

Delfino Corso V. Emanuele 67 ℡06.686.4053. Daily 8am–9pm. A fairly ordinary but very central and busy cafeteria right on Largo Argentina, with a huge choice of snacks and full meals. Good for a fast fill-up between sights.

Caffè Sant'Eustachio Piazza Sant'Eustachio 82. No phone. Tues–Sun 8.30am–1am. Just behind the Pantheon you'll find what many believe is absolutely Rome's best coffee, usually served Neapolitan-style – that is, very, very sweet. You can ask for it without sugar, but they'll think you're weird. They also do a good line in coffee-based sweets and cakes.

La Tazza d'Oro Via degli Orfani 84/86 ☏06.679.2768. Straight off Piazza del Pantheon, this place is well named, since it is by common consent the home of one of Rome's best cups of coffee, plus decent iced coffee and sinfully rich *granita di caffè*, with double dollops of whipped cream. Good pastries and sandwiches too.

Da Vezio Via Tor di Nona 37 ☏06.678.6036. Mon–Sat 7.30am–9pm. Visible from the flags outside, this tiny bar, tucked away by the river around the corner from Via dei Coronari, is a shrine to the Italian Left, Castro and all aspects of the workers' struggle. Not the most welcoming bar in town, but it's worth lingering over a coffee to study the memorabilia that coats the walls.

Lo Zozzone Via del Teatro Pace 32 ☏06.6880.8575. Mon–Fri 9am–9pm, Sat 10am–11pm. This Rome legend, just around the corner from Piazza Navona and with outside seating, serves the best *pizza bianca* in town, filled with whatever you want, as well as lots of delicious *pizza al taglio* choices.

Campo de' Fiori and the Ghetto

See map on pp.68–69.

Bernasconi Piazza Cairoli 16 ☏06.6880.6264. Tues–Sun 7am–8.30pm. Closed Aug. A great, family-run *pasticceria*, with *sfogliatelle* to die for and a host of other goodies including great one-bite panini. Good coffee, too, though standing-room only.

Bruschetteria degli Angeli Piazza Benedetto Cairoli 2a ☏06.6880.5789. Lunch and dinner during the week, evenings only weekends. Lovely and large *birreria* that does a great line on large bruschette with all kinds of toppings to soak up the ale. Lots of other choices, too. Very good, very central – a good bet for lunch or even dinner. You'll pay €8 or so for a large bruschetta, which is enough for two as a snack.

Caffè Farnese Piazza Farnese 106 ☏06.6880.2125. Daily 7am–2am. Popular with business types and beautiful young things, but actually not expensive, and a pleasant place to come for breakfast or lunch as well as evening drinks. Good cappuccino and cornetti, and excellent pizza and sandwiches. Free seating at the window bar, but you might want to pay to sit

outside on a warm evening for the view of Palazzo Farnese.

Il Forno di Campo de' Fiori Campo de' Fiori 22 ☏06.6880.6662. Mon–Sat 7am–1.30pm & 5.30–8pm; closed Sat evening in summer, Thurs evening in winter. Great Campo bakery that is always busy with devotees. The *pizza bianca* here (just drizzled with olive oil on top) is a Roman legend and their *pizza rossa* (with a smear of tomato sauce) follows close behind. Get it hot from the oven.

The Tridente

See map on p.79.

Antico Forno Via delle Muratte 8 ☏06.679.2866. Daily 7am–9pm. The last thing you'd expect just by the Trevi Fountain: fresh pizza, a sandwich bar, fresh fruits and salads, a bakery and grocery store, all rolled into one – and open on Sundays!

Babington's Tea Rooms Piazza di Spagna 23 ☏06.678.6027. Daily 9am–8.15pm. Over one hundred years of tradition in the very heart of Rome. Light lunches, and scones and other English delicacies for tea. Extremely expensive – €9 for a pot of tea for one, €13.50 for poached eggs on toast – but very handy, and it has a great selection of teas and does a great Sunday brunch too.

Le Baguette Via Tomacelli 24–25 (between Piazza di Spagna and the Tiber) ☏06.6880.7727. Tues–Sun 9am–midnight. Formely part of a Belgian chain, the wonderful organic breads, French cheeses and hearty soups – along with communal-style dining banquettes – have quickly found their way into Roman hearts. Weekend brunches are ever popular.

Ciampini al Café du Jardin Viale Trinità dei Monti (no street number) ☏06.678.5678. Daily 8am–midnight. A secluded outdoor setting with a view, opposite Villa Medici, just up the Spanish Steps, a perfect place to relax if you're not too hungry. Salads, sandwiches, ice cream, and, of course, coffee, don't come cheap – resting your feet in Rome's most fashionable quarter has its price – but the location can't be beaten.

Defa Via del Corso 51 ☏06.679.3548. Daily 8am–midnight. *Tavola calda* with *pizza al taglio*, to eat on the premises or take away.

Dolci & Doni Via delle Carrozze 85 ☏06.678.2913. Daily 8am–8pm. A truly sumptuous array of pastries right in the heart of the city, just a few steps away from

Piazza di Spagna. Don't miss the lemon cheesecake. Tea and other snacks, too.
Caffè Greco Via Condotti 86 ☎ 06.678.5474. **Mon–Sat 8am–9pm.** Founded in 1742, and patronized by, among others, Casanova, Byron, Goethe and Stendhal. Now, it's a rather dubious tourist joint, but Romans still use the stand-up area in the front. Curiosity value only, although the *granita di caffè* (iced coffee) is a hit on a hot summer day.
Herbier Via San Claudio 87 ☎ 06.678.5847. **Mon–Sat 8am–8pm.** Well located bar, just off Piazza San Silvestro in a small arcade and thus a real oasis of calm away from the hectic and fumey traffic. Offers snacks or even a full lunch.

🏃 **Da Michele Via dell'Umilta 31** ☎ 349.252.5347. **Sun & Mon–Thurs 9am–7.30pm, Fri 9am–2pm, closed Sat.** This classic Roman snack joint used to be in Jewish Ghetto but was replaced by a burger bar, and the Ghetto's loss is very much the Trevi area's gain. Under its changed name it still does kosher pizza to go – the house speciality is pizza with fresh anchovies and *indivia* (endives) – roast chicken and *suppli*.
Museo-Atelier Canova-Tadolini Via del Babuino 150a. It's a bit odd eating here amongst the grand sculptures of this café-cum-museum, and certainly not cheap. But it provides one of the few places to sit down along this busy street, and decent sandwiches, salads, and simple pasta dishes. There are a few outside tables, too, to watch the designer bags bustle by.
Pizza House Via della Mercede 46 ☎ 06.679.7584. **Daily 11am–11pm.** *Rosticceria* and *tavola calda* with seating inside. Good choices and prices, at least for this part of town.
Pizzeria-Tavola Calda Piazzale Flaminia. Daily except Tues 8.30am–11.30pm. Right by the #2 tram stop outside the Porta del Popolo, the *pizza al taglio*, roast chicken, roast potatoes and various *fritti* items at this long-established *tavola calda* are a godsend in a part of town not well served by cheap snack places. A few tables outside, too, though it's not the quietest place to eat.

Termini, Monti and San Giovanni

See map on pp.126–127.

🏃 **Antico Caffè di Brasile Via dei Serpenti 23** ☎ 06.488.2319. **Mon–Sat 6am–8.30pm, Sun 7am–2pm.** Reliable old Monti stand-by that has been selling great coffee, snacks

and cakes for around a century, and with a handful of seats and tables at the back should you want to take the weight off.
Dagnino Galleria Esedra, Via E. Orlando 75 ☎ 06.481.8660. **Daily 7.30am–10.30pm.** Good for both a coffee and snack or light lunch, this long-established Sicilian bakery is a peaceful retreat in the Termini area, with tables outside in this small shopping arcade.
Enoteca Cavour 313 Via Cavour 313 ☎ 06.678.5496. **Mon–Sat 12.30–2.30pm & 7.30pm–12.30am.** At the Forum end of Via Cavour, a lovely old wine bar that makes a handy retreat after seeing the ancient sites. Lots of wines and delicious (though not cheap) snacks and salads.
Self-Service Luncheonette Salita di San Nicola da Tolentino 19/21 ☎ 06.474.0029. **Mon–Sat 8am–3pm.** Just up from Bernini's spouting Triton fountain at Piazza Barberini, this place has great food served cafeteria-style. It caters to the office workers in the area and so is delicious and cheap. It can be very crowded, so best get there early.
Trimani Via Cernaia 37b ☎ 06.446.9630. **Mon–Sat noon–midnight.** Classy wine bar (Rome's biggest selection of Italian regional vintages) good for a lunchtime tipple and an indulgent snack. You'll spend around €15 to sample a range of good-quality cheeses and cured pork meat, or a soup and salad, including a glass of wine. It also has a wine shop outlet nearby – see p.276.

Trastevere

See map on pp.168–169.
Bibli Via dei Fienaroli 28 ☎ 06.588.4097. **Tues–Sun 11am–midnight; Mon 5.30pm–midnight.** Café and bookshop that does a good American brunch at the weekend, and decent food – lunch and dinner – the rest of the time. Internet access too.
Fidelio Via degli Stefaneschi 3/7. No phone. Daily noon–2am. Tucked away just behind Piazza Sonnino in Trastevere, a *vineria* with sandwiches, salads and plates of cheese and cold cuts – as well as a good selection of Italy's best wines and beer.
Frontoni dal 1921 Viale Trastevere 52 ☎ 06.581.2436. Great *fritti* and focaccia sandwiches among many other snacks at this bustling Trastevere bar-cum-*birreria*, which is busy at all hours of day and night.
Gianicolo Piazzale Aurelia 5 ☎ 06.580.6275. **Closed Mon.** Quite an ordinary bar, but in a

nice location and a bit of a hangout for Italian media stars, writers and academics from the nearby Spanish and American academies. Good sandwiches too.

Di Marzio Piazza di Santa Maria in Trastevere 15 ☎06.581.6095. Daily 7am–1am. This bar isn't much on the inside, but it's a friendly place whose terrace bang on Piazza Santa Maria makes it one of the best people-watching spots in Trastevere.

La Renella Via del Moro 15 ☎06.581.7265. Daily 9am–9pm. Arguably the best bakery in Rome, right in the heart of Trastevere, with great focaccia and superb *pizza al taglio*. Take a number and be prepared to wait at busy times. You can take away or eat on the premises at its long counter.

Sisini Via San Francesco a Ripa 137 ☎06.589.7110. Mon–Sat 11am–11pm, **closed hols**. Located just half a block from Viale Trastevere, there's no sign outside this *pizza al taglio* hole-in-the-wall, which is ironic as it may well have the best pizza by the slice in Rome. Also roast chickens and potatoes, *suppli* and all the usual *rosticceria* fare. Try their unique chopped spicy green olive pizza.

See map on pp.106–107.

Palombini Piazzale Adenauer 12 ☎06.591.1700. Great EUR café whose outside terrace and large interior are a haven amidst the brutal boulevards. Appropriately housed on the ground floor of EUR's official "restaurant building", it's a café, *tabacchi* and wine shop all rolled Into one, and serves excellent cakes and sandwiches.

Caffè del Seme e la Foglia Via Galvani 18 ☎06.574.3008. Mon–Sat 8am–1.30am, Sun 6pm–1.30am. Pleasantly low-key café popular with Testaccio trendies and students from the nearby music school. During the day it's good for sandwiches and big salad lunches – they do fairly exotic things such as avocados with shrimp or crab, and curried turkey sandwiches – and in the evenings a mellow place to relax before visiting the area's more energetic offerings.

Volpetti Piu Via A. Volta 8. No phone. Mon–Sat 11am–9pm. *Tavola calda* that's attached to the famous deli a few doors down. Great pizza, *suppli*, chicken, deep-fried veg and much more.

⑭

EATING | Coffee, pastries, sandwiches and snacks

Ice cream and fruit shakes

Il Gelato di San Crispino Via della Panetteria 42 ☎06.7045.0412. Wed–Mon noon–midnight, Fri & Sat until 1am. Not far from the Trevi Fountain, this is considered by many to make the best ice cream in Rome. They do interesting flavours like ginger and cinnamon, but you may not find common-or-garden strawberry and it's a bit more expensive than your average ice-cream joint. However, it will make the other *gelato* you've tried pale by comparison. Worth paying a bit extra for.

Giolitti Via Uffici del Vicario 40 ☎06.699.1243. Tues–Sun 7am–2am. An Italian institution that once had a reputation – now lost – for the country's top ice cream. Still pretty good, however, with a choice of seventy flavours. Always very busy.

Palazzo del Freddo di Giovanni Fassi Via Principe Eugenio 65/7 ☎06.446.4740. Tues–Sun midday–midnight, Sat until 12.30am. A wonderful, huge and airy 1920s ice-cream parlour that does brilliant fruit ice creams and good milk shakes.

Della Palma Via della Maddalena 20 ☎06.6880.6752. The city's largest selection of ice-cream flavours by some way – over 100 to choose from.

Pascucci Via di Torre Argentina 20 ☎06.686.4816. Mon–Fri 6.30am–midnight, Sat 6.30am–12.30am Sun 10am–midnight. This tiny stand-up bar is *frullati* central for the centro storico. Your choice of fresh fruit whipped up with ice and milk – the ultimate Roman refreshment on a hot day.

Alla Scala Via della Scala 51 ☎06.581.317. Daily 1pm–midnight, later in summer. This Sicilian-owned Trastevere joint has some of the very best ice cream in town. Sublime consistency and unusual flavours such as cinnamon and cassata. The amarena and coconut are also great.

Tre Scalini Piazza Navona 30 ☎06.6880.1996. Thurs–Tues 8am–1.30am. Piazza Navona institution that is renowned for its famous *tartufo* – death by dark chocolate.

Prati and the Vatican

See map on pp.180–181.

Borgo Antico Borgo Pio 21 ☎ **06.686.5967. Tues–Sat noon–3pm & 7.30–10.30pm. Sun noon–3pm.** Great old-fashioned wine bar right by St Peter's Square that does (mainly cold) food and great wine.

Del Frate Via degli Scipioni 118/124 ☎ **06.323.6437. Mon–Sat 1pm–3pm & 7.30pm–midnight.** This large wine and spirits shop is a wine bar, too, with a great selection of cheeses and cold meats as well as regular pasta dishes. Very handy for the Vatican, for lunch or at the end of the day.

Gran Caffe Borgo Borgo Pio 170–171. There are plenty of places to get something quick to eat on Borgo Pio, but this is a slight cut above the rest, with an excellent selection of *tramezzini*, panini and cakes, and a few inside seats.

Non Solo Pizza Via degli Scipioni 95–97 ☎ **06.372.5820. Tues–Sun 8.30am–10pm.** Pizza by the slice, of Roman fritters – *suppli*, *olive ascolane*, *fiori di zucca*, *crocchette*, etc – and a complete selection of hot dishes *tavola calda*-style; plus from 7pm they offer made-to-order round pizzas, too. No extra charge to sit, inside or out.

Restaurants and pizzerias

There are lots of good places to eat in the **centro storico**, and it's still surprisingly easy to find places that are not tourist traps – **prices** in all but the really swanky places remain pretty uniform throughout the city, as do menus, especially in traditional Roman-cuisine restaurants. **Tridente** and **Campo de'Fiori** and around are similarly well served, and of course there's the Jewish restaurants of the neighbouring **Ghetto**. The area around **Termini** is packed with cheap places to eat, although some of them are of dubious reliability, and, if you are not in a hurry, you might do better heading up to the nearby student area of **San Lorenzo**, where you can often eat far better for the same money. South of the centre, the **Testaccio** neighbourhood is well endowed with good, inexpensive trattorias, a few of the most traditional serving the best of Rome's offal specialities, while, across the river, **Trastevere** is Rome's traditional restaurant enclave and is accordingly thronged with eating options – and people. The number of authentic "Traste" trattorias has declined over recent years, but you'll still easily find good-to-great meals there, at all price levels.

Centro Storico

See map on p.53.

Da Alfredo e Ada Via dei Banchi Nuovi 14 ☎ **06.687.8842. Weekdays only, lunch and dinner.** There's no menu, and precious little choice, at this city-centre stalwart, at which Ada presides over an appreciative clientele of regulars, serving up pasta starters, followed by veal stew with peas, sausage and beans, or whatever they happen to have cooked that day. Dessert is biscuits from Ada's tin, dished out with grand-maternal generosity. Three courses cost less than €20, including half a litre of wine.

Armando al Pantheon Salita de' Crescenzi 30 ☎ **06.6880.3034. Mon–Fri 12.30–3pm & 7–11pm, Sat 12.30–3pm.** Closed Sat pm and all day Sun. Surprisingly unpretentious surroundings and moderately priced hearty food in this long-standing staple close by the Pantheon (open since 1961).

Il Bacaro Via degli Spagnoli 27 ☎ **06.686.4110. Mon–Fri 12.30–2.30pm & 8–11.30pm, Sat 8–11.30pm.** This tiny restaurant tucked away down a small side street off Via della Scrofa, has a small, focused menu featuring a delicious, interesting selection of antipasti and *primi*, and main courses focusing on meat dishes, particularly beef, in a variety of original sauces and servings. The feel of the place is rather romantic but it's really too cramped for a truly private liaison.

Da Baffetto Via del Governo Vecchio 114 ☎ **06.686.1617. Daily 7pm–midnight.** A tiny, highly authentic pizzeria that has long been a Rome institution, though it now tends to be swamped by tourists. Amazingly it's still good value, and has tables outside in summer, though you will always have to queue. Especially good bruschette. Another branch – *Baffetto 2* – is on Piazza del Teatro del Pompeo.

Bevitoria Navona Piazza Navona 72
⏱ **06.6880.1022. Daily 11am–midnight, until 1am in summer.** Right by the Fountain of Neptune, some people swear that this old wine bar and restaurant is the only place in Rome to really drink Italian wine, though as with everywhere on this renowned piazza it's grown hyper-touristy over the years and now is more of a restaurant than anything else. The food isn't bad though, and you don't pay too much over the odds for the unbeatable location.

Boccondivino Piazza in Campio Marzio 6
⏱ **06.6830.8626.** A nice setting with outdoor seating on Piazza Campo Marzio, a short walk from the Pantheon. *Boccondivino*'s aspirations for a more chic brand of diner is matched by the slightly higher prices, but not always by the food, which – like the service – can be a bit hit and miss. When it's good, though, it's excellent.

La Campana Vicolo della Campana 18
⏱ **06.686.7820. Tues–Sun 11.30am–3.30pm & 7.30pm–midnight.** Packed with politicians and journalists, this is truly a trattoria of habitués. To newcomers, service can seem almost surly, but the Roman specialities – in what is said to be the oldest trattoria in the capital – are dependably good and hearty, featuring an abundance of fresh vegetables and fish and home-made desserts. The soups are all delicious, including the signature *pasta e fagioli*.

Capranica Piazza Capranica 104 ⏱ **06.679.0860. Daily noon–midnight.** This restaurant, *enoteca*, taverna and pizzeria all in one is admirably located on a fairly quiet piazza near the Pantheon. Standard fare, well prepared and average prices, plus no serious limits on when you can eat.

Il Convivio da Troiani Vicolo dei Soldati 31
⏱ **06.686.9432. Daily except Sun 8–11pm.** Beautiful restaurant with tables set out in three vaulted rooms by the river near Piazza Navona. The food is adventurous, with variations on traditional Roman dishes, and the restaurant adopts a hard line in using seasonal ingredients – which means the menu changes several times a year. The prices make it one for a special night out.

Le Cornacchie Piazza Rondanini 53
⏱ **06.6819.2096.** Classic Roman dishes served on this quiet piazza bang in the centre of the city. The cooking is good, the service fast and the prices moderate: €8–9 for a *primo*, €10–15 for a *secondo* – in short, pretty much everything you could want from a restaurant.

La Focaccia Via della Pace 11 ⏱ **06.6880.3312. Daily noon–3.30pm & 7.30pm–1am.** A great location, just off Piazza Navona, and hearty, unusual dishes and, of course, a dozen different kinds of focaccia, plus different pizza offerings, big salads, original pasta dishes and a variety of *secondi*. The red house wine is good. Tables outside in summer.

🏃 **Da Francesco Piazza del Fico 29**
⏱ **06.686.4009. Mon & Wed–Sun 7pm–1am.** Not just delectable pizzas in this full-on pizzeria in the heart of trendy Rome, but good antipasti, *primi* and *secondi* too. The service can be slapdash, but the food and atmosphere are second-to-none.

Il Leoncino Via del Leoncino 28 ⏱ **06.687.6306. Mon–Fri 1–2.30pm & 7pm–midnight, Sat & Sun 7pm–midnight. Closed during Aug.** Cheap, hectic and genuine pizzeria, little known to out-of-towners. Really one of the very best for lovers of crispy Roman-style pizza, baked in wood ovens. Just off Via del Corso. No credit cards.

🏃 **Maccheroni Piazza delle Coppelle 44**
⏱ **06.6830.7895. Mon–Sat 12.30–3pm & 8pm–midnight.** A friendly, restaurant that enjoys a wonderful location on this quiet piazza right in the heart of the centro storico. Inside is spartan yet comfy, with basic furniture and marble-topped counters, while the outside tables make the most of the pretty square-cum-inter-section. The food is good, basic Italian fare, affordably priced and cheerfully served.

La Montecarlo Vicolo Savelli 12 ⏱ **06.686.1877. Daily noon–3pm & 6.30pm–1am.** Hectic pizzeria owned by the daughter of *Da Baffetto* (see above) and serving similar crisp, blistered pizza, along with good pasta dishes. Tables outside in summer, but be prepared to queue. Tucked off Corso Vittorio, not far from Piazza Navona.

Myosotis Via della Vaccarella 3–5
⏱ **06.686.5554. Mon–Sat 12.30–2.45pm & 8–11pm.** Excellent food, service and value at this upscale restaurant tucked away on a side street a short walk from the Pantheon,

with excellent pasta, fish and roast meat dishes. Kind of snooty – the sort of place you choose for a posh night out.

Obikà Via dei Prefetti 26 ⓣ06.683.2630. Daily 10am–midnight. The ultra-modern interior and pleasant outside terrace on secluded Piazza Firenze are home to the world's first restaurant specializing in mozzarella from Campania, served with everything from tomatoes to salami to anchovies and much more. There are a few salads and pasta dishes on offer too, but cheese is the main thing here, and as such it's a great place for lunch, though not perhaps dinner. Dishes start at about €8.

Riccioli Piazza della Coppelle 10 ⓣ06.6821.0313. Daily except Sun 5pm–2am. This swish modern restaurant does great sushi, oysters and other seafood, and its funky bar leads the way till late on this busy square in the heart of old Rome.

La Rosetta Via della Rosetta 9 ⓣ06.6830.8841. Mon–Sat 12.45–2.45pm & 7.30–11pm. Rome's premier fish restaurant, which all the others try to imitate. Set on a quiet side street a block from the Pantheon, it's an elegant dining experience, and well worth the – very expensive – prices.

Tapa Loca Via di Tor Millina, 4a–5 ⓣ06.683.2266. Daily 6pm–2am. Moderately priced Spanish restaurant serving four different paellas (including vegetarian), tapas of all sorts, gazpacho, meat, fish and fish soup, and Spanish tortilla. Just off Piazza Navona in a very busy area, so reservations are a good idea. During the day, it's a bar with snacks.

🏃 **Da Tonino Via del Governo Vecchio 18–19.** Closed Sun. There are no menus in this unmarked centro storico favourite, but usually they'll just tell you what they've got that day – basic Roman food, always freshly cooked, and always delicious, although the service can be a bit slow.

El Toulá Via della Lupa 29b ⓣ06.687.3498. Mon–Fri 1–3pm & 8–11pm, Sat 8–11pm. This is one of Rome's chicest and most beautiful restaurants, with a menu featuring some nostalgic Venetian recipes. Very expensive.

Campo de' Fiori and the Ghetto

See map on pp.68–69.

Acchiappafantasmi Via dei Cappellari 66 ⓣ06.687.3462. Daily 8pm–2am. Fine "ghost-shaped" pizzas – the name of the place is Italian for "Ghostbusters" – appetizers,

bruschette and *sfizosita*. Always busy, with a very lively atmosphere, and service can suffer as a result.

Arnaldo ai Satiri Via di Grotta Pinta 8 ⓣ06.686.1915. Wed–Mon 7.30pm–midnight. One of Rome's cosiest hideaways, near Piazza Navona and the Pantheon. Couples can enjoy the cosy, candlelit setting with ballet themed decor. Try the spaghetti sautéed with greens.

La Carbonara Campo de' Fiori 23 ⓣ06.686.4783. Wed–Mon noon–3.30pm & 7pm–midnight. The most expensive of the square's restaurants, but always busy, with plenty of outdoor seating and an excellent selection of antipasti – and great pasta (try the *papardelle* in wild boar sauce, or of course the *pasta alla carbonara. La Carbonara* tends to get mixed reviews these days but we believe it still offers value for money.

Il Drappo Vicolo del Malpasso 9 ⓣ06.687.7365. Mon–Sat 1–3pm & 7–11.30pm. This Sardinian restaurant just off Via Giulia has been going for years, and attracts large crowds of loyal regulars to sample its fish, seafood and suckling pig, along with wafer-thin flat Sardinian bread. Great Sardo desserts, too.

Dar Filletaro a Santa Barbara Largo dei Librari 88 ⓣ06.686.4018. Mon–Sat 6–10.30pm; closed in Aug. A fish-and-chip shop without the chips. Paper-covered Formica tables (outdoors in summer), cheap wine, beer and fried cod, a timeless Roman speciality. Located a short walk from Campo de' Fiori, off busy Via Giubbonari. Service can be offhand, to say the least.

🏃 **Ar Galletto Piazza Farnese 102** ⓣ06.686.1714. Mon–Sat 12.15–3pm & 7.30–11.15pm. This place is situated on one of Rome's stateliest piazzas, and just off one of its trendiest, too, and yet retains the feel of a provincial trattoria. It's been a local favourite for at least a quarter of a century and specializes in traditional Roman cookery with a homely touch. In winter, the atmospheric indoor setting is old Rome at its best; in warmer months, you can enjoy the magnificent Renaissance square from outside seating. Very good prices.

🏃 **Da Giggetto Via del Portico d'Ottavia 21a– 22** ⓣ06.686.1105. Tues–Sun noon– 3.30pm & 7.30pm–midnight. Roman-Jewish fare in the Jewish Ghetto, featuring deep-fried artichokes, *baccalá*, and *rigatoni con pajata*, along with good non-offal pasta dishes, eaten outside in summer by the ruins of the Portico d'Ottavia. Not cheap, but worth the splurge. It's usually very crowded, but so huge you can almost always get a table.

Da Giulio Via della Barchetta 18/19 ⊤06.6880.6466. Tues–Sun noon–3pm & 7– 11pm. Decent Roman food, well served in a nice atmosphere in the vaulted hall of an ancient palazzo.

Govinda Via Santa Maria del Pianto 15/17 ⊤06.689.1540. Mon–Fri 12.30am–3pm, Fri & Sat 7.30–10.30pm. This delightful, strictly Hindu vegetarian place is run by the Italian branch of the Hare Krishna movement. It does lunch during the week, for which you are asked for a donation, and a fixed-price dinner Fri and Sat (€15), for which you have to book. The food is always delicious, and the service gracious. No alcohol.

Grappolo d'Oro Piazza della Cancelleria 80 ⊤06.686.4118. Mon–Sat 12.30– 3.30pm & 8–11pm; closed Aug. This place has had a bit of a facelift recently but still remains relatively unscathed by the hordes in nearby Campo de' Fiori, and serves imaginative Roman cuisine in a traditional trattoria atmosphere at moderate prices.

L'Insalata Ricca Largo dei Chiavari 85/86 ⊤06.6880.3656. Daily noon–3.30pm & 7pm– 1am. An Anglo-American presence in a relaxed and slightly out-of-the-ordinary place, although it is just one of a Roman chain of six. A good choice for vegetarians, with inter-esting big salads, as the name suggests, wholefood options and reasonably priced Italian fare, including pizzas. The setting is nice too, next to a church, between Piazza Navona and Campo de' Fiori, and there are other branches, one nearby on Piazza Pasquino, and others in Prati – very handily situated for the Vatican Museums on Piazza del Risorgimento – and in Trastevere (on Via Santini, just off Viale Trastevere).

Der Pallaro Largo del Pallaro 15 ⊤06.6880.1488. Tues–Sun noon–3pm & 7pm–midnight. An old-fashioned trattoria serving a set four-course daily menu for €21, including wine (whether you want it or not). A good option when you're starving. Located in a quiet piazza between Campo de' Fiori and Largo Argentina. No credit cards.

Piperno Monte de Cenci 9 ⊤06.6880.6629. Tues–Sat 12.30– 2.15pm, Sun 12.30–2.15pm. Tucked away on the tiny piazza of Monte di Cenci, this rather formal restaurant makes for one of the best

opportunities to sample Jewish specialities. The cooking is exceptional, the prices moderate to high, but the location is special, with seats outside in summer. An excellent choice for a big night out.

Al Pompiere Via Santa Maria dei Calderari 38 ⊤06.686.8377. Closed Sun, otherwise noon–3pm & 7pm–midnight. Housed in a frescoed old palace in the heart of the Ghetto, this fusty, old-fashioned restaurant exudes tradition and serves up some of the best Roman-Jewish food you'll find at decent prices. Its warren of high-ceilinged rooms is usually crowded, especially late on, and it's a good place to try *carciofi alla giudea* and *fiori fritti*.

La Primavera Via del Sudario 37 ⊤06.687.5417. Daily noon–3pm & 7pm–midnight. Chinese food isn't great in Italy, but this is a decent enough and rather elegant (by Roman standards) Chinese restaurant, just off Largo Argentina. Reservations are recommended.

Roscioli Via dei Giubbonari 21/22 ⊤06.687.5287. Closed Sun. Is it a deli, a wine bar, or fully fledged restaurant? Actually it's all three, and you can either just have a glass of wine and some cheese or go for the full menu, which has great pasta dishes and *secondi* at lunchtime and in the evening. Nothing is cheap here, and the service can be on the snooty side, but once you've tasted the buffalo mozzarella you'll believe that everything you're served will only be the best. See p.276 for more.

Sciam Via del Pellegrino 55 ⊤06.6830.8957. Lovely, authentically Middle Eastern café and restaurant with lots of good, mainly Lebanese and Syrian food – a choice of meze dishes for €18, which can easily feed two – and hookahs to finish off for €6 for two. No alcohol.

Da Sergio Via delle Grotte 27 ⊤06.686.4293. Mon–Sat 11.30am– 3.30pm & 7pm–midnight. Towards the river from Campo de Fiori, this is an out-of-the-way, cosy trattoria with a traditional, limited menu and the deeply authentic feel of old Rome. Inexpensive, and with outdoor seating in summer.

Sora Margherita Piazza delle Cinque Scuole 30 ⊤06.686.4002. Tues–Sun 12.30–3pm, Sat & Sun also 8.30–11pm. A tiny and famous trattoria in the heart of the Jewish quarter serving reasonably priced home-made pasta, *gnocchi*, and desserts. Great artichokes, Jewish-style, and stuffed squash blossoms. For something rare and delicious, try *aliciotti*, a casserole of fresh anchovies and curly endive. No sign outside – look for the doorway on the northern side of the square. **Thien Kim Via Giulia 201** ℡ 06.6830.7832. **Mon–Sat 7.30–11pm.** Perhaps Rome's only Vietnamese restaurant, but it's been here since the 1970s so it must be doing something right. Not expensive, and good if you want something different, but it's very small so you should probably book.

The Tridente

See map on p.79.

🏃 **Antica Birreria Peroni Via San Marcello 19** ℡ 06.679.5310. **Mon–Sat noon–midnight, Fri & Sat until 12.30am.** Big bustling *birreria* with an excellent and cheap Italian-German fusion menu of simple food that's meant to soak up lots of beer. There are the usual starters and pasta dishes, plus a good selection of meat dishes, *scamorza* and wurstel specialities. Its walls are decorated with a frieze adorned by cherubs and slogans urging you to drink more beer – something that's very hard to resist in this lovely old wood-panelled turn-of-the-century restaurant full of photos of old Rome.

🏃 **Beltramme Via della Croce 39. No phone. Daily noon–3pm & 7–11pm.** Originally this place sold only wine, by the fiasco or flask. Now, a few blocks from the Spanish Steps, it is a full-blown restaurant and just about always packed. But if you want authentic Roman food and atmosphere at prices most people can afford – €10 for a *primo*, €15 for a *secondo* – then this is the place. Service can be a bit slow. No credit cards.

Dal Bolognese Piazza del Popolo 1 ℡ 06.361.1426. **Tues–Sun 12.45–3pm & 8.15–11pm.** An elegant restaurant that is the place to go if you want to treat yourself to good Emilian cuisine; *tortellini in brodo* is a must if you like chicken soup. Reservations are recommended, especially if you'd rather eat

outside and watch the passers-by in the piazza. Expensive.

Il Chianti Via del Lavatore 81–82a ℡ 06.678.7550. **Closed Sun.** In the heart of tourist Rome, just metres from Trevi Fountain, this Tuscan specialist, both in wine and food, is a good find in a part of town not generally known for its good-value food and drink. It calls itself a *vineria* so you can just stop by for a drink or a full meal. There are good spreads of Tuscan cheese and cold meats, a good selection of beef and other meat dishes, the usual pasta dishes and decent pizzas. Sit outside in summer if you can bear the travelling musicians who congregate to entertain the tourists.

Gina Via San Sebastianello 7a ℡ 06.678.0251. **Mon 11am–5pm, Tues–Sun 11am–10pm.** This slick white all-day restaurant is a good choice for lunch or dinner, just off Piazza di Spagna, with an easily digested menu of soups, salads and a couple of light pasta dishes.

🏃 **'Gusto Piazza Augusto Imperatore 9** ℡ 06.322.6273. **Daily 12.45–3pm & 7.45pm–1am.** A swish establishment that's more like something you might find in San Francisco or Sydney. However, the food is unique and often wonderful, and the atmosphere very chic. There's a downstairs pizzeria that does excellent pizzas and a reasonably priced Mediterranean buffet lunch every day that is very popular – great value at €8 a head, €13 at weekends – and a restaurant upstairs that offers more upscale and imaginative food at higher prices, including unusual, well-executed desserts, and a very complete wine list. See also *Osteria della Frezza* (below), and p.276 for details of the 'Gustoshop.

Hamasei Via della Mercede 35/36 ℡ 06.679.2134. **Tues–Sun noon–2.30pm & 7pm–10.30pm.** Medium-priced elegant Japanese restaurant right in the centre of town. Tranquil, refined atmosphere and a full range of Japanese dishes, including a sushi bar. A

Traditional Roman restaurants

la carte prices are high, but there are economical lunch specials.

Margutta Via Margutta 118 ☎06.3265.0577. Daily 12.30–3pm & 7.30–11.30pm. Good taste is not only about art and antiques on this famous street. There's also this upmarket, vegetarian restaurant that serves generous helpings – albeit at rather high prices. Try the Sun brunch.

Matricianella Via del Leone 4 ☎06.683.2100. Closed Sun. Very handily placed just off Via del Corso, this old favourite is perhaps the best place to try real Roman food in the city centre, with classic deep-fried dishes like *baccalá* and various vegetable *fritti*, classic Roman pasta dishes such as *cacio e pepe*, and a great wine list – all of which you can consume in the bustling main dining room or on the outside terrace.

Naturist Club Via della Vite 14 (just off Via del Corso, a block away from Piazza San Silvestro, up on the fourth floor) ☎06.679.2509. Mon–Sat 12.30–2.45pm & 7.30–10.30pm. A friendly, well-priced vegetarian fourth-floor restaurant, *Naturist Club* features wholegrain risottos, vegetable pies and fresh juices, wonderful organic wines, home-made ice creams and other delicious desserts. Lunch €10 a head, dinner €20.

Osteria della Frezza Via della Frezza 16 ☎06.322.6273. Daily 12.30–3pm & 7.30–midnight. Part of the super-cool – and ultra-successful-'Gusto empire, this place is equally good for snacks such as cheese or salami plates or for full meals. There's a large wine list, and the whole thing is carried with the usual 'Gusto panache – although the cool jazz sounds and gliding black-attired waiters tend to grate after a while. Not cheap, either.

Otello alla Concordia Via della Croce 81 ☎06.679.1178. Mon–Sat 12.30–3pm & 7.30–11pm. This place used to be one of Fellini's favourites – he lived just a few blocks away on Via Margutta – and remains an elegant yet affordable choice in the heart of Rome. A complete offering of Roman and Italian dishes, but ask for "spaghetti Otello" for a taste of pure tradition – fresh tomatoes and basil with garlic.

Pizza Ciro Via della Mercede 43/45 ☎06.678.6015. Daily noon–3pm & 7pm–midnight. Just up from Piazza San Silvestro, this is a big, friendly pizza place that also has first courses, main courses and desserts. Try the *linguine al ciro* which comes with seafood.

Pizza Re Via di Ripetta 14 ☎06.321.1468. Daily, except Sun lunch, 12.30–3pm & 7pm–midnight. Authentic Neapolitan pizzeria (thicker than Roman) made in a wood-stoked oven. Just up from Piazza del Popolo. Busy, so book. Another, larger branch is in Prati, at Via Oslavia 39 ☎06.372.1173, just north of Piazza Mazzini.

Recafé Piazza Augusto Imperatore 9 ☎06.6813.4730. Daily 12.45pm & 7.30pm–1am. The entrance on Via del Corso is a Neapolitan café, while on the Piazza Augusta Imperatore side you can enjoy proper Neapolitan pizzas, good pasta and salad dishes and excellent grilled *secondi* for moderate prices – €9 or so for a *primo*, €12–18 for a *secondo*. There are Neapolitan sweets and *fritti* too. The ambience is deliberately chic and the large outside terrace always has a buzz about it.

Supperclub Via de' Nari 14 ☎06.6880.7207. The original Dutch vision of this now international chain is alive and kicking in Rome. DJs, live music and performance artists complement the adventurous and sometimes downright bizarre food in a restaurant that is shamelessly contemporary yet feels like a throwback to imperial Rome.

Termini, Monti and San Giovanni

See map on pp.126–127 and pp.140–141.

Africa Via Gaeta 26 ☎06.494.1077. Tues–Sun noon–3.30pm & 7.30–11pm. Arguably the city's most interesting ethnic food – Eritrean – and the first culinary sign of Rome's mostly recently arrived Ethiopian and Somalian population.

Arancia Blu Via dei Latini 57 ☎06.445.4105. Daily 8.30pm–midnight. This ultra-trendy San Lorenzo vegetarian restaurant reckons itself a cut above. But in a city with very few vegetarians it doesn't have to try too hard. Good food using fresh ingredients in an imaginative fashion: specialities include various stuffed veggie pasta dishes – ravioli, cannelloni and the like – and decent salads.

Baia Chia Via Machiavelli 5 ☎06.7045.3452. Mon–Sat 12.30–3.30pm & 7.30pm–11.30pm; Closed Sun. Just off Via Merulana, this moderate Sardinian restaurant has lots of good fish starters and tasty first courses. The fish baked in salt is spectacular. For dessert don't fail to try the *sebadas*, hot

Rome doesn't have many specifically **vegetarian restaurants**: vegetarianism isn't particularly widely followed in Italy and in any case most traditional Italian places offer plenty of meatless options. However, the few that exist are excellent; as always, see the listings for full reviews.

Acqua e Farina? (p.246)
Arancia Blu (p.243)
Govinda (p.241)

L'Insalatiera 2 (p.248)
Margutta (p.243)
Naturist Club (p.243)

pastries stuffed with cheese and topped with Sardinian honey.

Il Bocconcino Via Ostilia 23 ☎06.7707.9175. **Daily except Wed noon–3pm & 7–11pm.** Not the greatest service, but a cut above most of the other places within earshot of the Colosseum, with high-quality Roman food served in an old-fashioned environment.

Alle Carrette Via Madonna dei Monti 95 ☎06.679.2770. **Daily 8pm–midnight.** Inexpensive large pizzeria just up Via Cavour from the Imperial Forums that is always crowded – expect to wait for the exceptional pizza here. Great home-made desserts too.

Charley's Sauciere Via San Giovanni in Laterano 270 ☎06.7049.5666. **Mon–Sat 12.30–3pm & 7.30–11pm.** This French–Swiss old-timer is a welcome place to indulge in some comfort food after a tiring day at the Forum – from which it is around ten minutes' walk. Moderate prices and very reliable French standards, and wine.

Colline Emiliane Via degli Avignonesi 22 ☎06.481.7538. **Tues–Sat 12.45am–2.45pm & 7.30–10.45pm, Sun 12.45am–2.45pm only; closed Mon.** Many Italians consider the cuisine of the Emilia Romagna region to be the country's best. Try it for yourself, lovingly prepared by a family, oddly enough, from Le Marche. Located just down from Piazza Barberini, on a quiet backstreet parallel to Via del Tritone. Moderate prices.

Il Dito e La Luna Via dei Sabelli 49/51 ☎06.494.0726. **Mon–Sat 7.45–11pm.** Creative Sicilian cuisine in a bistro-like San Lorenzo restaurant popular with thirty-something-ish Romans. Go early, as they tend to run out of dishes.

Formula 1 Via degli Equi 13 ☎06.445.3866. **Mon–Sat 7.30–midnight.** Cheap and justifiably popular San Lorenzo pizzeria, with tables outside in summer. Delicious *pizza all'Ortolana* (with courgettes, aubergines and peppers) and good courgette-flower fritters.

Il Guru Via Cimarra 4/6 ☎06.474.4110. **Daily 7pm–1am.** An elegant, inviting atmosphere and good northern Indian cuisine. Great location in an evocative, little-frequented neighbourhood, just above the Imperial Forums. Fixed menus vary from

Luzzi Via San Giovanni in Laterano 88 ☎06.709.6332. **Daily except Wed noon–3pm & 7pm–midnight.** Midway between San Giovanni in Laterano and the Colosseum, this bustling restaurant is a good choice amid the tourist joints of the neighbourhood. The food is hearty and simple, if unspectacular, there's outside seating and it's extremely cheap – *secondi* go for €6–9. There are pizzas too, but only in the evening.

Monti DOC Via G. Lanza 93 ☎06.487.2696. **Tues–Fri 1–3.30pm & 7pm–1am, Sat & Sun 7pm–1am.** Comfortable Santa Maria Maggiore neighbourhood wine bar, with a good wine list and some nice food: cold cuts and cheese, soups, quiches, salads and pastas, including some good veggie dishes, chalked on the blackboard daily.

Le Naumacchie Via Celimontana 7 ☎06.700.2764. **Daily noon–3pm & 7pm–midnight.** A good wine bar and restaurant just a couple of hundred yards from the Colosseum that is a higher priced but equally convivial alternative to *Luzzi* (see above) – though it has no outside seating.

Pommidoro Piazza dei Sanniti 44 ☎06.445.2692. **Mon–Sat noon–3pm & 7.30–11pm.** A typical, family-run Roman trattoria that's been around forever and was apparently the favoured haunt of Pasolini. It has a breezy open verandah in summer and a fireplace in winter. Try the tasty pappardelle with a wild-boar sauce, *cicoria ripassata* if you like vegetables, and *abbachio scotta-dito*, always perfectly grilled.

Tram Tram Via dei Reti 44–46 ☎06.490.416. **Tues–Sun noon–3pm &**

7.30pm–midnight. A grungy location but a cosy spot, this trendy, animated San Lorenzo restaurant serves good Pugliese pasta dishes, fish and seafood and unusual salads. Reservations are recommended. There's also a bar if you want to carry on drinking after dinner. €15 to 18.

Trattoria Monti Via di San Vito 13a ☎06.446.6573. **Tues–Sat noon–3pm & 7.30–11pm, Sun noon–3pm, closed Mon.** Small, family-run restaurant that specializes in the cuisine of the Marche region, which means hearty food from a short menu – great pasta and interesting cabbage-wrapped *torte* as starters, and mainly meat *secondi*, with beef, lamb and rabbit predominating. Close by Santa Maria Maggiore, this is close enough to the Termini hotel district to be convenient, but is as homely and friendly a restaurant as you could want – something places in this neighbourhood often aren't.

Wanted/Birreria Moretti Via dei Serpenti 166/168 ☎06.4788.1057. **Daily except Tues 11am–2am.** Pizzas from €5, pasta dishes from €6, and main courses for around €10 at this crowded Italian-Austrian Monti standby that is open all hours.

Trastevere

See map on pp.168–169.

Akropolis Via S. Francesco a Ripa 103 ☎06.5833.2600. **Tues–Sun noon–2.30pm & 7–11.30pm.** Small Greek restaurant and takeaway with good souvlaki and all the usual snacks and honeyed sweets.

Antico Arco Piazzale Aurelio 7 ☎06.581.5274. **Mon–Sat 7.30pm–midnight.** One of Rome's finest restaurants, and usually a truly wonderful dining experience. Superb dishes exquisitely presented, plus an enormous fine wine list. Located above Trastevere, next to the Janiculum Hill. Reservations are definitely required.

ATM Sushi Bar Via della Penitenza 7 ☎06.6830.7053. **Tues–Sun 7pm–midnight.** Tucked away in Trastevere, this cool yet cosy place comes as a real – and affordable – surprise, serving delicious sushi and sashimi, as well as lacy, perfect tempura. The sashimi salad is very special. Start off with a flawless miso soup and finish with home-made green tea ice cream, and a lime cocktail. There's a great wine list, too.

Da Augusto Piazza de Renzi 15 ☎06.580.3798. **Mon–Sat noon–3pm & 8–11pm.** Diner-style Trastevere stand-by serving Roman basics in an unpretentious, bustling atmosphere. Good pasta and soup starters, and daily meat and fish specials – not haute cuisine, but decent, hearty Roman cooking.

Casetta de' Trastevere Piazza de' Renzi 31a/32 ☎06.580.0158. **Tues–Sun noon–3.30pm & 7pm–1am.** A traditional Trastevere eatery in every way, with a beautiful setting, good food and lowish prices. Delicious *spaghetti alle vongole.*

Ci-Lin Via Fonte d'Olio 6 ☎06.581.3930. **Daily 11.30am–3.30pm & 7.30–11.30pm.** Excellent Cantonese cooking in a warm and friendly atmosphere – at very friendly prices, too. Handily located right off Trastevere's main piazza.

Ferrara Via del Moro 1a ☎06.5833.3920. **Daily 7.30pm–1am.** Just off Piazza Trilussa, this is Trastevere's most original spot, with an exciting, if pricey, regional menu, a sommelier who really knows the perfect wine for every course, and an inviting series of rooms elegantly stripped back to their medieval walls. The vegetarian antipasto selection is a great choice, and different every time, depending on the season and the chef's

Ethnic restaurants

Chinese restaurants – most of them pretty average – abound. Otherwise there's a slowly growing list of international options in and around the centre. See our listings for full reviews.

Africa (Eritrean) (p.243)
Akropolis (Greek) (p.245)
ATM Sushi Bar (Japanese) (p.245)
Charro Café (Tex-Mex) (p.247)
Ci-Lin (Chinese) (p.245)
Govinda (Indian) (p.241)

Il Guru (Indian) (p.244)
Hamasei (Japanese) (p.242)
La Primavera (Chinese) (p.241)
Sciam (Middle Eastern) (p.241)
Tapa Loca (Spanish) (p.240)
Thien Kim (Vietnamese) (p.242)

inspiration. Reservations are a must. Expect to spend at least €60 a head, including wine.

Ivo Via di San Francesco a Ripa 158
T 06.581.7082. Wed–Mon 7.30pm–1am. *The* Trastevere pizzeria, almost in danger of becoming a caricature, but still good and very reasonable. A nice assortment of desserts, too – try the *monte bianco* for the ultimate chestnut cream and meringue confection. Arrive early to avoid a chaotic queue.

Da Lucia Vicolo del Mettonate 2
T 06.580.3601. Tues–Sun noon–3pm & 7.30–11.30pm. Outdoor Trastevere dining in summer is at its traditional peak at this wonderful old Roman trattoria. *Spaghetti cacio e pepe* is the great speciality here – get there early to nab a table outside.

Ai Marmi Viale Trastevere 53/59
T 06.580.0919. Thurs–Tues 6.30pm–2.30am. Nicknamed "the mortuary" because of its stark interior and marble tables, this place serves unique "*suppli al telefono*" (so named because of the string of mozzarella it forms when you take a bite), fantastic fresh *baccalá* and the best pizza in Trastevere. Nice house red wine, too. Rapid service, despite the crowds. A lively, inexpensive feel of the real Rome.

Da Olindo Vicolo della Scala 8 T 06.581.8835. Mon–Sat noon–3pm & 8–11pm. Great, family-run Trastevere trattoria with traditional Roman fare. There's a small menu of staples, and prices are cheap and easy to remember: *primi* cost €7, *secondi* €9.

Da Paris Piazza San Calisto 7a
T 06.581.5378. Tues–Sat noon–3pm & 8–11.30pm, Sun noon–3pm. Fine Roman-Jewish cookery in one of Trastevere's most atmospheric piazzas, with tables outside in summer and a whole host of excellent traditional dishes. Moderate prices.

Il Ponentino Piazza del Drago 10 T 06.588.0680. This restaurant serves all the usual suspects – decent pasta, a full complement of pizzas, nice *secondi* – and does them all fairly well. But its main attraction is its location on peaceful Piazza del Drago and its pleasant outside terrace.

Dar Poeta Vicolo del Bologna 45 T 06.588.0516. Tues–Sun 7.30pm–1am. Without any doubts, one of the top-ten pizzerias in Rome. Don't expect the typical crusty Roman pizza here; the margherita (ask for it *con basilico* – with basil) comes out of the oven soft and with plenty of good mozzarella on top. They have good imported *birra rossa* – a rarity outside a pub – as well as a few outside tables.

Romolo Via Porta Settimiana 8 T 06.581.3873. Tues–Sun noon–3pm & 7–11pm. A Trastevere institution, apparently located in the very building where Raphael's lover, "La Fornarina", lived and serving a traditional Roman menu and nice house wines, albeit at relatively high prices. For all that, the menus are decorated with sketches by famous artists who have dined here, and the garden setting is great in fine weather.

Pizzeria San Calisto Piazza di San Calisto 9a T 06.581.8256. Tues–Sun 7.30pm–1am. Large pizzas at small prices. Friendly, fast service and a vibrant, welcoming atmosphere, whether you sit inside or out on the piazza.

La Scala Piazza della Scala 60 T 06.580.3763. Daily 7pm–2am. This place was originally just a *birreria* but gradually expanded its offerings and now has a very broad menu of classic Italian and Roman dishes at reasonable prices. A nice location on Piazza della Scala. Almost always packed, so go early or you'll have to wait.

South Central Rome

See map on pp.106–107.

Citta del Gusto

This industrial building by the river in the southern reaches of Trastevere (Via Enrico Fermi 161 T 06.551.1221) is a six-floor testimony to the success of the **Gambero Rosso food empire**, which has grown from a food and wine supplement in the communist newspaper *Manifesto* to Italy's most successful gourmet publisher, with a best-selling magazine, TV show and a series of restaurant guides. At their headquarters they hold food seminars and **wine tastings**, host a **wine bar** (Tues–Sat 7.30pm–midnight) and **restaurant** (Mon 9am–4pm, Tues–Fri 7.30–11.30pm; T 06.5511.2277), a **shop** selling cookbooks and kitchen equipment, and a theatre and TV studio.

Not all Rome's restaurants just serve **Roman specialities**; in fact Rome offers a good sampling of the varied *cucina* of Italy's many distinct regions. See the listings for the full rundown on these places.

Acchiappafantasmi (Calabrian) (p.240)
Baia Chia (Sardinian) (p.243)
Dal Bolognese (Emilian) (see p.242)
Il Chianti (Tuscan) (p.242)
Colline Emiliane (Emilian) (p.244)
Il Dito e La Luna (Sicilian) (p.244)

Ferrara (multiregional) (p.245)
Dal Toscano (Tuscan) (p.248)
El Toulá (Venetian) (p.240)
Tram Tram (Pugliese) (p.244)
Trattoria Monti (Le Marche) (p.245)

Acqua e Farina? Piazza O. Giustiniani 2 ☎06.574.1382. Daily noon–3pm & 8pm–midnight. Very reasonable Testaccio restaurant serving dishes that are unique: everything, from starters to desserts, is a variation on the theme of pastry creations – hence the name, "Water & Flour?". Ideal for a light meal, lunch or dinner, for as little as €10 a head. A very busy place in the middle of an area bustling with streetlife, especially in summer.

Augustarello Via G. Branca 98 ☎06.574.6585. Mon–Sat noon–3.30pm & 7.30–11.30pm. Moderately priced Testaccio standard serving genuine Roman cuisine in an old-fashioned atmosphere. A good place to come if you appreciate oxtail and sweetbreads, although, as with all Italian restaurants, even strict vegetarians can find good choices.

Charro Café Via Monte Testaccio 73 ☎06.578.3064. Tues–Sun 8.30–2am. Right in Testaccio's busiest stretch (look for the red-pepper-coloured lights in the tree to find it), this has a Tex-Mex menu with everything on it. Prices are higher than average, as with all establishments along this side of Monte Testaccio. But the lively, party atmosphere more than compensates, as does the salsa music.

Checchino dal 1887 Via Monte Testaccio 30 ☎06.574.6318. Tues–Sat noon–3pm & 8–11.30pm. A historic symbol of Testaccio cookery, with an excellent wine cellar, too – at the end of Via Galvani on the road that circles Monte Testaccio, lined with restaurants and nightspots. Expensive.

Felice Via Mastro Giorgio 29 ☎06.574.6800. Mon–Sat 12.30–2.45pm & 8–10.30pm. Don't be put off by the "riservato" signs on the tables – the owner likes to "select" his customers. Smile and make Felice understand that you're hungry and fond of Roman cooking. Try *bucatini*

cacio e pepe, or lamb, and, in winter, artichokes.

Ketumbar Via Galvani 24 ☎06.5730.5338. Daily 8–11.30pm; bar open till 2am; closed Aug. One of Rome's handful of fusion restaurants, where Mediterranean tradition meets Oriental pizzazz. The decor of the ultra-cool Testaccio venue is just as fused, with a most intriguing mix of world music to go with it, and very attitude-free service, despite its chic allure. Convenient for all the district's nightspots.

Da Remo Piazza Santa Maria Liberatrice 44 ☎06.574.6270. Mon–Sat 7.30pm–1am. *Remo* is the best kind of pizzeria: usually crowded with locals, very basic, and serving the thinnest, crispiest Roman pizza you'll find. Try also the heavenly bruschetta and other snacks like *suppli* and *fior di zucca*. Almost worth travelling out to Testaccio for – and very cheap.

Tuttifrutti Via Luca della Robbia 3a ☎06.575.7902. Tues–Sun 7.30–11.55pm. This Testaccio favourite is pretty much the perfect restaurant – family-run, with good food, decent prices and lots of customers. The menu changes daily, and offers inter-esting variations on traditional Roman dishes. Recommended.

Prati and the Vatican

See map on pp.180–181.

La Grotta Azzurra Via Cicerone 62a ☎06.323.4490. Fri–Wed noon–3.30pm & 7.30pm–midnight. Moderate, quiet, relaxing refuge after a day at Castel Sant'Angelo or the Vatican. Fish specialities and good service at moderate prices.

Les Etoiles Via G.Vitelleschi 34 ☎06.687.3233. Daily 12.30–2.30pm & 7–10.30pm. This ravishing roof-garden restaurant on the top floor of the

Atlante Star hotel, has magnificent views of Rome, especially St Peter's – perfect if you have something to celebrate. Great, Mediterranean food and friendly and courteous staff make this an unforgettable (though very expensive) experience.

L'Insalatiera 2 Via Trionfale 94 ☏ **06.3974.2975. Mon–Sat 1–4pm & 8pm–midnight.** Moderate vegetarian restaurant specializing in regional Italian cuisine, located right across from Rome's flower market. Try their *tagliolini alle noci* or *gnocchi al radicchio e gorgonzola*. For seconds go for the *rotolo di verdura al cartoccio*, the *focaccia napoletano* (with olives, pine nuts and raisins) or the *involtini di radicchio*. Everything is home-made, including the wonderful desserts, such as chocolate and ricotta pie.

Lingua Lunga Piazza dell' Unitá 25/27 ☏ **06.3260.0166.** A good menu for those paralyzed by indecision after the rigours of the Vatican Museums. Lots of *fritti* and *bruschette* and a full list of pizzas and classic pasta dishes, plus steaks in various forms, make it good choice for lunch. The food is nothing special, but the location is handy.

Osteria dell'Angelo Via G. Bettolo 24 ☏ **06.372.9470. Mon–Sat 8–11.15pm; plus Tues & Fri 12.45–2.30pm.** Above-average traditional Roman food, at extremely reasonable prices, in a highly popular restaurant run by an ex-rugby player. Booking is advisable, as it's often heaving with locals.

Ragno d'Oro Via Silla 26 ☏ **06.321.2362.** This family-run restaurant not only has great Roman cooking and good service, but it's also just five minutes' walk from the Vatican. Moderate prices too.

Dal Toscano Via Germanico 58/60 ☏ **06.3972.5717. Tues–Sun 12.30–3pm & 8–11pm.** Don't come here for a salad. This restaurant specializes in *fiorentine* (the famous thick Tuscan T-bone steaks), perfectly grilled on charcoal, and delicious *pici* (thick home-made spaghetti) or *ribollita* (veg and bread soup) – all at honest prices. Tremendously popular with Roman families, so reservations recommended for dinner. Near the Piazza del Risorgimento end of Via Germanico.

Paroli and north

See map on pp.154–155.

La Maremma Viale Parioli 93 ☏ **06.808.6002.** There are quite a few restaurants along the sweeping boulevard of Viale Parioli, but this chain is probably the most unpretentious – an all-day pizzeria with thin Roman or thicker Neapolitan pizzas, *fritti* and *crostini* and a few simple grilled dishes.

ReD Via Pietro de Coubertin 30 ☏ **06.8069.1630.** Part of the Auditorium complex on the northern edge of central Rome, this self-consciously sleek designer bar-restaurant is good for a drink or something to eat before or after a performance. During the day you might like to stop by for its €15 buffet lunch if you're in the area, but it's not worth a special trip.

La Scala Via dei Parioli 79d ☏ **06.808.4463.** One of Parioli's posh choices, but sedate rather than pretentious and serving excellent food in its cosy inside rooms and outdoor terrace. Great fish and seafood risotto. Always crowded.

Drinking

Drinking is not something Romans do a lot of, at least almost never to drunken excess. Despite that, you'll find plenty of bars in Rome, although, as with the rest of Italy, many are functional daytime haunts and not at all the kinds of places you'd want to spend an evening. (We've listed the best of these in Chapter 14.) However, partly due to the considerable presence of Brits and Americans in Rome, there are nowadays plenty of bars and pubs conducive to an evening's drinking; indeed, there's an Irish pub practically on every corner in the city centre. One of Rome's more traditional types of drinking establishment is the **wine bar**, known as an *enoteca* or *vineria*. The old ones have gained new cachet in recent years, and newer ones, with wine lists the size of unabridged dictionaries, are weighing in, too, often with gourmet menus to go with the superb wines they offer. There's also been a recent proliferation of wine-tastings (*degustazioni*), which offer a chance to sample some interesting vintages, often at no cost. Wine bars that also feature great **food**, or in which food is the major activity, have been listed in Chapter 14, either under "Snacks" or "Restaurants". Those that still concentrate on the fruit of the vine, however, are many in number, and we've listed the best here.

Many drinking spots are slick and expensive excuses for people to sit and pose, but most have the advantage of late **opening hours** – sometimes until 4am in summer, and almost always until around 1am. Remember there is sometimes considerable crossover between Rome's bars, restaurants and clubs. For the most part, the places listed in this chapter are drinking spots, but you can eat, sometimes quite substantially, at many of them, and several could be classed just as easily as nightclubs, with loud music and occasionally even an entrance charge. Although we've, again, divided these listings into **neighbourhoods**, the truth is that there are plenty of drinking venues all over Rome. However, Campo de' Fiori and the centro storico near Piazza Navona, plus, of course, Trastevere and Testaccio, are the densest and most happening areas. **Internet cafés** are listed in Basics on p.35.

Centro Storico

See map on p.53.

Anima Via Santa Maria dell' Anima 57 ☎06.6889.2806. Tues–Sun 10pm–3am. This late-night bar-club is at present one of the most popular spots in town, tricked out in post-modern-meets-The Flintstones chic and offering an assortment of elegant snacks to go with your cocktails. Music tends towards chill-out, lounge, and softer soul.

Bloom Via del Teatro Pace 29 ☎06.6880.2029. Mon–Sat. 8pm–2am. Perhaps the most self-consciously cool bar in the centre of Rome,

---

Opening hours have been given for all bars and cafés; note, however, that many places are closed during August.

from its leather banquettes to its curvy zinc counter. It serves food, too, but you'd do better to fill up elsewhere and come on here afterwards, saving your money for one of *Bloom*'s cocktails.

Le Coppelle Piazza delle Coppelle 52
06.683.2410. Mon–Sat 6pm–2am. Snazzy bar decked out in 1970s disco-style that very much functions outdoors during the warm months, when there's a nice array of sofas and pillows to sink into on the usually heaving small piazza.

Cul de Sac Piazza Pasquino 73
06.6880.1094. Daily noon–4pm & 7pm–12.30am. Busy, long-running wine bar with an excellent wine list, a great city-centre location with outside seating, and decent wine-bar food – cold meats, cheeses, salads and soups. One of the best centro storico locations for a snack.

Bar del Fico Piazza del Fico 26/28
06.686.5205. Daily 8am–2am. One of several long-standing hotspots in the area – just around the corner from *Bar della Pace*, and slightly cheaper. Outdoor heating in winter.

Jazz Café Via Zanardelli 10–12 06.6821.0119. Mon–Sat 8.30am–2am. Subdued lighting and a few touches of sleek, post-modern decor set the tone for judicious sipping and murmured conversation set to jazzy background music, veering towards hip-hop as the night wears on. A full (American) menu is served, too. And there's live music on Wed.

Jonathan's Angels Via della Fossa 18
06.689.3426. Daily 1pm–2am. This quirky bar, just behind Piazza Navona, certainly wins the "most decorated" award. Every inch (even the toilet, which is worth a visit in its own right) is plastered, painted or tricked out in outlandish style by the artist/proprietor.

Miscellanea Via delle Paste 110a.
No phone. Daily 12.30pm–3am. Located halfway between Via del Corso and the Pantheon, this was the first American-style bar in Rome, a boozy hangout of US students, and inevitably packed at night. Reasonable prices and the best-value sandwiches in town – jaw-breaking doorstops weighing in at about €3 as well as salads, various antipasti and the odd pasta dish. Outside seating too. Also open Christmas Eve and other holidays for lonesome ex-pats.

Bar della Pace Via della Pace 5
06.686.1216. Daily 10am–2am. Just off Piazza Navona, this is *the* summer bar, with outside tables full of Rome's self-consciously beautiful people. Quietest during the day, when you can enjoy the nineteenth-century interior – marble, mirrors, mahogany and plants – in peace.

La Trinchetta Via dei Banchi Nuovi 4
06.6830.0133. Mon–Sat 8pm–2am. This wine bar is tucked away in the warren of streets between Piazza Navona and the Tiber and is well worth seeking out. There's not only a great selection of wines, but also what may be Rome's most extensive list of *grappa* labels.

Trinity College Via del Collegio Romano 6
06.678.6472. Daily noon–3am. A warm and inviting establishment offering international beers and food. Its two levels can get quite loud and crowded. Food includes a bit of everything – pasta burgers, salads, Tex-Mex – and is served until 1am, plus there's a special brunch menu for around €12.

Campo de' Fiori and the Ghetto

See map on pp.68–69.

L'Angolo Divino Via dei Balestri 12
06.686.4413. Tues–Sun 11am–2.30pm & 5.30pm–2am. Quite a peaceful haven after the furore of Campo de' Fiori, this wine bar has a large selection of wine, and simple, typical wine bar food fare – bread, cheese, cold cuts and the like.

Le Bain Via delle Botteghe Oscure 32a/33
06.686.5673. Tues–Sun 8pm–2am. Popular with a trendy set, just off Largo Argentina, this bar-restaurant includes three spaces featuring art exhibitions, a cocktail bar and cool music – as well as food.

Bartaruga Piazza Mattei 7 06.689.2299. Daily except Sun 3pm–2am. This very theatrical bar attracts members of the city's entertainment *demimonde*, and even provides costumes for clients who feel like a change of persona. The setting is wonderfully camp, eclectically furnished with all sorts of eighteenth-century bits and pieces; nothing really matches and the feel is sumptuously comfy.

Black & White Piazza della Pollarola 32
348.364.8808. Daily 8pm–2am. Nestled in a small piazza between Corso Vittorio and the Campo, this fairly spacious pub draws a good mix of Americans and Romans, who come for the soul sounds and the

€2 shots. Often stays open well after hours, in keeping with the party zone it inhabits.

La Curia di Bacco Via del Biscione 79
T06.689.3893. Daily 4pm–2am. This long, thin, bustling wine bar was hollowed out of the ruins of Pompey's Theatre, near Campo de' Fiori. A very young crowd, some good wines, pricey beer and interesting snacks – crostini, bruschette, cheese plates and the like.

The Drunken Ship Campo de' Fiori 20–21
T06.6830.0535. Daily 11–2am. Standing-room only at this lively meeting-point, with great music – always tremendously popular with young Romans and foreign students. Happy Hour 7–8pm, brunch at weekends.

Mad Jack's Via Arenula 20 T06.6880.8223. Daily 11–2am. One of many Irish pubs, but one of the nicest and most authentic, as well as one of the easiest to find, right across from Piazza Cairoli. Guinness is a speciality, and there are light snacks, burgers and suchlike available, too, to go with the warm welcome. Frequented by Italians as well as tourists and ex-pats.

Rock Castle Café Via B. Cenci 8 T06.6880.7999. Daily 9pm–3am. In the Jewish Ghetto, just across from Trastevere, a basement hangout consisting of six medieval-style rooms, good for mingling while checking out the live music.

Taverna del Campo Campo de' Fiori 16
T06.687.4402. Tues–Sun 8–2am. Identifiable by the peanut shells that litter the floor, this busy wine bar is one of the many overflowing spots around this piazza. You will certainly have to contend for an outside table; but it's the only one that does fancy panini and little foodie treats as well. Good value considering the location.

Vineria Campo de' Fiori 15 T06.6880.3268. Mon–Sat 9–1am, Sun 5pm–1am. Long-established bar/wine shop right on the Campo, patronized by devoted regulars, while more recently making some concessions to comfort as well and offering light meals. Much cheaper if you sit or stand inside.

The Tridente

See map on p.79.

L'Enoteca Antica Via della Croce 76b
T06.679.0896. Daily 11–1am. An old Spanish Steps-area wine bar with a selection of hot and cold dishes, including soups and attractive desserts. Intriguing trompe l'oeil decorations inside, majolica-topped tables outside.

▽ Propping up the bar in *L'Enoteca Antica*

Canova Piazza del Popolo 16 T06.361.2231. Daily 8am–midnight. Once the haunt of the monied classes, but not really the place it was. Still it does all sorts of cocktails and reasonable food, and is a fine place to sit and take the air and watch the world go by on Piazza del Popolo. Politically, *Canova's* clientele was traditionally a right-wing one, while dyed-in-the-wool lefties patronized *Rosati* across the square (see below).

'Gusto Piazza Augusto Imperatore 9
T06.322.6273. Daily 10–2am. This stylish modern bar is part of the 'Gusto foodie empire that occupies this corner and serves drinks, sandwiches and Catalan one-bite tapas to the discerning chattering classes of Rome. Entrance to the bar is around the corner on Via della Frezza.

Lowenhaus Via della Fontanella 16d
T06.323.0410. Daily 11–2am. Just off Piazza del Popolo, a Bavarian-style drinking establishment with beer and snacks – and full meals too – to match.

Rosati Piazza del Popolo 5 T06.322.5859. Daily 8am–midnight. This was the bar that hosted left-wingers, bohemians and writers in years gone by, though now it's cocktails and food that draw the crowds to the outside terrace.

Shaki Via Maria de'Fiori 29 T06.679.1694. Daily 11am–11pm. Wine bar of the nearby gourmet store, and serving salads, soups, light lunches and snacks at outside tables, footsteps from Piazza di Spagna. Good wine, and very handy, if a little too self-consciously chic.

Quirinale, Termini, San Lorenzo

See maps on pp.126–127.
New Orleans Via XX Settembre 52,
T06.4201.4785.Daily except Sun 8am–2am.
More or less a regular Italian bar by day, but a loud pub at night, with American food, good German beer and live music.
Rive Gauche 2 Via dei Sabelli 43 T06.445.6722.
Daily 7pm–3am. The San Lorenzo district's smoky, noisy, cavernous evocation of intel-lectual Left Bank Paris – more or less. Lots of Irish beer choices and snacks to sustain your night of drinking. Happy Hour till 9pm.
Trimani Via Goito 20 T06.446.9661. **Mon–Sat 11am–midnight.** This fine *enoteca* has a truly vast wine list and has also lately been gleaning accolades for its interesting dining options. Mediterranean specialities such as octopus salad and black rice are hits, as well as some unusual cheeses.

Monti and San Giovanni

See map on pp.140–141.
Club Machiavelli Via Machiavelli 49
T06.9761.4348. **Wed–Sat 8pm–1am.** Located in an historic palace, which accounts for the beautiful vaulted ceilings, in up-and-coming Piazza Vittorio, this place serves wines, cocktails and home-made desserts and other treats. Piano bar-style evenings, with occasional live jazz combos and other cultural events.
The Druid's Den Via San Martino ai Monti 28
T06.4890.4781. **Mon–Thurs & Sun 6pm–1.30am, Fri & Sat 6pm–3am.** Appealing Irish pub near Santa Maria Maggiore with a genuine Celtic feel (and owners). It has a mixed expat/Italian clientele, and is not just for the homesick. Cheap and lively, with occasional impromptu Celtic music.
Fiddler's Elbow Via dell'Olmata 43
T06.487.2110. **Mon–Sat 5pm–1.15am, Sun 3pm–1.30am.** One of the two original Irish bars in Rome, one block closer to Santa Maria Maggiore than its rival, *The Druid's*, and roomier, with a decidedly more Latin feel.
Finnegan Via Leonina 66 T06.474.7026.
Decent Irish pub with live football on TV, pool, and a friendly ex-pat crowd. Seating outside, too, on this bustling Monti street.

Al Vino al Vino Via dei Serpenti 19 T06.485.803.
Daily 11.30am–1.30pm & 5pm–12.30am. The Monti district's most happening street offers this seriously good wine bar with a choice of over 500 labels, many by the glass. Snacks are generally Sicilian specialities.

Trastevere

See map on pp.168–169.
Art Café Friends Piazza Trilussa 34
T06.581.6111. **Mon–Sat 6–2am, Sun 5pm–2am.** Fashionable Trastevere bar on busy Piazza Trilussa, serving salads and light lunches as well as being a pleasant place to drink.
Artu Largo F. Biondi 5 T06.588.0398. **Tues–Sun 6pm–2am.** Trastevere bar and pub on one of the district's busiest corners. Its terrace is great for watching the world go by, plus there's a full menu if you're peckish.
Enoteca Ferrara Via del Moro 1a
T06.5833.3920. **Daily 7.30pm–1am.** This renowned restaurant, just off Piazza Trilussa, has a cosy wine bar out front where you can sit and sample from the establishment's excellent wine list while saving on the price of dinner. Nice snacks, too, to help it all go down.
Fidelio Via degli Stefaneschi 3/7
T06.9784.1585. **Daily 6pm–3am.** Just behind Piazza Sonino in Trastevere, this creakingly old *vineria* serves wine and beer and does good traditional food too – mainly pasta, salads and cheese and cold meat plates.
Mr Brown Vicolo del Cinque 29 T06.581.2913.
Mon–Sat 8pm–3am. This popular hangout is one of Trastevere's most charming detours, with a young, fun-loving crowd, happy hour from 9 to 10pm daily, cheap beer, and an assortment of salads, sandwiches and crepês.
Ombre Rosse Piazza Sant'Egidio 12
T06.588.4155. **Mon–Sat 7am–2.30am, Sun 5pm–2.30am.** Pubby yet very Italian café with a shady outside terrace and clubby interior that hosts live jazz and blues. Something of a Trastevere institution, and serving decent wine bar-style snacks and light meals. Along with *San Calisto* (see below), perhaps the neighbourhood's nicest bar.
San Calisto Piazza San Calisto 4
T06.583.5869.**Mon–Sat 6am–2am.** An old-guard Trastevere bar which attracts a huge crowd of just about everybody on late summer nights; the booze is cheap, and

Hotel Bars

Doney Via Veneto 145 ☎06.4708.2805. Mon–Sat noon–3.30pm & 7–11pm, Sun noon–3.30pm. The bar and restaurant of the Via Veneto's *Westin Excelsior* hotel is an elegant Dolce Vita-era institution, serving buffet lunch and dinner and Sunday brunch. Eat or drink inside or out on the famous street, full of promenaders dressed to kill.

Hotel Eden Via Ludovisi 49 ☎06.478.121. The top-floor piano bar here, with its outside terrace, boasts perhaps the best views that you can enjoy in Rome with a drink in your hand.

Hotel Forum Via Tor de' Conti 25–30 ☎06.679.2446. The American bar at this Monti four-star commands magical views over the Forum and Colosseum nearby – great for a drink just as the sun is setting.

Palazzetto International Wine Academy, Vicolo del Bottino 8 ☎06.699.0878. 7.30pm–1am. Just off Piazza di Spagna, Rome's wine academy has a hotel, restaurant and a rooftop bar that's open during August and September.

RipArte Café Via Orti di Trastevere 7 ☎06.586.1852. This cool, elegantly modern hotel bar – part of the trendy *Hotel Ripa* – also has food and live music, although you have to travel down to Trastevere's southerly quarters to enjoy it.

Rose Garden Palace Via Boncompagni 19 ☎06.421.741. Daily 7–9pm. This classy Via Veneto hotel lounge offers an unusual place to celebrate Happy Hour. It's elegant and understated and the band do their very best to bring back the swing era.

Hotel de Russie Via del Babuino 9 ☎06.328.881. The courtyard garden of this stylish hotel is as magical a place for a drink as you can find in Rome, with tables sheltered by the building's two wings and looking up to its terraced gardens and restaurant.

Zest Via Turati 171 ☎06.444.841. Rome's sleek Radisson-SAS hotel also sports one of the city's most elegant cocktail bars. Poolside drinks give top-floor views over the very much up-and-coming Esquiline district.

(15)

DRINKING

you can sit at outside tables for no extra cost. Things are slightly less *demimonde*-ish during the day, when it's simply a great spot to sip a cappuccino, read and take the sun.

Stardust Vicolo de' Renzi 4 ☎06.5832.0875. Mon–Sat 3.30pm–2am, Sun noon–2am. One of Trastevere's most authentic haunts, with good food as well as drink, including a buffet brunch on weekends between noon and 4.30pm. Just the place, too, for all-night partying – see p.258.

Enoteca Trastevere Via della Lungaretta 86 ☎06.588.5659. Mon, Tues, Thurs–Sat 5pm–2am, Sun 11am–1am. The district's largest *enoteca* is also a local favourite. Lots of mostly Italian wines to choose from, including some organic labels. Good choices, too, if you're into *grappa* and *amaro*.

Testaccio

See map on pp.106–107.

Caffe Emporio Piazza del'Emporio 1 ☎06.575.4532. Daily 8.30pm–2am. cool, sparsely furnished café-wine bar on the trendy Testaccio side of the Porta Portese (Trastevere) bridge, a good venue for a midday snack or evening drinks.

Oasi della Birra Piazza Testaccio 41 ☎06.574.6122. Mon–Sat 7.30pm–1am. Unassumingly situated under an *enoteca* on Piazza Testaccio – you wouldn't know this was there. But the cosy basement rooms here house an international selection of beers that rivals anywhere in the world – 500 in all, and plenty of wine to choose from as well. Food is generously assembled plates of cheese and salami, and a great selection of bruschetta and polenta dishes. It's not particularly Roman, but it's a very alluring place to get hammered and eat good food nonetheless.

On the Rox Via Galvani 54 ☎06.574.6013. Tues–Sat 8pm–4am, Sun 7pm–2am. Around the corner from the nightspots of Via di Monte Testaccio, and bang in the heart of the Via Galvani strip of night-time joints, this is as convivial a bar as you could imagine, run by a couple of Danes.

Picasso Via di Monte Testaccio 63
ⓣ06.574.2975. Tues–Sat 10.30pm–3am. A cool
but not too pretentious Testaccio bar
hosting the occasional art exhibition and
performance arts event, as well as playing
an interesting and eclectic mix of music.
Perch on a bar-stool rather than taking a
table to avoid paying extra for service. It's
also a pizzeria.

Prati

See map on pp.180–181.
All Brothers Via delle Fornaci 8–10 ⓣ06.630.011.
Daily 7–3am. Street level is a bar and popular
gelateria, as well, while live music holds forth
downstairs several evenings a week. See
p.256 for more details.
Fonclea Via Crescenzio 82a ⓣ06.689.6302.
Daily 7pm–2am. This historic basement
joint is loaded with devoted regulars and
those who have happily discovered that
there is life in the Vatican's sometimes

somnolent Borgo and Prati area. Live
music adds to the excitement (see p.257
for more info).
Four Green Fields Via C. Morin 42 ⓣ06.372.5091.
Daily 2pm–2am. A large Irish pub, decked out
in wood and terracotta, which stretches over
two floors, with live music downstairs every
evening. Draft Guinness and Kilkenny
complement the scene, along with OK pub
grub. See p.257 for more about the music.
Senza Fondo Via Germanico 168 ⓣ06.321.1415.
Open daily 9pm–3am. Convivial Prati
basement pub with a good choice of beers
and decent food. Sometimes live music, too.
Simposio di Piero Costantini Piazza Cavour 16
ⓣ06.321.1502. Mon–Sat 12.30–2.30pm & 7.30–
11pm. On the corner of Piazza Cavour right
behind the Castel Sant'Angelo, this old-
fasioned wine bar and restaurant has a fine
and authentic Art Nouveau feel. Look for the
wrought-iron grapes on the doors and
windows. Good food.

Nightlife

Roman **nightlife** retains some of the smart ethos satirized in Fellini's film *La Dolce Vita*, and designer-dressing-up is still very much a part of the mainstream scene. Entrance prices to the big **clubs** tend to be high, but there are a few smaller, more alternative nightspots, where your travel-crumpled clothes will be perfectly acceptable. To get around the licensing laws, some of Rome's night haunts are run as private clubs – usually known as *centro culturali* or *sociali*, a device that means you may be stung for a membership fee, particularly where there's music, but entry will be free – although as a one-off visitor some places will let you in without formalities, and others charge no fee at all to be a member. In recent decades these sorts of places have sprung up all over the city, particularly in the suburbs, and are becoming the focus of political activity and the more avant-garde elements of the music and arts scene. In general **entrance prices** vary hugely: sometimes entry is free or you just have to buy a drink, but mostly you won't pay more than €10 for "membership".

If you're after **live music**, there are regular summer festivals (see box on p.256), with several venues all over town, featuring concerts of every sort, including practically free events in Testaccio. However, the chances of catching major rock and pop acts are low, due to the lack of suitable venues. Big promoters book the cities up north, especially Milan and Bologna, and traditionally leave Rome entirely out of the loop. However, there is a chance you can catch up-and-coming US and UK indie bands playing some of the city's more alternative venues.

If you're heading out after dinner or a snack in a bar, Roman nightlife can be found all over the city, including neighbourhoods on the very edge of town. However, in the central zone the **best areas** tend to be Ostiense and Testaccio (especially in summer), Trastevere, and the centro storico from the Jewish Ghetto to the Pantheon. For what's-on information, there's *Romac'è*, with its helpful section in English. If you understand Italian, the main Rome newspaper, *Il Messaggero*, lists major musical events, and "TrovaRoma" in the Thursday edition of *La Repubblica* is another handy guide to current offerings.

Live music

Rome's **rock** scene is a relatively limp affair, especially compared to the cities of the north, focusing mainly on foreign bands and the big venues. Summer sees

See the next chapter, "Culture and entertainment", for details of Rome's more **highbrow entertainment** – classical music, opera and dance.

Live music festivals

Rome hosts a variety of music festivals especially during the summer. There are regular **jazz** concerts in the Villa Celimontana park as part of the Jazz & Image Festival, with evening performances starting at 10.15pm between early June and the end of August (☎06.589.7807 or ☎06.5833.5781; ⓦwww.villacelimontanajazz.com) – a great venue, with some big names. Later in the year there's the Rome Jazz Festival – ⓦwww.romajazzfestival.it – held from the end of October to the end of November at the Auditorium. There's a big **Latin music** scene, too, particularly Brazilian, which includes the Fiesta event in summer, held from mid-July to mid-August out at the Ippodromo delle Capannelle at Via Appia Nuova 1245 (tickets cost €10; ☎06.718.2139, ⓦwww.fiesta.it). The other main cultural event of the summer is Estate Romana (ⓦwww.estateromana.it), a collective name for a series of mainly outdoor events that last all summer, including the concerts and performances of Testaccio Village, which offers a different artist every night during the warm months, followed by three outdoor discos, all for free on production of a very low-priced weekly pass – available at the ticket booth near the entrance. Again, check *Romac'è* or *Time Out* for details.

Finally, look out for the **Notte Bianca** festival in September, when the whole city stays up all night and lots of little-used venues host all manner of entertainment.

local bands giving occasional free concerts in the piazzas, but the city is much more in its element with **jazz**, with lots of venues and a wide choice of styles performed by a healthy array of local talent.

Rome's big arenas

For information about events at either of these two **venues** – really the city's only options for big, internationally renowned visiting bands and solo acts – call the Orbis agency (details on p.261).

Palacisalfa Viale del Oceano Atlantico 271d ☎06.5728.8024. Metro B EUR Palasport or bus #706 or #714 from Termini. A giant tent-like structure 400m from Palaeur, this is one of two sports arenas where major acts tend to end up. It holds about 1500 people and has served up everything from sporting events to clubbing nights.

Palallotomatica Piazzale dello Sport. ☎199.128.800 Metro B EUR Palasport or bus #706 or #714 from Termini. This circular hall has recently undergone a total overhaul, including work on its acoustics, and hosts major acts that come to Rome.

Rock and pop

Akab/Cave Via Monte Testaccio 69 ☎06.5740.4485. Metro B Piramide or bus #23, #30, #75, #95, #280, #716, #719 or tram #3. Thurs–Sun 11pm–4.30am. Two venues in one. *Akab* is at ground level and usually plays house music. *Cave* is below ground and features R&B. Concerts are generally once or twice a week.

Alpheus Via del Commercio 36 ☎06.574.7826, ⓦwww.alpheus.it. Metro B Piramide or bus #23, #769, #770. Tues–Sun 10pm–4.30am. Housed in an ex-factory off Via Ostiense, a little way beyond Testaccio, the *Alpheus* has space for three simultaneous events – usually a disco, concert and exhibition or piece of theatre. Sat is Gorgeous – gay night.

Blue Knight Via delle Fornaci 8–10 ☎06.630.011. Metro A Ottaviano or bus #32, #34, #49, #81, #492, #590, #982 or tram #19. Daily 7–3am. Right near St Peter's, the main floor here is a bar and *gelateria*, while downstairs there are concerts – almost always acoustic music, ranging from rock to blues to pop, featuring some of Rome's best musicians and occasional foreign acts. Concerts usually start at 10.30pm. No admission charge.

Bluecheese Factory Via Caio Cestio 5b ☎06.5725.0032. Metro B Piramide or bus #23, #30, #75, #95, #280, #716, #719 or tram #3. Fri & Sat 11pm–5am. The top choice in town for more cutting-edge creativity, combining electronic music experimentation and multimedia performance work.

Circolo degli Artisti Via Casilina Vecchia 42 ☎06.7030.5684, ⓦwww.circoloartisti.it. Metro A

Re di Roma or San Giovanni or bus #105 from Termini, or #810 from Piazza Venezia. Tues–Sun 7.30pm–4am. A very large venue, located beyond Porta Maggiore, that was one of the first of the city's *centro sociali*. A good range of bands, with frequent discos and theme nights – hip-hop, electronic, house, ska, revival, etc. On Fri it hosts Omogenic – gay night.

Circolo Vizioso Vla dei Reti 25 ☎0347.814.6544. Bus #71, #492 or Tram #3, #19. Tues–Sun 9pm–2am. Multi-room multi-venue in the San Lorenzo district, featuring live rock, reggae and jazz, plus performance art, theatre and cabaret in the main hall. Elsewhere you can dine and chat.

Fonclea Via Crescenzio 82a. Metro A Ottaviano or bus #23, #32, #34, #49, #81, #492, #590, #982 or tram #19. Daily 7pm–2am. Happy Hour 7–8pm. Busy and happening basement bar in the Vatican area that hosts regular live music – usually jazz, soul and funk. Free Mon–Fri and Sun.

Forte Prenestino Via F. Delpino 100 ☎06.2180.7855, ⓦwww.forteprenestino.net. tram #5 or #19, bus #516 or #542. This early, twentieth-century fortress, and giant squat since 1986 is home to one of Rome's most active *centro sociali*, with regular live music, film screenings and other events held both inside and out in the castle courtyards. It also boasts a bookstore, various studios, even a body-piercing salon. Its Mayday "non-lavoro" events, held to celebrate the anniversary of the occupation of the building, are popular.

Four Green Fields Via C. Morin 42. Metro A Ottaviano or bus #23, #32, #34, #49, #81, #492, #590, #982 or Tram #19. Daily 2pm–2am. Mixed crowds visit this long-running, versatile Vatican-area pub, which also has a cocktail bar. Live music in the basement every night starting at 9.30pm. Free admission.

I Giardini di Adone Via dei Reti 38a ☎06.445.4382. bus #71, or #492 tram #3, or #19. Tues–Sun 8pm–3am. A San Lorenzo venue with rock acts every night, plus theme nights from time to time. Also food, cocktails and beer.

Il Locale Vicolo del Fico 3 ☎06.687.9075. Bus #30, #40, #46, #62, #64, #70, #81, #97, #189, #304, #492, #628, #916. Tues–Sun 10.30pm–2.30am. Centrally located close to Piazza Navona, this trendy joint enjoys a lively, if not chaotic, atmosphere, and English and American alternative bands and Italian

folk-rock. Not the trendsetter it once was, but still a fun, central venue.

The Place Via Alberico 27/29 ☎06.6830.7137. Bus #23, #34, #40, #62, or #280. Daily 8pm–2am. Singer-songwriters, jazz, Latin and R&B and – later – DJs at this Prati live music club. A restaurant too, interesting fusion cuisine, and admission is free with a drink.

Villaggio Globale Lungotevere Testaccio 22 ☎06.575.7233. Winter months only; opening hours depend on events. Bus #95, #170, #719, or #781. Situated in the old slaughterhouse along the river, the "global village" has something on almost every night, whether it's world music, indie rock or avant-garde performance art, in its *Spazio Boario*. Closed Aug.

Jazz, Latin and blues

Alexanderplatz Via Ostia 9 ☎06.5833.5781, ⓦwww.alexanderplatz.it. Daily 9pm–2am. Rome's top live jazz club/restaurant with reasonable membership (€10) and free entry, except when there's star-billing. Reservations recommended. Doors open at 8pm.

Big Mama Vicolo San Francesco a Ripa 18 ☎06.581.2551, ⓦwww.bigmama.it. Tues–Sat 9pm–2am. Trastevere-based jazz/blues club of long standing, hosting nightly acts. Membership €8, and free entry except for star attractions (when it's important to book ahead). Doors open 9pm.

Beba Do Samba Via dei Messapi 8 ☎339.361.9800. Tram #3 or #19. Daily 9pm–2.30am. Brazil Central in Rome, and each night they highlight a new group, with the focus on Latin sounds, while the chill-out room is replete with comfortable cushions and divans.

Caffé Latino Via Monte Testaccio 96 ☎06.5728.8556. Metro B Piramide or bus #23, #30, #75, #95, #170, #280, #716, #781 or tram #3. Tues–Sun 10pm–3am. Multi-event Testaccio club with varied live music almost every night, as well as cartoons, films and cabaret. There's also a disco playing a selection of funky, acid jazz and R&B music. Best at weekends when it gets more crowded.

Caruso/Caffé de Oriente Via Monte Testaccio 36 ☎06.574.5019. Metro B Piramide or Bus #23, #30, #75, #95, #170, #280, #716, #781 or tram #3. Tues–Sun 10pm–3am. Three rooms and a roof terrace for the warm months host Latin music most of the week, with soul, R&B and live cover groups at times. €8 monthly membership.

Casa del Jazz Viale di Porta Ardeatina 55 ⊕ 06.704.731, ⊛ www.casajazz.it. Metro B to Piramide or bus #714. Sponsored by the city, and very much the project of jazz-loving mayor Walter Veltroni, this converted villa in leafy surroundings is the ultimate jazz-lovers' complex, with a book and CD store and restaurant, recording studios and a 150-seat auditorium that hosts jazz names most nights of the week. Admission €5–10. **Escopazzo** Via d'Aracoeli 41 ⊕ 06.6920.0422. Bus #23, #30, #40, #46, #62, #63, #64, #81, #87, #280, #492, #628, #630, #780, H or tram #8. Daily 8.30pm–2.30am. Halfway between Piazza Venezia and Largo Argentina, this friendly bar attracts a crowd of thirty-somethings and offers food and wine along with live concerts or jam sessions most nights.

Gregory's Via Gregoriana 54d ⊕ 06.679.6386. Tues–Sun 8pm–3am. Just up the Spanish Steps and to the right, this elegant nightspot pulls in the crowds with its live jazz, improvised by Roman and international musicians. Tues–Sun 5.30pm–3am. **Stardust** Vicolo de' Renzi 4 ⊕ 06.5832.0875. Bus #23, #75, #280, #630, #780, H or tram #8. Mon–Sat 3.30pm–2am, Sun noon–2am, sometimes much later. One of Trastevere's most authentic haunts, this tiny jazz venue stays open as long as there's somebody there and organizes all-night jam sessions in the basement whenever the mood strikes – or the regulars demand (see also p.253).

△ DJing on Monte Testaccio

Clubs

Rome's **clubs** run the gamut. There are vast glitter palaces with stunning lights and sound systems, predictable dance music and an over-dressed, over-made-up clientele – good if you can afford it and just want to dance (and observe a good proportion of Romans in their natural Saturday-night element). But there are also places that are not much more than ritzy **bars** with music, and other, more down-to-earth places to dance, playing a more interesting selection of music to a younger, more cautious-spending crowd (we've listed some of these in Chapter 15 as well).

There is also a small group of clubs catering specifically to **gay or lesbian** customers (see Chapter 18 for details of these). Whichever you prefer, all tend to open and close late, and entrance fees vary from €10 to €20, though they often include a drink. During the hot summer months, many clubs close down or move to outdoor locations.

Alien Via Velletri 13/19 ⊕6.841.2212, ⊛www .aliendisco.it. Bus #63. Tues–Sun 11pm–4am. The two halls here feature starkly contrasting decor, one redolent of maharaja plushness, the other done up in modernistic black and white. Music is a mixture of house and techno. It also has a summer venue, *Alien 2 Mare*, at the nearby seaside resort of Fregene, at Piazzale Fregene 5 (⊕06.6656.4761).

Art Café Via del Galoppatoio 33 ⊕06.3600.6578. Housed in the underground car park at Villa Borghese, this is one of Rome's trendiest clubs. Expect to queue, and dress up – otherwise you might not get in.

Associazione Culturale Vecchio Mattatoio Via di Monte Testaccio 23 ⊕06.5823.8321. Bus #23, #30, #75, #95, #170, #280, #716, #781 or tram #3. Thurs–Sat 11pm–5am. This indoor-outdoor venue is actually several scenes in one, and they change constantly. The most consistent is called "Black Planet", which showcases soul, R&B, reggae and hip-hop. Full meals are also available until the wee hours.

Balic Via degli Aurunci 35 ⊕06.9761.2428. Tues–Sun 10pm–3am. Cool lounge bar and club that hosts occasional live music and "Black Betty" gay nights, and dance music on Fri and Sat. Modernist ethnic decor and a restaurant too.

Black Out Via Saturnia 18 ⊕06.7049.6791. Metro A San Giovanni or Re di Roma or bus #85. Thurs–Sat 11pm–4am. Murky industrial San Giovanni club that plays punk, heavy metal and Goth music, with occasional gigs by US and UK bands. Closed in summer.

Classico Village Via Libetta 3 ⊕06.5728.8857. Metro B Garbatella or Bus #29, #769, #770. Wed–Sun 9pm–2am. Industrial Ostiense location with a big dance floor, a venue for live music, often jazz, and a restaurant.

Gilda Via Mario de' Fiori 97 ⊕06.678.4838, ⊛www.gildabar.it. Metro A Spagna or bus #52, #53, #61, #71, #80, #85, #95, #116, #119, #160, #850. Tues–Sun 11.30pm–5am, and Sun 4.30–7.30pm. A few blocks from the Spanish Steps, this slick, stylish and expensive club is the focus for the city's minor celebs and wannabes, mainly of the middle-aged variety. Dress smart to get in. Their summer venue, *Gilda-on-the-Beach*, is in Fregene, at Lungomare di Ponente 1 (⊕06.6656.0649, ⊛www.gildaonthebeach.it).

Goa Via Libetta 13 ⊕06.574.8277. Metro B Garbatella or Bus #29, #769, #770. Tues & Thurs–Sat 11pm–5am. Long-running Ostiense club near the Basilica San Paolo that was opened by famous local DJ Giancarlino and is still playing techno, house, and jungle, Goa has an ethnic feel – a shop sells handmade items, there's incense burning – and also has sofas to help you recover after high-energy dancing.

Jackie O' Via Boncompagni 11 ⊕06.4288.5457. Bus #52, #53, #61, #62, #63, #80, #95, #116, #119, #175, #492. Daily 1.30pm–4.30am. Closed Mon in winter. Amazingly, this 1960s Via Veneto jet-set glitter palace is still going strong, even attracting its share of celebs from time to time. Long on attitude, it can actually be fun if you enjoy its rather retro notion of a night out, including a preponderance of mainstream Italian pop.

La Maison Vicolo dei Granari 4 ⊕06.683.3312. Tues–Sun 11pm–3am, until 5am on Fri & Sat. Ritzy club whose chandeliers and glossy decor attracts Rome's gilded youth. Sun – gay night – is the one to go for, although you'll need to book a table if you want to sit down.

Piper Via Tagliamento 9 ☎06.855.5398, ⍟www
.piperclub.it. bus #63, #86, #92, #217, 360 or
tram #3, #19. Tues–Sun 11pm–4am. Established back in the 1970s, but still going
strong, *Piper* has different nightly events
(fashion shows, art shows, gigs), and a wide
variety of music, having survived by undergoing a reincarnation every season. There
are two levels, a smart-but-casual mixed-
aged crowd, and a heavy pick-up scene. It's
hard to predict the kind of music you'll hear;
it varies hugely, depending on the night.
Piper also has a summer venue by the sea,
Aquapiper di Guidonia, Via Maremmana
(☎0774.326.538).

Qube Via Portonaccio 212 ☎06.4358.7454.
Metro B Tiburtina or bus #409. Thurs–Sat
10.30pm–4am. Big Tiburtina club hosting a
variety of different nights each week,
including live music. Not the most original
for music but its Fri gay and drag night –
Mucca Assassina ("Killer Cow") – draws a
big crowd.

Zoobar Via Bencivenga 1 ☎339.27.27.995. bus
#23, #30, #75, #95, #170, #280, #716, #781 or
tram #3. Thurs–Sat 11pm–3.30am. This club
is now in a new location out near
Nomentana station but still plays a wide
range of different music – oldies, ska, funk,
R&B and much more.

Culture and
entertainment

et's face it: Rome is a bit of a backwater for the **performing arts**. Northern Italy is where creativity in theatre and dance – and, of course, opera – flourishes, and very few international-class performers put in an appearance here. Nevertheless, the city does have a cultural life, and its quality is sometimes better than you might expect, and has perhaps improved in recent years, helped by the opening of the Auditorium, north of the centre. In any case, what the arts here may lack in professionalism they have always made up for in the charm of the city's settings.

Rome's **summer festival**, for example, organized by "Estate Romana", means that there's a good range of classical music, opera, theatre and cinema running throughout the warm months, often in picturesque locations – amidst ancient ruins with soaring columns, or perched on hills with brilliant panoramas of Rome by night – although obviously some of what's on is of little interest if you don't speak Italian.

During the winter season, you'll find a regular programme of **classical music** mounted by the city's principal orchestra, the Accademia Nazionale di Santa Cecilia and other sporadic musical offerings of mixed quality, sometimes in beautiful churches or palatial halls, and on occasions free. **Opera** is well established in Rome and now and again approaches world-class levels, though perhaps not often enough. Good **dance** is a rarity in

Information and ticket agencies

For current **information** about what's on where in English, consult the English section at the back of *Romac'è* (€1, Wed) or *Wanted in Rome*, the English-language bi-weekly (€0.75, every other Wed), which you can pick up at almost any newsstand in the centre. Otherwise, in Italian, the "TrovaRoma" booklet inserted in *La Repubblica*'s Thursday edition is your best bet.

Ticket agencies

Messaggerie Musicali Via del Corso 472 ☏06.684.401.

Orbis Piazza Esquilino 37 (Santa Maria Maggiore) ☏06.482.7403.

Ricordi Via del Corso 506 ☏06.320.2790; Viale Giulio Cesare 88 (Prati) ☏06.3750.0375.

Rome, although international companies do show up from time to time, usually at the Teatro Olimpico and the Teatro Argentina (see p.264). Finally, **cinema-lovers** will find an increasing number of films in the original language, as Italy gradually breaks away from its historic dubbing leanings.

Classical music and opera

Under new directors, Rome's own **orchestras** of late are approaching international standards, and although the city attracts far fewer prestigious artists than you might expect of a capital, it is becoming more and more a magnet for contemporary works – a sea-change that has been inspired by the completion of the new **Auditorium**. Critics say that beauty has been entirely sacrificed for acoustics here, but the three halls of various sizes certainly do deliver on sound quality, while the outdoor space can be used for anything from rock to opera.

Otherwise, check the listings and keep a look-out for posters advertising little-known **concerts** – a wide range of choral, chamber and organ recitals – in churches or other often spectacular venues, sometimes including the private halls in Renaissance or Baroque palaces. Otherwise, the many national academies and cultural institutes (Belgian, Austrian, Hungarian, British, American, French, et al) frequently offer free concerts as well, along with the Auditorium Cavour (℡06.721.9771). In the summer, concerts are staged in cloisters, in the Villa Giulia and Teatro di Marcello, just off Piazza Venezia, and

Music, opera and film festivals

Accademia d'Opera Italiana ℡06.784.2702, ⓦwww.accademiadoperaitaliana.it. Metro A Spagna or bus #117, #119. Held in All Saints Church on Via del Babuino, performances generally include popular standards such as *La Traviata*, *Tosca* and *Il Barbiere di Siviglia*, as well as the Mozart *Requiem* and *Carmina Burana*. Throughout Sept. Tickets €30.

Festa Internazionale di Roma Auditorium Via P. de Coubertin ⓦwww.romacinemafest .org. This new festival of film is held over nine days each Oct at the Auditorium and a variety of other venues around town. Tickets cost €7–10 and can be purchased from the Auditorium box office (see p.263).

Festival EuroMediterraneo Villa Adriana, Via di Villa Adriana, Tivoli ℡06.6880.9107. Seeing an opera amidst the monumental remains of this great emperor's city-sized pleasure dome is an unforgettable evening out. July–Aug only; take COTRAL bus from Ponte Mammolo (Metro B).

New Operafestival di Roma Basilica San Clemente Piazza San Clemente 1 ℡340.088.0077, ⓦwww.newoperafestivaldiroma.com. Metro B Colosseo or bus #60, #85, #87, #117, #810, #850 or tram #3. This festival brings together talented opera students from the US and around Italy to mount full productions, recitals and the like in the courtyard of the basilica of San Clemente and in the Roman theatre at Ostia Antica. Mid-June to mid-Aug.

La Notte Bianca One night in Sept when there are events all over town in all kinds of fantastic venues, both indoors and out. From 8pm until 8am churches, ancient sites, cinemas and theatres host everything from poetry to concerts to children's happenings at the zoo. It's a marvellous night, and you can plan your tour of the city with the free booklet or by visiting the website – ⓦwww.lanottebianca.it – which lists the main events and locations. Public transport runs all night to make things easier.

in the ancient Roman theatre at Ostia Antica. In addition there are sponsored Sunday-morning concert cycles, such as the Telecom Italia one at the Teatro Sistina, Via Sistina 129 (☎06.482.6841), between November and April. It may be that you'll just stumble across a concert-in-progress while out on an evening stroll, passing by some ancient church with all its lights on (a rarity not to be missed); Rome is a city where such magical musical moments can still happen.

The city's **opera scene** has long been overshadowed by that of Milan, Parma, and even Naples, grand opera's acknowledged birthplace, but it is improving. In summer, opera moves outdoors and ticket prices come down. Summer performances are now once again held in the stunning setting at the ancient **Baths of Caracalla**, as well as in the courtyard of the San Clemente basilica and in other churches and venues all around Rome, in the context of the various summer music festivals which have multiplied remarkably in recent years.

Classical music and opera venues

Auditorium/Parco della Musica Via P. de Coubertin 15 ☎199.109.783, ⓦwww.auditorium.com. Bus #53, #280, #910 or tram #2, #19. This new landmark musical complex is Rome's most prestigious venue. home to its premier orchestra, the Accademia Nazionale di Santa Cecilia, who are resident part of the year in its largest hall, while two smaller venues host smaller chamber, choral, recital and experimental works. The complex also hosts major rock and jazz names when they come to town. Daily 11am–6pm to visit; guided tours available €9. Box office Mon–Sun 11am–6pm.

Aula Magna dell'Università la Sapienza Piazzale Aldo Moro 5 ☎06.3600.1511, ⓦwww.concertiiuc .it. Bus #61, #490, #495 or tram #3, #19 or metro B Policlinico. The university's music Istituzione Universitaria dei Concerti is deliberately experimental and eclectic, with musical offerings ranging from Mozart to Miles Davis, and from Ravel to Kurt Weill. Tickets cost €10 to 25. The season here runs from Oct to April, and performances are usually held on Tues evenings and weekends.

Oratorio del Gonfalone Via del Gonfalone 32a ☎06.687.5952. Bus #64. This lovely theatre stages performances of chamber music, with an emphasis on the Baroque every Thurs at 9pm. The season here runs from Nov to early June. Tickets cost €15 and you can reserve by phone. Reservations are strongly recommended. For those

wishing to visit the Oratorio, or to pick up tickets in advance, the entrance is at Vicolo della Scimmia 1b, during office hours.

Teatro Ghione Via delle Fornaci 37 ☎06.637.2294, ⓦwww.ghione.it. Bus #34, #46, #64, #916. Box office hours daily 10am–1pm & 4–8pm. This traditional little theatre offers chamber music and recitals, often by well-known musical lights, some of whom are legends in their own lifetimes.

Teatro Olimpico Piazza Gentile da Fabriano ⓦwww.teatroolimpico.it, ⓦwww .filarmonicaromana.org. bus #53, #280, #910 or tram #2, #19. Classical standards, chamber music and ballet are performed here, by resident orchestra Accademia Filarmonica Romana, as well as occasional contemporary work. Tickets are cheap and relatively easy to come by. Performances are on Thursdays and run from October to early May. Tickets range from €15 to 30.

Teatro dell'Opera di Roma Piazza Beniamino Gigli 1 ☎06.481.601, ⓦwww.operaroma.it. Metro A Repubblica or Bus #40, #64, #70, #117, #170. Box office Mon–Sat 9am–5pm, Sun 9am–1.30pm. Nobody compares it to La Scala, but cheap tickets are a lot easier to come by at Rome's opera and ballet venue – they start at around €20 for opera, less for ballet – and important artists do sometimes perform here. If you buy the very cheapest tickets, bring some high-powered binoculars, as you'll need them in order to see anything at all.

Theatre, dance and cabaret

There is a great deal of **theatre** in Rome, but it's virtually all in Italian, or even dialect. Very occasional English-language musicals, usually put together by some travelling American company, come to town during the winter season. The venue for such rare events is almost always either the Teatro Olimpico or the Teatro Sistina, sometimes Teatro Argentina of late. Incidentally, virtually all Roman theatres close on Mondays. Again, check the usual sources for your options. As for **dance**, apart from the very occasional international company, home-grown Roman and Italian troupes do their thing on the city's stages, and it is rarely an inspiring sight. Though the origins of ballet can be traced back to eighteenth-century Italy, there are at present few Italian companies that rise above amateurish levels. See also Teatro dell'Opera (see p.263) for ballet.

Mainstream and English theatres

English Theatre of Rome Teatro L'Arciliuto Piazza Montevecchio 5 ☎06.444.1375, ⊛www .rometheatre.com. Metro B Cavour or bus #40, #64, #70, #71, #75, #84, #117, #170, H. There is one English-language theatre group, who perform five plays each season between Oct and June. Tickets cost €15.

Miracle Players ⊛www.miracleplayers.org. One of Rome's two English-language theatre companies, performing light-hearted renderings of the classics and lots of material with an ancient Rome theme, often in authentic venues – for example the Forum in summer.

Teatro di Argentina Largo Argentina 52 ☎06.6840.0345, ⊛www.teatrodiroma.net/ teatroArgentina. Box office daily 10am–2pm & 3–7pm. Bus #30, #40, #46, #62, #63, #64, #70, #81, #87, #492, #628, #810, #916 or tram #8. One of the city's most important theatres for dramatic works in Italian, as well as the occasional production in English, and for dance. Quality varies widely.

Teatro Greco Via R. Leoncavallo 10/16 ☎06.860.7513. bus #63, #135, #342, #630. Located well out of the centre, on the far side of Villa Ada, this theatre generally offers some of the best Italian dance and even has its own company, with tickets starting at €8. In Oct the Italian National Dance competition is often held here.

Teatro Olimpico Piazza Gentile da Fabriano 17 ☎06.326.5991, ⊛www.teatroolimpico.it. Bus #53, #280, #910 or tram #2, #19. Located well beyond Piazza del Popolo, this theatre tends to get Rome's best international dance and sometimes some important alternative performers. There's a decent snack bar, where you can sometimes spy the performers taking a break during the interval.

Teatro Sistina Via Sistina 129 ☎06.420.0711, ⊛www.ilsistina.com. Metro A Spagna or Barberini or Bus #52, #53, #61, #63, #71, #80, #95, #116, #119, #160, #175, #492, #630, #850.

Every now and then an English-language (American, very off-Broadway) musical revue blows into town and it generally ends up here, just up from Piazza di Spagna. Gershwin seems to be a perennial favourite, along with other jazzy-bluesy musical confections.

Teatro Valle Via del Teatro Valle 21 ☎06.6880.3794. Bus #30, #40, #46, #62, #63, #64, #70, #81, #87, #492, #628, #810, #916 or tram #8. Between Piazza Navona and the Pantheon, this theatre sometimes offers special works in English by visiting actors and companies.

Teatro Vittoria Piazza Santa Maria Liberatrice 8/11 ☎06.574.0170, ⊛www.teatrovittoria.it. Bus #23, #30, #75, #95, #170, #280, #716, #781 or tram #3. In Testaccio's main square, this large theatre sometimes books cabaret-like acts or dance-theatre companies that need no translation.

Other theatres

Teatro Agorà Via della Penitenza 33 ☎06.687.4167. Bus #23, #280. Once upon a time this Trastevere theatre sometimes produced English-language plays and other entertainments, and it could always happen again. Tickets start at €8.

Teatro Ambra Jovinelli Via G. Pepe 43/47 ☎06.4434.0262, ⊛www.ambrajovinelli.com. Metro A Vittorio or Bus #70, #71, #105, #360, #649 or tram #5, #14. Recently saved from terminal decay, this bastion of Rome's comic theatre tradition is now thriving, as is this entire neighbourhood. Concerts as well as theatrical works.

Teatro Brancaccio Via Merulana 244 ☎06.4782.4893, ⊛www.teatrobrancaccio.net. Bus #16, or #71. Musicals and comedies, sometimes featuring major Italian players, are generally the focus here. Not a top choice for good acoustics, so your Italian has to be excellent to follow the action, if not to enjoy the songs.

Teatro Colosseo Via Capo d'Africa 7 ☎06.700.4932, ⓦ www.teatrocolosseo.it. Metro B Colosseo or bus #75, #81, #85, #87, #117, #810, #850 or tram #3. Just up from the Colosseum, this theatre presents new, usually vaguely underground plays by contemporary Italian playwrights or translations. They have also been known to offer English-language one-acts in their small theatre downstairs. Tickets start at €6.

Teatro Eliseo Via Nazionale 183e ☎06.488.2114, ⓦ www.teatroeliseo.it. Bus #40, #60, #64, #70, #71, #170. One of Rome's main theatres, hosting plays by Italian playwrights, and adaptations into Italian of foreign works, and featuring some of the top dramatic talent Italy has to offer. Tickets start at €8.

Teatro Prati Via degli Scipione 98 ☎06.3974.0503, ⓦ www.teatroprati.it. Metro A Ottaviano or bus #32, #34, #49, #81, #492, #590, 982 or tram #19. A few blocks away from St Peter's, another small space that often features Italian comic classics. Tickets start at €10.

Teatro Romano di Ostia Antica Ostia Antica. Information ☎06.6880.4601; box office daily 10am–2pm & 3–6pm. Ostia train from Piramide. Metro B Piramide or bus #23, #30, #75, #95, #170, #280, #716, #781 or tram #3. In July and Aug specially scheduled performances of all kinds are offered in the restored ancient Roman theatre – a spectacular, unforgettable setting, even if you don't speak Italian. Performances begin at 8.45pm. Go early for a chance to visit the ruins. It's a twenty-minute train ride to Ostia Antica, then a short walk over the footbridge into the ruins. A great Roman summer experience.

Teatro Rossini Piazza Santa Chiara 14 ☎06.6821.6852. Bus #30, #40, #46, #62, #63, #64, #70, #81, #87, #492, #628, #810, #916 or tram #8. Traditional Roman-dialect productions are one of the main focuses in this atmospheric old theatre.

Salone Margherita Via Due Macelli 75 ☎06.679.1439. Metro A Spagna or Barberini or bus #52, #53, #61, #63, #71, #80, #95, #116, #119, #160, #175, #492, #630, #850. Traditional Roman political satire and cabaret – worth it for the atmosphere, even if you don't understand the admittedly difficult verbal sallies.

Film

There tends to be more **English-language cinema** on offer in Rome these days, partly due to foreign demand, though if your Italian is up to it, you'll naturally also find current Italian language productions available all over town. Look out for the words "version originale" if you want to be sure it's not dubbed. You'll find usually accurate **listings** in the English-language section of *Romac'è* and in all the newspapers, which also include a section on "film clubs" or "cinema d'essai", a euphemism for stifling rooms where two or three aficionados sit on hard wooden chairs in front of a tiny, blurred screen watching films in their original language. Also, the "Italy Daily" supplement to the *International Herald Tribune* lists current English-language films; and if you speak Italian there's also *Time Out Roma*. Tickets everywhere cost €6–10.

Screens

Alcazar Via Merry del Val 14 ☎06.588.0099. Bus #75, #780, H or tram #3, #8. Trastevere cinema featuring mainstream American and English films, with the occasional weird one slipping in.

Casa del Cinema Largo Marce llo Mastroianni 1 ☎06.423.601, ⓦ www.casadelcinema.it. bus #490, #491 #495, #116. Right by the Porta Pinciana entrance to the Villa Borghese, this building epitomizes Rome's cultural renaissance under Walter Veltroni, opened in 2004 as a venue for re-runs and retrospectives

and dedicated to Italy's most famous international film actor.

Filmstudio Via degli Orti d'Alibert 1c ☎06.6819.2987. Arty films and themed retrospectives in this newly renovated old cinema in the nether reaches of Trastevere.

Metropolitan Via del Corso 7 ☎06.320.0933. Metro A Flaminio or bus #88, #95, #117, #119, #495, #628, #926 or tram #2. Lots of mainstream and the occasional quirky choice, with at least one of the four screens showing the undubbed version.

Nuovo Olimpia Via in Lucina 16 ☎06.686.1068. bus #63, or #492. Very central, just off Via del

Corso, with two screens, and they sometimes feature at least one foreign film in the original language.

Nuovo Sacher Largo Ascianghi 1 ☎06.581.8116. bus #44, #75, #780, H or tram #3, #8. Again in Trastevere, this film theatre, oddly enough housed in the old fascist youth HQ, shows current films in their original version on Mon and Tues. Their choices tend toward independent, Left-leaning works from around the world – as you might expect from film director and owner Nanni Moretti, the scourge of Berlusconi.

Pasquino Piazza Sant'Egidio 10 ☎581.5208 bus #23, #75, #280, #780, H or tram #8. Long-established in Trastevere as Rome's premier English-language cinema, with three screens showing recent general releases and the odd indie. The programme changes every Fri, and they also mount their own mini-festivals from time to time. A word of warning: avoid screen three unless you're really dying to see the film – the screen is terrible, the sound worse.

Quattro Fontane Via Quattro Fontane 23 ☎06.474.1515. Bus #40, #60, #64, #70, #170. Lots of mainstream and the occasional quirky choice, with at least one of the four screens showing the undubbed version.

Warner Village Moderno Piazza della Repubblica 45–46 ☎06.4777.9202. Metro A Repubblica or bus #40, #60, #61, #62, #64, #90, #170, #175, #492, #910, H. This American-style multiplex occasionally shows a Hollywood block-buster in the original undubbed version on one of its five screens.

Gay and lesbian Rome

E ver since "World Pride 2000" broke down the closet door, **gay and lesbian Rome** seems to have come into its own. Italy has never had any laws prohibiting same-sex couplings, but until recently the overwhelming pressure was enough to keep everyone suitably zipped up, and even now Italy has quite a bit of catching up to do before it is quite as laid-back about gay sex as much of the rest of Europe. Nonetheless, these days Rome has not just generic gay clubs, but specialist bars, restaurants and hotels, and all sorts of regular clubs are organizing gay nights to cater for the growing scene. There's also the tremendously successful **Gay Village** – ⑩ www.gayvillage.it – which holds events throughout the summer at an open-air venue in Testaccio.

Still, discretion is important in the community at large; Rome remains a city where a man walking around in the historic centre without a shirt on will almost certainly be stopped by the police and told to cover up, and the city is not quite ready for hand-holding and kissing in public. As yet there is no particularly gay part of town; clubs and bars are spread far and wide. Also, choices exclusively for women remain very few, although most places welcome both gay men and lesbians.

Contacts, shops, services

ARCI-Gay Ora Via Goito 35b ☎ 06.6450.1102, ⑩ www.arcigayroma.it. **Mon–Fri 4–8pm.** Rome branch of the nationwide Italian gay organization that runs a gay help line on ☎ 800.713.713 Mon and Wed (5–9pm) and Sat (4–8pm); has gatherings for those new to the city on Thurs (6–9pm); and social events every Fri (6–9pm). Annual membership costs €14 and can be useful for getting into clubs and bars (there's also a cheaper monthly version available).
Casa Internazionale delle Donne Via della Lungara 19 ☎ 06.6880.9723. Not a gay organization but rather a group of facilities for women only,

including a bookstore, library, restaurant and café, housed, appropriately enough, in an old convent. It also has accommodation in its *Orsa Maggiore* hostel.
Circolo Mario Mieli di Cultura Omosessuale Via Efeso 2a ☎ 06.541.3985, ⑩ www.mariomieli.org. Rome's most important gay activist organization offers a broad range of social and health services, including counselling and a help line. Weekly welcome group, political group and volunteer group meetings; call for details. Their magazine, *Aut*, features interesting articles, as well as listings, and is free at many gay spots.

Libreria Babele Via dei Banchi Vecchi 116,
T 06.687.6628. W www.libreriababeleroma.it.
Daily except Sun and Mon morning 11am–7pm.
Just off Corso Vittorio Emanuele, this is
Rome's gay and lesbian bookshop, with lots
of gay-themed books, some in English, plus
gadgets, posters, videos, guides and
postcards.
Zipper Via Castelfidardo 18, 2F T 06.488.2730,
W www.zippertravel.it. **Mon–Fri 9.30am–**
6.30pm. Gay travel agent, located near
Termini, brokering round-the-world or
round-Italy travel for gay and lesbian groups
and individuals.

Bars and clubs

L'Alibi Via Monte Testaccio 44 T 06.574.3448.
Tues–Sun midnight–5am. This predominantly –
but by no means exclusively – male venue is
one of Rome's oldest gay clubs, situated in
the heart of the city's alternative night scene
in Testaccio. It's no longer quite cutting
edge, but is a good, all-round venue, with a
multi-room cellar disco and an upstairs
open-air bar and big terrace to enjoy in the
warm months. Free admission with a drink
Wed–Fri, Sat €15 including drink.
La Buca di Bacco Via San Francesco a Ripa 165
T 0348.764.7388. This cocktail bar, wine bar
and tearoom is one of the new breed of
openly gay establishments. Quiet during the
day, gayer by night.
Coming Out Via San Giovanni in Laterano 8
T 06.700.9871. **Daily 5pm–2am.** If any area is

developing as Rome's gay zone, it may be
the stretch between the Colosseum and
Piazza Vittorio. This little pub is the newest
addition to the scene, frequented mostly by
a younger clientele.
Gay Village Mattatoio, Testaccio, W www
.gayvillage.it. July and Aug see gay
performers and events take over Testaccio
in the annual Gay Village festival. See the
website and flyers for what's on.
Garbo Vicolo di Santa Margherita 1a
T 06.581.6700. **Wed–Mon 10pm–2am.** Friendly
Trastevere bar, just behind the main piazza,
with a relaxed atmosphere and a nice setting.
L'Hangar Via in Selci 69 T 06.488.1397. About
halfway between Termini and the Roman
Forum, just off Via Cavour, this is one of
Rome's oldest and least expensive gay
spots, always crammed with young people.
No charge with an Arcigay card; without a
card, you have to pay for at least one drink,
whether you had one or not.
Max's Bar Via A. Grandi 7a T 06.7030.1599.
Daily except Wed 10.30pm–3.30am, Fri & Sat
until 5am. A very friendly bar with dance-floor
in the Esquiline/San Giovanni area, popular
with a broad cross-section of gay Romans.
Qube Via di Portonaccio 212 T 06.438.5445.
Thurs–Sat 10.30pm–4am. This club plays host
to the extremely successful *Mucca
Assassina* ("Killer Cow") gay night every
Friday. See p.260.
Skyline Via Pontremoli 36 T 06.700.9431. **Tues–**
Thurs & Sun 10.30pm–3am, Fri & Sat
10.30pm–5am. Gay male strippers, dark

Gay nights

Many Rome clubs have a devoted **gay night,** plus there are specifically gay nights
that move around from venue to venue. For contact details of most of the clubs
mentioned here, see the Nightlife chapter, and for up-to-date details of specific gay
nights, check out the relevant websites.

Black Betty W www.blackbetty.it. This is a black gay night that moves around from
club to club; most recently it has set up home at *Balic* on Tues.

Kinder Gaarten Sat at *Alpheus.*

Muccassassina Fri at *Qube.*

Omogenic Fri at *Circolo degli Artisti.*

Queer Sat at *Piper.*

Leather Club Roma Second Sat of the month at *Sphinx.*

Venus Rising Lesbian night, last Sun of the month at *Goa.*

zones, and the decidedly macho decor make this San Giovanni club a magnet for various creatures of the night, possibly drawn by the heavy cruising along the balcony. Various regular theme nights, including "Bears" every third Thurs.

Sphinx Piazza M. Fanti 40 ☎06.444.1312. Daily except Mon 11pm–4am. Leather and bear club that's been going about five years and is now well established, with regular bear nights on Sat. Some nights can be a riot.

Restaurants

Asinocotto Via dei Vascellari 48 ☎06.589.8985. One of the first restaurants to hang the rainbow flag above its door, this Trastevere restaurant is run by a gay couple and has a great, Proust-inspired menu of moderately priced pasta, meat and fish dishes. Worth a visit whatever your non-culinary preferences.
La Taverna di Edoardo II Vicolo Margana 14 ☎06.6994.2419. Daily except Tues 7pm–12.30am. Right in the middle of the old Jewish Ghetto, just off Piazza Venezia, this

place used to be a medieval torture chamber theme bar, and was named after the infamously gay English king. It's now a gay restaurant and still attracts the same young and cruisy crowd. Membership is required, but it's free.
Le Sorellastre Via San Francesco di Sales 1b ☎340.486.2295. Tues–Sat 7pm–midnight. This Trastevere bar and restaurant, serving Italian and international cuisine, is the only exclusively lesbian place in town.

Saunas

Europa Multiclub Via Aurelliana 40 ☎06.482.3650. Mon–Thurs 1pm–2am, Fri–Sun 1pm–6am. Near Termini, this has pleasantly stylish, clean facilities, and a snack bar. €14 per visit, €12 after 11pm.
Mediterraneo Via Pasquale Villari 3, ☎06.7720.5934, ⊛www.saunamediterraneo.it.

Daily 1pm–midnight. Close by Piazza Vittorio, this is a sauna on three levels, with all the usual choices, including a snack bar. Notably clean and attracts all ages. €14 entrance.

Accommodation

B&B 58 Le Real De Luxe Via Cavour 58, 4F ☎06.482.3566. Double rooms from around €85 in this small gay-friendly Via Cavour *pensione*.

Gayopen Via dello Statuto 44 ☎06.482.0013. Centrally situated gay B&B right on Piazza Vittorio Emanuele, with doubles for around €100.

Shops and markets

A t first glance, you may wonder where to start when it comes to **shopping** in a big, chaotic city like Rome. In fact the city is a more appealing shopping experience than you might think, abounding with pleasant shopping streets and colourful markets, most of which are in the city centre. Many shopping areas have been pedestrianized, and, perhaps best of all, the city hasn't yet been entirely overrun by department stores and shopping malls, or by the international chain stores that characterize most European city centres. One-stop shopping opportunities are rare, but you will find corners of the city that have been colonized by stores featuring the same sort of merchandise – fashion, antiques, food – making it easy for you to check out the competition's products and prices. You will also find true artisans in central Rome, who take great pride in their crafts.

You can find the best of Italy in Rome. **Fashion** straight from the catwalk is well represented on the fashionable streets close to the Spanish Steps – Via Condotti, Via Borgognona, Via Frattina and Via del Babuino – where you'll find chic boutiques such as Gucci, Prada and Valentino. If you want to do more than window-shop, head to Via del Tritone, Via Nazionale or Via Cola di Rienzo, near the Vatican, for more mid-range and affordable fashion. The stores on and around Via del Corso are a mixture, selling both mainstream and youth-orien-tated fashions, as are those on Via dei Gubbonari near Campo de' Fiori, while Via Veneto, off Piazza Barberini, caters to those who were youthful when Fellini's *La Dolce Vita* opened, and are now the fashionably well-off patrons of the street's expensive leather shops and boutiques. **Antiques** shops – a huge selection – line Via dei Coronari and neighbouring Via dell' Orso and Via dei Soldati, just north of Piazza Navona; and Via Giulia, southwest of Campo de' Fiori, and Via del Babuino and Via Margutta, between Piazza del Popolo and the Spanish Steps, are also good sources of art and antiques. As for **food**, if you

Opening hours

These days quite a few shops in the centre of Rome stay open all day and are open on Sunday too. However, many still observe the city's traditional **opening hours** – roughly Monday 3.30–7.30pm, Tuesday–Saturday 9.30am–1.30pm & 3.30–7.30pm, and closed on Sunday. Food shops are also often closed on Thursday afternoon in the winter and Saturday afternoon during the summer; and most shops close for at least two weeks in summer, usually in August. Most places accept all major credit **cards. Markets** tend to open up early – around 7am – and close at 2pm. Supermar-kets are generally open all day from 8am until 8pm. Bear in mind as ever that a lot of stores close down during August for their annual holiday.

want to take home a bottle of extra virgin olive oil or some vacuum-packed porcini mushrooms, end your day visiting the food shops and markets around Campo de' Fiori or Via Cola di Rienzo across the river. The city's many **markets** offer a change of pace from Rome's busy shopping streets. Many of these are bustling local food markets and, even in the centre, are still very much part of Roman life. The Campo de' Fiori market is probably the most central of these but we've listed others on p.278. Otherwise there's Trastevere's **Porta Portese** flea market, a venue for antiques, clothing, books, and indeed virtually anything else, every Sunday morning.

Shops

Antiques

Antichità Via del Babuino 83 ☎06.320.7585. Mon–Sat 9.30am–1.30pm & 4–7.30pm. One of the several fine antique stores in the area, with a large collection of stunning Italian furnishings from the 1700s. There is also an entrance on Via Margutta.

Antichità Archeologia Largo Fontanella Borghese 76 ☎06.687.6656. Mon 3.30–7pm, Tues–Sat 9am–1pm & 3.30–7.30pm. If you want to take home your own piece of ancient Rome, this is the place for you. Genuine, certified Greek, Etruscan and Roman antiquities, such as terracotta oil lamps, figurines and incised jewels, start at about €100.

Antiquetrade Via del Boschetto 4 ☎06.4782.5539. Mon 3.30–7pm, Tues–Sat 9am–1pm & 3.30–7.30pm. Antiques of all kinds and eras can turn up here. However, the speciality is fine old prints. A satisfying place to browse through Rome's history.

Arabesco Via del Panico 14 ☎06.686.9659. Mon–Sat 9.30am–8pm. One of a couple of such stores on this street, around the corner from Via dei Coronari, this has old Turkish carpets and kilims, oriental glassware and other bits and pieces from the East.

La Bottega del Principino Via Margutta 59b ☎06.320.7979. Mon–Sat 9.30am–7.30pm. An interesting little shop, quite different from the fancy antique shops that surround it, offering quite an eclectic array of bric-a-brac – everything from eighteenth-century farm equipment to crystal chandeliers from the 1940s.

Papadato Antichità Roma Piazza di Pietra 41 ☎06.679.6931. Tues–Sat 10.30am–7pm. Friendly store that has both Italian and English antiques. The store is mostly known for its large selection of European fans from the sixteenth and seventeenth centuries.

Valerio Turchi Via Margutta, 91a ☎06.323.5047. Mon 3.30pm–7pm, Tues–Sat 10.30am–7pm. A bit different from the other antique shops on Via Margutta, with exquisite pieces from Rome's past – various pieces of Roman statues and sarcophagi dating from as early as 300 AD.

Books

The Almost Corner Bookshop Via del Moro 45 ☎06.583.6942. Mon–Sat 10am–1.30pm & 3.30pm–8pm, Sun 11am–1.30pm & 3.30–8pm. Closed Sun in Aug. Under new ownership and also shifted to a larger space a few doors away from the corner, this shop, of all Rome's English bookshops, is perhaps the best bet for almost certainly having the very latest titles on your list of must-reads.

Anglo-American Bookshop Via delle Vite 102 ☎06.679.5222. Mon 3.30–7.30pm, Tues–Sat 9am–1pm & 3.30–7.30pm. One of the best selections of new English books in Rome, especially good on history and academic books.

Arion Via V. Veneto 42 ☎06.482.5308. Daily 9.30am–1am. This excellent bookshop boasts a fine stock of books about Rome – in English and Italian – and has the benefit of being open late so you can browse into the small hours.

Bibli Via dei Fienaroli 28 ☎06.588.4097. ⊛www.bibli.it. Mon 5.30pm–midnight, Tues–Sun 11am–midnight. Bookstore, cultural centre and café that has only a small selection of English books, but they do have Internet access, and a helpful bulletin board with many ads in English for those looking for work, apartments, etc.

Feltrinelli International Via Emanuele Orlando 84 ☎06.482.7878. Mon–Sat 9am–8pm, Sun 10.30am–1.30pm & 4–8pm. Opposite the *Hotel Gran Bretagna*, this international branch of the nationwide chain has an excellent stock of books in English, as well as French, German, Spanish and Portuguese. There's an ordinary Feltrinelli next door, while other city-centre branches include a smaller shop at Via del Babuino 39/40 (Mon 2–7.30pm, Tues–Sat 10am–7.30pm; ☎06.3600.1842), and two superstores selling books (including English ones) and music at Largo Argentina 5 (Mon–Fri 9am–9pm, Sat 9am–11pm, Sun 10am–8pm; ☎06.6880.32480), and in the Galleria Sordi, off Via del Corso (Sun–Thurs 10am–9pm, Fri & Sat 10am–10pm; ☎06.6975.5001).

Libreria del Cinema Via dei Fienaroli 31d ☎06.581.7724, ⓦwww.libreriadelcinema.roma.it. Mon 4–11pm, Tues–Fri 10am–1.30pm & 4–11pm, Sat & Sun 11am–11pm. Books, DVDs, magazines on film and everything related to it – many in English. There's a small café too to browse your purchases with other film buffs.

Libreria del Viaggatore Via del pellegrino 78 ☎06.6880.1048. Mon 4–8pm, Tues–Sat 10am–2pm & 4–8pm. A small store, but central Rome's best stock of guides and travel books, many of which are in English.

Lion Bookshop Via dei Greci 33 ☎06.3265.4007. Mon 3.30–7.30pm, Tues–Sat 10am–7.30pm. The comfortable location of this veteran English bookshop has a lounge area where you can take a break from browsing and enjoy a coffee or tea. A great store, and one of Rome's longest-established outlets for books in English.

Mel Bookstore Via Nazionale 252–255 ☎06.488.5405, ⓦwww.melbookstore.it. Mon 9am–Sat 8pm, Sun 10am–1.30pm & 4–8pm. One of Rome's largest book outlets, this pleasant store is one of a chain of megastores throughout Italy. It carries a good selection of books in English (off to the left as you enter), and a handful of used English titles in the basement, as well as CDs and DVDs. It also has an inviting café on its upper floors.

Mel Giannino Stopanni A great kids' bookstore. See p.287 for details.

Open Door Bookshop Via della Lungaretta 23 ☎06.589.6478, ⓦwww.books-in-italy.com. Mon 4.30–8.30pm,Tues–Fri 10.30am–8.30pm, Sat 10.30am–midnight, Sun noon–6pm. Summer hours – afternoons and evenings only. Although they do have some new titles, especially on Rome and Roman history, used books dominate the shelves at this friendly Trastevere bookshop, where you never know what treasures you might turn up. They also have a selection of books in Italian, German, French and Spanish.

Remainders Piazza San Silvestro 27–28 ☎06.679.2824. Mon–Sat 9.30am–8m, Sun 10am–1pm & 4–7.30pm. Thousands of remaindered books turn up here at a fraction of their original cost, many of them having something to do with art, so it's a wonderful place to flesh out your library with beautiful tomes. Not much in English, though.

TCI (Touring Club Italiano) Bookstore Via del Babuino 19–20 ☎06.3600.5281. Tues–Fri 9am–7.30pm, Sat 9am–1.30pm & 2.30–7.30pm. The city-centre shop of the nationwide organization is in fact a great travel bookstore, with an excellent selection of maps and guides – in Italian and in English – on Rome and Italy, and on overseas destinations too.

Clothes, hats, shoes, underwear

Arsenale Via del Governo Vecchio 64 ☎06.686.1380. Mon 3.30–7.30pm, Tues–Sat 10am–7.30pm. This large store is one of the main cool boutiques along this funky stretch, with great dresses by the owner Patrizia Pieroni and lots of other stuff by small independent designers.

Borsalino Piazza di Campo Marzio 72 ☎06.679.6120. Mon 3–7.30pm, Tues–Sat 9.30am–1.30pm & 3–7.30pm. Home of the classic fedora as sported by Jean-Paul Belmondo and others, as well as a whole host of other kinds of hats. Other branches on Piazza del Popolo and by the Trevi Fountain.

La Cravatta su Misura Via Seminario 93 ☎06.6994.2199. Mon 3.30–7.30pm, Tues–Sat 10am–7.30pm. Ezio Pellicano sells only one thing: ties, made by Ezio himself or his daughter. You can buy any of the hundreds of ties you see on display, or you can choose from one of the hundreds of rolls of material and have your own made up in about a week.

Davide Cenci Via di Campo Marzio 1/7 ☎06.699.0681. Mon 3.30–7.30pm, Tues–Fri 9.30am–1.30pm & 3.30–7.30pm, Sat 10am–7.30pm. This is one of the city's longest-established purveyors of elegant and refined clothing, offering conservative high-quality fashion to men, women and children for the past 75 years.

Diesel Via del Corso 186 ☎06.678.3933. Mon–Sat 9.30am–7.30pm. Well known now around the world, this Italian manufacturer of very trendy styles for posy, disaffected youth sports a major outlet in the heart of Rome, where the window displays can always be depended upon to make a statement.

Dress Agency Donna Via del Vantaggio 1b ☎06.321.0898. **Mon 4–7.30pm, Tues–Sat 10am–1pm & 4–7.30pm.** Used women's clothing and accessories from Versace, Armani and all the big-name Italian

▽ *Energie*, Via del Corso

designers. Not as cheap as you might expect, but still worth a rummage.

Energie Via del Corso 179 & 486 ☎06.322.7046. **Mon–Sun 10am–8pm.** One of the city's most popular clothing stores, mainly aimed at teenagers, with expensive trendy clothes, loud music and an omnipresent group of kids hanging out around the entrance. Definitely the place to be seen if you're loaded and under 21. Another branch at Via Cola di Rienzo 143/147.

Fiorucci Via Nazionale 236 ☎06.488.3175. The bright and funky clothes of this icon of 1980s Italian fashion still shine as brightly in this flagship Rome store. Particularly good for jeans and tops, and also stocking other like-minded young and sexy brands.

Gallinelle Via del Boschetto 76 ☎06.488.1017. **Mon 4–8pm, Tues–Sat 10am–1pm & 4–8pm.** Vintage clothing, stage costumes and stylish own-brand designs at this cool Monti store.

Giorgio Sermoneta Gloves Piazza di Spagna 61 ☎06.679.960. **Mon–Sat 9am–8pm, Sun 10am–7pm.** This long-standing glove specialist has a large collection of Italian gloves in every price range, and has catered to celebrities, politicians and tourists for 35 years.

Intimissimi There are several city-centre branches of this stylish yet affordable Italian lingerie chain, the most central of which is at Via del Corso 167.

Loco Via dei Baullari ☎06.6880.8216. **Mon 3.30–8.30pm, Tues–Sat 10.30am–8.30pm.**

The big designers

Giorgio Armani Via Condotti 76 ☎06.699.1460.
Bulgari Via Condotti 10 ☎06.679.3876.
Roberto Cavalli Via Borgognona 7a. ☎06.6938.0130.
Dolce & Gabbana Piazza di Spagna 82/83 ☎06.679.2294.
Fendi Largo Goldoni 420 ☎06.696.661.
Ferre Via Borgognona 6 ☎06.679.7445.
Gucci Via Condotti 8 ☎06.679.1882.
Krizia Piazza di Spagna 87 ☎06.679.3772.
Max Mara Via Condotti 17/19 ☎06. 6992.2104.
Missoni Piazza di Spagna 78 ☎06.679.2555.
Moschino Via Belsiana 53/57 ☎06.6920.0415.
Prada Via Condotti 91/93 ☎06.679.0897.
Salvatore Ferragamo Via Condotti 73 ☎06.679.5180.
Valentino Via Condotti 13 ☎06.679.5862.
Gianni Versace Via Bocca di Leone 26 ☎06.678.0521.

Eccentrically designed shoes, the like of which you won't find anywhere else.

Maga Morgana Via del Governo Vecchio 27 & 98 ⊤06.687.9995. Mon–Sat 9.30am–7.30pm.Two shops selling nice, original women's tops, skirts and knitwear, and great dresses.

NuYorica Piazza Pollarola 36/37 ⊤06.6889.1243. Mon–Sat 10.30am–7.30pm. Just a few steps form Campo de' Fiori, this stylish shop specializes in clothes, bags and shoes by contemporary designers. Not at all cheap.

La Perla Via Condotti 79 ⊤06.6994.1934. The flagship store of this now international designer lingerie and beachwear chain is the last word in underwear.

Vestiti Usati Cinzia Via del Governo Vecchio 45 ⊤06.686.1791. Mon 3.30–7.30pm, Tues–Sat 10am–2pm & 3.30–7.30pm. The best of the several used clothing shops along this street, where you can find anything from an elegant raincoat to black leather biker jeans, and much more.

Accessories: bags, jewellery, hair and toiletries

Bozart Via Bocca di Leone 4 ⊤06.678.1026. Mon 4–8pm Tues–Sat 9.30am–8pm. These fakes are truly fabulous, each necklace or bracelet making its own rich statement. Semiprecious stones, as well as Swarovski crystal pieces and resin and wooden elements are freely used to create dazzlingly alluring costume jewellery, ranging in price from €25 to 300.

ElleEffe Via di San Calisto 6–6a ⊤06.5833.3875 or 06.5834.3483. Mon–Sat 9.30am–8pm. If you want the perfect new haircut to go with your fresh Roman fashions, let Fabio, one of Rome's top hair stylists, take care of you. His English is as perfect as his taste and his cutting skills. All the usual salon services as well.

Fabio Piccioni Via del Boschetto 148 ⊤06.474.1697. Mon–Sat 10.30am–8pm, except closed Mon morning. Original Art Nouveau and especially Art Deco pieces are impressively displayed here, as are exquisite reproductions and inspired one-of-a-kind adornments made by this workshop.

Lefevre Via Colonna Antonina 50 ⊤06.678.3885. Mon 4–8pm Tues–Sat 9.30am–1.30pm & 4–8pm. Exclusive designs here include seed pearl ropes hung with cut crystals of ruby, emerald and sapphire matrix, for under €100. Silver frames are also featured, as well as fine porcelains.

Ibiz Via dei Charivari 39 ⊤06.6830.7297. Mon–Sat 10am–7.30pm. Great leather bags, purses and rucksacks in exciting contemporary designs made on the premises.

Mandarina Duck Via Due Macelli 59 ⊤06.678.6414. Mon 3.30–7.30pm, Tues–Sat 10am–7.30pm. The main branch of the trendy Bologna bag company is a two-tier homage to how to be both practical and stylish at the same time.

Materozzoli Piazza San Lorenzo in Lucina 5 ⊤06.6889.2686. Mon 3–7.30pm, Tues–Sat 10am–1pm & 3–7.30pm. Ancient city-centre perfume store selling classic scents from all over the world, toiletries and shaving products.

Roma-Store Via della Lungaretta 63 ⊤06.581.8789. Mon 4–8pm Tues–Sat 9.30am–1.30pm & 4–8pm. Not a football merchandise store but in fact a shop selling classic perfumes – Acqua di Parma, Penhaligons and suchlike – scented soaps, lotions and candles. Only the very finest from Italy, France and England.

Siragusa Via delle Carrozze 64 ⊤06.679.7085. Mon 4–8pm Tues–Sat 9.30am–1.30pm & 4–8pm. As much a museum and antiques gallery as it is a jewellery shop; the gems set into rings and things here are almost all ancient sardonyxes, carnelians and other carved semiprecious and precious stones. Also sells ancient coins.

Department stores and malls

COIN Piazza Appio 7 ⊤06.708.0020. Mon 3.30–8pm, Tues–Sat 9.30am–1.30pm & 3.30–8pm. Inexpensive clothes, accessories, and a great place to find stylish kitchenware at bargain prices.

Forum Stazione Termini Daily 8am–10pm. Since the refurbishment of Termini, this is probably the city centre's best shopping centre, with branches of all the big Italian chains, and an excellent bookstore.

M.A.S. Piazza Vittorio Emanuele 138 ⊤06.446.8078. Mon–Sat 9am–1pm & 3.45–7.45pm. It doesn't get any cheaper than this. The "Magazzini allo Statuto" (Statutory Warehouses) are like one vast, multi-level rummage sale, but take your time and you'll find something you want. There's everything from clothing to housewares.

La Rinascente Largo Chigi 20 ⊤06.679.7691. Mon–Sat 9am–9pm, Sun 10.30am–8pm. Part of a national chain, this is the closest Rome gets to an upscale department store, with several floors of high-quality merchandise displayed in an architecturally interesting setting.

TAD Via del Babuino 155a ⓣ06.3269.5131. **Mon noon–8pm, Tues–Sat 10am–8pm.** This stylish store look's tiny from the outside, but in fact its one level houses departments selling clothes, perfume and cosmetics, flowers and home furnishings, as well as having a hairdressing salon and ultra-cool café. It's as sleek and expensive as it gets for the most part, but it does have some clothes and accessories at prices most people can afford – unlike most of the other shops on the street – and the café is a nice spot for a designer lunch.

UPIM Via del Tritone 172 ⓣ06.678.3336. Mon noon–8pm, Tues–Sat 9am–8pm. The most inexpensive of the chain stores, good for cheap clothes and household goods, as well as basic toiletries and other necessities for travellers. Another branch on Piazza Santa Maggiore (ⓣ06.446.5579).

Food and wine

Buccone Via di Ripetta 19 ⓣ06.361.2154. **Mon–Thurs 9am–8.30pm, Fri & Sat 9am–midnight, Sun 10am–5pm.** Every alcoholic beverage you could dream of, with a large selection of wines from all over the world, spirits, even ten-litre bottles of *grappa*.

Castroni Via Cola di Rienzo 196 ⓣ06.687.4383. **Mon–Sat 8am–8pm.** Huge labyrinthine food store with a large selection of Italian treats including chocolates, pastas, sauces, and olive oils, as well as hard-to-find international favourites such as plum pudding and Mexican specialities – plus a café with coffee, cakes and sandwiches. There's another branch nearby at Via Ottaviano 55 and one just off Via Nazionale on Via delle Quattro Fontane, both of which also have cafés.

Centro Macrobiotico Italiano Via della Vite 14 &06.679.2509. **Mon–Fri noon–4pm and 7–11pm, Sat 7–11pm.** If you love authentic Italian food but are also a devotee of natural foods, this is Rome's most central option for stocking up on wholegrain pastas and other *integrali* products from Italy's rich countryside.

La Dolceroma Via Portico d'Ottavia 20b ⓣ06.689.2196. **Tues–Sat 8.30am–8pm, Sun 10am–1.30pm.** First-class Austrian and American sweet classics – brownies, blueberry muffins and, best of all, white chocolate chip cookies.

Il Forno del Ghetto Via del Portico d'Ottavia 1 ⓣ06.687.8637. **Sun–Thurs 8am–7.30pm, Fri 8am–3.30pm.** This marvellous tiny kosher Jewish bakery, unmarked but in the heart of the Ghetto, has unforgettable ricotta pies and *pizza giudia* (a hard cake, crammed with dried and candied fruit) that draw quite a crowd.

Franchi Via Cola di Rienzo 200 ⓣ06.686.4576. Mon–Sat 8am–9pm. One of the best delis in Rome – a triumph of cheeses, sausages and an ample choice of cold or hot food to go, including delicious *torta rustica* and roast chicken. They'll make up customized lunches for you, and they also have the wines to go with it.

Del Frate Via degli Scipioni 118/124 ⓣ06.321.1612. **Mon–Sat 8am–8pm.** This large wine and spirits shop is located on a quiet street near the Vatican, and has all the Barolos and Chiantis you could want, alongside shelves full of *grappa* in all shapes and sizes. See also p.238.

Innocenti Via della Luce 21 ⓣ06.580.3926. Mon–Sat 9am–1pm & 4–7.30pm, Sun 9am–1pm; closed Aug 15–Sept 15. Trastevere's – and maybe Rome's – best *biscottificio*, a family operation for 100 years. Wonderful, chewy *croccantini* – half chocolate, half vanilla. Plus *amaretti* (almond biscuits), *brutti ma buoni* (hazelnut biscuits), *straccetti* (almond and hazelnut biscuits) and dozens more varieties.

Innocenzi Piazza San Cosimato 66 ⓣ06.581.2725. A great dry goods grocer, with all the usual rice and pasta and Italian goodies but also a great selection of stuff from around the world – tomato ketchup. teas, peanut butter, the works. A good option for homesick ex-pats and foodies alike.

Moriondi & Gariglio Via Pie di Marmo 21/22 ⓣ06.699.0856. **Mon–Sat 9.30am–1pm & 3.30–7.30pm.** Just a short walk from the Pantheon, this is perhaps the city centre's most sumptuous and refined handmade chocolate shop – great for exquisitely wrapped gifts.

Panella Via Merulana 54 ⓣ06.487.2435, ⓕ06.487.2344. **Mon–Fri 8am–1.30pm & 5–8pm, Sat 8am–1.30pm & 4.30–8pm Sun 8.30am–1.30pm.** The art of bread-making is the speciality here, as well as pasta, like colourful *sombrerini* (hats), packaged to take home.

Quetzalcoatl Via delle Carrozze 26 ⓣ06.6920.2191, ⓕ06.6929.1932. **Mon–Sat 10am–7.30pm.** This shop stocks some of Rome's most sublime chocolates, presented as if they were art. Once you taste them, you'll probably feel that they are. All sizes of gifts boxes available.

Roscioli Via dei Giubbonari 21–23 ⊕06.687.5287. Daily 8.30am–8pm. Cheeses, salamis and a very good selection of wine. Plus food is served at lunch and early evening. *Roscioli* also has its own bakery across the street at Via dei Charivari 34 (⊕06.686.4045). .

Shaki Piazza di Spagna 65 ⊕06.678.6605 Mon–Sat 9am–8pm, Sun 10.30am–1.30pm & 2.30–7pm. Located right in Piazza di Spagna to make it easy for visitors to stock up on the entire range of canned sauces and delectables Italy has to offer. A unique selection of Italian pottery and other handicrafts, as well. See also p.251 for details of its wine bar around the corner.

Teichner Piazza San Lorenzo in Lucina 17 ⊕06.679.0612. Daily 7.30am–9pm. Good all-round foodotoro and deli that has stocks of all those Italian goodies you want to take home with you. Also with a branch outside the city centre at Porta San Giovanni.

Trimani Via Goito 20 ⊕06.446.9661. Mon–Sat 11am–midnight. One of the city's best wine shops, and handily close to Termini if you want to stock up before heading off to the airport.

Valzani Via del Moro 37 ⊕06.580.3792. Wed–Sun 10am–8.30pm; closed June–Sept 15; extended hours at Christmas and Easter. One of the oldest of the city's confectioners, still keeping up tradition with marvellous *mostaccioli* and *pangiallo* (both are traditional dried fruit and nut honey bars, the former chocolate-covered), *torrone*, *sachertorte* (classic Viennese double-chocolate cake with apricot filling), and, at Easter time, huge, gift-filled chocolate eggs which you can have your name etched on.

🏃 **Volpetti** Via Marmorata 47 ⊕06.574.2352. Mon–Sat 8am–2pm & 5–8pm. It's worth seeking out this Testaccio deli, which is truly

one of Rome's very best. If you're lucky, one of the staff will give you samples of their truly incredible *mozzarella di bufala*. There's another, city-centre branch at Via della Scrofa 31–2 (⊕06.686.1940), open the same hours, but it's much smaller. *Volpetti* also has its own eatery round the corner; see p.237.

Household goods

Art'e Piazza Rondanini 32 ⊕06.683.3907. Mon 1–7.30pm, Tues–Sat 9.30am–7.30pm. Ultra-modern kitchenware and home furnishings, including lamps, clocks and kitchen utensils and appliances in flashy neon colours and shiny stainless steel. The perfect stylish gift to yourself from Italy.

Azi Via Manara 7 ⊕06.581.8699. Mon 3.30–7.30pm, Tues–Sat 9.30am–1.30pm & 3.30–7.30pm. Anything curiously or cunningly designed for the home is likely to be found here. The owners comb the earth for trendy, generally high-tech treasures, and the result is a truly unique shop – in two locations, around the corner from each other in Trastevere.

C.U.C.I.N.A. Via Mario de' Fiori 65 ⊕06.679.1275. Mon 3.30–7.30pm, Tues–Sat 10am–7.30pm. A shop filled with modern kitchen appliances, including a large selection of Italian caffetterie.

'Gusto Piazza Augusto Imperatore 7 ⊕06.323.6363. Daily 10.30am–2am. Everything for the aspirant gourmet: wines, decanters, glasses, and all the top-of-the-line kitchen gadgets you could ever hope to find. Also a large selection of cookbooks in English.

Spazio Sette Via dei Barbieri 7 ⊕06.686.9747. Mon 3.30–7pm, Tues–Sat 9.30am–1pm & 3.30–7.30pm. Designer housewares of all sorts are the speciality here, for decades the shop of choice for Romans who want something chic and stylish for their home or as a gift.

City-centre supermarkets

Rome's food stores and delis are so good that you shouldn't need to use a **supermarket** too often, but for pasta and other basics the supermarkets that there are in the city centre can be enormously useful, especially if you're self-catering. Here's a list of some conveniently located ones:

DiperDi Via del Gesu 56; Via Monterone 5; Via Poli 47; Via Vittoria 22.

De Spar Corso V. Emanuele 42; Vicolo di Moretta x; Via San Bartolomeo di Caccinari 78.

Standa Via Cola di Rienzo 173; Viale Trastevere 60.

Miscellaneous: art, gifts and crafts

La Bottega del Marmoraro Via Margutta 53b
☎ 06.320.7660. Mon–Sat 8.30am–7.30pm.
Enrico and Sandro Fiorentini, a father-and-son team, are skilled artisans, creating personalized marble plaques for every occasion, as well as statuary, both ancient and modern repros.

Campo Marzio Penne Via Campo Marzio 41
☎ 06.6880.7877. Daily 10am–1pm & 2–7pm.
Small shop dedicated to really cool pens and writing accessories, briefcases and pencil cases.

Carmignani Via della Colonna Antonina 42–43
☎ 06.679.5449. Tues–Sat 10am–2pm and 3–7.30pm. Even if you don't smoke, you will appreciate the beauty of the handmade pipes, shiny silver cigar holders and cutters, and poker sets, in this small shop a few minutes from the Pantheon.

Cesare Diomedi Via E. Orlando 96/97
☎ 06.488.4822. Mon–Sat 9am–7.30pm. A few minutes' walk from Piazza della Repubblica, two floors filled with luxury leather goods, Versace clocks, Cartier wallets, and all sorts of other fancy gifts for every occasion.

Ditta G. Poggi Via del Ges' 74/75 ☎ 06.678.4477.
Mon–Sat 10am–1pm & 4–7.30pm. Fantastic long-established art materials shop, with a huge range of specialist paints and accessories but more mainstream pens, pencils and stationery too.

Ferrari Store Via Tomacelli 147/152
☎ 06.689.2979. Daily 10am–7.30pm. What better souvenir to take back than an accessory from this Italian motor racing icon? It's not a cheap store, by any means, but there's a range of things to buy whatever your budget – from a €30 remote-control car to pricey Ferrari-themed jewellery.

Fratelli Alinari Via Alibert 16a ☎ 06.679.2923,
🌐 www.alinari.it. Mon–Sat 3.30–7.30pm. If you want to know what Rome's piazzas looked like before McDonald's came to town, come here for a fine selection of black-and-white photographs of Rome from at least 100 years ago. Branches in Milan and Florence, too.

Frette Piazza di Spagna 11 ☎ 06.679.0673. Mon 3.30–7.30pm, Tues–Sat 9.30am–1.30pm & 3.30–7.30pm. This famous luxury linen shop is located among all the designer shops in Piazza di Spagna. They are happy to fill custom orders and will ship their products anywhere.

Il Gancio Via del Seminario 82/83
☎ 06.679.6646. Mon 3.30–7.30pm, Tues–Sat 10am–1pm and 3.30–7.30pm. High-quality leather bags, purses, shoes all made right here, in the workshop on the premises.

Il Giardino di Domenico Persiani Via Torino 92
☎ 06.488.1967. Mon 3.30–7.30pm, Tues–Sat 10am–1pm and 3.30–7.30pm. An experience not to be missed – a quiet garden setting filled to the brim with all sorts of creations of the ceramicist's art. Everything from glazed tiles to full-sized copies of famous statuary. Pieces made to order.

Ai Monasteri Corso del Rinascimento 72
☎ 06.6880.2783. Mon 3.30–7.30pm, Tues–Sat 10am–1.30pm & 3.30–7.30pm. Cakes, spirits, toiletries and other items made by monks in monasteries.

Nostalgica Via di Ripetta 30 ☎ 06.321.9448. Old-fashioned Italian football shirts from around €70 – ironically enough, made in England.

Il Papiro Via del Pantheon 50 ☎ 06.679.5597.
Daily 10am–8pm. The most central branch of this originally Tuscan chain which stocks fine paper, notelets and notebooks, as well as the fancy pens to go with it.

Pineider Via Due Macelli 68 ☎ 06.239.344,
☎ 06.239.447. Mon 3.30–7.30pm, Tues–Sat 10am–1.30pm & 3.30–7.30pm. This exclusive store has been selling beautiful handmade paper, invitations, and writing materials for Roman society since 1774. Another branch at Via di Fontanella Borghese 22 (☎ 06.687.8369).

Polvere di Tempo Via del Moro 59
☎ 06.5880.0704. Mon 3.30–8pm, Tues–Sat 10am–1pm & 4–8pm. For that astrolabe you've always dreamed of, as well as a huge array of ancient and medieval devices for telling time, stop by this arcane little shop. Also, alchemists' rings that double as sundials and loads of oddities and curiosities.

Vacanze Romane Via dei Pastini 18a
☎ 06.6992.5056. Mon–Fri 11am–11pm, Sat 11am–midnight, closed between 2pm & 3pm.
Upscale gift shop with fun and often tacky "art" souvenirs – suitcases decorated with Raphael's angels, Michelangelo lampshades and suchlike.

Music

Disfunzioni Musicali Via degli Etruschi 4–14
☎ 06.446.1984. Mon 3–8pm, Tues–Sat 10.30am–8pm. Supplying nearby college students with a huge collection of both new

Food markets

Rome's **food markets** are a perfect place to stop to pick up a snack or picnic provisions. The one on Piazza di Campo de' Fiori is the city's most famous and picturesque, and has been around for the last four hundred years. Other central options include: the market between the Termini railway tracks and Piazza Vittorio Emanuele, off Via Lamarmora; Piazza Mastai in Trastevere; Piazza della Unitá in Prati; and Piazza Testaccio in Testaccio. Most are open Mon–Sat 6am–2pm.

and used music. A large selection of underground, rare and bootlegged recordings. **Messagerie Musicali** Via del Corso 472 ℡06.684.401. Mon–Sat 10am–11pm, Sun 10am–8.30pm. One of the city's best mainstream collections of CDs, plus a wide array of foreign magazines and books. **Metropoli Rock** Via Cavour 72 ℡06.488.0443. Mon–Sat 9am–1pm & 4–8pm. The place to come if you are looking for old and out-of-print recordings, whether it's classical, rock, or jazz. Two floors stocked floor-to-ceiling with vinyl, 33rpm and 45rpm, as well as new and used CDs. **Ricordi** Via del Corso 506 120 ℡06.361.2370. Mon–Sat 9.30am–8pm, Sun 10am–1pm & 3–8pm. Rome's largest and most complete

music store, with a good array of CDs, plus books on music, scores, musical instruments, DVDs, sound equipment – and concert tickets. **La Rinascita** Via Botteghe Oscure 1/3 ℡06.679.7136. Mon–Sat 10am–8pm. The old HQ of the Italian communist party is a good, basic CD (and book) store, especially good on Italian artists. **Soul Food** Via San Giovanni in Laterano 192–194 ℡06.7045.2025. Tues–Sat 10.30am–1.30pm & 3.30–8pm. This vinyl junky's paradise is the city centre's only CD-free zone when it comes to music. Lots of stuff from the pre-digital ages of the 1960s and 1970s, and genuinely enthusiastic staff too.

Markets

Borghetto Flaminio Piazza della Marina 32. Sept–July Sun 10am–7pm; entrance €1.60. A partly covered flea market with plenty of knick-knacks, designer clothing and antiques. Rummage alongside Rome's upper classes and celebrities.
Fontanella Borghese Piazza Fontanella Borghese. Sat & Sun 9am–7pm. A small print and book market off Via del Corso, where you can find expensive antique prints and etchings along with inexpensive reproductions.
Galleria delle Stimmate Largo delle Stimmate 1. Sept–May last Sun of the month 10am–7pm. Mostly household goods, and some jewellery, with some great finds like antique lace, silver serving dishes, and old cutlery.
Piazza Vittorio Emanuele The market that used to take place here in fact goes on now over by the Termini railway tracks in a couple of buildings between Via Lamarmora and Via Ricasoli, one housing clothes and household goods, the other fresh fruit and veg and other food stalls.
Porta Portese Sun 5am–2pm. By far, Rome's most famous and largest market, stretching

from Porta Portese a mile or so down Via Portuense and into the streets around, with hundreds of stalls selling myriad goods, including antiques, oriental artefacts, clothing, carpets, art, tools, appliances, fake brand-name jeans, underwear, linens, and even puppies.
La Soffitta Sotto I Portici Piazza Augusto Imperatore ℡06.3600.5345. Sept–July third Sun of every month 9am–7pm. Flea market selling a diverse mix of clothing, household items and antiques.
Underground Via Francesco Crispi 96. Oct–June first Sun of each month and the Sat before: 10.30am–7.30pm. Located in an underground parking garage near Piazza di Spagna, and selling all the usual flea market finds, but with a special section for children's goods.
Via Sannio Via Sannio. Mon–Fri 9am–1.30pm, Sat 9am–6pm. Centrally located market selling mostly new and used clothing, including lots of fake brand names. To get to the extensive secondhand section, continue past all the stalls selling new things.

Sports and outdoor activities

S pectator sports are popular in Italy; the hallowed *calcio*, or football, is far and away the most popular, and tends to overshadow everything else. Rome, with two clubs in the top division (Serie A), is no exception. As for **participation** in sport, there isn't quite the same compulsion to hit the hell out of a squash ball or sweat your way through an aerobics class after work as there is, say, in Britain or the US. However, the notion of keeping fit and being active is becoming as fashionable here as it is in most European countries, especially when it offers the opportunity to wear the latest designer gear.

Cycling

The month of May sees the *Giro d'Italia* (Italy's national race) spin through Rome's cobbled lanes, but for most visitors **cycling** is far too daunting to be enjoyable. However, the Appia Antica is ideal for a ride, especially on Sundays when it's (theoretically) closed to automobile traffic. See "Travel Essentials" in Basics for places you can rent bikes.

Football

Rome's two big **football** teams, AS Roma and SS Lazio, play on alternate Sundays between September and May at the Olympic Stadium, northwest of the city centre. Unsurprisingly, feelings run extremely high between the two teams, and derby games are big – and sometimes violent – occasions. **Roma**, traditionally the team of the inner-city urban working class, were, until relatively recently, perennially the better of the two sides, while traditionally right-wing Lazio trailed. However, in 2000 **Lazio** won the championship, only to have Roma then bounce back in 2001 to take their third *scudetto*. Needless to say, it's a breathless rivalry that can go either way, despite Lazio's recent financial ills.

We've given **ticket** details on p.280, but bear in mind that the **Stadio Olimpico** is enormous, with a capacity of 100,000, and at most games, except perhaps Roma-Lazio clashes, you should be able to get a ticket for all but the cheapest seats on the night. Take your passport with you to buy a ticket as they always want some sort of ID. The diehard fans traditionally occupy the Curva areas at each end of the ground (Lazio in the Curva Nord, Roma in Curba Sud), and tickets in these areas cost €15–25 (if you can get one). It's usually easier to pick up seats in the corner stands, or *distinti*, for €25–35; seats in the side stands, or *tribuna*, cost €60–100. You can get seats for matches at Ⓦ www.romantickets .com but you'll pay for the convenience – prices are around fifty percent higher than what you'll pay if you buy direct. **Getting there** on public transport, you can reach the Olympic Stadium by taking tram #2 from Piazzale Flaminio to Piazza Mancini or bus #910 from Termini and then walking across the river to the stadium. Or take bus #32 from Piazza Risorgimento or #271 from Piazza Venezia direct to the stadium.

Lazio Ⓦ www.sslazio.it. To book ahead, try *Lazio Point*, Via Farini 34 (Mon–Sat 9am–7pm; ☎ 06.482.6768), the Lazio ticket office ☎ 06.323.7333, up to 48 hours before the game, or, after that, the Lazio shop, Via Calderini 66, close to Piazza Mancini, or the stadium itself. Lazio supporters traditionally occupy the Curva Nord end of the ground (colours blue and white, symbol, the eagle), where you can get seats for around €15–25; seats in the *distinti*, or corners of the ground, or the *tribuna*, along the sides, are more expensive; and you should reckon on paying around €60–100 for a reasonable *tribuna* ticket.

Roma Ⓦ www.asromacalcio.it. The *As Roma Store* sells tickets, as well as fan supplies (Piazza Colonna 360 ☎ 06.6920.0642; Piazza Indipendiente 8 ☎ 06.4470.2689; both daily 10am–6pm), again up to 48 hours before a game; after that you need to go to Orbis at Piazza Esquilino 37 (Mon–Sat 9.30am–1pm & 4–7.30pm; ☎ 06.482.7403, no credit cards). Fans of Roma (symbol, the wolf, colours red and yellow) occupy the Curva Sud, which is usually completely sold out to season-ticket holders, making a visit to a Roma game a slightly more expensive business, since the cheapest seat you'll find will be in the *distinti*, for €25–35.

Golf

If you simply can't go a week or two without hitting a ball, it's worth knowing that **golf** is slowly becoming a popular sport in Italy. Most clubs welcome non-members but you must be able to produce a membership card from your hometown club. For more information, call the *Federazione Italiana Golf*, Viale Tiziano 74 (☎ 06.323.1825, Ⓦ www.federgolf.it). All of the following offer an eighteen-hole course and a driving range:

Circolo del Golf di Roma Via Appia Nuova 716a ☎ 06.780.3407, Ⓦ www.golfroma.it; closed Mon. Eighteen-hole course south of Rome.
Golf Club Parco de' Medici Viale Parco de' Medici 22 ☎ 06.655.3477, Ⓦ www.golfparcomedici.com; closed Tues. Southwest of the centre, towards Fiumicino, with eighteen holes, plus a driving range.

Country Club Castel Gandolfo Via Santo Spirito 13, Castel Gandolfo ☎ 06.931.2301, Ⓦ www .countryclubcastelgandolfo.it. Down in the Castelli Romani, this is the pope's local course and has excellent facilities, including a restaurant and bar.

If you want more **information** about the Italian football season in general, the *Federazione Italiana Gioco Calcio* (Ⓦ www.figc.it) has information (in English) about all the season's games. Or, if your Italian is good enough, get hold of one of the Italian sports newspapers, which are published daily and focus heavily on football. The Rome paper is the *Corriere dello Sport* and will have details of any upcoming games, as will the other two papers: the pink *Gazzeto dello Sport* and *Tuttosport*.

Gyms

If you're in the habit of a regular workout and want to keep it up even while you're checking Rome's sights off your list, here are a few handily located facilities:

Farnese Fitness Vicolo delle Grotte 35 ☎06.687.6931, ⓦwww.farnesefitness.com. Mon–Fri 9am–10pm, Sat 11am–6pm, Sun 10am–1pm; closed Aug. Decent gym bang in the centre of town. Aerobics classes included in the daily fee. €10 per day.

Fitness First Via Giolitti Giovanni 44 ☎06.4782.6300, ⓦwww.fitnessfirst.it. Mon–Fri 8am–11pm, Sat & Sun 9am–8pm. Not far from Termini, this branch of the chain offers a variety of classes, such as yoga, spinning and Thai kickboxing, on offer in this spanking clean establishment. €16 per day.

Fitnext Piazza Mignanelli 23 ☎06.679.6003 or 06.679.6003; Mon–Fri 8am–10pm, Sat 11am–7pm; closed Aug. Choice of one class included in the fee, including yoga and Pilates. €20 per day.

Roman Sports Center Viale del Galoppatoio 33 ☎06.320.1667, 06.321.8096 or 06.322.3665. Mon–Sat 8am–10pm, Sun 9am–3pm; closed Sun Jun–Aug. Rome's largest, oldest and most prestigious fitness centre, with a host of offerings, including Olympic-sized pools, squash courts and hydromassage and saunas. €26 per day.

Jogging

The **Rome Marathon** – ⓦwww.maratondiroma.it – circles around the city's most famous monuments on the third Sunday in March, and is a nice opportunity to run through the city centre free of cars and crazy drivers. It starts and finishes on Via dei Fori Imperiali and the course follows the river, going as far north as the Ponte Milvio and as far south as the Basilica of San Paolo. Other annual races you might want to take part in include the **Rome–Ostia half-marathon** every February, and the **Roma–Appia 14k** each April, which takes you past all the sights of the Appian Way.

The rest of the time the traffic and congestion make it impossible, and sometimes even dangerous, to jog in Rome, but luckily there are plenty of **green spaces** to escape the traffic. The most popular is Villa Borghese, where there are plenty of places to jog, including the Piazza di Siena, a grass horsetrack in the centre of the park. Other good options include the Villa Ada, a lush and vast green space some kilometres north of the city centre, which has a running track, and the Villa Doria Pamphilj above Trastevere, which offers nice paths with exercise stations along the way. For more central – and public – jogging, the Circo Massimo is the perfect size, and shape, although it gets busy with tourists early on.

Riding

There are not very many options for those who are looking to go **horse riding** in Rome. The only place really is *Il Galoppatoio*, Via del Galoppatoio (☎06.322.6797), a posh riding club that offers expensive lessons in an idyllic atmosphere deep in the heart of Villa Borghese. Lessons last an hour but you have to sign up for ten – at a cost of around €150. More feasibly, there's also the *Maneggio Cavalieri dell'Appia Antica*, Via dei Cernenii 15 (☎06.780.1214) where you pay around €25 for a gentle one-hour trot. Groups only though.

Swimming

If you feel like cooling off from a hot summer day, a dip in a **pool** may be the perfect cure. Unfortunately, most of Rome's pools are privately run and can be quite expensive, though there are a couple of affordable public pools (see also "Gyms"). If you fancy a spot of real pampering it's worth booking a day at a hotel spa.

Public pools

Oasi della Pace Via degli Eugenii 2 ☎06.718.4550; June–Sept daily 9.30am–6pm. The "Oasis of Peace" is just off the Via Appia – an atmospheric place to take a dip in this lovely open-air pool.

La Piscina delle Rose Viale America 20 ☎06.592.6717, ⓦwww.piscinadellerose.it. Mon–Fri 10am–10pm, Sat & Sun 9am–7pm. Down in EUR, and easily reachable on metro line #B, this is Rome's largest public pool, accessible for a rate of €13 a half-day, €16 a day, or €45 a week.

Hotel pools

Cavalieri Hilton Via Cadloro 101 ☎06.3509.2950, ⓦwww.cavalieri-hilton.it. Mon–Fri 7am–11pm, Sat & Sun 8am–9pm. Luxury outside and indoor pools – the outdoor pool is Olympic size. But it will cost you around €49 to use it.

Parco dei Principi Via Frescobaldi 5 ☎06.854.421, ⓦwww.parcodeiprincipi.com. This outdoor pool is set in its own gardens right on the edge of Villa Borghese and as such a lovely central choice for a dip. €50 or so and it's yours.

Tennis

The massive **Foro Italico** sports complex (see p.166) hosts the Italian Open, or Rome Masters as it's now known, one of the city's biggest annual sporting events, held during the first two weeks of May. For more information contact the Federazione Italiana Tennis, Via Eustachio 9 (☎06.855.894, ⓦwww.federtennis.it), or the Foro Italico itself (☎06.3685.8218). If you want to hire courts to play, the Foro Italico also has public courts, or there's the Circolo della Stampa, Piazza Mancini 9 (☎06.323.2454) and Tennis Belle Arte, Via Flaminia 158 (☎06.323.3355). Courts cost €10–12 an hour.

Kids' Rome

talians love **children**. Don't be surprised by how much attention people pay yours here: peeking into buggies and cheek-pinching are quite normal, as is help lugging pushchairs up steps and giving up a seat for you and your child on public transport. That said, Rome has a surprisingly limited number of activities specifically geared towards children, though there have been significant improvements of late. Luckily, touring the sights of Rome is something that children can enjoy if it's approached in the right way – hopping on and off one of the several open-top bus tours (see p.27) is a great way of giving them a fun introduction to the city's highlights, while certain places are especially interesting for kids – Castel Sant'Angelo with its park and playground, the Colosseum (where there are usually Roman soldiers dressed up in full costume), and of course throwing coins into the Trevi Fountain and sticking your hand in the Bocca della Verità and daring to tell a fib. There is also a handful of relatively new attractions, aimed directly at children, notably the Time Elevator, Explora – Museo dei Bambini di Roma, and the Bioparco (zoo). Of Rome's parks, the Villa Borghese is the most convenient, and has a lot to offer kids – rowboats, a little train, pony rides, bikes, and, on its northeastern side, the zoo. If all else fails, there's always LUNEUR Park, a large, old-fashioned amusement park in EUR.

Eating out with kids in Rome is easy – Roman food appeals to kids and the numerous pasta and pizza options ensure that there's something for even the fussiest of eaters (failing that the kitchen is almost always willing to rustle you up a plate of plain spaghetti with butter and parmesan), while the relaxed waiting staff go out of their way to charm and amuse the kids. And, if you're on the go, you can always head to the nearest *gelato* stand, or grab a slice of juicy pizza to keep them quiet. For more information, *Romacè's* (see Basics, p.36) English section often has details of what's on for children that week.

Babysitting services

If you simply have to have a break from the kids one day or for an evening, English-speaking **babysitters** are available through a firm called Angels, Via dei Fienili 98 ⊤06.678.2877, ⑤06.678.9246, ⑥eaupairs65@hotmail.com.

Books and maps

Pick up the English version of *ConosciRoma*, available free from any tourist kiosk; it's a children's **map** of the centre with interesting facts about sights, daily

If it's hot and you're having a hellish time in the city, it might just be best to call it a day and get away, either for a picnic or an energy-releasing romp. **Day-trips** kids might enjoy include Ostia Antica (see p.209), Villa d'Este and Villa Adriana in Tivoli (see p.208), and, further afield, the charming town of Bracciano (see p.213) with its beautiful lake offering swimming and boating, and the Parco dei Mostri (Park of Monsters) at Bomarzo (℡0761.924.029, ⊛www.bomarzo.net, daily 8am–sunset; €9, 4–8yrs €7), 93km north of Rome – basically a garden, but with crazy sculptures, weird buildings and surreal conceits that make it one of Lazio's top tourist attractions. You can get to Bomarzo by bus from Viterbo, which in turn is easily reached by train from either Rome San Pietro or the Laziale platform at Termini.

Finally, the sandy beaches at Anzio and Nettuno (see p.217) are only 40km south of the city or an hour by train, and easily reached on a day-trip.

life of ancient Rome, and stickers. While you're there grab a copy of the free *ConosciRoma* booklet (Italian only) "*La città per ogni età*" which has details of what to do with your kids in Rome usefully divided by age group. The "then and now" books of ancient sites with overlay transparencies can also work wonders to bring piles of weathered stones to life; they're available at most city-centre bookstores.

Parks and outdoor activities

Bioparco Via del Giardino Zoologico, Villa Borghese ℡06.360.8211, ⊛www.bioparco.it. Daily: Jan–March & Nov–Dec 9.30am–5pm; April–Oct 9.30am–6pm, open till 7pm Sat & Sun April–Sept; €8.50 adults, €6.50 3- to 12-year-olds. Rome's zoo, on the northern edge of the Villa Borghese (see below) is a large, typical city-centre zoo, recently much improved and reinvented as the "Bioparco" and focusing on conservation and education yet still providing the usual animals kids are after – tigers, apes, giraffes, elephants, hippos and much more – though the separate *Rettilario* (Reptile house) for some reason costs an extra €2.50, a bit of a rip-off. The zoological museum next door – see below – has also been revamped.

Gianicolo This park, high up on Janiculum Hill, is a good place to keep kids amused, with pony rides, carousels, balloon sellers and puppet shows, while adults enjoy a great view of the city below. The puppet shows (see box, p.286) are top-notch and kids can choose to take their favourite character home with them from the colourful selection on sale. You might want to time your visit to coincide with the daily firing of the cannon at noon. See also p.174.

LUNEUR Park Via delle Tre Fontane ℡06.592.5933, ⊛www.luneur.it. Mon–Fri

4pm–midnight, Sat 4pm–1am, Sun 4pm–midnight; free entrance, rides cost €1–3. This amusement park in the EUR district is the only place in Rome that you'll find big-scale amusements – a rollercoaster, haunted house, Ferris wheel and the like. It's a bit dated, but is still very popular with families, and there are loads of diversions aimed at pint-sized clients.

Orto Botanico Via Corsini. Tues–Sat 9.30am–6.30pm, adults €4, children under 6 free, 6–11 years €2. A peaceful oasis in the heart of Trastevere, the city's botanical gardens have palm-lined paths, fountains, a meandering rose garden, towering bamboo patches and lush greenhouses to keep the kids amused for a while. The benches and paths around the Fountain of Tritons, near the entrance, are a meeting place for local mothers, nannies and toddlers. See also p.173.

Villa Ada Beautiful grounds just north of the city with plenty to keep youngsters amused, including a roller-skating rink, bike paths, two playgrounds and ponds.

Villa Borghese As well as the Bioparco (see above), this huge park offers plenty of entertainment for young ones. Enter at the northern side, via the Viale delle Belle Arti entrance, to find pony rides, a children's train, swings and paddleboats on the lake complete with Greek temple. On the southern side of the park, the Pincio Gardens have a playground and carousels. You can also take a fifteen-minute ride in a tethered hot-air balloon from next to Il Galoppatoio during certain months (T06.321.1511) and hire bikes and rollerblades (see p.153).

Villa Celimontana Up on the Celian Hill, these public gardens have nice views over the river, a playground and pony rides. See also p.108.

Villa Doria Pamphili Main entrance on Via di San Pancrazio. A ten-minute walk east from the Janiculum Hill, Rome's largest park is a great place for kids to let off steam – more like real countryside in parts, it's the perfect walking, cycling or picnic spot and has a pretty lake filled with basking turtles and surrounded by woods. See also p.178.

Villa Sciarra Entrances on Via Calandrelli and Viale Mura Gianicolensi. A little way to the south of the Janiculum Hill, this small park is a bit out of the way but has a lovely little playground, though the adjacent aviary has seen better days and is now populated largely by pigeons.

Museums and attractions

Castel Sant'Angelo Lungotevere Castello 50. Tues–Sun 9am–7.30pm, adults €8, children free, free guided tours in English Sat & Sun 4.30pm. Along with the Colosseum this is one of the most exciting of the city's ancient monuments for kids. Hadrian's mausoleum has through the centuries served as a papal escape route in times of trouble and the city's prison and has all the grisly, dungeon-like spookiness you'd expect from such a history – fortifications, drawbridges, lots of suits of armour and swords, plus a wide, spiral ramp leading to the mausoleum itself add to the atmosphere. There are also great views over the city from the top.

Colosseum Daily 8.30am to one hour before sunset; adults €11, children from EU countries under 18 free, non-EU countries €6.50. Loaded with atmosphere given its setting as the stage for many a grisly end for both humans and beasts, Rome's most famous ancient monument can't fail to capture kids' imaginations. For €5 they can have their picture taken with one of the gladiators outside. See also p.102.

Explora – Museo dei Bambini di Roma Via Flaminia 82 T06.361.3776, Wwww.mdbr.it. Timed entry for 1hr 45min slots: Jan–June & Oct–Dec Tues–Fri at 9.30am, 11.30am, 3pm & 5pm, Sat & Sun 10am, noon, 3pm & 5pm; July & Sept Tues–Sun at 10am, noon, 3pm & 5pm; Aug Tues–Sun at noon, 3pm & 5pm; advance booking recommended. Adults €6, children €7, 0–3 years free. Geared towards kids under 12, this learn-as-you-play centre aims to teach children about themselves and the world they live in through hands-on activities. It's all laid out in the form of a small city

---

Piazzas, playgrounds and pussycats.

Rome's abundant **piazzas** with their cobbled expanses, fountains and cafés are often just as much fun for kids to run around in as **playgrounds** – especially in the early evening when everyone's out for a stroll and the street sellers and buskers liven things up even more. Piazza Santa Maria in Trastevere is always a lively place, as is Piazza Navona (with the added attraction of two toy shops, see p.286–287) and Piazza di Spagna. Villa Borghese, Villa Sciarra, Villa Ada and Villa Celimontana all have playgrounds; there's also a very good play area in Testaccio, at Piazza Santa Maria Liberatrice and a smaller play area in Piazza San Cosimato in Trastevere.

The city's **cat colonies** are usually a big hit with kids – check out the one at Largo Argentina where cat-spotting among the ancient ruins is a popular pastime while, at the cat sanctuary alongside it, kids can get close up to some of the inhabitants that are up for adoption. The volunteers who look after the cats here also take care of various other colonies around the city – notable ones to visit are those at the Colosseum, at Piazza Vittorio Emanuele II in Monti (see p.146) and around the Piramide Cestia in Testaccio (see p.144). You can find out more at Wwww.romancats.com.

– kids can shop in the mini-supermarket, pay cheques in at the bank, fill up their car at the garage and post mail in the post office. There's also plenty of purely fun stuff, such as a puppet theatre and a playground. **Museo della Civiltà Romana & Planetario e Museo Astronomico Piazza Agnelli 10, EUR** ☎06.592.6041. Tues–Sat 9am–2pm, Sun 9am–1.30pm; adults € 6.50, €8.50 including planetarium, children free. On your way to LUNEUR Park, stop by this Roman Civilization museum, where you can see replicas of Rome's famous statues and buildings, as well as more everyday artefacts. Kids will love the model of Rome in the time of Constantine, which takes up a whole room. On the same site, there's also a planetarium and astronomy exhibition (€6.50, €8.50 including Roman museum) but it's not as thrilling as you'd expect and audio shows are only in Italian.

Museo di Zoologia Via Aldovrandi 18 ☎06.6710.9270. Tues–Sun 9am–5pm; €4.50, kids under 18 free. Located next to the Bioparco, this museum, like the zoo, has had a recent facelift. A new permanent exhibit, *Animals and their Habitats*, is on

display in a new wing, while a variety of stuffed animals fill the older part of the museum, and the "bear cave" is always a scary treat.

Ostia Antica Viale dei Romagnoli, Ostia Antica. April–Oct Tues–Sun 8.30am–6pm; March 8.30am–5pm; Nov–Feb 8.30am–4pm. Adults €4, children free. Every bit as atmospheric and mesmerizing as Pompeii, the ruins of Rome's ancient port will give kids a great feel for what a Roman city was like. It's a must-see for any child who has read *The Thieves of Ostia*, the first in the Roman Mysteries series by Caroline Lawrence, in which a sea captain's daughter and her pals set about solving a mystery in 79AD Ostia.

Time Elevator Via dei Santissimi Apostoli 20 ☎06.977.46243, ⓦwww.time-elevator.it. Daily 10.30am–7.30pm; €11, 5–12s €8. Flight-simulator seats and headphones (English audio available) set the stage for a 45-minute virtual tour of three thousand years of Roman history; an excellent way to prime the kids for the sights they will be seeing, not to mention their parents. Shows every 30min; not suitable for children under 5.

Shops: books, toys and clothing

Benetton Via Cesare Battisti 129 ☎06.6992.4010. Mon 3.30–7.30pm, Tues–Sat 9.30am–1pm & 3.30–7.30pm. Just one of the several locations of this famous Italian chain store that sells fairly expensive clothes for children and adults. This one

conveniently has a children's hairdresser on the second floor.

Bertè Piazza Navona 108 ☎06.687.5011. Mon 3.30–7.30pm, Tues–Sat 9.30am–1pm & 3.30–7.30pm. One of Rome's oldest toy stores at the other end of the piazza from Al Sogno

Rome's puppet theatres

Puppetry has been delighting Italian children for hundreds of years, and Rome has a few venues for viewing true puppeteers in action. Sometimes you can find a show in English, but the storyline is visually explanatory and kids don't seem to care whether they understand the words or not.

The **outdoor theatres** on the Janiculum Hill (see p.174), and in EUR on Largo K. Ataturk, are said to be the only places to view the true puppeteers left in Rome. Both are free, although a small donation is expected. You can also see shows near the Janiculum at Teatro Verde, Circonvallazione Gianicolense 10 (☎06.588.2034, ⓦwww .teatroverde.it), a children's theatre where they also put on musicals and marionette shows (€6.80). Most puppet shows run from around 4pm till 7pm on weekdays and from 10.30am until 1pm at weekends. The Puppet Theatre, Piazza dei Satiri (☎06.589.6201), puts on familiar fairy tales at 5pm on Sunday afternoons, while Testaccio's Teatro Vittoria (see p.264) has been known to mount variety shows that children can easily enjoy.

La Befana

There are many stories about **La Befana**, always depicted as an ugly old woman who flies along on a broom draped in black. The most recognized version is that she was outside sweeping when the three kings walked by; she stopped them and asked where they were going. The kings responded that they were following a star, in search of a newborn baby. They invited her to come along, but she declined, saying she had too much sweeping and cleaning to do. When she found out who it was the kings were off to find, her regret for not having joined them was so great that she has spent eternity rewarding good children with presents and sweets and bad children with pieces of coal on the day of Epiphany, January 6. Each year, from early December until January 6, Piazza Navona sets up the Befana toy fair, where endless stalls tempt children with every sort of sticky sweet and even chunks of black sugar made to look like coal. There are also toy stands and several manger scenes where children sometimes leave letters for La Befana, asking her for specific presents and toys.

(see below), that has a complete range of toys for children of all ages.

La Bottega di Marinella Via Margutta 34 ℡06.324.4793, ℉06.361.4143. Mon 3.30–7.30pm, Tues–Sat 9.30am–7.30pm. Adorable children's store on swanky Via Margutta, selling their own designs of infant and young children's clothes, plus fabrics to brighten up any child's bedroom.

La Cicogna Via Frattina 138 ℡06.679.1912; Via Cola di Rienzo 268 ℡06.689.6557. Mon–Sat 10.30am–7.30pm, Sun 11am–7pm. From newborns to adolescents, these stylish outlets of the national chain ("The Stork") carry designer everything for kids, and maternity wear for expectant mothers, too. Not cheap.

Città del Sole Via della Scrofa 66 ℡06.6880.3805. Mon 3.30–7.30pm, Tues–Sat 11am–1.30pm. Toys, games and books for kids in a great central location.

IANA Via Cola di Rienzo 182 ℡06.6889.2668. Mon 3.30–7.30pm, Tues–Sat 10am–1.30pm &

3.30–7.30pm. Popular Italian chain store offering moderately priced kids' clothes.

Marina Menasci Via del Lavatore 87 ℡06.678.1981. Mon 3.30–7.30pm, Tues–Sat 9.30am–1pm & 3.30–7.30pm. Toy store that sells exclusively wooden toys, in a great location a few steps from the Trevi Fountain.

Mel Giannino Stoppani Piazza Santi Apostoli 59/62 ℡06.6994.1045. Mon–Sat 10–8pm, Sun 10.30am–1.30pm & 4.30–6.30pm. Fantastic specialist kids bookstore, mainly Italian but with a small stock of books in foreign languages, as well as DVDs and puzzles and games too.

Al Sogno Piazza Navona 53 ℡06.686.4198. Mon 3.30–7.30pm, Tues–Sat 9.30am–1pm & 3.30–7.30pm. Perfectly located at the north end of Piazza Navona, two floors of stuffed animals, handmade dolls, board games, and replicas of Roman soldiers.

Contexts

Contexts

History

T
he history of Rome is almost the history of the western world, and as such is hard to encapsulate in a potted guidebook form. Inevitably the best we can do here is provide the basic framework. However, knowing at least some Roman history is crucial to an understanding of the city – its sights and monuments are often interconnected and will mean much more if you have a basic grasp of the continuum of events and their relationships to each other. We've tried to contextualize as much of the information in the guide as possible, but we recommend you take a look at some of the historical texts we list in "Books", p.319 – Edward Gibbon or Tom Holland on ancient Rome and the empire, and perhaps the novels of Robert Graves or Allan Massie for a dramatized take on the same. For a general and very readable overview, Christopher Hibbert's "biography" of the city is excellent, and Christopher Duggan's *History Of Italy* gives a good account of key events in Italian history and how they shaped and affected the capital.

Beginnings

No one knows precisely when Rome was founded, though excavations on the Palatine Hill have revealed the traces of an **Iron Age** village dating back to the ninth or eighth century BC. The **legends** relating to Rome's earliest history tell it slightly differently. Rea Silvia, a Vestal Virgin and daughter of a local king, Numitor, had twin sons – the product, she alleged, of a rape by Mars. They were supposed to be sacrificed to the gods but instead the two boys were abandoned and found by a wolf, which nursed them until their adoption by a shepherd, who named them **Romulus and Remus**. Later they laid out the boundaries of the city on the Palatine Hill (after arguing as to its exact location Remus chose the Aventine Hill and Romulus the Palatine Hill, and the latter won), but it soon became apparent that there was only room for one ruler, and, unable to agree on the signs given to them by the gods, they quarrelled, Romulus killing Remus and becoming the city's first ruler, in 753 BC.

Whatever the truth of this, there's no doubt that Rome was an obvious spot to build a city: the Palatine and Capitoline hills provided security, and there was, of course, the **River Tiber**, which could be easily crossed here by way of the Isola Tiberina, making this a key location on the trade routes between the neighbouring regions of Etruria and Campania.

The Etruscans

The **Etruscans** dominated Etruria – the area of Italy from the northern part of the peninsula as far south as Rome. Little of their history is known, their language was of non Indo-European origin, the architecture that survives is almost exclusively that of tombs, and their art has a particular and personal quality quite unlike that of the Romans or even the Greeks. Long before other Italic tribes, they took the important steps towards creating central urban nuclei, with twelve city-states, and at the height of their civilization in the sixth century BC one of their greatest cities, Cerveteri (or Caere) had a population of over 25,000. Rome may or may not have been an Etruscan town, but the Etruscans' influence on the kingdom of Rome was very strong, and three of its legendary seven kings were Etruscan, the first being **Tarquinius Priscus** (616–579 BC). Under his rule, Rome began to develop as a city: the first buildings of the Forum were raised, the rudiments of the city's sewage and water system – the *Cloaca Maxima* – were put in place, and the walls of the Capitoline Hill were built. Rich finds from this period include the contents of the Regolini-Calassi tomb, displayed in the Vatican museum, and there are numerous artefacts from all over northern Lazio in the city's marvellous Villa Giulia. Although the Romans finally overcame the Etruscans (see below) and obliterated much of their history, it is likely that the Etruscan influence on Rome continued long into the Republic – indeed it was an Etruscan soothsayer, Spurinna, who warned Julius Caesar about the ides of March.

The Roman Republic

Rome as a kingdom lasted until about 509 BC, when the people rose up against the last, tyrannical Etruscan monarch, **Tarquinius Superbus**. Tarquinius was a brutal, unpopular ruler, but the crunch came when his son, Sextus, raped a Roman noblewoman, Lucretia. She committed suicide shortly after, and her husband, along with one Lucius Junius Brutus, helped to lead an uprising that led eventually to the establishment of a **Republic** – a reaction, basically, against the autocratic rule of the Etruscan monarchs. The Roman Republic was to last nearly five hundred years, and was a surprisingly modern, and democratic, form of government, based on the acknowledged fact that the fate of the Roman people and its patrician classes were inextricably bound up together (the acronym SPQR, which you still see everywhere, stands for "Senatus Populusque Romanus" or "The Roman Senate and People" or as the French cartoon character Obelix would have it "Sono Pazzi Questi Romani" – "these Romans are crazy"). The **Senate** represented the patrician families, and elected two consuls from their number to lead Rome – in itself a forward-thinking act after years of absolute rule – while the people were allowed to elect two tribunes to represent their interests, even vetoing the appointment of senators they disagreed with. The city prospered under the Republic, growing greatly in size and subduing the various tribes of the surrounding areas – the Volsci and Etruscans to the north, the Sabines to the east, the Samnites to the south. The Etruscans were finally beaten in 474 BC, at the battle of Cumae, and the Volsci and Sabines soon after. Rome later drew up its first set of laws, in 451 BC, inscribing them on bronze tablets and displaying them prominently in the Forum – by now the city's most important central space.

Despite a heavy defeat by the **Gauls** in 390 BC, when they took the entire city except for the Capitoline Hill (a night assault was reputedly foiled by the cackling of sacred geese kept on the hill which woke the besieged soldiers), by the following century the city had begun to extend its influence beyond the boundaries of what is now mainland Italy, pushing south into Sicily and across the ocean to Africa and Carthage. In the meantime Rome was also trying to subdue the **Samnites**, who occupied most of the land in the southern part of what is now Italy, waging wars on and off between 343 BC and 290 BC that led eventually to the Romans occupying most of the region that is now Campania, south of Rome. Beyond mainland Italy, the next hundred years or so were taken up by the **Punic Wars**, against **Carthage**, the other dominant force in the Mediterranean at the time, and really the only thing standing between Rome and total dominance of the region. The First Punic War, fought over Sicily, began in 264 BC, and continued for around twenty years until Carthage surrendered all rights to the island, while the Second Punic War was famously started in 218 BC by Hannibal's march across the Alps by elephant, and ended, after years of skirmishes in southern Italy, in 202 BC. By the time Rome had fought and won the Third Punic War, in 146 BC, it had become the dominant power in the Mediterranean, subsequently taking control of present-day Greece and the Middle East, and expanding north, also, into what is now France, Germany and Britain.

Domestically, the Romans built **roads** – notably the Via Appia, which dates back to 312 BC and was built as a means of moving around troops during the Samnite wars – and developed their civic structure, with new laws and far-sighted political reforms, one of which cannily brought all of the Republic's vanquished enemies into the fold as **Roman citizens**. However, the history of the Republic was also one of internal strife, marked by factional fighting among the patrician ruling classes, as everyone tried to grab a slice of the riches that were pouring into the city from its plundering expeditions abroad – and the ordinary people, or plebeians, enjoying little more justice than they had under the Roman monarchs. In 87 BC, a power struggle between two consuls, Lucius Cornelius Sulla and Gaius Marius, led to a **civil war** in which Sulla, in 82 BC, eventually emerged as the sole leader of Rome. He initiated terrifying revenge against his opponents and introduced laws which greatly reduced the powers of the city's elected and appointed officials. Gaius Marius's nephew, **Julius Caesar**, later emerged as a powerful military leader and over the course of eight long years he conquered Gaul and Britain, and then returned to fight another civil war against his rival Pompey, which he won. Following this victory, he was proclaimed "dictator of Rome". It was the last straw for those eager to restore some semblance of the republican vision, and Caesar was murdered in the Theatre of Pompey on March 15, 44 BC, by conspirators concerned at the growing concentration of power into one man's hands.

However, rather than returning Rome to the glorious days of the Republic, the murder of Caesar in fact threw it back into turmoil. After his death, Julius Caesar's deputy, **Mark Antony**, briefly took control, joining forces with Lepidus and Caesar's adopted son, Octavian, in a **triumvirate**. Their armies fought against, and defeated those controlled by, Caesar's assassins, Brutus and Cassius, in a famous battle at Philippi, in modern-day Greece, in 42 BC. Their alliance was further cemented by Antony's marriage to Octavian's sister, Octavia, in 40 AD, but in spite of this things did not go well for the triumvirate. Lepidus was imprisoned and Antony, unable to put his political ambitions before his emotional bond with the queen of Egypt, Cleopatra, was defeated by Octavian at the battle of Actium in 31 BC. Antony escaped to Alexandria, where he committed suicide, with his lover, the queen, leaving Octavian in command.

The Imperial era

A triumph for the new democrats over the old guard, **Augustus** (27 BC–14 AD) – as Octavian became known – was the first true Roman emperor, in firm control of Rome and its dominions; indeed "Augustus" became the name by which all future Roman emperors were known. Responsible more than anyone

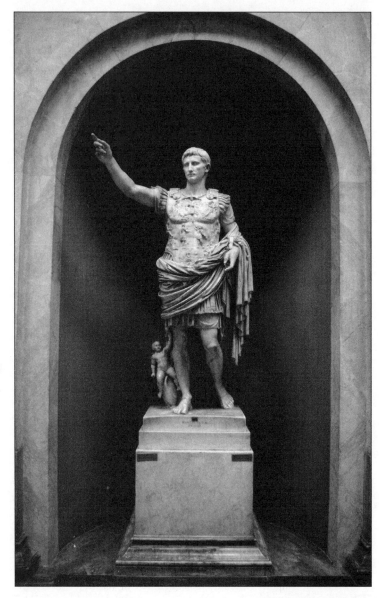

△ Augustus, the Vatican Museums

for heaving Rome into the Imperial era, Augustus was determined to turn the city – as he claimed – from one of stone to one of marble, building arches, theatres and monuments of a magnificence suited to the capital of an expanding empire. Perhaps the best and certainly the most politically canny of Rome's many emperors, Augustus reigned for forty years.

Augustus was succeeded by his stepson, **Tiberius** (14–37 AD) who ruled from the island of Capri for the last years of his reign, and he in turn by **Caligula** (37–41 AD), a poor and possibly insane ruler who was assassinated after just four years in power. **Claudius** (41–54 AD), his uncle, followed, at first reluctantly, and proved to be a wise ruler, only to be succeeded by his stepson, **Nero** (54–68 AD), whose reign became more notorious for its excess than its prudence, and led to a brief period of warring and infighting after his murder in 68 AD, with Vitellius, Galba and Vespasian all vying for the position of emperor.

Vespasian (69–79 AD) was eventually proclaimed emperor, thus starting a dynasty – the **Flavian** – which was to restore some stability to Rome and its empire. Vespasian started as he meant to go on, doing his best to obliterate all traces of Nero, not least with an enormous amphitheatre in the grounds of Nero's palace, later known as the Colosseum. Vespasian was succeeded by his son, **Titus** (79–81 AD), and soon after by his other son – Titus's brother – **Domitian** (81–96 AD), who reverted to imperial type, becoming an ever more paranoid and despotic ruler until his murder in 96 AD, when all his decrees were declared void. **Nerva** was declared emperor (96–98 AD) thus beginning the rule of the "five good emperors" who were known for their moderate policies and for giving Rome much needed stability under the Pax Romana. He was succeeded by his adopted son (successors being chosen by merit), **Trajan** (98–117 AD), whose enlightened leadership once again allowed Rome and its colonies to settle to some sort of stability. Trajan also expanded the empire greatly, conquering the lands to the east – Turkey and modern-day Romania – and it was under his rule that the empire reached its maximum limits. Trajan died in 117 AD, giving way to his cousin, **Hadrian** (117–38 AD), who continued the grand and expansionist agenda of his predecessor, and arguably provided the empire's greatest years. The city swelled to a population of a million or more, its people housed in cramped apartment blocks or *insulae*; crime in the city was rife, and the traffic problem apparently on a par with today's, prompting one contemporary writer to complain that the din on the streets made it impossible to get a good night's sleep. But it was a time of peace and prosperity, the Roman upper classes living a life of indolent luxury, in sumptuous residences with proper plumbing and central heating such as Hadrian's own villa at Tivoli. Hadrian's successor, **Antoninus Pius** (138–61 AD), and then **Marcus Aurelius** (161–80 AD), ruled over a largely peaceful and economically successful empire, until 180 AD, when Marcus Aurelius's son, **Commodus** (180–192 AD), assumed the throne but wasn't up to the task, and Rome entered a more fragile phase. Predictably, Commodus was murdered, and eventually replaced by **Septimius Severus** (193–211 AD), thus initiating the Severan dynasty – again a time of relative calm, although the political and military skills of Severus unfortunately weren't matched by those of his sons, Geta and Caracalla. **Caracalla** (211–17 AD) murdered his brother before assuming power for himself in 211 AD.

The **decline of Rome** is hard to date precisely, but it could be said to have started with the emperor **Diocletian** (284–305 AD), an army officer from present-day Croatia who assumed power in 284 AD and, in an attempt to consolidate the empire, divided it into two parts, east and west. Known also for his relentless persecution of Christians, Diocletian abdicated in 305 AD, retiring to the vast palace he had built for himself in what is now Split, on the Dalmatian coast, giving rise to a power struggle that concluded with the battle of the Ponte Milvio in Rome, in which Constantine defeated his rival, Maxentius, at the same time as converting to Christianity due to a vision of a cross in the sky he saw the evening before the battle. The first Christian emperor, **Constantine** (306–37 AD), ended Diocletian's persecution of the

The Rulers of Rome

Roman Kings
Romulus (753 BC–716 BC)
Numa Pompilius (715 BC–674 BC)
Tullus Hostilius (673 BC–642 BC)
Ancus Marcius (642 BC–617 BC)
Lucius Tarquinius Priscus (616 BC–579 BC)
Servius Tullius (578 BC–535 BC)
Lucius Tarquinius Superbus (535 BC–509 BC)

Roman Republic
c.509 BC–82 BC (death of Marius)

Roman Dictators and Triumvirs
Sulla (82–78 BC)
Triumvirate of Julius Caesar, **Pompey** and **Crassus** (60–53 BC)
Pompey (52–47 BC)
Julius Caesar (45–44 BC)
Triumvirate of Antony, **Octavian Caesar (Augustus)** and **Lepidus** (43–27 BC)

Roman Emperors
Augustus (27 BC–AD 14)
Tiberius (14–37)
Caligula (37–41)
Claudius (41–54)
Nero (54–68)
Galba (68–69)
Otho (69)
Vitellius (69)
Vespasian (69–79)
Titus (79–81)

Domitian (81–96)
Nerva (96–98)
Trajan (98–117)
Hadrian (117–138)
Antonius Pius (138–161)
Lucius Verus (161–169) co-emperor with **Marcus Aurelius** (161–180) co-emperor with **Commodus** (177–192)
Pertinax (192–193)
Didius Julianus (193)
Septimius Severus (193–211) co-emperor with **Geta** (209–211) co-emperor with **Caracalla** (211–217)
Macrinus (217–218)
Elagabalus (218–222)
Alexander Severus (222–235)
Maximinus Thrax (235–238)
Gordian III (238–244)
Marcus Philippus (244–249)
Decius (249–251)
Trebonianus Gallus (251–253)
Aemilianus (253)
Valerian (253–260) co-emperor with **Gallienus** (253–268)
Claudius II (268–270)
Quintillus (270)
Aurelian (270–275)
Marcus Claudius Tacitus (275–276)
Florianus (276)
Probus (276–282)
Carus (282–283)
Carinus (283–285) in competition with **Diocletian** (284–305)
Constantine I (306–337)

faith, and shifted the seat of power to Byzantium in 325 AD, renaming it Constantinople. Rome's heady period as capital of the world was over, and the wealthier members of the population moved east. A series of invasions by Goths in 410 AD and Vandals about forty years later only served to quicken the city's ruin. The imperial buildings decayed and became buried, the Roman Forum languishing beneath the Campo Vaccino or "cow pasture", and by the sixth century the city was a devastated and infection-ridden shadow of its former self, with a population of just twenty thousand.

The rise of the papacy

It was the **papacy**, under Pope **Gregory I** ("the Great"; 590–604) in 590, that rescued Rome from its demise. Thomas Hobbes described the papacy as none other than "the Ghost of the deceased Roman Empire, sitting crowned upon the grave" and in an eerie echo of the empire, Gregory sent missions all over Europe to spread the word of the Church. The missions publicized its holy relics, so drawing pilgrims, and their money, back to the city, and in time making the papacy the natural authority in Rome. The pope took the name "Pontifex Maximus" after the title of the high priest of classical times (literally "the keeper of the bridges", which were vital to the city's well-being). Four of the city's great basilicas were built during this time, along with a great many other early Christian churches, underlining the city's phoenix-like resurrection under the popes, who as well as building their own new structures converted those Roman buildings that were still standing – for example fortifying the Castel Sant'Angelo to repel invaders and converting the Pantheon into a Christian church. The crowning a couple of centuries later of Charlemagne as **Holy Roman Emperor**, with dominions spread Europe-wide but answerable to the pope, intensified the city's revival, and the pope and city became recognized as head of the Christian world.

There were times over the next few hundred years when the power of Rome and the papacy was weakened. Conflict between the pope and the Holy Roman Emperor raged. While the Holy Roman Emperor could claim absolute power over the secular world, the pope claimed not only spiritual power but also the right to crown and therefore validate the emperor. At times popes excommunicated emperors, at other times emperors imprisoned popes. The Ghibellines (supporters of the emperor) and the Guelphs (supporters of the pope) ravaged many Italian cities and Rome was attacked on several occasions. Robert Guiscard, the Norman king, sacked the city in 1084; a century later, a dispute between the city and the papacy led to a series of popes relocating in Viterbo. Things became so unstable that in 1308 the French-born Pope **Clement V** (1305–14) transferred his court to Avignon. In the mid-fourteenth century, Cola di Rienzo, a self-styled "tribune" of Rome, seized power, setting himself up as the people's saviour from the decadent ways of the city's rulers and forming a new Roman republic. But the increasingly autocratic ways of the new ruler soon lost popularity; Cola di Rienzo was deposed, and in 1376 Pope **Gregory XI** (1370–78) returned to Rome. However, things got distinctly worse shortly after Gregory's death when a dispute over his successor's election led to the Great Schism and the unnerving proposition of two popes – one in Rome and the other in Avignon. This was finally resolved in 1417, with the election of the Colonna family pope, Martin V, but the battling popes had taken their toll on the fabric of Rome.

The Renaissance and Counter Reformation

As time went on, power gradually became concentrated in a handful of wealthy Roman **families**, who swapped the top jobs, including the papacy itself, between them. Under the burgeoning power of these popes, the city began to take on a new aspect. The names of the families are etched on the city's buildings – Villa Borghese, Piazza Barberini, Palazzo Farnese. Churches were built, the city's pagan monuments rediscovered and preserved, and artists began to arrive in Rome to work on commissions for the latest pope, who would invariably try to outdo his predecessor's efforts with ever more glorious self-aggrandizing buildings and works of art.

This process reached a head during the **Renaissance**; Bramante, Raphael and Michelangelo all worked in the city, on and off, throughout their careers. The reigns of Pope **Julius II** (1503–13) and his successor, the Medici pope, **Leo X** (1513–21), were something of a golden age: the city was at the centre of Italian cultural and artistic life and site of the creation of great works of art like Michelangelo's frescoes in the Sistine Chapel, Raphael's Stanze in the Vatican Palace and fine buildings like the Villa Farnesina, Palazzo Farnese and Palazzo Spada, not to mention the commissioning of a new St Peter's as well as any number of other churches. Many of the capital's national art collections began life under these patrons of the arts. The city was once again at the centre of things, and its population had increased to a hundred thousand. However, in 1527 all this was brought abruptly to an end, when the armies of the Habsburg monarch and Holy Roman Emperor, **Charles V**, swept into the city determined to avenge himself after having been excommunicated by Pope Clement VII (1523-34). He occupied the city and wreaked havoc for a year while the pope cowered in the Castel Sant'Angelo, witnessing the end to the splendours of Renaissance Rome.

The ensuing years were ones of yet more restoration, and perhaps because of this it's the **seventeenth century** that has left the most tangible impression on Rome today, the vigour of the **Counter Reformation** throwing up huge, sensational monuments like the Gesù church that were designed to confound the scepticism of the new Protestant thinking, and again using pagan artefacts (like obelisks), not to mention the ready supply of building materials provided by the city's ruins, in ever more extravagant displays of wealth. The Farnese pope, **Paul III** (1534–49), was perhaps the most efficient at quashing anti-Catholic feeling, while, later, Pope **Sixtus V** (1585–90) was perhaps the most determined to mould the city in his own image, ploughing roads through the centre and laying out bold new squares at their intersections. This period also saw the completion of St Peter's under **Paul V** (1605–21), and the ascendancy of Gian Lorenzo Bernini as the city's principal architect and sculptor under the Barberini pope, **Urban VIII** (1623–44) – a patronage that was extended under the Pamphilj pope, **Innocent X** (1644–55).

The eighteenth and nineteenth centuries

The **eighteenth century** saw the decline of the papacy as a political force, a phenomenon marked by the occupation of the city in 1798 by Napoleon's forces; **Pius VI** (1775–1800) was unceremoniously sent off to France as a prisoner, and Napoleon declared another Roman republic, with himself at its head, which lasted until 1815, when papal rule was restored under **Pius VII** (1800–23). The years that followed were fairly quiet in Rome, if not in the rest of Italy, where the relatively despotic rules of the various city-states and fiefdoms that made up what we now know as Italy were at odds with the new ideas of centralization and modernization of the **reunification movement**, led by Giuseppe Mazzini. The revolutionary year of 1848, when popular revolts were sparked all over Europe, led to widespread unrest in Italy. In 1849 a pro-Unification caucus under **Mazzini** declared the city a republic and forced Pope Pius IX to leave Rome in disguise. However, Mazzini was chased out after a short four months by Napoleon III, who restored the papacy. There was further fighting

Papal Reigns

Celestine III (1191–1198)
Innocent III (1198–1216)
Honorius III (1216–1127)
Gregory IX (1227–1241)
Celestine IV (1241)
Innocent IV (1243–1254)
Alexander IV (1254–1261)
Urban IV (1261–1264)
Clement IV (1265–1268)
Gregory X (1271–1276)
Innocent V (1276)
Adrian V (1276)
John XXI (1276–1277)
Nicholas III (l277–1280)
Martin IV (1281–1285)
Honorlus IV (1285–1287)
Nicholas IV (1288–1292)
Celestine V (1294)
Boniface VIII (1294–1303)
Benedict XI (1303–1304)
Clement V (1305–1314)
John XXII (1316–1334)
Benedict XII (1334–1342)
Clement VI (1342–1352)
Innocent VI (1352–1362)
Urban V (1362–1370)
Gregory XI (1370–1378)
Urban VI (1378–1389)
Boniface IX (1389–1404)
Innocent VII (1404–1406)
Gregory XII (1406–1415)
Martin V (1417–1431)
Eugenius IV (1431–1447)
Nicholas V (1447–1455)
Callixtus III (1455-1458)
Pius II (1458–1464)
Paul II (1464–1467)
Sixtus IV (1471–1484)
Innocent VIII (1484–1492)
Alexander VI (1492–1503)
Pius III (1503)
Julius II (1503–1513)
Leo X (1513–1521)
Adrian VI (l522–1523)
Clement VII (1523–1534)
Paul III (1534–1549)

Julius III (1550–1555)
Marcellus II (1555)
Paul IV (155-1159)
Pius IV (l559–1565)
Pius V (1566–1572)
Gregory XIII (1572–1585)
Sixtus V (1585–1590)
Urban VII (1590)
Gregory XIV (1590–1591)
Innocent IX (1591)
Clement VIII (1592–1605)
Leo XI (1605)
Paul V (1605–1621)
Gregory XV (1621–1623)
Urban VIII (1623–1644)
Innocent X (1644–1655)
Alexander VII (1655–1667)
Clement IX (1667–1669)
Clement X (1670–1676)
Innocent XI (1676–1689)
Alexander VIII (1689–1691)
Innocent XII (1691–1700)
Clement XI (l700–1721)
Innocent XIII (1721–1724)
Benedict XIII (1724–1730)
Clement XII (l730–1740)
Benedict XIV (1740–1758)
Clement XIII (1758–1769)
Clement XIV (1769–1774)
Pius VI (1775–1799)
Pius VII (1800–1823)
Leo XII (1823–1829)
Pius VIII (1829–1830)
Gregory XVI (1831–1846)
Pius IX (1846–1878)
Leo XIII (1878–1903)
Pius X (1903–1914)
Benedict XV (1914–1922)
Pius XI (1922–1939)
Pius XII (1939–1958)
John XXIII (1958–1963)
Paul VI (1963–1978)
John Paul I (1978)
John Paul II (1978–2005)
Benedict XVI (2005–)

all over Italy in 1859 and 1860 as forces for the Risorgimento or Unification of Italy gathered strength. Victor Emanuele of Savoy and his prime minster, Camillo Benso, Conte di Cavour, managed to bring the French on board against the Austrians who had control of the Lombardy-Venetia region. But, despite winning the second war of independence, they were betrayed by the French, who made a private settlement with the Austrians whereby the Austrians would hold on to Venetia while giving up Lombardy. This came to nothing, but growing anger at this outrage galvanized the movement still further and forces under Giuseppe **Garibaldi**, who had defended Rome with Mazzini in 1849, waged an effective guerrilla campaign in Sicily and southern Italy, which ceded the territories to King Victor Emmanuel. Eventually Florence became the capital of the new kingdom in 1864. Garibaldi made repeated attempts to capture Rome – occupied by Pope Pius IX and protected by the French – but he was arrested and sidelined by the new regime, embarrassed by his growing power and charisma. In 1870 French troops were withdrawn from Rome to fight the Franco-Prussian war, allowing Italian forces to storm the walls at Porta Pia and retake the city. Rome was declared the capital of the new Italy under Victor Emmanuel II (who moved into the Quirinale Palace), and the by now powerless pontiff, **Pius IX** (1846–78), was confined in the Vatican until agreement was reached on a way to coexist. The initial **Law of Guarantees** drawn up by the new government defined the relationship between the state and the papacy, and acknowledged the pope as sovereign within the Vatican but no further; it was rejected by the pope, leaving the status of the Vatican in limbo for years to come. In the meantime **Agostino Depretis** became the first prime minister of the new Italian state, and one of its greatest politicians, remaining in power until 1887, and seeing the new country through the difficult early years.

Modern times

As capital of a modern European country, Rome was (some would say still is) totally ill-equipped. The **Piemontese rulers**, from the region in northwest Italy, set about building a city fit to govern from, cutting new streets through Rome's central core (Via Nazionale, Via del Tritone) and constructing grandiose buildings like the Altar of the Nation. **Mussolini** took up residence in Rome in 1922, and in 1929 signed the **Lateran Pact** with Pope **Pius XI** (1922–39), a compromise which finally forced the Vatican to accept the new Italian state and in return recognized the Vatican City as sovereign territory, together with the key basilicas and papal palaces in Rome, which remain technically independent of Italy to this day. Mussolini had typically bombastic visions for the city, and not only constructed new buildings and neighbourhoods such as Foro Italico, the University, EUR and Cinecittà, but also new thoroughfares and views within the historic centre itself. He created grand avenues, the better to march his troops along, including Via della Conciliazione, which connected St Peter's to the river, a scheme going back to the times of Pope Nicholas V (1447-55). Mussolini also "liberated" the monuments of Imperial Rome from the surrounding mess of buildings – the Arch of Janus, the Temple of Vesta, the Theatre of Marcellus. But he also bulldozed his way through ancient sites such as the Roman Forum and medieval borghi of the city to achieve this, behaving not unlike the popes and families of old. Rome was declared an "open city" during **World War II**, and as such emerged from the war relatively unscathed. However, after Mussolini's death, and the end of the war, the Italian king, Vittorio Emanuele III, was forced to abdicate and Italy was declared a republic – still, however, with its capital in Rome.

After the war Italy became renowned as a country which changes its government, if not its politicians, every few months, and for the rest of Italy Rome came to symbolize the inertia of their nation's government – at odds with both the slick, efficient north, and the poor, corrupt south. Despite this, the city's growth was phenomenal in the postwar years, its population soaring to close on four million and its centre becoming ever more choked by traffic. Rome was in the spotlight for fifteen minutes during the **Sixties**, when it was the (cinematic) home of Fellini's *Dolce Vita* and Italy's bright young things. However, in the **Seventies**, when the so-called Anni Piombi or "years of lead" arrived, Rome became a focus for the polarization and terrorism that was going on nationwide in Italian politics – a period when there were troops on the streets and the country often seemed on the brink of civil disruption. Since then, beginning with the "mani puliti" or "clean hands" enquiries of the **early 1990s**, the landscape of Italian politics has changed massively, and Rome in particular saw a period of stable government under the Green party mayor, Franceso Rutelli. Great efforts were made to prepare the city for the arrival of the **Millennium**, and the millions of visitors who came to celebrate the Jubilee (Holy Year) declared by the pope: buildings and monuments that had been closed for decades were reopened, restoration was completed, and as a result the city is looking better than ever. Rome's mayor, **Walter Veltroni**, elected in 2001 and confirmed again in 2006, has worked to improve cultural life and public services. A journalist and friend of the film director Nani Moretti, he has an accessible style and enjoys an easy-going popularity in the city. He has organized free concerts at the Colosseum and launched Rome's first annual film festival. The Italian architect, Renzo Piano, was commissioned to build a large auditorium – actually three concert halls and an outdoor theatre – on the north side of the city centre, which opened to great fanfare in 2006. Other **cultural initiatives** include the Casa del Jazz and Casa del Cinema, and the Sala Santa Rita, recently restored and reopened as a temporary exhibition space. The metro is to be extended with an extra line (metro C) at a cost of three billion euros, an enormously difficult project which keeps having to be stopped for archeological investigation. As a result it is not expected to open until 2015.

Nonetheless, in many ways Rome hasn't altered a bit. It's still clogged with traffic and, even by Italian standards, remains a relatively provincial place, and one which is in some ways still trying to lug itself into the twenty-first century. It will do so – eventually; and the city is already changing fast in lots of obvious ways, with rundown neighbourhoods like Ostiense becoming gentrified, rents and other prices shooting up with the advent of the euro, and long-closed galleries and attractions becoming ever more accessible. But, perhaps uniquely among European capitals, it retains a feel in its central districts that is still peculiarly local – and defiantly Roman. Visit now while it still exists.

Writing on Rome

There has been so much written about Rome over the years that picking out something that encapsulates the city in a few words is a hard if not impossible task. There's nothing, however, quite like the reaction that Rome induces in first-time visitors. However much they may have read, and no matter how well travelled they are, no one is ever quite prepared for the exuberant confusion of the city. The three pieces we have chosen are all about coming to Rome for the first or second time; all were written in the modern era, and as such are still highly relevant to what you see today; but they were written long enough ago to be also enjoyed as history.

Elizabeth Bowen

A novelist and travel writer, Elizabeth Bowen was born in Dublin in 1899. Her book, *A Time in Rome*, from which the following extract was taken, was first published in 1960.

The Confusion

Too much time in too little space, I thought, sitting on the edge of my bed at the end of the train journey from Paris. Never have I heard Rome so quiet before or since. I had asked for a quiet room, this was it. It was on the fourth floor, at the back. The bed was low, the window was set high up, one half of it framing neutral sky, the other a shabby projection of the building. Colour seemed, like sound, to be drained away. The hour was half-past four, the day Tuesday, the month February. I knew myself to be not far from the Spanish Steps, which had flashed past the taxi like a postcard. These anti-climactic first minutes became eternal. My bedroom's old-fashioned double room, with key in the lock and the tab dangling, had been shut behind him by the outgoing porter; stacked on trestles at the foot of the bed here was my luggage for three months. Through a smaller doorway showed the tiles of a bathroom wanly reflecting electric light. I was alone with my tired senses.

The hotel, from what I had seen of it, was estimable and dignified, nothing gimcrack. The corridor, dark and extremely long, had been lined with noble old-fashioned furniture, and in here was more of it, on top of me, Close to my pillows was the telephone, sharing the marble top of a commode with a lamp with the Campidoglio on its shade. After my one thought I felt unequal to any others and lay down flat. The bedhead was in a corner, so I switched on the lamp and tipped up the shade, to continue my reading of a detective story – interrupted just at the crucial point by my train's arrival at Rome station.

When I emerged from the story, darkness had fallen and I was hungry. Taking with me the *Walks of Rome* of Augustus Hare, I left the hotel to look for dinner. In these surrounding little streets, lit up like aquariums and tonight anonymous, saunterers passed me in vague shoals. Restaurant after restaurant was empty; blue-white electricity, hatless hatstands, as chalky and void as the tables' napery. Here and there a waiter posed like a waxwork. Spying through glass doors or over blinds, I began to fear something had gone wrong – actually all that had happened was, I was ahead of the Roman dinner-hour. So I ended in yellow-brocaded

Ranieri's, where they showed a polished lack of surprise, among foreigners other than myself. Great gilt candelabra were on the chimney-piece, and for each of us a little vase of anemones. But here I was afflicted by something else: it seemed uncouth to read while dinner was served. Stealing a glance now and then at Augustus Hare, I never succeeded in getting further than Dr Arnold's 1840 letter to his wife: "Again this date of Rome; the most solemn and interesting that my hand can write, and even now more interesting than when I saw it last." This was not my first visit to Rome either.

Next day, I changed my room for an outside corner one, a floor higher. This, with the freshness following on what seemed more absolute than a mere night's sleep, altered the feeling of everything like magic. I found myself up in a universe, my own, of sun-coloured tiled floor, sunny starchy curtains. Noise, like the morning, rushed in at the open windows, to be contained by the room in its gay tranquillity. Roses, bleached by seasons of light, rambled over the cretonne coverings of the two beds. The idea of Rome, yesterday so like lead, this noonday lay on me lighter than a feather. Life at this level had a society of its own: windows across the way, their shutters clamped back, looked pensively, speakingly in at mine.

The quarter in which the Hotel Inghilterra stands is early nineteenth century. It fills the slight declivity, shallow as the hollow of a hand, between the Pincio and the Corso, and is bisected by the *de luxe* Via Condotti, apart from which the quarter is unassuming. It has acoustics of its own, echoes and refractions of steps and voices, now and then of the throb of a car in low gear nosing its way among the pedestrians. Every narrow street in this network is one-way; the system is dementing to motorists, who do not embroil themselves in it willingly. Radio jazz, a fervent young singer at her exercises, a sewing-machine tearing along, and the frenetic song of a small-caged bird, hooked to my sill, were my sound-neighbours. From top-but-one storey windows I beheld one crinkled continuous tawny roofline: all the buildings fitted into this quarter, like segments of a finally solved jigsaw, are one in height as they are in age. They are ochre, which was giving off a kind of August glow on to the mild spring-winter morning: on throughout the chilliest time of year smoulders the afterglow of Rome's summers. And my streets, on a grid plan, sunken deep between buildings, also are all alike: sunless, down there, for the greater part of the day, they stretch so far that they fade away at the ends. Small shops, workshops, bars and restaurants line them, with apartments or offices above. Banal, affable, ripe to become familiar, this was the ideal Rome to be installed in: everything seemed to brim with associations, if not (so far) any of my own. I began to attach myself by so much as looking. Here I was, centred. I dared to hope that all else might prove as simple. It did not.

One trouble is that Rome's north-south axis, Via del Corso, does not run due north, due south. It slants, thereby throwing one's sense of direction, insofar as one has one, out of the true. The Piazza Venezia, at one end, is east of Piazza del Popolo at the other. Then, there are the exaggerated S-curvings of the Tiber; one minute the river is at one's elbow, the next lost. A stroll along the embankment is one of the least enjoyable in Rome; the dustiest, baldest, most unrewarding. (To stand on a bridge is another thing.) The Tiber is not intended to be followed; only trams do so, and those in very great numbers. They grind by unceasingly, and one does well to take one.

Then again, there are far more than seven hills: how is one to be clear which the seven are? This seems to be one of the primal facts which guidebooks are obstinate in withholding. Viewed from above, from the Janiculum lighthouse or a terrace of the Pincio gardens, Rome as a whole appears absolutely flat, or, if anything, sunken in the middle like a golden-brown pudding or cake which has failed to rise. Down again in the city, you register gradients in aching foot muscles – this does establish that Rome is hilly. Knowledge of Rome must be physical, sweated into the system, worked up into the brain through the tinning shoe-leather. Substantiality comes through touch and smell, and taste, the tastes of different dusts. When it comes to knowing, the senses are more honest than the intelligence. Nothing is more real than the first wall you lean up against sobbing with exhaustion. Rome no more than beheld (that is, taken in through the eyes only) could still be a masterpiece in cardboard – the eye I suppose being of all the organs the most easily infatuated and then jaded and so tricked. Seeing is pleasure, but not knowledge.

In shape the Capitoline and the Palatine are hills unmistakably; so is the Aventine, at the other side of the trough of the Circo Massimo. But the Caelian, Esquiline, Viminal and Quirinal are ambiguously webbed together by ridges. On the whole I have come to suppose that these *are* the Seven – but if so, what of the Pincian, "hill of gardens" and Janiculum, bastion across the river? I asked a number of friends, but no two gave me the same answer; some did not want to be pinned down, others put forward their own candidates. That I should be set on compiling a definitive list of the Seven Hills, eager to check on all, to locate each, was, I can see, disillusioning to people who had hoped I might show more advanced tastes. So, given the equal unwillingness of guidebooks to disgorge anything like a list, I left Rome, when the end of my time came, no more certain as to the Seven Hills.

An excerpt from *A Time in Rome*, reprinted with the kind permission of Curtis Brown Group Ltd on behalf of the estate of Elizabeth Bowen. ©Elizabeth Bowen 1959

William Weaver

William Weaver served as an ambulance driver during World War II and first visited Rome a few years later. He became the most sought-after translator of Italian literature of the second half of the twentieth century, translating most of the modern Italian literary greats at one time or another. The following extract, part of his introduction to Steerforth Press's anthology of modern Roman literature, details his first impressions of the city, and his relationships with some of the writers he later came to work with.

Open City

It was raining when we arrived, and the rickety bus finally emptied us – me and my Neapolitan friend Raffaele – into a small, dark square near the Borsa. This was Rome? True, there were some scarred ancient columns along a street-front, but they were grimy with soot. I had imagined a city of snowy white, elegant classical forms, resembling perhaps the columned Citizens National Bank in Front Royal, Virginia, my childhood paragon of fine architecture. Rome, I saw, in shock, was different from the black-and-white Alinari photographs of art history courses; it was orange, yellow; rust-color; there were even a few neon signs blinking on baroque facades in the early winter dusk.

From the Piazza di Pietra we went to our pensione. Again, with reminiscences of E.M. Forster in my head, I imagined a place of relaxed conversation and, of course, a room with a view. The Pensione Sieben had once been a solid, spacious, middle-class apartment. Now the Siebens (he was an elderly German, a retired translator) lived in the kitchen and in a crammed bedroom next to it. An old lady, Herr Sieben's mother, occupied the next bedroom. In the front of the apartment, my friends Peppino and Mario shared the former salon, a once-splendid room now almost empty save for two cots, a desk, and a wood-burning stove, jutting from what was a formerly decorative fireplace.

Across the vestibule was a much smaller room, where I was to sleep. It also contained two cots, but the few square meters could not accommodate even a small desk. The cot farther from the door was occupied by Achille, another Neapolitan friend, an actor just getting his first small roles in a repertory company specializing in new Italian plays (they were not usually very good, so the bill changed often; Achille was building a large, useless repertory). Until the previous week, my cot had been occupied by yet another Neapolitan, Francesco Rosi, an aspiring film-maker; now he had landed an enviable job, as assistant to Luchino Visconti, and had just gone off to Sicily to join the director in working on what was to prove an enduring masterpiece, *La terra trema*. The room's single window gave on an air-shaft and a blank wall.

Achille was a trying roommate. Unless he had a rehearsal, he slept until midday (so I had to dress in the dark). Afternoons, he received his lovely and long-suffering girl-friend, and I was expected to go out for an extended walk – it was a rainy winter – and stay out until dark. He was a hypochondriac, and when he discovered my super-giant family-size bottle of aspirin – calculated to last me for my whole Italian stay – he began happily popping pills; the aspirin level in the big jar descended at an alarming rate. He was also fascinated by my clothes, ordinary as they were, and constantly borrowed them, with or without asking me first. He particularly liked to wear them on stage; so I became used to seeing my Princeton sweatshirt or my favorite striped pyjamas turn up on a set representing an Italian living room.

After a few days in Rome, I dutifully made my way to the University, planning to enroll in some courses, to justify and, presumably, enrich my Italian stay. My first real tangle with Italian bureaucracy ensued: a nightmare of waiting in the wrong line, lacking this or that document, failing to understand angry, shouted directions from the grouchy staff behind the windows or the confusing attempts at help from equally beleaguered Italian students.

I gave up (two years later, thanks to a Fulbright, I actually enrolled at the University and attended a few classes), and determined to dedicate myself to my other Roman project: the novel I expected to write. Having published two stories in national magazines (*Harper's Bazaar* and *Mademoiselle*, which had published stories of Truman Capote and other rising stars), I – and my friends – assumed that a novel was the next step. There was just one difficulty: I had nothing I particularly wanted to write about. But I didn't let that stop me. Mornings, when Peppino had gone off to his job at the Rai, the Italian State Radio, and Mario to his classes at the Accademia di Arte Drammatica, I moved into the former salon, sat at their desk, opened my copious notebooks (a Gide fan, I could not contemplate writing a novel without keeping journals, *cahiers*), and tried to work. I had never been successfully self-critical. But even permissive me soon had to concede that the novel was a dud.

If the rain let up, I soon found an excuse to go out. The excuse was always the same: my determination to get to know Rome. It was not a matter of visiting churches, studying frescoes, deciphering inscriptions. I wanted to gulp down real Roman coffee in the morning, eat real Roman pasta at lunch, drink all the real Roman wine I could afford. I wanted to read the newspapers, see the movies and the plays, hear the music.

I was perfectly situated. Dreary as the Pensione Sieben looked at first, it turned out to be a hive of cultural, and social activity; a center of fun. The big salon of Peppino and Mario served as a gathering-place for a host of young people from the Accademia, writers from the Rai, and other newly-arrived Neapolitans aiming to break into film or journalism.

And I had a trump-card of my own. I was an American, and to the Italians – whatever their ages or degree of fame – that nationality inspired endless curiosity. For many I was the first American they had encountered, except perhaps for a stray GI a few years earlier. And so I was consulted as the expert on everything American: my opinion on William Wyler was seriously pondered. I was asked whether I would place Gershwin in the mainstream of white jazz or in the area of classical music (the question, for me, was unanswerable, as I knew far more about Puccini than about my popular compatriot). I was invited to contribute to nascent literary magazines, some of them born only to die after the first issue, which perhaps included my little piece on Karl Shapiro or John O'Hara.

Through a visiting American I met the Italian painter and writer Dario Cecchi, a few years my senior, scion of an Italian literary/artistic family with ramifications extending into every area of Italy's cultural life. Dario's father was the eminent and powerful critic Emilio Cecchi; his sister was Suso Cecchi d'Amico, the script-writer of Visconti and others, and her husband, Fedele d'Amico, was a brilliant, polemical music critic and polymath, eventually to become a treasured friend and colleague.

The chain of acquaintances grew, link by link, creating degrees not of separation but of connection. And some of these connections soon became hubs, branching off in one direction after another. It was Dario who took me first to meet Princess Marguerite Caetani. He told me little about her beyond the fact that she was American-born (a Chapin from Connecticut), a patron of the arts who had lived for many years in France, but had returned to Italy with her musician husband before the second world war and had remained in Rome. In Palazzo Caetani she edited an international literary review, *Botteghe Oscure*, after the name of the street where the Palazzo had stood for many centuries. The fact that Communist Party Headquarters now stood in that same street, making its name a synonym for the pci, was a minor nuisance that the Principessa airily dismissed.

We stepped into the dark courtyard of the great, grim palace, took an elevator to the piano nobile, and were shown into a huge, high-ceilinged hall, hung with dusty portraits (I looked around for Boniface VIII, the Caetani pope pilloried by Dante, but I couldn't identify him): then Dario, who knew his way around the palace, led me to a modern corkscrew staircase in a corner of the room. We climbed it and, passing through a plain little door at its top, stepped into a large, but cozy, New England living room: sofas covered in beige monkscloth, low tables, a fire in the fireplace, French windows revealing a broad terrace beyond. A large tea-pot stood on one table, and plates of sandwiches circulated.

The Principessa, in heather tweeds, only a few wisps of her gray hair out of place (to hint at her artistic side?), welcomed me warmly. And the welcome was equally warm from other guests, all clearly frequenters of the house. They were not many, and I remember almost all of them, as they all became friends of mine very soon: Elena Croce, the daughter of the philosopher but with a lively mind of her own; Umberto Morra, an aristocratic anti-Fascist and old friend of Bernard Berenson; Ignazio Silone – whose works I had read in translation – with his beautiful, ebullient Irish wife Darina, whom I had already met for a fleeting moment. And Giorgio Bassani, titular editor of *Botteghe Oscure*, though Marguerite clearly made all the operative decisions, while encouraging Bassani to propose new writers, especially for the Italian section of the magazine. At that time, Bassani was known, if he was known at all, as a poet; he had just published the first of what were to become the now classic *Five Stories of Ferrara*.

After that first visit, I returned to Palazzo Caetani countless times, and each visit was memorable, especially those when I was alone with Marguerite, who soon discovered – and exploited – my boarding-school experience as a proof-reader. The Italian printers, excellent artisans, inevitably made gibberish of some of the magazine's English and French texts, and complaining authors drove Marguerite to despair ("Alfred Chester called me this morning from Paris, he cried all last night because of the mistakes in his story.") My work was unpaid – and I put in long hours – but I had ample occasion to appreciate Marguerite's real generosity. Not only did she soon publish my work: she also invited me to any number of meals. Food at the Caetani table was plain, but as I lived from day to day, a steak gained was a steak earned.

And the company! For foreign literary visitors of a certain level, Palazzo Caetani was an obligatory stop. One week there would be a tea-party for "Cousin Tom" (known to me as T.S. Eliot), in Rome to give a reading at the British Council, but also to enjoy a honeymoon with his new wife Valerie. The great poet's radiant happiness was evident, irrepressible. For much of the party he and his wife sat side-by-side on one of Marguerite's comfortable low sofas, and he could not refrain from touching her, patting her hand, pressing her arm, like an enamored schoolboy. Standing not far away, I pointed out Eliot's enraptured behavior to Alberto Moravia. "Senile sexuality," the novelist commented tartly. I remembered this remark some decades later when Moravia himself, by then close to eighty, married Carmen Llera, forty-odd years his junior.

Between the world wars, Marguerite had lived much of the time in Paris, where her house just outside the city was also an intellectual gathering place (Berenson's letters tell of visits there from the Armistice meetings, which he was attending). So the Palazzo in Rome welcomed many French visitors, among them René Char, Francis Ponge, Henri Sauguet. And there were also musicians, partly because of Prince Roffredo's background as a composer (he was Liszt's godson and had known the Wagners); in the Caetani salon I first heard Gian Carlo Menotti and Tommy Schippers discuss a festival they were beginning to think about, a place for young artists in some Umbrian town, perhaps Todi, or perhaps Spoleto.

Umberto Morra, a Piedmontese count, whose family had been close to the royal family (Umberto's father, a general, had served as the Savoys' ambassador to the court of the Czar), lived in a single room in Rome, in the apartment of some old friends. But he led an intense social life, and he particularly enjoyed entertaining new arrivals to Rome, arranging introductions. Often he would invite a new acquaintance, with perhaps one or at most two old friends, to tea at Babington's tea rooms in Piazza di Spagna. The atmosphere at Babington's certainly belonged to another world, but what world was it? I suppose the unpretentious setting was meant to evoke pre-war England (pre-first war, that is), and the motherly old ladies with their starched frilly caps who brought the tea and scones and cake looked like Margaret Rutherford stand-ins, imported directly from some Staffordshire village. But then you realized they spoke little English, and that smattering came out with a thick Italian accent.

In any case, the tea was authentic and delicious, the scones came with home-made jams; and the company was always stimulating. Whether at Babington or, for grander luncheons, at the Stanze dell'Eliseo, a quirkish private club, with Morra you were always sure to meet someone who was not just interesting but was actually a person you were eager to know: Jimmy Merrill was a Morra gift to me, and so – in Florence – was Bernard Berenson. Later, when Morra headed the Italian Institute in London, he introduced me to the great Maurice Bowra, to the equally legendary Judge Learned Hand. His was a mobile salon. When you came to know him really well, he would invite you for a weekend at his comfortable, slightly shabby villa in Tuscany (Moravia "stole" the villa to use as the setting of his novel *Conjugal Love*). Again the house party was always varied, relaxed, unexpected. Even the occasional bore – the garrulous widow of a distinguished anti-Fascist friend, for example – was, somehow, a bore you were glad to meet.

Morra seemed to be a friend of every Italian I encountered. But I soon realized he was unusual, if not unique in his pan-amicability. By some of my new literary acquaintances, the Cecchi family was considered tainted. For, while never an aggressive Fascist, Cecchi had been something of a social and political opportunist, not above putting his pen to the regime's service, while not compromising his high literary standards or marring the beauty of his jeweled prose. Still, his name appeared on the scenario of the absurdly, blatantly racist film *Harlem*, and his biased book *America amara* was virtually a gift to the anti-USA dictatorship. So at the Cecchis', while you might meet important writers, including the art historian Cesare Brandi or the once-notorious, feminist poet Sibilla Aleramo, you would not find Silone or Moravia. Hence my young Neapolitan friends, and their Roman acquaintances, looked somewhat askance at my association with the Cecchis, though my friendship was with the Cecchi son and daughter rather than the writer himself.

When I first arrived in Italy, in the fall of 1943, I knew the name of only one living Italian writer: Ignazio Silone, and that name was one I had learned only a few months earlier. For my generation – I was born in July 1923 – my knowledge of Italian culture was, I should think, typical. Though a couple of Alberto Moravia's books had been translated before the war, they had not attracted much attention, had not established him as the literary leader he had long been in Italy. A few Americans perhaps knew of the poems of Montale and Ungaretti, but I was not one of them.

I had discovered Silone's works in the Western Desert, in Libya. Isolated with the other thirty-odd members of my company, idle, I spent all my time reading. But books were scarce, and so there was a constant trading. I even read *Winnie the Pooh* for the first time (my father's stern literary standards would not allow the coy Milne in our house, and, after reading him, I agreed with my father). Then a fellow-driver – I forget who it was – lent me the Penguin edition of *Fontamara*, the stark title printed on a white band between two orange ones; when I had read that, the same friend handed me the Harper first US edition of *Bread and Wine*. When I came across a copy of that same edition recently in the Bard College library, it was like running into a long-lost wartime buddy; I could almost feel grains of Libyan sand between the pages.

Silone represented much more than simply my introduction to contemporary Italian fiction; those first two novels of his served also as a political primer. Though I was involved in a great war against Fascism, I had only a vague notion of what the word meant. Silone's fiction led me beyond the headlines, newsreel parades and balcony histrionics to the human facts, the meaning of Fascism in terms of daily bread and loss of freedom.

In Rome, three years later, shortly before I met Silone at Palazzo Caetani, I met – for an unforgettable instant – his beautiful, captivating Irish wife Darina. I had had a drink at the Caffè Greco with Stephen Spender (whom I had met in New York through Chester Kallman and Auden – another of the radial paths of my cultural landscape). He was on his way to a dinner party at the nearby Palazzo Torlonia, at the residence of the Irish ambassador, the elegant poet Denis

Devlin. I walked Stephen to the door of the Palazzo; as we were saying good night, a taxi squealed to a stop, and from it, in breathless haste, a tall, blonde Viking of a woman descended, her face half-covered by a light veil. I was introduced, and I heard her soft, melodious accent for the first of many times.

Of course, I was envious. I wished with all my heart that I had been invited to Denis Devlin's party, and I imagined all sorts of beautiful and brilliant guests, as I saw Stephen and Darina disappear inside the massive portal. A moment later, when I was alone in the Via Bocca di Leone, I grasped the irony of seeing a Silone enter the palace of the Torlonia family, the landlords of southern Italy, who are the ultimate villains of Silone's peasant world.

I met Darina soon again at Marguerite's, and at the same time I met Silone. At a first encounter, he was a forbidding presence, taciturn and – this was my impression – disapproving. This impression persisted after I had been invited to several dinners and parties at the Silone apartment, in an anonymous, outlying part of the city near Piazza Bologna. The foreign visitors who gravitated there were often different from the Botteghe Oscure salon. At the Silones, in addition to a small group of left-wing dissidents, among them Nicola Chiaramonte and his delightful American wife Miriam, you might encounter *Partisan Review* people, Philip Rahv, William Phillips or Dwight Macdonald, or (separately) Edmund Wilson or Mary McCarthy.

One day, after I had been there several times, never exchanging more than a few formal remarks with my host, Darina called with another dinner invitation. Unfortunately I was already engaged for that evening, and so expressed my regrets. "What a pity!" Darina exclaimed. "Silone always enjoys himself so much when you're here."

I was dumbfounded. True, at the Silones', as elsewhere, I liked to talk (and also listen): I told stories, asked questions, ventured opinions, sometimes shaky ones. And then, more often than not, the next morning, if I didn't have an out-and-out hangover, I had the nagging suspicion that I had talked too much and maybe even made a fool of myself. Remembered, Silone's stern silence took on an accusatory quality. But now I could slough off those qualms, and speak to the admired writer more easily. At about this time I made another parallel discovery. Reading a book about anti-Fascists in exile, I found a reference to Silone's humor, which kept his companions' spirits up, making the table in some humble Swiss beer-hall rock with laughter.

Incredulous, I asked Morra about this Silone, so different from the one I knew. "Oh, yes," Umberto confirmed. "Silone has a wonderful, quick wit. He can be very funny indeed."

Eventually, I came to appreciate this side of him (I should have sensed it also from his novels, rich in sly irony). After some years of our acquaintance, he asked me to translate a book of his, an old work, *The School for Dictators*, written in exile and first published in 1938, in German. Darina, herself a first-rate translator, had been responsible for some English versions of his works; but for personal reasons about which she remained vague, she preferred to pass the assignment on to me.

I set to work happily, although the text – a Platonic dialogue on the subject of power, rule, authority – was not the sort of thing I had translated thus far. But both Darina and Silone were separately helpful. I went a number of times to the Piazza Bologna apartment and, over tea, discussed my problems. When I had almost finished a last revision, Darina had to go off to London, and I began to see Silone alone.

Often between a translator and the author a kind of subtle conflict can grow up. (In some cases, as with Italo Calvino, it was not all that subtle.)

That competitiveness did not develop with Silone, but, all the same, I was a bit pleased with myself when I uncovered a couple of minor factual errors in the Italian text (Hitler's birthplace was given as Brunau, which I corrected to Braunau). I was also smugly amused to discover that a book by Napoleon III, which Silone referred to as *Rêveries poetiques*, was, in reality, entitled *Rêveries politiques*, a more plausible but less entertaining title. I pointed out Silone's mistake tactfully; he thanked me for the information and, in an apologetic tone, he murmured. "You see, I didn't have any libraries at hand." Ashamed of myself, I realized he had written the book in exile, perhaps in the Davos sanatorium or even in prison, under conditions that other writers would consider heroic.

But that same evening, as we went out to dinner, I had a glimpse of Silone's humorous side; in fact, I provoked it, insisting that he be my guest. To convince him to accept my invitation, I used a Jesuitical argument, explaining that paying the bill would be an excellent spiritual exercise for me. In the past, I had always considered myself poor, but recently I had been awarded a Fulbright fellowship, so I should stop thinking of myself as needy. And anyway I wanted to repay – or, at least, make a gesture of gratitude – after months of Silone's hospitality.

"Ah, but paying would be a splendid spiritual exercise for me, too," Silone, said, immediately picking up the spirit of the discussion. And, as he really had been educated by Jesuits (I, by mere Franciscans), his arguments were much more dazzling and elaborate – and funny – than mine. And, to cap them, as we finished the meal, he added: "And besides, this is an Abruzzese restaurant; they'd never let a guest pay." Actually, I'm not even sure they let him pay. I didn't see a bill.

When I settled into the Pensione Sieben where I stayed most of the winter of '47–'48, Alberto Moravia and Elsa Morante had only recently moved nearby, into the apartment that was to be their home for the rest of their marriage (and Elsa's chief residence, after the separation, almost until her death). It was in Via dell'Oca, an oddly broad, but short street, running the two or three blocks from Piazza del Popolo to the embankment at the Tiber. Though they had been married for over five years (and had been together for some time before the marriage), Alberto and Elsa had never had a proper house of their own. Now thanks to Alberto's foreign royalties and the film work he continued to do, they were able to fit out the house comfortably, with many sofas and easy chairs in white or cream slipcovers, with paintings on the walls (at this time largely by Moravia's sister Adriana Pincherle, later by Elsa's tragic infatuation Bill Morrow), and with a varying number of Siamese cats, long ruled over by the imperious Gatto Tit.

For Elsa, who had grown up in grimly respectable poverty, the Via dell'Oca house represented luxury; and, to crown this elegance, she engaged a cook. Thus – probably for the first time in her life – she gave dinner parties. For the rest, Alberto and Elsa almost never ate alone, even in earlier times, when they went every evening to some trattoria. Then, if you called up during the day to ask Alberto for supper, his characteristic reply was "come by around eight and we'll go out somewhere."

Sometimes – but very rarely – I'd be able to go out to dinner with just Alberto and Elsa. More often, I would find other friends with them, or indeed I would find strangers, anybody who had called either him or her in the course of the day to ask what they were doing for dinner. When that evening's group had collected, there would be a discussion, sometimes heated, about where to go. La Campana? Too crowded. Trastevere? Too noisy. Another trattoria was regularly rejected because, according to Elsa, the proprietor treated his cat badly. Sometimes we would end up at La Carbonara, in Campo de' Fiori, not because anyone was particularly fond of the place,

△ Piazza del Popolo in the early twentieth century

but because there was always room. I remember those big impromptu dinners with mixed emotions. Moravia's circle of acquaintance included a few inevitable hangers-on, whom he treated, I felt, with more consideration than they deserved, especially since some of them – trying to assert a factitious independence – openly criticized him and belittled him. One particularly aggressive Communist art critic I found insufferable, and ill-luck sometimes placed me beside or opposite him at the long table, with Elsa and Moravia at separate, unbreachable distance from me.

But once in a while it would be just the three of us. Still, these more intimate nights were also fraught with risk. Speaking of Elsa once, some time after her death, Moravia – who continued to refer to her with affection and understanding long after their separation – said, "Elsa was profoundly ingiusta." "Unfair" is too mild a translation, and "unjust" sounds too juridical. What Moravia meant, I think, was "Elsa liked to deal low blows." And I have to agree with him. She could also be impulsive, and the blows could hit the innocent.

To make matters worse, Elsa – at least, in certain frequent moods – loved to quarrel, and to cast blame, almost always on Alberto: if the chosen restaurant happened to be closed, or the service was poor, or if a special dish was absent from that night's menu, the fault was somehow Alberto's. Elsa had a piercing voice that could cut, knife-like, through normal restaurant hum. Whether or not the deafness that later affected Alberto was already incipient in those days, he also tended to speak in a louder voice in restaurants. So their debates were, willy-nilly, overheard by fellow diners.

There is one restaurant in Rome – *Romolo* at Porta Settimiana – that I still enter with hesitation, though the embarrassing argument must have taken place fifty years ago. Unlikely as it now seems, the argument, as I recall, was about motherhood or perhaps about Southern Italian peasants. What I indelibly remember is Elsa's culminating retort: "Don't talk nonsense, Alberto, in the south peasant mothers masturbate their children to put them to sleep at night." The crucial verb was uttered in a shrill, loud cry, which seemed to echo interminably beneath the low vaults of the restaurant ceiling. The other diners had long since suspended their conversations in order to listen to ours. We ate the rest of our meal surrounded by silence and by the total attention of everyone in the place, customer or waiter or host. Only Elsa remained supremely unaffected.

Often I saw Alberto and Elsa separately, as did all their friends (for that matter, each also had separate friends, whom they saw on their own). It was easy to run into Alberto on the street, not only because Rome was small in those days and we lived in the same neighborhood, but also because Alberto was an indefatigable walker, his lame, rollicking gait recognizable blocks off. For a long period, when he was suffering from some form of sciatica, he took long, therapeutic walks for hours every afternoon on doctor's orders. When you encountered him, he would invariably ask you to accompany him for a while, as walking seemed to stimulate his conversation (not that it needed stimulation: it flowed naturally, with fascinating shifts and turns, unexpected aperçus).

In those immediate post-war years, Rome was a walker's paradise. There was barely any traffic, and the cluttering crowds of tourists were yet to return. At that time, American tourists were still afraid of drinking the water or of running out of toilet-paper. Often, in the course of that first winter, when I went to see the Sistine ceiling or the Caravaggios in San Luigi dei Francesi, I would find myself totally alone.

Taking walks was also a recognized convivial activity. At lunch-time, on a fine day, a friend might call up and suggest a walk later in the afternoon, as he or she might invite you for tea or a cocktail. One particularly enjoyable walking companion was Elena Croce, whose quirkish conversation (never a received idea) and irreverent opinions made the walks such fun that often I remained unaware of the streets we passed, the monuments, the genre scenes that are still an integral part of Roman outdoor life.

For one season, while she was at the American Academy, I went on walks with Eleanor Clark. Either I would take a bus up to the Janiculum and we would stroll among Risorgimento memories, the places where Bixio and Manara fought, perhaps where Jessie White or Margaret Fuller tended the wounded. Or we would walk downhill, to follow the curving alleys of Trastevere. But these walks were never aimless, and our attention never flagged: Eleanor had a list of things to be seen that day, and she ticked off the palazzo or the church or the historic spot. Later, when I first read Rome and a Villa, I recognized some of the ticked-off places, now caught in a double light: the illumination of Eleanor's recorded perceptions and the warm recollection of sharing with her the external experience if not necessarily also her intellectual epiphany.

I don't remember ever sight-seeing with Elsa, though any reader of her novel *History* will realize that she knew her native city stone by stone. But, in the early years of our friendship, I remember many occasions where I saw her alone – or, rather, without Moravia. For a time, around 1950, I was lent an elegant apartment near Piazza di Spagna, and there I also could do some entertaining at last.

I quickly learned the protocol to adopt in inviting Elsa. The important thing not to do was issue a double invitation. You were never to say, "Could you and Alberto come – ?" Even the use of the plural voi was a grave infraction of Elsa's personal rules. Sometimes Elsa's reply would be a simple no. More often she would say curtly, "Ah, you want Alberto? Call him at –" And she would supply the number of his studio.

The proper course was to invite Elsa: Can you – tu – come for dinner on Thursday? Almost invariably Elsa would accept, and set a time. In later years, she would perhaps inform you of the restrictions of her diet, never the same on successive occasions. Then, when all was agreed, you could venture, in as offhand a tone as possible: "If Alberto's free, tell him to join us. "I'll tell him," she would reply, audibly dubious. But then Alberto never failed to show up; or, if he really couldn't come, he would telephone separately and explain.

Elsa, socially, had a low boredom threshold. One evening, in my elegant borrowed apartment, she discovered a complete run of *Connaissance des Arts* in a living-room bookcase. For the entire evening, without a word to any of the other guests (or to me), she sat on the floor in a corner and, with almost scholarly attention, went through one number of the review after another, dutifully reading the texts as well as studying the illustrations.

But, on another occasion in the same apartment, when boredom threatened, she reacted in an entirely different way. She took charge of the guests – most of them old friends – and invented a series of guessing games, *bouts rimés*, the anti-social game of the tower, enjoying herself hugely but also inspiring the others. I had a moment of overweening pride when a verse of mine won her praise. There was this childish side of Elsa, rarely allowed to shine forth, yet irresistible when given free rein.

The child-Elsa could also be naughty; and like other naughty children, she liked to cause discomfiture. For this the tower game was ideal: the game consisted simply of obliging the player to imagine him (or her) self on a high tower with two people one of whom he had to push off. Elsa would insist on dreadful choices (herself? or Alberto?), always among people present at the table; and she would become truly angry at any waffling on the part of her victim.

At one of her dinners, she had invited Marco Visconti, a younger cousin of Luchino's, with his fiancée, the only other woman present, who was meeting Elsa for the first time. Wilfully, Elsa directed the conversation to sex and, specifically, to Lesbianism.

"I know, I know," she said, "some people say that I'm attracted to members of my own sex. Absolutely false. I do not like women. What's more, I don't like men who like women."

The three or four male guests exchanged impassive looks and tried hard not to glance at Moravia, the most impassive of all.

Elsa answered the unasked question. "Yes, even Alberto. Though I know he hasn't had any such experience... still he would have a strong tendency."

Moravia's blank astonishment made all of us laugh, and enabled someone to change the subject.

An excerpt from *Open City: Seven Writers in Postwar Rome*, edited by William Weaver, published by Steerforth Press of Hanover, NH. ©William Weaver 1999

William Murray

William Murray wrote regularly on Italy for the *New Yorker*. The following piece – one of many from his now out-of-print collection of Italian writings, *Italy: The Fatal Gift,* records his early years living in the city at the start of the 1950s, in particular a Campo de' Fiori that perhaps no longer exists but is still eminently recognizable today.

Voices

I don't think I began to understand Rome, and my own involvement in Italian life, until I moved to the apartment on the fourth floor of a run-down Renaissance palazzo at one end of a piazza called the Campo de' Fiori. The piazza is in the middle of the old papal city, surrounded by narrow, twisting little streets that thread their way among blocks of ancient houses dating back, many of them, to the fourteenth century. The rooms of my apartment were huge, with beamed and frescoed ceilings, thick walls, and tiled floors, and there was a terrace, awash in flowers and trellised ivy. I slept, or tried to, in a front room with a large window looking out over the piazza. At first, I was startled by the noise. There were lulls, but never long periods of uninterrupted silence. In the very early morning hours, I would sometimes be wakened by the explosive buzzing of a motor scooter, the rumbling of cart wheels over the cobblestones, the crash of some unbelievably heavy objects onto the pavement. Mostly, however, even at night, the sounds consisted of voices, individual and concerted, blending into and succeeding each other in a never ending choral composition of pure cacophony. It was astonishing.

Actually the sheer volume of sound at certain periods of the day didn't surprise me. I had known all along that the Campo de' Fiori was the site, six days a week, of a large open-air market. I would get up in the morning and open my shutters to look down over a sea of gray canvas umbrellas sheltering perhaps as many as two hundred stands. A great crowd of shoppers ambled and pushed down narrow aisles between rows of heaped edibles of all kinds. Directly beneath my window alone, at the northwestern end, of the piazza, I counted thirteen vendors of vegetables and several selling preserves, cheeses, and sausages. On my way across the piazza to a café where I often had breakfast and read the morning paper, I would pass pushcarts of fresh vegetables piled into great green mounds, tables buried under soft white and brown mushrooms, pyramids of cherries, apples, oranges sliced to reveal their dripping interiors, pears, apricots, bunches of white and green asparagus, enormous beets and onions, tiny round potatoes, huge heads of fresh lettuce, green and red peppers, artichokes, tomatoes, carrots and wild strawberries. Along one whole side of the piazza stretched a seemingly endless line of butcher stands, behind which the butchers themselves, in soiled white smocks, wielded their cleavers and large flat knives under the plucked bodies of chickens and the bloody carcasses of of lambs and kids hanging in rows from steel hooks. There were also bunches of pigs' feet, chunks of tripe, chains of plump sausages. At the far end of the piazza, the fishmongers presided over damp boxes and baskets of the day's catch – fish of all shapes, flaming red, blue, and silver, soft masses of squid and small octopuses, mountains of white-and-gray minnows with tiny, dead bright-button eyes, dozens of small, dark-red clawless Mediterranean lobsters. And scattered along the periphery of these crowded rows of comestibles were still other stands, selling pots and pans, dishes, glassware, cheap toys, shoes, and clothing. The stone face of the piazza, roughly rectangular and roughly the same size as football field, disappeared every morning of the week but Sundays and holidays under umbrellas, the tons of merchandise, the shuffling feet of thousands of shoppers.

Many other voices besides those of the market invaded my room. The most insistent and violent one belonged, I guessed, to a woman in her thirties. She lived in one of the apartments near the corner of Via dei Cappellari, somewhere behind the lines of laundry that hung, dripping relentlessly, across the street. Her voice was shrill and hard and piercing: it would come soaring across the piazza from behind the wall of laundry like a battle cry from the ranks of an army advancing behind flapping pennants. "Ah Massimo-o-o" it would scream. "Massimo-o-o, where the hell are you, you dirty monkey? Get the hell up here right this minute! Massimo-o-o! If you aren't home in two minutes, you little bastard, I'll break your head! Massimo-o-o imbecile! You hear me? Get right up here now before I come down and break your arm! Ah Massimo-o-o! Massimo-o-o! Cretino! Imbecille! A' vie' qua-a-a!" These tirades often became so vituperative, menacing and foul-mouthed that I'd find myself wondering how the woman could keep it up. I'd go to the window and gaze down into the piazza, hoping to spot Massimo among the hordes of children swarming through the market or, on Sunday, around the base of Bruno's statue. The voice would scream on, threatening mayhem and the vengeance of heaven on the object of its wrath, but no little boy would separate himself from his fellows and go running across the cobblestones. At least, I never noticed him.

Massimo apparently did hear, however, and eventually he would come home. The voice would cease its screaming imprecations and remain silent for some time. After a while, though, I'd hear it again – usually around two o'clock in the afternoon, when the market had closed up and the commercial uproar had abated somewhat. The intensity and depth of emotion would still be evident in the voice, but the tone had altered dramatically. "Massimo! Massimo!" I would hear it shout. "Treasure of my heart, flower of my life, why don't you eat? Eat, eat! You want to die of hunger? You want your mother to perish of grief? You want your papa to die of shame, to tell me I don't cook like I used to? My love, my sweet, my angel, have another tomato, eat your bread, drink your milk. Eat, eat, love of my life! Here, Mama will give you a big hug and a kiss! You eat now! Massimo-o-o! Tesoro! Amore! Mangia, che ti fa bene! Cocco! Angelo!"

I tried often to imagine what Massimo looked like. I saw a small boy of seven or eight with dirty knees and scuffed shoes, black hair and red eyes, red cheeks, and sturdy shoulders, but too fat for his age. I'd see him climb the stairs to the sounds of threats and fury, bursting in to be met by a hug and a light cuff and a mound of steaming spaghetti. Who, anywhere around the Campo, would not have heard of him? At the newsstand, I once idly enquired about him, but the young man who sold me my newspaper couldn't identify him, either. "Ah, Signore, it could be any one of them," he said, indicating with a flick of his hand a crowd of urchins then engaged in kicking a soccer ball around the piazza. "Masimo? A common enough name. And here everyone shouts from the windows all the time. Do you not notice?"

This young man's name was Remo. He and his family had been tending their stand, on the corner of Via dei Baullari, for thirty-five years. They would take turns sitting like benevolent gnomes inside a very small wooden booth festooned with magazines and newspapers. Nothing escaped their vigilant attention. Remo rarely smiled, and he thought that life in the piazza had deteriorated a good deal since he first began to observe its goings-on. "Ah Signore," he said to me one day, "you like this market? It is not what it was. No indeed it isn't. On Saturdays you had to fight your way into the piazza, that's what

I remember. Now – ". He shrugged. "Now, it's nothing. People are moving out. The ones who were brought up in this quarter, they do not like the old palazzi. When they have money, they move away. The rich and the foreigners are moving into the buildings now, but they don't buy in the market. They go to the supermarkets in the Parioli – drive all the way out there rather than buy in the piazza. No, it's not what it was." He was unhappy, too, about the crime in the area. "Dirty people," he said. "Gentaccia, that's what they are. The quarter is full of them. Every thief in town lives here. Do you have a car?" I told him I didn't.

"That's lucky for you," he said. "It would be stolen. Don't trust anyone you meet in the piazza. Anyone can see you're an American." At the time, I had seen no evidence of crime in the piazza, and I paid no attention to Remo's advice.

One night at about 2am I was awakened by the sound of loud masculine laughter and conversation outside my window. I looked down and saw a group of men directly below. They were talking and joking, making no effort to keep from disturbing the neighbourhood. I shouted down at them to keep quiet. One of them looked up briefly, but otherwise paid no attention. Their hoarse, merry voices continued to resound in the night air. After about ten minutes more of this, I went to the kitchen and came back with a large pot full of water. I asked them one more time to keep quiet, but I was ignored. I then leaned out of the window and poured cold water on their heads. Bellowing and cursing, they quickly scattered out and regrouped beyond the fountain, out in the piazza and well out of range. Through the slats in my shutters I saw them conferring angrily and occasionally pointing up toward my window. Slightly uneasy, I went back to bed.

The next morning, when I stepped out into the piazza, I was greeted by a young tough in wrinkled slacks and a torn jersey. He was unshaven, with close-set eyes and a snarl of oily-looking curls, and he had evidently been lounging against the wall of my building, waiting for me. "Hey you," he said hoarsely. "Hey, are you the one who threw water on us last night?"

The market was in full swing and the piazza crowded with people. I made up my mind not to be intimidated. "Yes," I said. "You woke me up." The youth shook his head gravely.

"That was a very stupid thing to do."

"Listen," I said. "I have some rights. I asked you twice to keep quiet and you paid no attention. You have no right to wake everybody up." "And you have no right to throw water on people."

This seemed a rather weak rejoinder to me, so I pressed my luck a little. "I could have called the police, you know."

The tough smiled, revealing a bright row of gold teeth. "No, no," he said, shaking his head. "You would not do that. No one in this quarter would do such a stupid thing. You have to live here – no?"

"I don't live here all the time," I said. "Besides, I don't like to be threatened."

The tough smiled again and spread his hands out wide. "Threatening you? Who is threatening you, Signore? I? I merely wish to protest against being doused with water in the middle of the night, that's all. That's not unreasonable, is it?"

"Mario, introduce me to the gentleman," I heard someone say.

I turned, and was confronted by a short, stocky, bald Roman in a rumpled but well-tailored brown suit. He had a round, affable face with large brown eyes and a strong, prominent, straight nose. He was smiling broadly. "Mario does not know my name," I said, and I introduced myself.

"Of course he does," the new arrival declared. "You are the American who lives on the fourth floor. Everyone knows who you are. I myself have often seen you in the piazza. Pleased to meet you. My name is Domenico. My friends call me Memmo."

"Were you also in the piazza last night?" I asked.

Memmo laughed. "Alas, yes," he admitted, "Luckily, you missed me. Mario, here, was soaked. That probably accounts for his sour face." He turned to Mario and clapped him roughly on the shoulder. "Hey Mario, cheer up! The bath did you good, eh? The first one you've had in weeks."

Mario made an effort to smile, but it did not seem entirely genuine. I concentrated on Memmo. "I'm sorry about it," I said. "But I was tired and wanted to get some sleep. You were directly under my window, and I asked you all several times to be quiet."

"Right," said Memmo. "Quite right. I think we will not chat there again. However, caro Signore" – he took my arm confidentially and pulled me a few feet off to one side – "don't do such a thing again. For your own good, Signore. No one would harm you, of course – Dio Mio, an American! But Mario and his friends can play such tricks, Signore! The apartment is so full of beautiful things. I have not seen it, but I know that it is. Apartments can be broken into, Signore, and even the most beautiful object can be made to disappear. What is the sense in playing tricks on people like Mario, eh?"

I looked back at Mario, who was still standing by the entrance to the building and regarding me sourly. "And you?" I asked. "What about you?"

"I?" he said. "Oh, I'm a friend of Mario's. He runs little errands for me. I have a shop here, just around the corner. You've passed it many times. Electrical equipment – radios, iceboxes, toasters, things like that. You've seen my shop, haven't you?"

I said that I had passed it often.

"Well, of course you have," Memmo said. "It's a very well-known store. Everyone in the neighbourhood knows me. Ask anyone."

"It's very kind of you to warn me," I said.

Memmo looked astonished. "Warn you?" he said. "Signore, I would not think of presuming to warn you. Still, it is important that you know how things are here on the piazza, eh?"

"Yes, I understand," I said. "Thanks very much."

"Forget it," Memmo said. "Forget the whole thing. And don't worry about Mario. Nothing will happen. Come and see me in the shop. Drop in any time – right there, just around the corner." He shook my hand and departed in the direction of his store. As he went, I saw him nod almost imperceptibly to Mario, who went off with him, not casting so much as a backward glance in my direction.

A couple of days later, I did drop in on Memmo. From the outside, the store looked like any other small shop dealing in electrical housewares, but since my encounter with Mario and Memmo and our oblique conversation, I had become curious about it. When I stepped inside the door, I discovered that the place was all but empty of merchandise. The window display featured a cheap washing machine and a secondhand refrigerator, but except for a couple of toasters and a small radio or two the store looked cleaned out. Mario and a couple of other shady-looking men lounged against the walls, smoking American cigarettes, while Memmo sat behind a small wooden desk. He had been talking into the telephone, but he hung up immediately when I came in. "Ah, buon giorno, buon giorno," he said, coming out from behind his desk and rubbing his hands briskly together. "How nice to see you! Thanks for dropping in."

"Business seems to be a little slow," I said.

"On the contrary," Memmo answered, smiling broadly. "Business could not be better."

"You've sold everything in the shop, then?"

"Well, not quite," Memmo said. "Come back here."

Memmo led me back to his desk, opened a top drawer, and pulled out a large, flat box full of Swiss wristwatches. "Look at this," he said, holding one up by the strap. "Fifty thousand lire, this watch costs. I sell it for thirty. Would you like it?"

I told Memmo that I already had a watch.

He put the watch back in the drawer and closed it. "Well, then, how about this?" he opened another drawer and showed me a pile of cigarette lighters. "Or these?" He produced boxes of cufflinks, tie clasps, studs, men's and women's bracelets, earrings, electric razors, razor blades, small bottles of cheap cologne, key rings, charms. Finally, with an elaborate little flourish of one hand, he opened still another drawer and took out a long, thin, expensive-looking case. "Perhaps there is a lady in your life?" He opened the box to reveal a handsome pearly necklace. "For you," he said, "for my friend the American, only a hundred thousand lire, eh?"

"No, thanks," I said. "I can't afford it."

Memmo sighed, cheerfully stuffed the box back into the drawer, and closed it.

"You seem to be selling everything here," I said.

Memmo smiled and shrugged. "Well, Signore, I believe in floating with the traffic, eh?" What you Americans call, I believe, the laws of supply and demand."

"How can you afford to sell these things so cheaply?" I asked.

"Signore, we have our own direct sources of supply," Memmo said. "We eliminate the middleman, as you would say. We import everything directly. You understand?"

"I think so," I said.

After that, I became increasingly aware of Memmo and his boys. Mario and half a dozen other young toughs strolled in and out of the shop, and several times I noticed them peddling objects through the marketplace. Once, I found Mario and a friend presiding at the corner of Via dei Baullari over a large stack of shoeboxes. They were selling sandals for five hundred lire a pair – a ridiculously low price. Occasionally, they would operate out of the back of a panel truck, selling everything from shirts to hardware. I never saw Memmo anywhere except inside his store, usually on the phone or in deep conversation with one of his young men.

One day, at the newsstand, I asked Remo about Memmo and his friends. Remo glanced sharply at me, then looked around to see if we were alone. "Stay away from them, Signore," he said in an undertone. "They are no good, that bunch. I let everything I hear go in one ear and out the other. It is better that way. But I tell you this Signore – the police drop in there from time to time, and it is not to pass the hours chatting, Memmo wasn't around for a long time last year, and that Mario – you know him?"

I said that I did.

"A bad one," Remo said. "He was a carpenter. Then he killed a man one day just because the fellow clapped him too hard on the back, or something. He did three and a half years. A hood, *un vero teppista*. Don't have anything to do with them."

"But who are they? Are they from around here?"

"All from this quarter, Signore, every one of them," Remo said sadly. "They give it a bad name. All over Rome, people say the Campo de' Fiori is a den of thieves. Memmo and his crowd – they're responsible for that. It's really too bad."

An excerpt from Italy: The Fatal Gift, reprinted with the kind permission of the author. ©William Murray

Books

T here have been an enormous number of books published about Rome over the years, both in English, and of course in Italian, and the list below is inevitably extremely selective, concentrating on the odd travelogue, key texts on history and art, and on works of fiction that might be instructive – or fun – to read while you're in Rome. Particular favourites are marked with the ☀ symbol. To help find the books, we've listed the publisher, with the British publisher first, and the US publisher second, except when the publisher is the same in both territories, when we've only mentioned it once; where a book is published in only one territory, we've said so.

History, art and architecture

R.J.B. Bosworth *Mussolini's Italy* (Penguin). Bosworth's book gets to the heart of the Fascist period in Italy, and its effect on life in Rome, from the bulldozing and rebuilding of parts of the city centre to the vicious reprisals in the Ardeatine caves of 1944.

Jerome Carcopino *Daily Life in Ancient Rome* (Penguin/Yale). Originally published in 1941, and consistently in print since, Carcopino's book is a classic, bringing to life the beliefs, social life and customs of ordinary Romans during the first two centuries AD, at the height of the Roman Empire.

Amanda Claridge *Oxford Archeological Guides: Rome* (OUP). A well-conceived and excellently written concise guide to the archeology of the ancient city – a good investment if this is your particular area of interest.

Christopher Duggan *A Concise History of Italy* (CUP). The best all-round history of the Italian nation that you can buy, concise and well-written, covering everything from the fall of the Roman Empire to Unification and beyond. For a more visual, though less portable, alternative, OUP's *Illustrated History of Italy* is edited by George Holmes.

Edward Gibbon *The History of the Decline and Fall of the Roman Empire* (Penguin). If you can't manage all six volumes, this abridged version is your best chance to read this classic text, conceived amidst the ruins of the Roman Forum in the latter part of the eighteenth century and covering the period from the second century AD to the fall of Constantinople in 1453. If the shortened version isn't enough for you, Everyman publishes the whole thing in three volumes.

☀ **Christopher Hibbert** *Rome: The Biography of a City* (Penguin). Simply put, the most entertaining and accessible historical introduction to Rome that you can buy – no less than you would expect from this most prolific of popular historians.

Tom Holland *Rubicon* (Abacus/Anchor). Tom Holland's readable book pinpoints a specific but crucial period of Roman history, beginning with the Roman Republic at the height of its greatness and charting its decline, starting in around 140 BC and ending with the death of Augustus in AD 14. Good narrative history, documenting a fascinating era.

Keith Hopkins and **Mary Beard** *The Colosseum* (Profile). An extremely readable history of the famous monument, full of architectural, literary and often very funny anecdotes. Not only does it give you the background to its construction, demise and resurrection but also advice on site visits.

Anthony Majanlahti *The Families Who Made Rome* (Pimlico). Majanlahti's approach to his subject matter has produced a book that is part history and part on-the-ground itinerary. It brings the buildings to life with "strange but true" histories of families such as the Borghese, Chighi and Farnese, whose stamp is all over Rome.

Borden W. Painter Jr. *Mussolini's Rome* (MacMillan Press). A scholarly but accessible take on how one man changed the face of Rome, bulldozing his way through medieval sites to "liberate" the monuments of Imperial Rome and so create a suitable backdrop to the new Fascist Empire.

Ingrid D. Rowland *The Culture of the High Renaissance: Ancients and Moderns in Sixteenth-Century Rome* (CUP). A relatively expensive but highly regarded and scholarly evocation of the high Renaissance in Rome – looking not only at the art and architecture of the period, but also at its economics, culture and sociology.

Charles L. Stinger *The Renaissance in Rome* (Indiana UP). The best-value book to focus exclusively on the Renaissance period in Rome, documenting the rehabilitation of the city under the papacy.

Giorgio Vasari *The Lives of the Artists* (OUP). There is no better background work on the artists of the Renaissance, written by a contemporary and correspondent of his subjects, who include Raphael, Michelangelo, and others less relevant to Rome. Available in a very readable English translation.

Margaret Visser *The Geometry of Love* (Penguin/North Point Press). This book is basically an extended tour of the church of Sant'Agnese fuori le Mura, and is an absorbing study not just of the building and its history but also of the iconography and architecture of all Christian churches. Visser looks at things that are often taken for granted when looking at churches, and gets deep into the meaning of why they are as they are, as well as digging back into the history of Sant'Agnese specifically and the ancient times that created it.

Travel and impressions

Elizabeth Bowen *A Time in Rome* (Vintage). Though written in the 1960s, Bowen's book endures because it is so engaging, and because it summarizes so well the longevity and continuity of Rome.

Tobias Jones *The Dark Heart of Italy* (Faber/North Point Press). Jones's book is immediately different from other books on Italy because it's about how Italians live now – not what happened centuries ago. As such, it's a good book to take with you on any Italian trip, focusing as it does on football, politics, terrorism, religion – all the things that surround you when in Rome or indeed any other Italian city. A refreshing guide to the sleaze, corruption and dysfunctionality that make up the contemporary nation.

H.V. Morton *A Traveller in Rome.* Like all Morton's books, this is a marvellously personal stroll around the sights, reflecting on history, architecture and culture. Rather dated, and currently out of print, but it should be relatively easy to get hold of.

William Murray *Italy: The Fatal Gift.* Out of print, but worth trying to get hold of for its perceptive essays on history and contemporary Italian life and culture, especially with regard to Rome, where Murray lived for many years – first as a child, then as an aspiring opera singer and later as a writer and journalist, filing regular pieces for the *New Yorker*. He writes with flair and enthusiasm, and,

best of all, knows the city intimately. Try also the in-print *City of the Soul* (Crown Journeys, US), Murray's latest slim volume of essays, walks and musings on the city.

Literature

Lyndsey Davies *Shadows in Bronze* (Arrow/Ballantine). Davies's second novel is perhaps the best introduction to the ancient Roman thrillers in which she specializes, following the doings of her sleuth, Marcus Didius Falco, during the period of the emperor Vespasian. Like later volumes, it has pace and humour, and is creditably well researched and nicely written. In the UK, *Falco on his Metal* (Arrow) incorporates three Falco novels, and as such makes for a good sample of Davies's work.

Robert Graves *I Claudius*; *Claudius the God* (Penguin/Vintage). Graves's two-volume pseudo-autobiography is perhaps the definitive dramatized account of Rome in the early years of its decline: both books are a thumping good read.

David Hewson *A Season for the Dead; The Sacred Cut* (Pan/Dell). Hewson writes thrillers set in Rome, and these two are full of local colour. One is full of murders in the manner – and locations – of local Christian martyrdoms, the other starts with a gruesome death in the Pantheon before a labyrinthine citywide conspiracy ensues.

Conn Iggulden *The Gates of Rome; The Death of Kings; The Field of Swords; The Gods of War* (HarperCollins/Dell). Iggulden's highly success-ful and engaging four-book series, *Emperor*, is a tub-thumping historical romp that documents the rise and fall of Julius Caesar, from the rites of passage of the young man during the turmoil of the last decades of the Republic through his campaigns

in Gaul and his eventual murder in Pompey's theatre.

Allan Massie *Augustus; Tiberius; Caesar, Caligula* (Sceptre/Carroll & Graff). Massie's series of novels aspires to recreate the Roman empire at its height through the imagined memoirs of its key figures, and does so with great success, in a series of novels that offers a wonderfully palatable way into the minutiae of the era.

Alberto Moravia *A Woman of Rome* (Steerforth Press, US). Probably the most pre-eminent postwar Roman novelist, Moravia uses the Rome of the Mussolini era as a delicate back-drop for this detached yet compas-sionate tale of a Roman model and prostitute. See also *Roman Tales* (OUP), a varied collection of short stories that has the lives of ordinary Romans of the 1950s as its thread.

Margaret Mazzantini *Don't Move* (Chatto & Windus). This intense psychological novel of mid-life crisis, sex and obsession in Rome was a massive best-seller in Italy and made into a movie directed by the author's husband. The city and its outskirts form a bleak, rain-soaked backdrop.

Iain Pears *The Raphael Affair; The Bernini Bust; The Titian Commit-tee* (HarperCollins/Berkeley). Pears writes thrillers with an art histori-cal theme, of which these, primarily Rome-based examples, make great holiday reading. Plenty of local colour, not to mention fast-paced art-world intrigue concerning robbery, forgery and general skull-duggery.

Stephen Saylor *The House of the Vestal*; *Arms of Nemesis*; *A Mist of Prophecies*; *The Judgement of Caesar* (Constable & Robinson/St Martin's Press). Light detective yarns set in the days of the Roman republic, in which Saylor's fictional detective, Giordanius the Finder, solves mysteries with consummate ease.

John Varriano (ed.) *A Literary Companion to Rome* (John Murray/St Martin's Press). Arranged as a series of walking tours, this picks out the best of the many observations made about the city over the years. Entertaining in itself, but also a taster for many other writers and books on Rome that you may not have yet come across.

William Weaver (ed.) *Open City: Seven Writers in Postwar Rome* (Steerforth Press, US). An anthology of pieces by some of the best modern Italian novelists – Bassani, Silone, Moravia, Ginzburg, among others – selected and with an introduction by one of the most eminent postwar Italian translators.

Marguerite Yourcenar *Memoirs of Hadrian* (Penguin/FSG). Yourcenar's slow-moving, reflective narrative, most of it in the form of letters to his nephew, Marcus Aurelius, details the main events of the emperor Hadrian's rule, documenting at once the Roman Empire at its height and the very human anxieties of perhaps its wisest and most accomplished leader. See also Yourcenar's conceptual Roman novel, *A Coin in Nine Hands* (Harvill, UK).

Language

Language

Italian

The ability to speak English confers prestige in Italy, and there's often no shortage of people willing to show off their knowledge, especially in Rome. But using at least some Italian, however tentatively, can mark you out from the masses in a city used to hordes of tourists, and having a little more can open up the city no end. The words and phrases below should help you master the basics. If you want a decent phrasebook, look no further than the *Rough Guide Italian Phrasebook*, which packs a huge amount of phrases and vocabulary into a handy dictionary format. There are lots of good pocket dictionaries – the Collins range represents probably the best all-round choice, with their Gem or Pocket formats perfect for travelling purposes.

Pronunciation

Italian is one of the easiest European languages to learn, especially if you already have a smattering of French or Spanish. Easiest of all is the **pronunciation**, since every word is spoken exactly as it's written, and usually enunciated with exaggerated, open-mouthed clarity. All Italian words are stressed on the penultimate syllable unless an accent (´ or `) denotes otherwise. The only difficulties you're likely to encounter are the few consonants that are different from English:

c before e or i is pronounced as in **ch**urch, while **ch** before the same vowels is hard, as in **c**at.

sci or **sce** are pronounced as in **sh**eet and **sh**elter respectively.

The same goes with **g** – soft before e or i, as in **g**eranium; hard before h, as in **g**arlic.

gn has the ni sound of o**ni**on.

gl in Italian is softened to something like li in English, as in stal**li**on.

h is not aspirated, as in **h**onour.

When **speaking** to strangers, the third person is the polite form (ie lei instead of tu for "you"); using the second person is a mark of disrespect or stupidity. It's also worth remembering that Italians don't use "please" and "thank you" half as much as we do: it's all implied in the tone, though, if in doubt, err on the polite side.

Words and phrases

Basics

Buongiorno	Good morning	**Ciao** (informal; to strangers use phrases above)	Hello/goodbye
Buonasera	Good afternoon /evening		
Buonanotte	Good night	**Arrivederci**	Goodbye

Si	Yes	Più tardi	Later
No	No	Aspetta!	Wait a minute!
Per favore	Please	Andiamo!	Let's go!
Grázie (molte/ mille grazie)	Thank you (very much)	Di mattina	In the morning
Prego	You're welcome	Nel pomeriggio	In the afternoon
Va bene	All right/that's OK	Di sera	In the evening
Come stai/sta?	How are you? (informal/formal)	Qui/Là	Here/There
		Buono/Cattivo	Good/Bad
Bene	I'm fine	Grande/Píccolo	Big/Small
Pàrla inglese?	Do you speak English?	Economico/Caro	Cheap/Expensive
Non ho capito	I don't understand	Presto/Tardi	Early/Late
Non lo so	I don't know	Caldo/Freddo	Hot/Cold
Mi scusi	Excuse me	Vicino/Lontano	Near/Far
Permesso (in a crowd)	Excuse me	Velocemente/ Lentamente	Quickly/Slowly
Mi dispiace	I'm sorry	Con/Senza	With/Without
Sono qui in vacanza	I'm here on holiday	Più/Meno	More/Less
Sono inglese	I'm English	Basta	Enough, no more
scozzese	Scottish	Signor/Signora/ Signorina	Mr/Mrs/Miss
gallese	Welsh	Entrata/Uscita	Entrance/Exit
irlandese	Irish	Ingresso libero	Free entrance
americano/a (masculine/feminine)	American	Signori/Signore	Gentlemen/Ladies
australiano/a (masculine/feminine)	Australian	Vietato fumare	No smoking
		Gabinetto/Bagno	WC/Bathroom
neozelandese	a New Zealander	Aperto/Chiuso	Open/Closed
Oggi	Today	Chiuso per restauro	Closed for restoration
Domani	Tomorrow	Chiuso per ferie	Closed for holidays
Dopodomani	Day after tomorrow	Tirare/Spingere	Pull/Push
Ieri	Yesterday	Cassa	Cash desk
Adesso	Now	Avanti	Go, walk
		Alt	Stop, halt

Accommodation

Albergo	Hotel	con una doccia/ un bagno	with a shower/bath
C'è un albergo qui vicino?	Is there a hotel nearby?	con balcone	with a balcony
Ha una cámera ...	Do you have a room...	acqua calda/fredda	hot/cold water
per una/due/tre persona/e	for one/two/three person/people	Quanto costa?	How much is it?
		È caro	It's expensive
per una/due/tre notte/i	for one/two/three night/s	È compresa la prima colazione?	Is breakfast included?
per una/due settimana/e	for one/two week/s	Ha qualcosa che costa di meno?	Do you have anything cheaper?
con un letto matrimoniale	with a double bed	Pensione completa/ mezza pensione	Full/half board

Posso vedere la camera?	Can I see the room?	Vorrei prenotare una camera	I'd like to book a room
La prendo	I'll take it	Ho una prenotazione	I have a booking

Questions and directions

Dove?	Where?	Per arrivare a...?	How do I get to ... ?
(Dov'è/Dove sono ... ?)	(Where is/where are ... ?)	Quant'è lontano....?	How far is it to ... ?
Quando?	When?	Mi può dire dove scendere?	Can you tell me when to get off?
Cosa? (Cos'è?)	What? (What is it?)	A che ora apre?	What time does it open?
Quanto/Quanti?	How much/many?	A che ora chiude?	What time does it close?
Perché?	Why?	Quanto costa?	How much does it cost
C'e ... ?	It is/there is (Is it/is there ... ?)	(... Quanto costano?)	(... do they cost?)
Che ore sono?	What time is it?	Come si chiama in italiano?	What's it called in Italian?

Numbers

uno	1	venti	20
due	2	ventuno	21
tre	3	ventidue	22
quattro	4	trenta	30
cinque	5	quaranta	40
sei	6	cinquanta	50
sette	7	sessanta	60
otto	8	settanta	70
nove	9	ottanta	80
dieci	10	novanta	90
undici	11	cento	100
dodici	12	centuno	101
tredici	13	centodieci	110
quattordici	14	duecento	200
quindici	15	cinquecento	500
sedici	16	mille	1,000
diciassette	17	cinquemila	5,000
diciotto	18	diecimila	10,000
diciannove	19	cinquantamila	50,000

Menu reader

Basics and snacks

Aceto	Vinegar	Caramelle	Sweets
Aglio	Garlic	Cioccolato	Chocolate
Biscotti	Biscuits	Formaggio	Cheese
Burro	Butter	Frittata	Omelette

Marmellata	Jam	Sale	Salt
Olio	Oil	Uova	Eggs
Olive	Olives	Yogurt	Yoghurt
Pane	Bread	Zucchero	Sugar
Pepe	Pepper	Zuppa	Soup
Riso	Rice		

The first course (*il primo*)

Brodo	Clear broth	Pastina in brodo	Pasta pieces in clear broth
Farfalle	Butterfly-shaped pasta	Penne	Smaller version of rigatoni
Fettuccine	Narrow pasta ribbons		
Gnocchi	Small potato and dough dumplings	Rigatoni	Large, grooved tubular pasta
Maccheroni	Macaroni (tubular pasta)	Risotto	Cooked rice dish, with sauce
Minestrina	Clear broth with small pasta shapes	Stracciatella	Broth with egg
Minestrone	Thick vegetable soup	Tagliatelle	Pasta ribbons, another word for fettucine
Pasta al forno	Pasta baked with minced meat, eggs, tomato and cheese	Tortellini	Rings of pasta, stuffed with meat or cheese
Pasta e fagioli	Pasta with beans	Vermicelli	Thin spaghetti ("little worms")

... and pasta sauce (*salsa*)

Amatriciana	Cubed bacon and tomato sauce	Peperoncino	Olive oil, garlic and fresh chillies
Arrabbiata	Spicy tomato sauce, with chillies ("Angry")	Pesto	Sauce with ground basil, garlic and pine nuts
Bolognese	Meat sauce		
Burro	Butter	Pomodoro	Tomato sauce
Carbonara	Cream, ham and beaten egg	Puttanesca	Tomato, anchovy, olive oil and oregano ("Whorish")
Funghi	Mushroom		
Panna	Cream	Ragù	Meat sauce
Parmigiano	Parmesan cheese	Vongole	Sauce with clams

The second course (*il secondo*): meat (*carne*) ...

Agnello	Lamb	Maiale	Pork
Bistecca	Steak	Manzo	Beef
Carpaccio	Slices of raw beef	Ossobuco	Shin of veal
Cervello	Brain, usually calves'	Pancetta	Bacon
Cinghiale	Wild boar	Pollo	Chicken
Coniglio	Rabbit	Polpette	Meatballs
Costolette	Cutlet, chop	Rognoni	Kidneys
Fegato	Liver	Salsiccia	Sausage

| Saltimbocca | Veal with ham | Trippa | Tripe |
| Spezzatino | Stew | Vitello | Veal |

... fish (*pesce*) and shellfish (*crostacei*)

Acciughe	Anchovies	Merluzzo	Cod
Anguilla	Eel	Ostriche	Oysters
Aragosta	Lobster	Pesce spada	Swordfish
Baccalà	Dried salted cod	Polpo	Octopus
Calamari	Squid	Rospo	Monkfish
Cefalo	Grey mullet	Sampiero	John Dory
Cozze	Mussels	Sarde	Sardines
Dentice	Sea bream	Sogliola	Sole
Gamberetti	Shrimps	Tonno	Tuna
Gamberi	Prawns	Trota	Trout
Granchio	Crab	Vongole	Clams

Vegetables (*contorni*), herbs (*erbe aromatiche*) and salad (*insalata*)

Asparagi	Asparagus	Insalata verde/mista	Green salad/mixed salad
Carciofi	Artichokes		
Carciofini	Artichoke hearts	Lenticchie	Lentils
Cavolfiori	Cauliflower	Melanzane	Aubergine
Cavolo	Cabbage	Patate	Potatoes
Cipolla	Onion	Peperoni	Peppers
Fagioli	Beans	Piselli	Peas
Fagiolini	Green beans	Pomodori	Tomatoes
Finocchio	Fennel	Radicchio	Red salad leaves
Funghi	Mushrooms	Spinaci	Spinach

Some terms and useful words

Arrosto	Roast	Alla griglia	Grilled
Ben cotto	Well done	Alla milanese	Fried in egg and breadcrumbs
Bollito/lesso	Boiled		
Alla brace	Barbecued	Pizzaiola	Cooked with tomato sauce
Cotto	Cooked (not raw)		
Crudo	Raw	Ripieno	Stuffed
Al dente	Firm, not overcooked	Al sangue	Rare
Al ferri	Grilled without oil	Allo spiedo	On the spit
Al forno	Baked	Stracotto	Braised, stewed
Fritto	Fried	In umido	Stewed

Cheese (*formaggi*)

Dolcelatte	Creamy blue cheese	Pecorino	Strong, hard sheep's cheese
Fontina	Northern Italian cheese, often used in cooking	Provola/Provolone	Smooth, round mild cheese, made from buffalo or sheep's milk; sometimes smoked
Gorgonzola	Soft, strong, blue-veined cheese		
Mozzarella	Soft white cheese, traditionally made from buffalo's milk	Ricotta	Soft, white sheep's cheese

Sweets (*dolci*), fruit (*frutta*) and nuts (*noci*)

Amaretti	Macaroons	Mándorle	Almonds
Ananas	Pineapple	Mele	Apples
Anguria/Coccomero	Watermelon	Melone	Melon
Arance	Oranges	Pere	Pears
Banane	Bananas	Pesche	Peaches
Cacchi	Persimmons	Pinoli	Pine nuts
Ciliegie	Cherries	Pistacchio	Pistachio nut
Fichi	Figs	Torta	Cake, tart
Fichi d'India	Prickly pears	Uva	Grapes
Frágole	Strawberries	Zabaglione	Dessert made with eggs, sugar and marsala wine
Gelato	Ice cream		
Limone	Lemon		
Macedonia	Fruit salad	Zuppa Inglese	Trifle

Drinks

Acqua minerale	Mineral water	Succo	Concentrated fruit juice with sugar
Aranciata	Orangeade		
Bicchiere	Glass	Tè	Tea
Birra	Beer	Tonica	Tonic water
Bottiglia	Bottle	Vino	Wine
Caffè	Coffee	Rosso	Red
Cioccolata calda	Hot chocolate	Bianco	White
Ghiaccio	Ice	Rosato	Rosé
Granita	Iced drink, with coffee or fruit	Secco	Dry
		Dolce	Sweet
Latte	Milk	Litro	Litre
Limonata	Lemonade	Mezzo	Half
Selz	Soda water	Quarto	Quarter
Spremuta	Fresh fruit juice	Caraffa	Carafe
Spumante	Sparkling wine	Salute!	Cheers!

Glossary of artistic and architectural terms

agora Square or market place in an ancient Greek city.

ambo A kind of simple pulpit, popular in Italian medieval churches.

ambulatory A semi-circular aisle around the sanctuary or apse of a church.

anfiteatro Amphitheatre.

apse Semicircular recess at the altar (usually eastern) end of a church.

architrave The lowest part of the entablature.

atrium Inner courtyard.

baldachino A canopy on columns, usually placed over the altar in a church.

basilica Originally a Roman administrative building, adapted for early churches; distinguished by lack of transepts.

belvedere A terrace or lookout point.

caldarium The steam room of a Roman bath.

campanile Belltower, sometimes detached, usually of a church.

capital Top of a column.

chiaroscuro The balance of light and shade in a painting, and the skill of the artist in depicting the contrast between the two.

chiesa Church.

cistae Drum-like engraved Etruscan containers that accompany the dead, holding toiletries and the like.

chancel Part of a church containing the altar.

ciborium Another word for "baldachino", see above.

cornice The top section of a classical facade.

cortile Galleried courtyard or cloisters.

cosmati work Decorative mosaic work on marble, usually highly coloured, found in early Christian Italian churches, especially in Rome. Derives from the name "Cosma", a common name among families of marble workers at the time.

crypt Burial place in a church, usually under the choir.

cryptoporticus Underground passageway.

cyclopean walls Fortifications built of huge, rough stone blocks, common in the pre-Roman settlements of Lazio.

dalmatic A wide-sleeved tunic worn by officiating priests.

decumanus maximus The main street of a Roman town. The second cross-street was known as the Decumanus Inferiore.

entablature The section above the capital on a classical building, below the cornice.

ex-voto Artefact designed in thanksgiving to a saint. The adjective is ex-votive.

fresco Wall-painting technique in which the artist applies paint to wet plaster for a more permanent finish.

frigidarium The cold room of a Roman baths.

largo Square.

loggia Roofed gallery or balcony.

metope A panel on the frieze of a Greek temple.

mithraism Pre-Christian cult associated with the Persian god of light, who slew a bull and fertilized the world with its blood.

narthex The vestibule at the west end of a Christian basilica.

nave Central space in a church, usually flanked by aisles.

palazzo Palace, mansion, or block of flats.

pantocrator Usually refers to an image of Christ, portrayed with outstretched arms.

piano nobile Main floor of a palace, usually the first.

piazza Square.

polyptych Painting on several joined wooden panels.

ponte Bridge.

porphyry A reddish-pink kind of marble.

portico Covered entrance to a building, or porch.

presepio A Christmas crib.

putti Cherubs.

reliquary Receptacle for a saint's relics, usually bones. Often highly decorated.

sgraffito Decorative technique whereby one layer of plaster is scratched to form a pattern. Popular in sixteenth-century Italy.

stereobate Visible base of any building, usually a Greek temple.

stucco Plaster made from water, lime, sand and powdered marble, used for decorative work.

thermae Baths, usually elaborate buildings in Roman villas.

triptych Painting on three joined wooden panels.

trompe l'oeil Work of art that deceives the viewer by means of tricks with perspective.

Travel store

D: Rough Guide
DIRECTIONS for
short breaks

Available from all good bookstores

Kenya
Marrakesh **D**
Morocco
South Africa, Lesotho
& Swaziland
Syria
Tanzania
Tunisia
West Africa
Zanzibar

Travel Specials
First-Time Africa
First-Time Around
the World
First-Time Asia
First-Time Europe
First-Time Latin
America
Travel Health
Travel Online
Travel Survival
Walks in London
& SE England
Women Travel
World Party

Maps
Algarve
Amsterdam
Andalucia
& Costa del Sol
Argentina
Athens
Australia
Barcelona
Berlin
Boston & Cambridge
Brittany
Brussels
California
Chicago
Chile
Corsica
Costa Rica
& Panama
Crete
Croatia
Cuba
Cyprus
Czech Republic
Dominican Republic
Dubai & UAE
Dublin
Egypt

Florence & Siena
Florida
France
Frankfurt
Germany
Greece
Guatemala & Belize
Iceland
India
Ireland
Italy
Kenya & Northern
Tanzania
Lisbon
London
Los Angeles
Madrid
Malaysia
Mallorca
Marrakesh
Mexico
Miami & Key West
Morocco
New England
New York City
New Zealand
Northern Spain
Paris
Peru
Portugal
Prague
Pyrenees & Andorra
Rome
San Francisco
Sicily
South Africa
South India
Spain & Portugal
Sri Lanka
Tenerife
Thailand
Toronto
Trinidad & Tobago
Tunisia
Turkey
Tuscany
Venice
Vietnam, Laos
& Cambodia
Washington DC
Yucatán Peninsula

**Dictionary
Phrasebooks**
Croatian
Czech
Dutch
Egyptian Arabic
French
German
Greek
Hindi & Urdu
Italian
Japanese
Latin American
Spanish
Mandarin Chinese
Mexican Spanish
Polish
Portuguese
Russian
Spanish
Swahili
Thai
Turkish
Vietnamese

Computers
Blogging
eBay
iPhone
iPods, iTunes
& music online
The Internet
Macs & OS X
MySpace
PCs and Windows
PlayStation Portable
Website Directory

Film & TV
American
Independent Film
British Cult Comedy
Chick Flicks
Comedy Movies
Cult Movies
Film
Film Musicals
Film Noir
Gangster Movies
Horror Movies
Kids' Movies
Sci-Fi Movies
Westerns

Lifestyle
Babies
Ethical Living
Pregnancy & Birth
Running

Music Guides
The Beatles
Blues
Bob Dylan
Book of Playlists
Classical Music
Elvis
Frank Sinatra
Heavy Metal
Hip-Hop
Jazz
Led Zeppelin
Opera
Pink Floyd
Punk
Reggae
Rock
The Rolling Stones
Soul and R&B
Velvet Underground
World Music
(2 vols)

Popular Culture
Books for Teenagers
Children's Books,
5-11
Conspiracy Theories
Crime Fiction
Cult Fiction
The Da Vinci Code
His Dark Materials
Lord of the Rings
Shakespeare
Superheroes
The Templars
Unexplained
Phenomena

Science
The Brain
Climate Change
The Earth
Genes & Cloning
The Universe
Weather

For more information go to www.roughguides.com

Avoid Guilt Trips

Buy fair trade coffee + bananas ✓

Save energy – use low energy bulbs ✓
- don't leave tv on standby ✓

Offset carbon emissions from flight to Madrid ✓

Send goat to Africa ✓

Join Tourism Concern today ✓

Slowly, the world is changing.
Together we can, and will, make a difference.

Tourism Concern is the only UK registered charity fighting exploitation in one of the largest industries on earth: people forced from their homes in order that holiday resorts can be built, sweatshop labour conditions in hotels and destruction of the environment are just some of the issues that we tackle.

Sending people on a guilt trip is not something we do. We know as well as anyone that holidays are precious. But you can help us to ensure that tourism always benefits the local communities involved.

Call 020 7133 3330
or visit **tourismconcern.org.uk** to find out how.

A year's membership of Tourism Concern costs just £20 (£12 unwaged) – that's 38 pence a week, less than the cost of a pint of milk, organic of course.

Fighting Exploitation in Tourism

TourismConcern

Small print and

Index

A Rough Guide to Rough Guides

Published in 1982, the first Rough Guide – to Greece – was a student scheme that became a publishing phenomenon. Mark Ellingham, a recent graduate in English from Bristol University, had been travelling in Greece the previous summer and couldn't find the right guidebook. With a small group of friends he wrote his own guide, combining a highly contemporary, journalistic style with a thoroughly practical approach to travellers' needs.

The immediate success of the book spawned a series that rapidly covered dozens of destinations. And, in addition to impecunious backpackers, Rough Guides soon acquired a much broader and older readership that relished the guides' wit and inquisitiveness as much as their enthusiastic, critical approach and value-for-money ethos.

These days, Rough Guides include recommendations from shoestring to luxury and cover more than 200 destinations around the globe, including almost every country in the Americas and Europe, more than half of Africa and most of Asia and Australasia. Our ever-growing team of authors and photographers is spread all over the world, particularly in Europe, the USA and Australia.

In the early 1990s, Rough Guides branched out of travel, with the publication of Rough Guides to World Music, Classical Music and the Internet. All three have become benchmark titles in their fields, spearheading the publication of a wide range of books under the Rough Guide name.

Including the travel series, Rough Guides now number more than 350 titles, covering: phrasebooks, waterproof maps, music guides from Opera to Heavy Metal, reference works as diverse as Conspiracy Theories and Shakespeare, and popular culture books from iPods to Poker. Rough Guides also produce a series of more than 120 World Music CDs in partnership with World Music Network.

Visit www.roughguides.com to see our latest publications.

Rough Guide travel images are available for commercial licensing at www.roughguidespictures.com

Rough Guide credits

Text editors: James Smart, Helena Smith
Layout: Ankur Guha
Cartography: Maxine Repath, Jotinkumar Athokpam
Picture editor: Mark Thomas
Production: Aimee Hampson
Proofreader: Helen Castell
Cover design: Chloë Roberts
Photographer: James McConnachie
Editorial: **London** Kate Berens, Claire Saunders, Ruth Blackmore, Polly Thomas, Richard Lim, Alison Murchie, Karoline Densley, Andy Turner, Keith Drew, Edward Aves, Nikki Birrell, Alice Park, Sarah Eno, Lucy White, Jo Kirby, Samantha Cook, Natasha Foges, Róisín Cameron, Joe Staines, Duncan Clark, Peter Buckley, Matthew Milton, Tracy Hopkins, Ruth Tidball; **New York** Andrew Rosenberg, Steven Horak, AnneLise Sorensen, Amy Hegarty, April Isaacs, Ella Steim, Anna Owens, Joseph Petta, Sean Mahoney
Design & Pictures: **London** Scott Stickland, Dan May, Diana Jarvis, Jj Luck, Harriet Mills, Chloë Roberts, Nicole Newman; **Delhi** Umesh Aggarwal, Ajay Verma, Jessica Subramanian, Pradeep Thapliyal, Sachin Tanwar, Anita Singh,
Madhavi Singh, Karen D'Souza
Production: Vicky Baldwin
Cartography: **London** Ed Wright, Katie Lloyd-Jones; **Delhi** Jai Prakash Mishra, Rajesh Chhibber, Ashutosh Bharti, Rajesh Mishra, Animesh Pathak, Jasbir Sandhu, Karobi Gogoi, Amod Singh, Alakananda Bhattacharya,
Online: **New York** Jennifer Gold, Kristin Mingrone; **Delhi** Manik Chauhan, Narender Kumar, Rakesh Kumar, Amit Kumar, Amit Verma, Rahul Kumar, Ganesh Sharma, Debojit Borah
Marketing & Publicity: **London** Liz Statham, Niki Hanmer, Louise Maher, Jess Carter, Vanessa Godden, Vivienne Watton, Anna Paynton, Libby Jellie, Rachel Sprackett, Lenalisa Fornberg; **New York** Geoff Colquitt, Megan Kennedy, Katy Ball; **Delhi** Reem Khokhar
Editorial Coordinator: Emma Traynor
Manager India: Punita Singh
Series Editor: Mark Ellingham
Reference Director: Andrew Lockett
PA to MD and Publishing Director: Helen Phillips
Publishing Director: Martin Dunford
Commercial Manager: Gino Magnotta
Managing Director: John Duhigg

Publishing information

This third edition published June 2007 by
Rough Guides Ltd,
80 Strand, London WC2R 0RL
345 Hudson St, 4th Floor,
New York, NY 10014, USA
14 Local Shopping Centre, Panchsheel Park,
New Delhi 110017, India
Distributed by the Penguin Group
Penguin Books Ltd,
80 Strand, London WC2R 0RL
Penguin Group (USA)
375 Hudson Street, NY 10014, USA
Penguin Group (Australia)
250 Camberwell Road, Camberwell,
Victoria 3124, Australia
Penguin Books Canada Ltd,
10 Alcorn Avenue, Toronto, Ontario,
Canada M4V 1E4
Penguin Group (NZ)
67 Apollo Drive, Mairangi Bay, Auckland 1310,
New Zealand

Cover concept by Peter Dyer.
Typeset in Bembo and Helvetica to an original design by Henry Iles.
Printed in Italy by LegoPrint S.p.A
© Martin Dunford 2007

352pp includes index
A catalogue record for this book is available from the British Library
ISBN: 978-1-84353-854-7

1   3   5   7   9   8   6   4   2

ROUGH GUIDES

SMALL PRINT

Help us update

We've gone to a lot of effort to ensure that the third edition of **The Rough Guide to Rome** is accurate and up to date. However, things change – places get "discovered", opening hours are notoriously fickle, restaurants and rooms raise prices or lower standards. If you feel we've got it wrong or left something out, we'd like to know, and if you can remember the address, the price, the time, the phone number, so much the better. We'll credit all contributions, and send a copy of the next edition (or any other Rough Guide if you prefer) for the best letters. Everyone who

writes to us and isn't already a subscriber will receive a copy of our full-colour thrice-yearly newsletter. Please mark letters: "**Rough Guide Rome Update**" and send to: Rough Guides, 80 Strand, London WC2R 0RL, or Rough Guides, 345 Hudson St, 4th Floor, New York, NY 10014. Or send an email to **mail@roughguides.com** Have your questions answered and tell others about your trip at
www.roughguides.atinfopop.com

Acknowledgements

Thanks to Flo Austin for helping out with Contexts, Victor Townley for information on life beyond Rome, James Smart for patient and astute editing, Natasha Foges for the benefit of her superior Italian and Bo Lundin for pointing out some gaps. Also to Katia and Sabrina at At Home, the Austin-Tarrys for happy days in Bracciano, and to Caroline and Daisy for being there every step of the way.

Readers' letters

Thanks to all the readers who have taken the time to write in with comments and suggestions (and apologies if we've inadvertently omitted or misspelt anyone's name):

Antoinette Sutto, Mark Lloyd, Martin Oldsberg, Andrew Young, Martin Kenzie, Dr René Brouwer, Douglas Smith, Jeffrey Robson, J Plumtree, Denise Cookson, Craig Wright, Michelle Villeneau, Alison Harris, G Tillson, Jonathan Sidaway and Stephen Dunn, Bill and Margaret Gray, James Bigus and Kimberly Lomax, Gary Elflett, Miranda Gardner, Kay and Enda Bannon, Michael Upshall, Iain Baker, Maria Laffey, John Newton, Judy Wood, Philip Melville, Bill and Carolyn Thomas, Emma Fletcher-Jones, Ana Belen-Martin, Joanne Carter, Peter Lawton, Bruno and Jelbrich Forment, Hans Kleinen Hammans, Rosemary O'Connor, Michael Wyatt, Helen Ryan, Mike Quirke.

Photo credits

All photos © Rough Guides except the following:

Title page
Romans on scooter © Ian Cumming/Axiom

Full page
Fontana del Nettuno © Peter Wilson/Axiom

Introduction
Vittorio Emanuele Mounument © Allessandro Bianchi/Corbis
Café in Rome © Peter Horree/Alamy
The Auditorium © Enzo Signorelli/CuboImages/Alamy

Things not to miss
01 Roma vs Lazio © Ettore Ferrari/Corbis
02 Bust of Hadrian, Museo Nazionale Romano (pallazo Massiomo alle Terme) © Foto Scala, Firenze – su concessione Ministero Beni e Attivita Culturali
03 Sistine Chapel ceiling: The Prophet Ezekiel, 1510 (fresco) © Michelangelo Buonarroti/The Bridgeman Art Library/Getty Images

04 Lady with Unicorn by Raphael (1483–1520), Galleria Borghese © Foto Scal, Firenze – su concessione Ministero Beni e Attivita Culturali
05 Hand of Constantine, fragment of colossal statue, Capitoline Museums © Foto Scala, Firenze
06 Making Pizza © Jon Spaull/Axiom

Black and whites
p.199 The Sistine Chapel ceiling © Michelangelo Buonarroti/The Bridgeman Art Library/Getty Images
p.294 Statue of Augustus in the Vatican Museums © Imagery and Imagination/Alamy
p.311 Piazza del Popolo © Corbis

Colour insert: Food and drink
People eating on Piazza della Rotonda © Travelpix Ltd/Getty Images

Index

Map entries are in colour.

I

INDEX

Q

Map symbols

maps are listed in the full index using coloured text

- - -	Chapter boundary	▣	Restaurant
▬▬	Motorway	T	Toilets
═══	Major road	ⓘ	Information office
───	Minor road	∴	Ruins
▬▬	Pedestrianized road	✈	Airport
▥▥▥	Steps	Ⓜ	Metro station
- - - -	Path	✡	Synagogue
──■──	Railway	✉	Post office
~~	River	⊞	Hospital
───	Wall	P	Parking
⌣	Bridge	▬	Building
⊠—⊠	Gate	╅	Church
△	Pyramid	◯	Stadium
⚠	Campsite	⁺₊⁺	Christian cemetery
◆	Place of interest	▦	Park
⟟	Fountain		

ROME AND AROUND

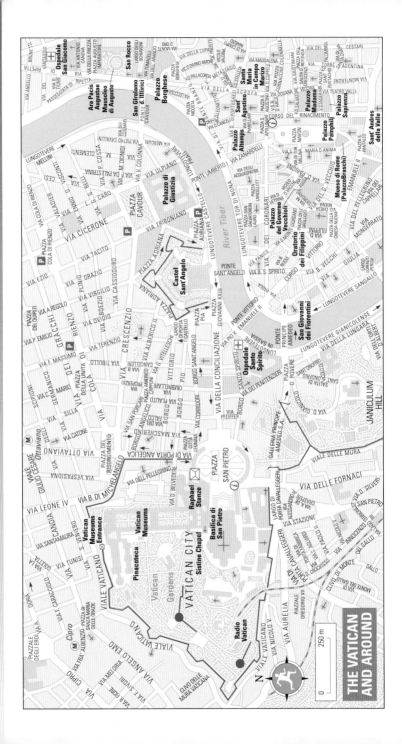

THE VATICAN
AND AROUND

N

0   250 m

TRASTEVERE AND TESTACCIO